83 ODYSSEY

83 ODYSSEY

An Adventure Down the Spine of America on U.S. Highway 83

-CHARLES ROAMER-

atmosphere press

This book is dedicated to all the good people I met on my 83 Odyssey, and everywhere else in my travels.

And to Norman Holtaway—my late, great high school English teacher—who liked and encouraged my writing and to "keep pushing that unusual curiosity."

© 2024 Charles Roamer

Published by Atmosphere Press

Cover design by Ronaldo Alves

All photos by author

No part of this book may be reproduced without permission from the author except in brief quotations and in reviews.

Atmospherepress.com

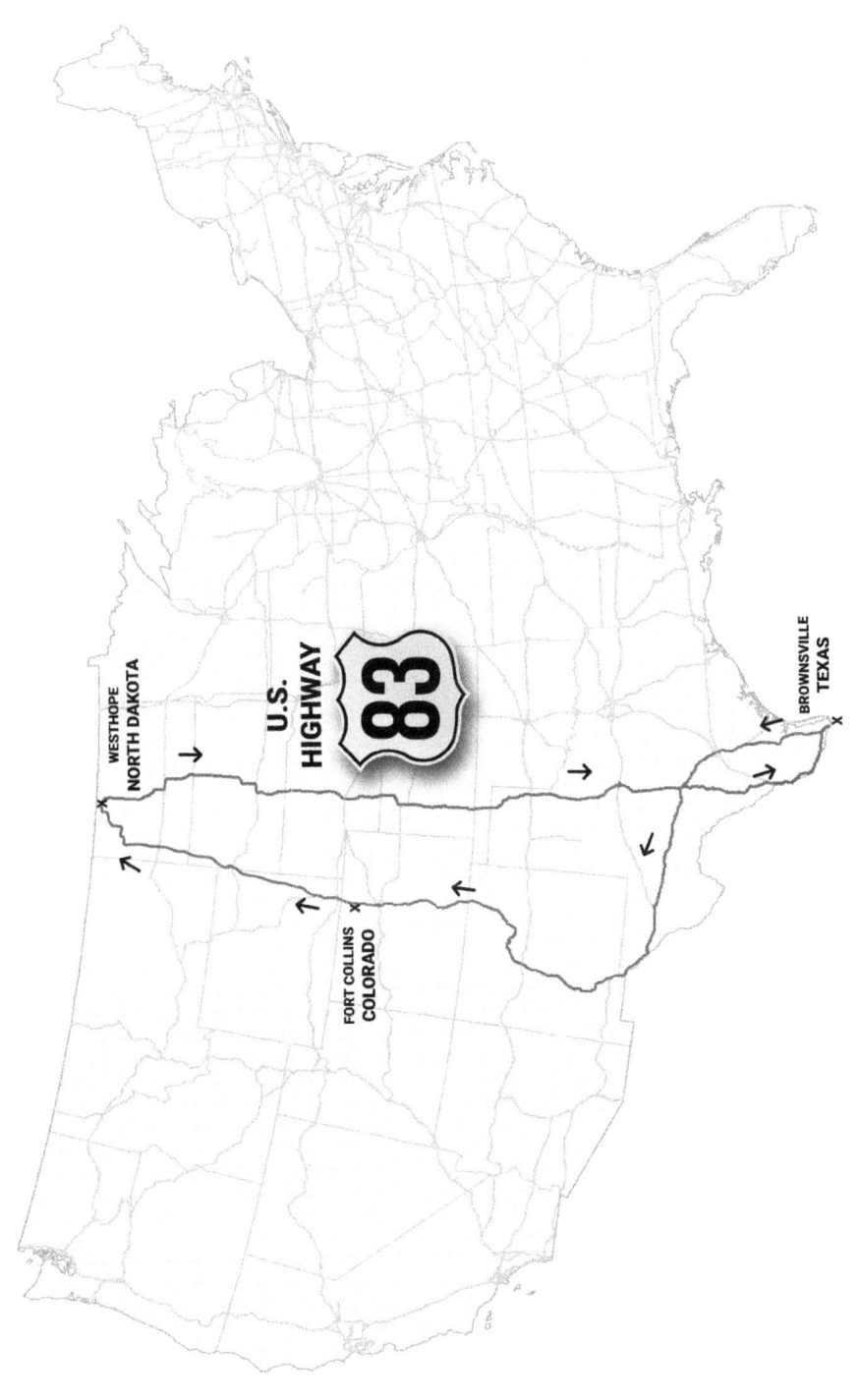

Author's Note

My journey down the entire length of U.S. Highway 83 was made in the autumn of 2014. So, some of the factual information I provide about the places I traveled through and some other subjects may have become somewhat dated. It's been my goal to present basic facts accurately. But not being an experienced researcher, and having relied on non-primary sources, there may be some minor inaccuracies. However, I believe that my fact-checking was careful enough for the information presented to be basically accurate.

Also, I've changed the names and some other details of some of the people I encountered along the road to protect their privacy when appropriate.

Table of Contents

Prologue to a Journey 3

DAYS 1-4	Journey to 83 10
DAY 5	Starting down the Spine of America 20
DAY 6	Magic City, Lewis and Clark, and the Capital 32
DAY 7	Meeting more North Dakotans 50
DAY 8	A Blachenda, Lawrence Welk, and South Dakota 66
DAY 9	A Day in Selby 82
DAY 10	The Land of John Deere, and a night in "Peer" 92
DAY 11	A museum, the Capitol, more bar-hopping 107
DAY 12	LaFramboise Island, the dam, and a walleye dinner 119
DAY 13	Into West River 131
DAY 14	The Big Show, Rosebud Reservation, a kiss in Valentine 141
DAY 15	The amazing Niobrara, sunset and moon rise in the Sandhills 158
DAY 16	A forest in Nebraska, some company in North Platte 173
DAY 17	"We're friends forever," Buffalo Bill, and the Golden Spike Tower 183
DAY 18	McCook, in Kansas, a night in Oberlin 199
DAY 19	Monument Rocks, and the smell of money 212
PHOTOS	 226
DAY 20	More of Kansas, the Land of OZ, two state panhandles 240
DAY 21	Down the Texas Panhandle 268

DAY 22	A walk in Childress, mesquite, cotton, an unfriendly cop	287
DAY 23	Anson, Abilene, a bed in Ballinger	304
DAY 24	"The Greatest Little Town in Texas," in Eden, Motel 83	318
DAY 25	Menard and the Hill Country	332
DAY 26	Garner State Park, palm trees and blackbirds	347
DAY 27	Uvalde, meeting Popeye, some great brisket	356
DAY 28	Laredo, along the Border, a Motel 6	366
DAY 29	Gunning for Brownsville, the finish line of 83	392
DAY 30	The Brownsville Flood, a jungle, and the Coast	410
DAYS 31-32	In the light and warmth of SPI, homeward bound	417
DAYS 33	San Antonio, The Alamo, back in the Hill Country	426
DAY 34	Into West Texas, Good Samaritans, an "old" twenty-five-year-old	431
DAY 35	El Paso and "The Land of Enchantment"	440
DAY 36	The Big Push, "There's no place like home."	448

Epilogue 458

"...While I know the standard claim is that Yosemite, Niagara Falls, the Upper Yellowstone and the like, afford the greatest natural shows, I am not so sure but the Prairies and the Plains, while less stunning at first sight, last longer, fill the esthetic sense fuller, precede all the rest, and make North America's characteristic landscape."

—Walt Whitman

Prologue to a Journey

I've had a long love for long road trips and a fascination with roads themselves—especially the old U.S. highways, also known as U.S. routes and federal highways. These predecessors of the modern interstate highways were planned in the mid-1920s—still early in the automobile age—when there was a confusing network of over 250 named highways around the U.S.

The early roads were also known as auto trails, which had been established by private auto clubs to meet the growing demand for better roads as the number of automobiles increased. In 1925, the Federal-Aid Highway Act was passed, and for the first time in history, a national standard was set for roads to eliminate confusion, which resulted in the development of the U.S. Highway System. The new system was administered by the states instead of private clubs, and the roads were given standard numbering—a novel idea at the time that had opposition from those who thought it would give the roads' designations a mathematical coldness compared to the character of individual names. Standard signs were planned with road numbers within white shields that are still the symbol used today, whereas many of the auto trails' routes were marked by colored bands on telephone poles. By November 1926, a final plan for the U.S. highways was approved, and the roads were eventually constructed.

Originally, these were mainly two-lane roads sufficient for the relatively light traffic of the times. But as traffic increased through the years, there arose a need for wider and better roads to avoid being hindered by slow vehicles and plodding through towns and cities. In 1944, the Bureau of Public Roads, headed by Thomas H. MacDonald, authorized another federal act to modernize the system, which was insufficiently funded, however. By the 1950s, President Dwight D. Eisenhower—who'd been impressed by the multi-lane expressways of the German Autobahn during World War II—was instrumental in passing the Federal-Aid Highway Act of 1956, which established the Interstate Highway System thirty years after the U.S highways. This vast network of modern roads that was administered by the federal government, but owned and maintained by the states that received federal funds, wasn't officially completed until 1992 and was one of the largest public works projects in the nation's history. Some U.S. highways were largely unaffected by the interstates, while others were integrated with the new multi-lane roads for long or short distances. Others were eventually rerouted, decommissioned, or recommissioned as other roads. But overall, the old system remained intact in the interstate era, and there have even been additions to it.

For over forty years, I'd taken many road trips around the U.S. by car, van, camper, motorcycle, hitch-hiking, and one coast-to-coast bus trip—traveling sections of many U.S. highways, which vary greatly in distance. Some years back I started thinking about journeying the whole length of one of the long and largely two-lane ones to better experience what extensive road trips were like before the express travel of the interstates, and there were a lot of old roads to choose from. It was a matter of which one.

Then, one day in 2010, when I was gazing at a map of the lower forty-eight states, I noticed a long road with the U.S. highway symbol that had a rather straight, north-south course near the center of the country through the Plains states. Its number was 83, and it ran all the way from the Canadian border in North Dakota to the Mexican border in Brownsville, Texas. I had to have crossed or possibly traveled parts of it on past road trips without giving it much thought. But now I had an inspiration for the kind of old highway I wanted to travel someday.

U.S. 83 traverses the whole length of the Great Plains in the U.S.—a vast hinterland commonly regarded as flat, empty, and boring. But I've had a fascination with the region and had traveled through all the Plains states, though generally in an east-west direction while headed somewhere else. I wondered what it would be like to journey through these states in a north-south direction and experience the plains for many hundreds of miles.

Some months after my initial inspiration, I had another one when I discovered a used book while browsing in a thrift shop, titled, *Road Trip USA*, by Jamie Jensen. It was a guidebook with lengthy descriptions of eleven very interesting routes around the country, and one chapter really grabbed my attention: "U.S. 83: The Road to Nowhere." This moniker for the road seemed to express the popular impression of the region that the old highway courses through, and it heightened my perhaps strange interest in exploring a region considered "nowhere." So, for a few bucks, I bought what looked like a well-researched guidebook that was perfect for the trip that had hatched in my mind. It was now just a matter of when I would begin my own adventure on 1,885 miles (3,034 km)-long U.S. 83—one of the original U.S. Highways and one of the least changed.

This was around the time that I—an old Child of the Sixties—had entered the sixties decade of my own life. I was still living in New Jersey, my home state, and working as a paratransit driver for the elderly and disabled—an occupation I'd fallen into in 1985 after having a variety of jobs, which I eventually regarded as a calling. I was employed by a county department that offered the golden carrot of a pension, which along with my upcoming eligibility for Social Security made retirement at age sixty-two possible. Although I found satisfaction in a type of work that genuinely helped people, I was anxious to retire from employment as early as I could for the personal freedom I always longed for—including the freedom to travel without time constraints. Having avoided the constraints of marriage also enabled such personal freedom. So, I planned on driving all of U.S. 83 during my upcoming retirement when it could be a more leisurely journey.

Meanwhile, I had plans to retire out West in the thriving city of Fort Collins, Colorado, about sixty-five miles north of Denver, and had even bought a small house there that was being rented until I could move in. But it wouldn't be the first time I lived in the West, since back in my youth I'd heard the old call: "Go West, young man,"— partly because of all the TV and movie Westerns I watched growing up as a Baby Boomer—which I heeded by attending the University of Wyoming for a while. Now the call had become: "Go West, old man,"— having reached the chronologically advanced age of sixty. My plans inspired my two years younger sister, who'd lived in Las Vegas for thirty years, to also consider relocating to Fort Collins. We had lost our parents recently; she was already retired; and she'd been through a recent divorce and was ready to start a new chapter in her life, which began when she made the move to Colorado in September 2011, over a year before I was able to.

My retirement came at the end of February 2012, shortly after I turned sixty-two. But complications from trying to sell a small log cabin I lived in by Lake Hopatcong, NJ, delayed my move to Colorado till near the end of that year. And about six weeks before the move, I had to deal with monstrous Hurricane Sandy, which knocked out power in my neighborhood for almost two weeks and caused a real ordeal during the final stretch of my long life in New Jersey. For the big move, I hired a national moving company, but would also cram whatever I could in my '06 Toyota Corolla that I would drive to Colorado.

After stressful preparations, I was ready to hit the road on December 17, 2012, and I'd lived just five miles from Interstate 80, which was a very direct route for most of my over 1,700-mile journey. The trip went smoothly until I was west of Omaha, Nebraska, where I encountered a snowstorm that swept in from the Rockies and gained strength eastward across the plains. Road conditions, including visibility, became very hazardous and slowed my progress to a crawl. I got off the interstate when I could by the town of York, Nebraska and checked into a Motel 6. The storm didn't let up, and there was news that I-80 had been closed in Nebraska. So, I wound up spending another night at the motel and learned that the snowstorm had even been given the name Draco, meaning "dragon" in Latin, and that it was affecting a vast area. It was less than two months after my experience with Sandy.

Blue skies glowed over Nebraska on Friday, December 21, and I-80 had reopened. The date happened to be the Winter Solstice, and the one that supposedly marked the end of the Mayan calendar, which had received a lot of publicity and even generated some anxieties. For me, the significant date looked like the one I could make it to Fort Collins if the highway was clear enough, and I was back on the road early that day but had to proceed slowly on long stretches with remaining snow. However, conditions improved further west across the broad Plains state, and I was able to accelerate my pace. When I reached the town of North Platte, I-80 intersected with U.S. 83, running north-south, which made me muse about my anticipated journey on the old highway. But for now, I stayed westbound on this big move of my life along the same route as many of the old pioneers and others who have been part of the historical westward movement of the nation.

I arrived in Fort Collins soon after dark that evening at my vacant new home, with the big moving truck a couple of days behind. My sister, now well-settled and living just several miles away, was soon there to greet me with some Fat Tire beer from the well-known New Belgium brewery in town. The Winter Solstice and the date that was claimed to be the end of the Mayan calendar, which some feared might even bring the end of the world, ironically wound up being the beginning of a big new chapter of my life. All because of a blizzard in Nebraska that delayed me.

Living in my new hometown even exceeded my expectations, and the proximity to my sister after being separated by great distance for many years worked out very well. I also made many new friends and engaged in some of the abundant activities that the area offered, while enjoying its great natural beauty. As much as I loved the Rockies just to the west, the plains to the east were also alluring, and I often mused about U.S. 83 running out there beyond the horizon, waiting for me to venture on it. However, 2013 came and went as I got more settled and didn't set out for the highway. After 2014 arrived, I decided to make the journey sometime that year, and after some deliberation thought that early autumn would be a good time to avoid the extremes of the Plains' climate. I also thought that season would have less of the tornado danger that the region is infamous for. In my younger years, I might have made the journey on my 1976 R75/6 BMW motorcycle, which I'd owned for decades since it was brand new and toured much of the U.S with. But the machine's age and the greater hardships of motorcycle travel discouraged me, and I was set on taking my Toyota Corolla, which I could even sleep in with my 5'6" stature. When the summer arrived, I planned a departure date for September 23—the first full day of autumn. I had no strict time limits, and expected to be gone for at least a month. My plan was to connect with U.S. 83 at its northern end in North Dakota and drive south before the northern plains became freezing and to avoid Texas while it still might be having severe heat.

Meanwhile, I learned more about places along the highway from *Road Trip USA* and online information. Near departure time, I had some service on my car that included an oil change and pre-trip inspection, and the Corolla's reputation for reliability and parts availability gave me more confidence. I named the '06 model "Wander" when I bought it pre-owned in 2010, since I planned to do a lot of wandering with it, and retirement offered the freedom to really wander in contrast to haste-filled traveling.

I packed the car according to a system I'd used on some shorter trips, with my mummy sleeping bag unrolled on the back seat under a pillow and two duffle bags containing most of my clothing. My footwear was stored on the rear floor beside two gallon-sized plastic water bottles for washing purposes and a large canteen for drinking water. I also had a water bottle in a small holder by the driver's seat. On the front passenger seat, I placed a tote bag with my small Nikon camera, binoculars, a few books including *Road Trip USA*, some CDs and a few miscellaneous items. The back of the seat had a large pocket for my maps, notebooks, and some other printed materials. The trunk was packed with a mid-sized plastic cooler, a two-person tent, small folding chair, a couple of large cloth shopping bags full of eating and drinking utensils and some packaged food, and a small crate and large tote bag full of assorted items that included a first aid kit and tool bag. The remaining trunk space had my raincoat and some other outerwear, a couple of brimmed hats, two towels, a small basket with nutritional supplements, and some other loose items. Along with these provisions was a compact spare tire and its accessories. I also carried jumper cables and triangle reflectors for the possibility of a breakdown.

Not just relying on two credit cards, I stored some cash under the driver's seat and would use ATMs when necessary—one of the great modern-era conveniences that weren't around in my early travels. For communications, I had a flip phone, since as an older, not very techie, and frugal guy, I still hadn't invested in a smartphone. I also did without a GPS.

On the day before my planned departure, I had my mail held at the post office, gassed up, got a haircut, cut the grass, paid some bills, and took care of some other business. The autumn equinox arrived that evening, and as I tried to sleep that night, I was kept awake longer than usual by my excitement over the long-awaited adventure.

It included some traveler's anxiety because I couldn't help thinking about all the mileage ahead, venturing alone into the unknown, and giving up the comforts and security of my new home. Then the big question on the most important matter—Would this be a safe trip? I'm most concerned about safety before motorcycle trips. But any mode of travel obviously involves dangers, and there were others on this trip besides the possibility of accidents and tornados.

I also felt excited about all the new places I would see and the people I was destined to meet. I wondered just who they would be and what circumstances would lead to our paths crossing. Eventually, fatigue overcame such musings, and I fell into a sound sleep.

DAYS 1-4

Journey to 83

Tuesday, September 23—the first full day of autumn—was fair and comfortably warm when I pulled out of my driveway early in the afternoon without any cheers or other fanfare. Some seasonal color had started in my neighborhood's hardwood trees that had been planted on what was once a largely treeless area on the western edge of the High Plains.

Heading for Interstate 25, which runs north-south along the eastern side of Fort Collins, I savored the sight of the snow-patched peaks of the Front Range of the Rockies to the west while still in view. Cruising north on I-25, I soon crossed the Wyoming line and passed through Cheyenne—the capital and largest city of the nation's least populated state with over 60,000 people, where U.S. 85 joined the interstate briefly. North of the city, I took an exit where 85 branched off as a two-lane highway, and I would stay on this close relative of U.S. 83 for many miles toward my destination road. A distinction of U.S. 85 is that it was designated as a major part of the Can Am Highway that connects Canada with Mexico like 83 does.

This highway is numbered higher than 83 because it's further west, and the general plan of the U.S. Highway System gives largely north-south routes odd numbers that increase from east to west; whereas the east-west routes have even numbers that increase from north to south. When the interstates were built, a reverse numbering system was devised to avoid confusion with the U.S. highways, though the odd-numbered roads are also north-south, and the even ones also east-west. Both systems also have three-numbered auxiliary routes that include the numbers of the main roads.

I drove on through sparsely populated, immense spaces with scattered outcrops, bluffs, and hills, where I spotted some bands of pronghorn antelope. The Laramie Mountains—the easternmost range of the Rockies in this region—were visible to the west. U.S. 85 crossed the North Platte River by the cow town of Torrington, east of historic Fort Laramie, and continued north through the darkening plains. I preferred to avoid night driving but wanted to make Newcastle further north for the night. Before the push, I stopped for a meal at a Subway chain store in the small ranching community of Lusk, where U.S. 85 crossed paths with U.S. 18 and U.S. 20. Ahead was a long, empty stretch with no services for eighty-one miles. Closer to Newcastle, the sprawling Thunder Basin National Grassland lay to the west in the darkness, which includes some of the most intact native prairies in North America.

I arrived in Newcastle quite late and turned west on U.S. 16 into the center of town and found what looked like a safe spot in a small grocery store lot to park overnight legally and sleep in the car. One reason I wanted to stay in the town and explore it a little was because it was the hometown I'd heard about of an old dorm-mate from the bygone days when I attended the University of Wyoming, who I'd reconnected with after forty-five years during the recent summer in western Wyoming, where he now lives seasonally. Newcastle is on the Wyoming side of the Black Hills and was established in 1889, with railroad and coal-mining origins, and named after Newcastle, England of coal-mining fame. Mining and other extractive industries have continued in this part of Wyoming, and there was an oil refinery near the center of Newcastle close to where I'd parked.

It felt good to set out on foot after the long drive, and I imbibed a couple of beers at Perkins Tavern in the downtown area—a quaint watering hole with some Western character inside. I had my first real conversation of the journey there with a friendly, young local guy when he was taking breaks from shooting pool, who admirably was a volunteer on the local fire department and rescue squad, besides having a job as a subcontractor for the state highway department.

After roaming more of the town, I was ready to get into my sleeping bag on the backseat of Wander. I had some concerns about being awakened and hassled by a bored, small-town cop, even though my parking was legal, since some towns have ordinances against sleeping in vehicles. But I was tired enough to doze off and was undisturbed this first night on the road.

In the morning, my legs had become stiff from having to bend them in the backseat sleeping position, which was relieved by some movement. Sleeping in a compact car would be more comfortable for someone only five feet tall, but the temporary discomfort seems worth it to me because of the money saved by beating a system in a country where lodgings are generally expensive and geared more toward luxury or non-essential conveniences in our culture of excess. I also love the sense of freedom from being able to live out of and sleep in a car—though certainly not every night on this journey. I wanted to hold off from paying for lodging, though, until I reached U.S. 83.

Donna's Main Street Diner in downtown Newcastle touted "World Famous Food," and the small Western omelet I ordered there for breakfast was excellent. My server was a mature woman originally from town, who had left and come back, and she remembered my old college friend. The eatery looked like a big local hangout that also attracted a lot of tourists because Newcastle is at a crossroads between many popular attractions in this part of the West. There was even a hanging notebook with the invitation, "Use this book to tell us about your journey and how your path crossed with ours," which had many signatures and comments from travelers around the country. I sure couldn't pass up making an entry about my being bound for U.S. 83.

Another sunny day was feeling more summer-like, and I followed U.S. 85 as it ascended into the Black Hills, where the scenery became dominated by pine trees, with breaks of grassy meadows and vistas of desolate land to the west. The Black Hills were named for the visual effect of the dark evergreens that cover much of the range, which rises 3,000-4,000 feet above the base elevation. Despite their proximity, the Black Hills are not considered part of the Rockies and have their own complex geology, with rocks as old as 2.8 billion years. These hills, which are the highest elevations east of the Rockies, were considered sacred to the indigenous Sioux; and there were many violations of the 1868 Treaty of Fort Laramie that prohibited non-Native settlement in the region, which started when gold was discovered there in 1874 and attracted prospectors and settlers.

The road wound through a diverse environment with some rugged features like the Rockies, but a scale that was more like the Appalachians. Some aspens mixed with pines had already turned gloriously gold. I crossed the state line that announced, "South Dakota—Great Faces, Great Places," with an image of Mount Rushmore which is located in another part of the Black Hills. After going over O'Neill Pass, U.S. 85 began a very scenic descent along Spearfish Creek, where there were many limestone formations, though some of the evergreens were denuded by bark beetle damage.

I temporarily left U.S. 85 at Cheyenne Crossing to drive U.S. 14A through spectacular Spearfish Canyon and was awed by its 1,000-foot limestone walls. Then, I reconnected with 85 near the town of Spearfish off transcontinental Interstate 90, and the old U.S. highway expanded to four lanes before the next town of Belle Fourche, which in the 1890s shipped the largest number of livestock in the world by rail. This is also the closest town to what's been determined to be the geographical center of the non-contiguous U.S. (including Alaska and Hawaii), which is about twenty miles to the north. U.S. 85 became a two-laner again, and I was back on the grassy plains with a panorama of the receding Black Hills to the south.

After a flaming sunset, I was driving in the dark again and passed through a few very small towns near a couple of sections of the widespread Custer National Forest. Then a sign proclaimed, "Welcome to North Dakota—Legendary," and I'd made it to the state where I would connect with U.S. 83, though it was still a good distance away. After a restful stop at the Frontier Travel Center in the community of Bowman at a junction with U.S. 12, I drove further north into the night.

Belfield, at the intersection of Interstate 94, is where I decided to spend the night, and instead of being seduced by one of the motels in this small town, I found a quiet trailer park outside an old downtown area that looked safe and legal to park in overnight. After driving to a nearby truck stop to use their facilities, I returned to my haven and wrote in a journal that I'd started in the car with the aid of a battery-powered lamp. The sound of a train horn blared from some distance, and I could hear a murmur of traffic from I-94.

The North Dakota sky was dazzling that night, with the majesty of the Milky Way sprawling across its center. Viewing the center of our galaxy so clearly in an area away from light pollution really made my day. But rising in the east in the late hour was the familiar and auspicious constellation of Orion the Hunter—the most prominent one of winter, already appearing soon after the start of autumn as a harbinger of the next season. The peace and grandeur of the heavens eased and uplifted my mind and spirit before I slipped into my sleeping bag again on the back seat of Wander.

After a breakfast of raisin bran with powdered milk and bread and almond butter at a table in a small local park, I was back on U.S. 85 and heading north through the expansive landscape. I wondered if the "Discover the Spirit" slogan I noticed on North Dakota license plates pertained to something real, however intangible. To the west was an area on my map marked as the Little Missouri National Grasslands. which are the largest grasslands in the U.S. The name refers to a tributary of the much longer and more famous Missouri River. I passed through cultivated stretches with sunflowers, golden wheat, dried corn, and hay bales, and there were also oil and gas operations. The outside temperature on my car's gauge was up to ninety-one degrees.

The landscape changed as the highway led into the badlands that western North Dakota is known for, and I started seeing massive, colorful rock formations that had been sculpted into varied forms by Nature's forces over time. I crossed a bridge over the Little Missouri River and entered the Central Time Zone, which was right by the entrance of the North Unit of Theodore Roosevelt National Park. I couldn't pass by a national park I'd never visited and turned west into it. The entrance station was unattended, and a visitor center was closed.

As I headed into the park's interior on a fourteen-mile scenic drive, the outside temperature had climbed to ninety-seven degrees in a strange, early autumn heat wave, and I'd changed to my shortest shorts and a light tank top. The road coursed near the Little Missouri River through rugged badlands that looked more dramatic and displayed their stark beauty under a clear sky. A sign warned about the presence of bison in the park, which can be dangerous at close range; but I wasn't lucky enough to see any. I drove to the end of the road, stopping for photos at overlooks, and didn't see many other vehicles. On the return, the sun was descending and giving the captivating landscape a golden quality with lengthening shadows. I pulled into the Juniper Campground and decided to camp there for a very low $5 fee with my national parks senior pass—one of the best deals in America for citizens or permanent residents aged sixty-two and up.

From an abundance of empty campsites, I chose one with a field behind it and a great view of impressive rock formations. It was delightful to be in a national park that was so uncrowded, and I put up my old Eureka two-person tent that I'd been using since the last century. Afterwards, I sipped a Coors Extra Gold, which went down very smoothly in the still sultry air. There was a splendid sunset through the trees, and the rocks glowed with color. After quaffing another beer at a picnic table as it was getting dark, I opened a can of Eden organic Cajun brown rice and beans and emptied it into a plastic bowl, which I didn't mind eating cold on such a warm evening.

Some mosquitos started buzzing me, which I discouraged by using repellent. The more benign sound of chanting crickets also carried in the evening air, and an immense amount of stars came out, including the Milky Way again. I gazed at its density through my binoculars and contemplated the mind-blowing scale of the cosmos and our planet's minuteness. But what wonders and beauty in this tiny world!—like what I'd seen in this national park. And as the vastness of the badlands humbles the human presence, our galaxy humbles the Earth.

A nearby restroom had flush toilets and faucets, and I was reminded of what an old acquaintance once said to me: "The challenge of camping is to be comfortable. Anybody can camp and be miserable." Inside my tent I appreciated the comfort of being able to fully stretch my legs after two relatively cramped nights in the car, and I used a compact camping mattress to lightly cushion most of my body.

Sleep came easily at the end of the third day of the journey, but I awoke after a disturbing dream about Wander not being able to start—perhaps a sign of a deeper anxiety. I was able to resume the slumber, however.

***

After another cold cereal breakfast, I walked to the restroom building. It didn't have any showers, but I gave my upper body a good washcloth rinse and even managed to shampoo under a high sink faucet, then crouched to use a hot-air hand dryer to blow dry my hair.

It was a cloudless day and close to eighty degrees when I drove off from the campsite, but I soon parked to walk a short trail to the Little Missouri River. Some of its bed was dry, but there was a strong flow that carried a kayaker. I also saw a flock of always delightful Eastern bluebirds flitting around the brush. Back on the park road, I stopped at the Longhorn Pull Out and scanned the terrain for longhorn cattle that a sign said were there and related to herds introduced in the region from Texas in the 1880s after the bison had declined. But I had no more luck seeing longhorns than the bison in the park.

Both bovines have a connection with the park's namesake—Theodore "Teddy" Roosevelt. The twenty-sixth president of the U.S. spent much time in these badlands as a young man in the 1880s—first hunting the declining bison, then as a cattle rancher with a principal residence at Elkhorn ranch, now between the North and South units of the national park. Though he left the cattle business, this Easterner's Western experience molded his character, as expressed by his later quote: "I never would have been president if it had not been for my experiences in North Dakota." Long after his death in 1919, his known love for the badlands and dedication to conservation inspired the establishment of Theodore Roosevelt National Memorial Park here in 1947, which was upgraded to a national park in 1978—making it the only national park named after a person.

The temperature had climbed to the nineties again when I rejoined U.S. 85, and I was back in grasslands and landscapes with hay bales, wheat fields, and oil wells. Just up the road was the rapidly growing community of Watford City that's located in the bustling "Oil Patch." I stopped there and had a mediocre lunch at a Chinese restaurant in a large shopping center, then bought some food, beer, and ice for my cooler at a big grocery store.

Watford City was where I departed from U.S. 85 and made a ninety-degree turn on North Dakota Highway 23, heading east. It's also where I had to deal with terrible truck traffic from the oil industry that was backed up because of road work. While moping through the congestion, it was hard to believe that the silence and wildness of the badlands was only about twenty miles away.

Finally, I was cruising about sixty-five miles per hour again on the two-lane road through more grasslands and fields, occupied by many oil wells, pumps, flares, and trucks moving in both directions, often with cylindrical tandem trailers marked "flammable." I had thoughts about the highly contentious issue of fossil fuel extraction as I ventured well into the region of the Bakken shale formation that also extends into parts of Montana and Canada. By 2013, the Bakken had become the source of more than ten percent of all U.S. oil production, and in 2014 North Dakota became the second-highest oil-producing state after Texas—all because of advances in hydraulic fracturing, or fracking, which extracts from the subsurface of the formation. I thought about the conflict between job creation, economic growth, less dependence on oil imports, and the downsides of serious air and water pollution, immense water consumption, and industrialization of bucolic landscapes I was seeing firsthand, besides new problems for boomtowns. But as with most such conflicts, there seemed to be no easy solutions. I couldn't help thinking, though, that if all the brains, money, and efforts spent on dirty and unsustainable energy were directed toward developing cleaner and renewable sources, the latter would have progressed much further. But dirty energy is Big Business that has Big Influence.

I followed ND 23 north, then east toward the Fort Berthold Indian Reservation, and saw the first sign for the Lewis and Clark Trail as I approached the Missouri River, which carried the famed expedition through a vast region of the continent. The reservation was established in 1870 and is inhabited by the Mandan, Hidatsa, and Arikara tribes, and it's another sad story of Native peoples getting short changed. For the size of the reservation allotted by the 1851 Fort Laramie Treaty became greatly reduced over time, and the construction of the huge Garrison Dam further down the Missouri River between 1947 and 1953 displaced many Native farmers and ranchers under eminent domain who had dwelled for generations in the rich bottomland areas that became flooded.

I crossed the Missouri on the almost mile-long Four Bears Bridge, where it's part of a long arm of massive Lake Sakakawea created from the river by the Garrison Dam. Ahead was New Town—the largest town and administrative center of the Fort Berthold Reservation that was a planned replacement community for residents of some of the small towns that were flooded out of existence by the dam.

Soon, I turned north on ND 8 and left the reservation. It was getting dark, but I was set on making it to U.S. 83 before the day's end. An empty stretch was ahead, where I saw more fracking activity before the town of Stanley. There, I headed east on U.S. 2—a long, old U.S. highway that was a four-lane expressway on this section. After cruising at higher speed, I took an exit for two-lane ND 28 heading north, where there were few other vehicles; and it was the type of road with slim shoulders I sure wouldn't want to have a flat tire or other mishap on, especially at night. U.S. 52 intersected in tiny Carpio, and there were no towns on a long stretch between there and a junction with ND 5, which would lead to U.S. 83.

I turned east on ND 5 and was now very excited about being so close to my big destination road. Past the small town of Mohall, at 9:47pm, after four days on the road and traveling 776 miles from Fort Collins, I reached the intersection with "The Road to Nowhere" and saw the number 83 on the familiar white shield of a U.S. highway sign. I headed toward the northern end of the highway at the Canadian border over twenty miles away. My day's destination, though, was the town of Westhope, about six miles south of the border, and I followed 83 toward the town.

I arrived in the small community in minutes and might have been more excited about it than any visitor in Westhope's history, since it was the town closest to the northern terminus of 83, where my main journey would begin. I found the Gateway Motel—probably named for its proximity to the border—and was ready to pay for a room after three nights of roughing it. The office had closed, and there was a strange way of checking in with a phone inside and dialing a message center; and I found out the person I talked to was in Michigan, and that this was a city-owned motel. A room was available for the reasonable single rate of $58, and I was given a code for a keypad to get the room key from a locked compartment.

Room 101 was good-sized with two double beds, and seemed palatial compared to my recent accommodations. Elated by the comfort zone I was now in, I uncapped a bottle of Pabst Blue Ribbon and poured it into a glass, then just relaxed in a nice, upholstered chair and zoned out for a while, not bothering to turn on the TV or do anything else. Then I made and ate two almond butter sandwiches along with half of a large orange.

I took an overdue shower that I lingered in much longer than usual, which gave me a born-again feeling because of my civilized sensibilities about feeling clean. After this self-renewal, I wrote for a while in my journal at a large desk. Later, when I got into one of the beds, I appreciated a bed as much as I ever had and thought about how the only way to really appreciate comfort is to experience some discomfort. Before falling soundly asleep, I had enthused thoughts about the big highway adventure awaiting me.

DAY

Starting down the Spine of America

Comfort made it harder to get out of bed. But once up, I was excited about the day ahead. While having another raisin bran breakfast in the room, I watched a TV weather channel that said a lot of the mid-section of the country was experiencing record-high temperatures from the jet stream circulating lower. But big changes were on the way that could bring unseasonably low temperatures soon.

Before checking out, I called my sister in Fort Collins and left a message that I'd made it to U.S. 83. Outside, the day was cloudless again and breezy, but it felt much cooler with a more seasonable sixty-two degrees, which urged me to wear jeans instead of shorts along with my denim jacket.

I talked to a fiftyish couple in the motel lot from south-central North Dakota. The man mentioned working for the state park system, and I asked about the tornado danger at this time of year.

"It's still serious enough," he said, "and in the late nineties we had a tornado right before Thanksgiving, and a blizzard right after that. That's how this climate can be."

"Very volatile then," I added, and felt uneasy about hearing that there was still a real tornado danger on the northern plains. Then the woman mentioned a time they started a road trip to Florida and got caught in a blizzard on an interstate before leaving North Dakota.

"It was a whiteout," she said, "where vehicles were immobilized and there were huge back-ups. It could even snow here now, but usually not until October."

"I'm heading far south now," I said, "and hope I have better luck than the beginning of your Florida trip. I'm driving 83 all the way to the bottom of Texas, which should be about as warm as Florida."

"That's quite a trip, and have a safe one," the man said. And the woman also wished me well.

After a long look at the metallic, silver water tower behind the motel that declared WESTHOPE, and a stop at a Cenex gas pump by the Farmers Union Oil store across the street from a noisy grain elevator, I was off to the Canadian border.

North of Westhope on 83, the last short stretch of the U.S. looked fertile and flat, and I soon approached a Port of Entry to the nation's giant but much less populated northern neighbor. A sign stated, "Canada–United States Boundary–¼ mile," and shortly after it another: "Last Turnaround Before Border." It was that close to the forty-ninth parallel—the latitudinal line that was designated the border between the two countries for 1,260 miles (2,030 km) in agreements with Great Britain in 1818 and 1846, which controlled Canada at the time. It's a major part of the longest boundary between two countries in the world.

The U.S. and Canadian Immigration and Customs stations were ahead, and the U.S. one was in view. I'd considered crossing the border, then heading right back into the U.S. to cover every bit of U.S. 83, but I didn't feel like hassling with officials from both countries and having to explain the eccentricity of such a move. So, I used a big right shoulder to turn around before both stations. In Canada, the road maintains its number and continues into the province of Manitoba as Provincial Trunk Highway 83 for another 250 miles (402 km) north to the town of Swan River. Both 83s make up the longest continuously numbered north-south highway in North America, with a total distance of 2,140 miles (3,450 km). Perhaps some future wanderlust will compel me to travel the much shorter Canadian 83, but this journey was to be a completely American one.

Wander was now aimed toward the southern border on the Rio Grande, close to 1,900 miles away down the "Border to Border Highway," as it's been called, along what I regard as the "Spine of America" because of its proximity to the center of the country. A sign proclaimed, "Welcome to North Dakota," and shortly ahead was another: "Veterans of Foreign Wars Memorial Highway"—a dedication to the nation's war veterans that all six states along U.S. 83 have made.

Backtracking to Westhope, the horizontal landscape featured some dried wetlands, with abundant cattails on both sides of the two-lane road. Lake Souris once existed here in pre-historic times—a giant, glacial lake that was about 170 miles long and almost seventy miles wide—which occupied the basin of the present-day Souris River that I'd crossed the night before. The Souris is an international river with its source in the province of Saskatchewan, which makes a good dip into North Dakota before curving back into Canada in Manitoba. Its name means "mouse" in French, and it's also called the Mouse River in the U.S. The landscape here looked more Midwestern compared to the high, dry plains I'd crossed to get here, with a flatness and more fertile appearance and more trees, though often distant. Originally, there was mixed-grass prairie here in a transition zone between the higher moisture tallgrass prairies to the east and the more arid short-grass prairies to the west. I passed cultivated fields and crops, farmhouses and metal sheds, and some windbreaker trees lining both sides of the road. Traffic was light on this first stretch of 83, and the older-looking road surface was a bit bumpy with horizontal streaks in the pavement. Westhope's grain elevator and water tower were back in view, and outside town was a sign touting Westhope as the "'Top' location in the USA," with its position just under the forty-ninth parallel marked on an outline of the lower forty-eight states.

In town, I came to an intersection with an attractive wooden sign and the greeting: "Welcome to Westhope—Est. 1904." The sign had an image of an old steam locomotive, and Westhope did develop along a branch of the Great Northern Railway. Its name was given by railroad officials who promoted the new community as the "Hope of the West." From a historic high of 824 inhabitants in 1960, its population had declined to 429 in the 2010 census—very typical for small rural towns that haven't been affected by the oil boom in the region. I parked on a side street near the small business district to explore more of the town on foot.

One of the first businesses I encountered was a bar with a Pabst sign outside. Since it was now afternoon and late enough for me to imbibe a brew without much guilt, I walked in thinking that such watering holes are one of the easiest places in small town America to have conversations with the locals. However, there was no one seated at a long bar or the side booths, but a twenty-something lady was behind the bar, and I thought I'd give her some business. She was somewhat attractive but not particularly friendly at first, perhaps because I had an unfamiliar face in a town where most were probably familiar. It was a basic small-town bar with a pool table in the back area and a pull tabs machine on one side—a game of chance that's legal in North Dakota. Behind the bar were some witty expressions displayed by mirrors, along with a sign about a happy hour. There were no draft beers, so I bought a bottle of Rolling Rock, which used to be a much better beer when it was brewed in Latrobe, Pennsylvania, but is still drinkable and economical. After a couple of sips, I broke the silence with the reserved young woman, who had a few small tattoos on one arm and wasn't wearing any rings.

"Did you have really hot temperatures here lately?"—another indication that I was a visitor in town.

"Yes."

"It must be more seasonable today,"

"It is, and they're predicting a very cold winter here, but with less snow. We usually get a lot of snow."

"Such predictions must involve enough guesswork," I commented. Then my curiosity about small-town people led me to ask: "So how do you like living here?"

"It's alright. But sometimes I wonder what I'm still doing here."

"Are you from Westhope originally?"

"Yes, and my parents are still in the area."

"If you left and lived in a bigger town, maybe you'd miss the quiet here."

"I did live in Minot awhile. I liked it but didn't know enough people there, and it's grown a lot. I spent some time in Dickinson and Fargo too. Crime has gotten bad in Dickinson in the past ten years, and I thought Fargo was too big."

I wondered what she'd think of a really big city, then asked if it was the fracking boom that had made towns like Dickinson less safe because of all the growth, and she thought it did.

"There's not much fracking in this area, though," she added.

The young woman had opened up quite a bit in a manner that was direct and unpretentious. She didn't show any curiosity about me, however, even after I mentioned being from Colorado and intended to drive all of U.S. 83. When I brought up staying at the Gateway Motel, she said the old lounge there had banquets where she and other bartenders from this place also worked, and that the town library was in the Gateway. I asked about where I could have lunch, and she said a place across the street that served pizza, burgers, and wraps was the only eatery in town after a diner next door had closed a while ago. But the place was closed for the day. The bar had a limited menu of some real pub grub posted on the wall that I didn't care for, and it didn't seem like the kitchen was open anyway. Westhope obviously wasn't a foodie's town.

Although I made some connection with the lady behind the bar, it wasn't enough of an energy exchange that led to introducing ourselves. After finishing my beer, I left her a tip, got up to leave, and said, "Nice talking to you, and I hope the coming winter isn't too cold and snowy here."

"It'll be at least one,"

"Happy Trails," was my parting remark as I continued my own very long one.

Soon after I left, I thought maybe I should have been a little more inquisitive with the Westhope native since I'm curious about what makes people tick, and just what keeps some in small towns like this. I'd barely scratched the young woman's surface.

U.S. and Canadian flags, and the North Dakota flag, waved behind a senior center on Main Street. I also walked by a Peoples State Bank, a small city hall, and a post office, where I asked a middle-aged guy coming out if the old railroad was still around since I hadn't seen any tracks.

"The tracks of a spur were removed about ten years ago," he answered in an amiable manner.

"So how does mail delivery work here?"

"The people in town have to pick up their mail like I'm doing, and those in the outlying area have deliveries."

I went into the modest-sized Opdahl's grocery store—apparently the only real food store in town—and bought a cup of yogurt. A young girl smiled at me, and an older check-out lady was also pleasant, which made me feel more welcome in town. Then I wandered some side streets with tidy homes of assorted ages, sizes, and styles, which were well shaded by hardwood trees changing to autumn colors and starting to shed leaves. There were also some evergreens that must have been planted with the hardwoods on what was originally prairie. I came to a Lutheran church and thought of that denomination's association with German and Scandinavian groups that I knew had been early settlers in North Dakota, which was evident in some of the business names in town and a few kids I saw on the walk with Nordic features. I also saw Catholic and Presbyterian churches—so three churches for a town with well under 500 people and the surrounding area that I assumed was quite religious like most rural areas in the U.S. I later checked the racial demographics of Westhope, which said the town was about ninety-eight percent White, not surprisingly. When a teenage girl bicycling one of the quiet side streets greeted me with a friendly "Hi," I wondered what reactions I might have received if I wasn't Caucasian.

I drove to a park I'd seen a sign for and noticed a public swimming pool that was closed for the season, and I parked by a weathered picnic table right next to an old baseball field where the diamond wasn't maintained very well, but the field had a groomed appearance. I sat at the table to eat the yogurt I'd bought, along with some bread, paprika-flavored peanuts, and a banana. But prairie breezes got gusty and drove me back into the car to finish eating. Other than the sound of some wind, the open park was very quiet, with not another soul around, even on a Saturday.

The ballfield, without having much of a resemblance, still made me reflect about the one right across the street from the house where I grew up in New Jersey—a very ordinary and small field, but my memories of it are huge. This now quiet small-town field must also have seen plenty of life through the years. Whose "field of dreams" was this?

The park also had a football field, which was proclaimed the "Home of the Sioux." Back in the small business center I'd seen colored window markings with slogans like: "Sioux Pride," "Go Sioux," and "We

Love the Sioux."—no doubt referring to the local high school football team during football season, which was another appropriation of the name of a famous large Native group that had once roamed the Northern plains. I supposed the high school games provided some of the biggest excitement in Westhope.

My solitude ended when a classic 1960s muscle car pulled in and parked by the football field, and a couple got out and ran two dogs on the field. Strong breezes blew in from the north, carrying the smell of manure from the surrounding farmlands into this little town on the prairie. I was ready to depart from Westhope and resume my own movement south.

I passed the town's municipal airport—another link with the outside world besides U.S. 83—and observed the level landscape that I couldn't see well the night before, which was largely cultivated with colorful wheat, corn, sunflowers, and a lot of round hay bales that I always find visually appealing. Sometimes the hand of man can enhance a landscape instead of degrading it. There were also some thick stands of cattails near the road, and a few small fracking operations in the bucolic surroundings. A noisy green combine was moving sluggishly in an expanse of golden wheat before the intersection where 83 joined ND 5 for a short distance. When 83 split off, it would run an almost totally straight course, like Plains highways often do, to the eastern end of Lake Sakakawea. There were wide shoulders on the first part of this long stretch, with "no stopping" signs and a good road surface. The larger width was soon appreciated when a big combine heading north looked to be approaching a little too close for comfort, and I veered onto the right shoulder. The landscape continued to feature more farming than ranching, though I did see a few grazing Angus cattle in some open pastures. This was a terrain that was scoured by glaciers in the last ice age, with a mix of sand, clay, and gravel called drift.

The sun was getting low as I approached the city of Minot. The highway expanded to four lanes and I passed two gates for the Minot Air Force Base. Opened in 1957, it's long been a powerhouse of national defense at this strategic location close to the northern border. From a major Strategic Air Command base during the long years of the Cold War, the base developed into part of the U.S. Air Force's Global Strike

Command, with bomber and missile wings. Mighty B-52 bombers were still operating here, and scores of Minuteman III ICBMs—among the worst weapons of mass destruction—are submerged in silos beneath the plains miles from the base, though their numbers were reduced after the Cold War. The insignia of the 91st Missile Wing includes the ironic slogan: "Poised for Peace."

Four lanes soon got me to the Minot city limit, where a sign read: "Minot—proud home of Minot Air Force Base." By now I knew that North Dakotans pronounce the city's name to rhyme with "why not." Soon, the road narrowed to two lanes again, and I later realized I'd taken the 83 Bypass instead of staying on the main highway that continues through the center of the city. My intention had been to stay on 83 itself for the whole journey, wherever it led, but I didn't feel like backtracking now and decided to make an exception. I came to the Souris, or Mouse, River, which winds through Minot and crossed a bridge over it. The city's recent growth that the bartender in Westhope had mentioned already made an impression on me, and I saw a lot of new housing developments along the bypass. At the end of the route, I crossed paths with U.S. 2 again and turned east, then took an exit that led into a huge shopping complex where I parked to get my bearings. It was a busy commercial environment full of names like Target, McDonald's, Applebee's, Pizza Hut, Best Buy, and Best Western, which seemed a world away from sleepy Westhope. A Canadian flag hung by an American one over one of the stores, and many Canadians must drive down here to shop.

Back in 1992, I'd stayed in a motel in Minot while on a motorcycle odyssey from New Jersey to Alaska to celebrate the fiftieth anniversary of the Alaska Highway that year. I decided on a second sojourn here since it was late in the day, though not in the luxury of a motel this time. I followed U.S. 2 back to 83 and found a smaller shopping center with a Walmart and turned in, knowing that this mega chain store is usually what I consider "vagabond friendly" and allows overnight parking—including for RV "boondockers" who stay somewhere without hook-ups. I still checked the lot for any restrictions and only saw a sign with "no extended stay" close to the store, and I parked in a corner at the far end of the lot by a small divider for more privacy. When not traveling, I'm not a big patron of Walmart. But their hospitable parking policy, facilities and supplies make the nation-wide stores a great resource for travelers, especially since many are twenty-four-hour stores like this one. There were also other stores and eateries in the shopping center, and I noticed a racial mix around here that included some Blacks, Hispanics, and Asians. I felt relieved to have found a place to spend the night that seemed safe; and to enhance my good mood, I pulled out a bottle of PBR from the cooler, poured it into a plastic glass, and sipped the beer in the front passenger seat.

It had gotten dark and cooler, and I discerned some clouds moving in from the west and sensed a cold front approaching. A striking crescent moon hung in a clear part of the sky. The brew whetted my appetite as usual, and I gravitated to a Mexican restaurant near my parking space called Mi Mexico, which claimed to be an "Authentic Mexican Restaurant." The place had a new look and some attractive decor inside, with a colorful mural depicting scenes from Mexico's history dating back to the Aztecs and Spanish Conquistadors. There was a cantina, but I chose to get seated in a dining area in the middle of a Saturday night crowd. My choice from the menu was a double burrito with chicken, rice and beans, lettuce, tomato, and guacamole—a basic Mexican dish that turned out to be substantial with excellent, home-made quality and reasonably priced. I thought there must now be some immigrants from south of the other border that I was headed toward who had migrated this far north; and quite a few people in the restaurant had Mexican features, including my server, who was an attractive, dark-haired young woman who was very poised. With just a slight Spanish accent, she told me she'd lived in the area less than three months and that the local economy was booming. No doubt the oil boom had affected Minot for better or worse.

On the way out, I complimented the excellent meal to a guy at the checkout, who said the restaurant had been open seven years. He had a south-of-the-other-border accent, and I asked how he felt about the North Dakota winters. His rather surprising reply was, "They're not that bad," and he was "getting used to them." I wondered if I could adapt as well.

I was interested in finding a bar in Minot mentioned in *Road Trip USA* called Blue Rider. I had the address and asked a young guy in front of the Walmart if he knew its whereabouts. He said he'd heard of it, then looked at his smartphone, and in not many seconds informed me that its distance was 2.8 miles toward the downtown area up Broadway, which the shopping center was on. The ubiquitousness of these ingenious devices and the helpfulness of many users is one reason I still didn't have one of my own. I was ready to walk the distance to the bar for the exercise.

The night sky had become overcast, and I stored my light raincoat and small umbrella in my backpack in case of any precipitation; and put on some warmer clothing, since the temperature had dipped into the fifties with some wind picking up. It now felt like autumn after the unseasonably high temperatures, and the change was rather abrupt. I paced briskly up Broadway, which was also U.S. 83, with a great footloose feeling. The area continued to be very commercial, with restaurants, motels, car dealers, and big box stores like Home Depot and Menards. Eventually, I came to 1st Avenue where the bar was and turned east through the downtown area, where part of a main street was closed for a street festival that had a blaring band. I paused my march to soak up some of the festive atmosphere, then moved on toward the Blue Rider, which I found to be somewhat isolated, with an illuminated Grain Belt Beer sign on a quaint Victorian exterior.

The inside was small and had a high period ceiling, old, thin-paneled wood, a carpeted floor, and walls adorned with paintings and pictures of different subjects. There was also moose and deer head taxidermy that gave the place some character of a country bar. Some of the small crowd was seated at tables, and I found a seat at the bar near a group of young guys. My guidebook was right about a huge selection of bottled beers, but the drafts were limited, and they apparently didn't serve liquor. I wanted to try a local beer, but the bartender said there weren't any, despite the variety. So, I wound up choosing a pint of Hefeweizen wheat beer—one of the drafts—from a brewery in Portland, Oregon, which the bartender told me was popular. I found it to be very smooth and flavorful, and savored each sip while enjoying a cozy, laid-back atmosphere in this full of character watering hole that was worth the walk.

Soon, a very fine-featured, thirtyish blonde, who looked like she might be one of the many locals with Scandinavian ancestry, stood close to me and said: "I don't mean to invade your body space. I just want a better view of the selection."

Suddenly, I felt a surge of physical attraction and replied, "I don't mind at all," then commented on the size of the selection. Not surprisingly, she seemed to be with a big guy about her age wearing a baseball cap. If she didn't have such company, I might have offered to buy her a beer of her choice. But it looked like her male companion had the honor. When she sat in view at another part of the bar, I continued to discreetly eye the rather stunning, much younger woman, with thoughts about the role of pulchritude in natural selection and how it's good for an older male's circulation.

A middle-aged guy sitting next to me was preoccupied with his phone, and to try and engage him in a little conversation, I said, "Excuse me, do you know what that street festival near here is about?"

"It's part of a high school homecoming celebration."

"Minot seems to have grown a lot in the twenty-two years since I was last here."

"It's grown a lot even in the three years I've been here."

"That must have pros and cons."

He didn't give much of a response and went back to being fixated on his phone, apparently preferring a gadget over a little conversation with a friendly stranger, which has become rampant in our age of technological excess. After finishing my beer, I made a visit to the bar's quaint and undersized restroom, where the sink had old-fashioned faucet handles.

It was after midnight when I began the hike back to the Walmart, and the street festival was breaking up when I passed by again. Soon I was back on Broadway, where a few young motorcyclists without helmets and wearing only short sleeves thundered by. The sky was still overcast, with no visible stars, in contrast to the great clarity of previous nights. As I marched up the main street, I stopped to pick up some litter to improve the appearance of Minot, however minutely, as I do in many places I pass through, as well as at home.

Back at the car, I found the Walmart had closed at midnight and wouldn't reopen until noon because of a Sunday blue law. Such laws still exist in about twenty-eight states and probably originated to encourage churchgoing instead of shopping on Sunday mornings. Since I was unable to use the Walmart restroom, I took care of a biological urge behind the store—vagabond style—and brushed my teeth by the car. The night was chilly enough for me to leave my jeans and a sweater on when I got snug in my sleeping bag and rolled up the windows, except for a little ventilation. It sure wasn't like the bed at the Gateway Motel, but I felt I'd developed a little more character, besides saving money, by not being enticed by one of Minot's motels.

DAY 6

Magic City, Lewis and Clark, and the Capital

I managed to sleep quite well and awoke to see a dome of gray overcast that rained lightly, then quite heavily. The outside temperature had fallen below fifty degrees, and the rain made me feel captive in the car. The Walmart lot wasn't crowded since the store hadn't reopened yet because of the Sunday blue law. Before 1967 these laws used to be stricter in North Dakota, when no businesses were allowed to be open at all on Sundays, including gas stations.

I drove off in the rain for a Denny's Restaurant I'd seen on the night walk, with the windshield wipers working for the first time on the journey. When I arrived, I was welcomed by the pleasing aroma of pancakes and other breakfast foods cooking. The place was filled with a Sunday morning crowd, and a large group was waiting to be seated. I was given a fifteen minute estimate for a single seating but didn't mind and shared a bench with some other patient people and noticed the age diversity in the crowd—from a cradled infant to a very geriatric gentleman tethered to a nasal breathing tube. Many of the guys were wearing the quite ubiquitous baseball-style caps, and an older gent was more conspicuous with a cowboy hat. Two teenage girls sat on my left, fixated on their phones as their age group is especially known for in this day and age, which seemed no different in North Dakota. I tried to make a little contact with the girl right next to me with a "good day to be inside," to which she responded with a curt "yeah," and continued to be captivated by her small screen. Her assumed companion looked equally lost in her own cloud of cyberspace. To occupy myself, I looked at a free print publication about current issues in the Bakken oil fields, which presented the industry favorably and had ads from companies involved in it.

Soon a booth was available for me that could have seated four, but some smaller ones were still occupied. My server was a pleasant, lanky young lady who quickly brought me a cup of hot water that I requested for the small, bottled green tea concentrate that I travel with. There was a separate menu for ages fifty-five plus, and since I don't mind the senior identity when it comes to discounts, I opted for a "Senior Starter" with one scrambled egg, a chicken sausage patty, red skin potato wedges, and whole wheat toast. The meal was satisfying and was the first one I had at a Denny's in a long time. The huge chain touts itself as "America's Diner" and has over 1,700 locations, also in eleven other countries and territories. Though I'm one who prefers supporting much smaller and locally-owned businesses, the big food chains can still have their place, especially for predictable meals. When I left, the rain had stopped, but it remained chilly enough to turn on Wander's heater when just a couple of days before I had the AC on.

The rapidly growing old river, railroad, and highway town I was in, which also has an international airport, had become the fourth largest city in North Dakota, with about a 48,000 population. Minot is also the seat of Ward County, and its beginnings go back to 1886 when the construction of the Great Northern Railway halted here for the winter, and a tent town quickly sprung up. The speed of development and rapid growth of the population to over 5,000 in five months led to the new community being called "Magic City," and it became incorporated—or an official municipality with its own government—in less than a year. The name Minot came from Henry D. Minot, who hailed from Massachusetts and was a railroad executive and investor, and interestingly also an ornithologist who'd been a classmate and friend of Theodore Roosevelt while attending Harvard. Ironically, this major railroad man was killed in a train crash in 1890 at the young age of thirty-one.

Settlers continued to arrive in Minot on the rails, with many drawn by land that became available after the famous Homestead Act of 1862, which offered ownership of 160 acres of undeveloped federally-owned land to settlers who resided on it and worked it for five years. The arrivals also included unsavory characters, which led to a period of high criminal activity and lawlessness that gave the town a reputation as the "crime capital of North Dakota." Between 1917 and 1920, a determined state attorney general named William Langer, who later became governor of North Dakota and also a U.S. senator, helped to rectify matters. But then Prohibition started, and due to its location near the Canadian border, Minot became a big hub of bootlegging that supplied a lot of Al Capone's illicit business, earning it another moniker—"Little Chicago." Booze flowed down from north of the border, with U.S. 83 and its predecessor, ND Highway 6, being the main conduit. Actually, North Dakota had been a dry state since it was established from the Dakota Territory in 1889, and bootlegging was nothing new. But the scale increased tremendously with national prohibition in 1920. Smugglers even had a system of underground tunnels to move and store their contraband.

Some natural and man-made disasters are also notable in Minot's history. In 1969, a major flood of the Souris River had very damaging effects on the city, which led to a big U.S. Army Corps of Engineers flood control project; and on January 18, 2002, a freight train carrying anhydrous ammonia had a disastrous derailment near the city, releasing a poisonous cloud that was one of the most serious chemical accidents in the nation's history. There was one fatality, but scores were sickened and harmed by the toxic gas. Then, in 2011, another serious flood struck the region that was worse than any previous ones. Whatever efforts had been made to prevent the river from becoming destructive still resulted in about twenty percent of the city suffering damage. One of the buildings affected was the Minot Amtrak station, which had been modernized in 1975 from the old Northern Railway depot built in 1905. Fortunately, it was repaired, and passenger service continues in Minot as a stop for Amtrak's daily Empire Builder, which also serves six other towns in North Dakota, with Minot being the busiest stop.

I saw no signs of disaster in town in late September of 2014, unless its growth becomes out of control. Besides a busy commercial center, Minot is a college town and is the home of Minot State University and the University of North Dakota School of Medicine. It also has some culture that includes an art museum, symphony orchestra, and opera company. Before leaving town, I wanted to check out the Scandinavian Heritage Park on 83, and when I arrived it felt chilly enough to wear my long underwear bottoms, which I awkwardly changed into on the front passenger seat. While changing, I heard a train in the distance, which was a reminder of what brought Minot into existence and continues today.

The Scandinavian Heritage Center is an impressive tribute to an ethnicity that's played a significant role in North Dakota's history. It's thought to be the only park in the world that honors the Nordic countries of Norway, Sweden, Denmark, Finland, and Iceland as a whole, where the flags of these nations wave with those of the U.S. and Canada above spacious, well-maintained grounds. I walked paved paths leading to different examples of Scandinavian culture, including a reconstruction of a Danish windmill, a traditional Finnish sauna, a thirty-foot wooden replica of a Swedish Dala horse—the national symbol of Sweden; and bronze statues of Leif Erikson—the legendary Viking explorer; Hans Christian Andersen—the Danish author; and Sondre Norheim—the Norwegian-born "father of modern skiing." The Plaza Scandinavia featured an impressionistic map of the Nordic countries set in granite, and the Observatory had a four-foot diameter spinning marble globe over a fountain. There were also interesting structures like the 230-year-old log Sigdal House that was relocated from Norway, and a replica of a Norwegian farm storehouse with a traditional sod roof and second level oddly larger than the one below. But most impressive was a replica of the medieval Gol Stave Church in Oslo, Norway. This imposing, rustic wooden structure looked like no church I'd ever seen, having a strange, four-tiered, triangular-like shape and steeply pitched roof sections. At its summit, four wing-like extensions added a final touch of Scandinavian character and craftsmanship.

Had I arrived in Minot just two days later, I could have caught the big annual Norsk Hostfest, which is sponsored by the Scandinavian Heritage Association and said to be "North America's largest Scandinavian festival" that's held at the state fairgrounds. Minot is an appropriate host since close to forty percent of its population has

Norwegian and Swedish ancestry.

Back on the highway, the rain resumed, and I soon left the bustle of Minot and was back in colorful cropland with expanses of sunflowers. U.S. 83 continued its perfectly straight, four-lane course with a smooth surface. An array of wind turbines appeared on the landscape, and if the Bakken oil formation is a huge resource for dirty energy in North Dakota, the state's winds provide plenty of a much cleaner source. As I've gotten more used to the sight of these increasingly common, towering structures, I've come to regard them as having their own kind of aesthetic on the plains, and less as unnatural-looking eyesores. And I'd rather see a type of windmill than bellowing smokestacks. I'm optimistic that human ingenuity will find solutions to the big problem of the turbines' massive blades killing large numbers of birds.

Some small water bodies became visible along both sides of the road, which I thought were signs of probably entering part of the Prairie Pothole region, with wetlands that were formed by the last ice age. When the great Wisconsin glacier retreated about 10,000 years ago, it left depressions in the terrain of this region that fill with water in the spring, largely from snowmelt and sometimes groundwater, which vary in the duration that water is retained, with some being rather permanent wetlands. These potholes, also called kettles, cover a broad belt across the northern Great Plains that extends into Canada. More than half of the potholes in this range—up to ninety percent in some places—have been drained and converted for agricultural purposes. But what remains provides a critically important habitat for waterfowl and other wildlife. In fact, fifty percent of North America's migratory waterfowl depend on the surviving wetlands, which also play a leading role in duck reproduction. Although the pothole region includes only about a tenth of the continent's suitable habitat for waterfowl breeding, about half of its main game duck species breed there.

The rain let up again, and I stopped for a photo of a large pond just off the road to the west. It was a peaceful place where greenstalked cattails lined the shore, but no waterfowl were around at the time.

I turned off the highway in a town called Max, which tallied 334 residents in the most recent count. The community was founded in 1906, and its name came from the first name of the eldest son of its first postmaster. There was a colorful "welcome" sign with a grain symbol, and near another body of water stood a row of grain elevators with the name EQUITY FARMERS' ELEV. CO on a gray structure. The elevator was along the old Soo rail line, and a long freight train was parked there. I went into the Max Farm Service Store to use the restroom and also bought a small bag of sunflower seeds grown in the Dakota earth.

After leaving Max, it rained lightly again, and I noticed a sign for a walleye tournament—referring to a popular local game fish—which indicated I was getting near sprawling Lake Sakakawea for the second time. Angling for walleye and other fish, and hunting waterfowl and other game must be a pastime for many prairie people and visitors to this region. Ahead were colorful crops and more watery potholes of different shapes and sizes, with many very close to the road. I came to the turnoff for the town of Garrison, six miles to the west—the namesake of the huge dam on the other side of Lake Sakakawea that created the enormous body of water. This community, with under 1,500 residents that began with the arrival of the Soo Line Railroad in 1905, is the home of the North Dakota Fishing Hall of Fame and Museum. A city park there features a twenty-six-foot fiberglass likeness of a walleye—size greatly exaggerated—named "Wally" in the town that claims to be the "Walleye Capital of the World." I stayed on 83, however, and saw a sign for the Lewis and Clark Trail that I was reconnecting with.

A long causeway was ahead on an embankment across Lake Sakakawea that separates its eastern end called Lake Audubon. A railroad track ran just west of the road, and on the east side were towering transmission lines that were no doubt part of the hydroelectric power system generated at the Garrison Dam. Along the shore of Lake Audubon and on its multiple little islands is the Audubon National Wildlife Refuge—a great haven for migratory waterfowl, shore and upland game birds, and deer.

Across the causeway, a tiny town called Coleharbor lay just off the east side of the road, with a population of seventy-nine that had decreased from 315 in 1950—another diminished Plains community with rail origins dating to 1904; and part of its name came from a Soo line official, W. A. Cole. I passed through a piney area before a turn-off for the Garrison Dam and power station, twelve miles to the west. The monumental dam was constructed by the U.S. Army Corps of Engineers between 1947 and 1953 to control flooding on the Missouri River and generate electrical power, and it's the third largest earth-filled dam in the nation and the fifth in the world—over two miles in length. The power supplies four states, and the giant reservoir also provides many recreational opportunities. But the historic losers were the three Native American tribes at the Fort Berthold Reservation, who fought the project to no avail, and about 1,700 of their people were forced to relocate. Eventually, the tribes received $12.5 million in compensation, but lost ninety-four percent of their farm and ranch lands, and consequently their self-sustaining, traditional way of life.

Adjacent to the dam and power station is the Garrison Dam National Fish Hatchery, which produces more walleye and northern pike than any other facility in the world, besides other species. On another route along the western bank of the Missouri River, which re-emerges from the reservoir below the Garrison Dam, is the Knife River Indian Villages National Historic Site, with remnants and reconstructions of the Mandan and Hidatsa villages that existed at the location for centuries before the Lewis and Clark expedition arrived there in late October 1804. And further downstream is the Fort Clark Historic Site—a state-owned site of a major fur trading post established by the American Fur Company in 1830. As interesting as these places seemed, I didn't want to stray much from 83 at this point in the journey. And in situations like this, when I feel like I might be missing out on something, I've learned to repeat to myself: "You can't see and do it all, and you shouldn't even try."

I cruised into a sea of cultivated sunflowers that sprawled on both sides of the highway. The rain took another break, and I stopped to get some photos at an unpaved turnoff by the single railroad track that had been running close to the road since the causeway. Another car was parked there, but I didn't see anyone else. To the west, sunflowers stretched to the horizon. The stalks were tall, and some of the dark brown flower heads were huge, with many drooping from their weight. The overall color of this cropland was a pale green, and not the dazzling yellow I thought must occur earlier in the season when the flower rays were in bloom. I learned that late September is the start of harvest time for the highly consumed seeds and that two basic types are cultivated. Black seeds produce the oil used for culinary purposes, and striped seeds—also called confectionery—are the food variety. Seeds are produced in the large, dark flower heads, and one sunflower can hold up to 2,000. Crops are usually planted in a four-year or more rotation and have a typical growing season of 120 days, with some reaching twelve feet in height. The cultivated sunflower's relative—the wild sunflower—originated in North America, and there are about seventy species worldwide. These have multiple branches and flowers, in contrast to the taller, single stemmed, large-headed cultivated varieties. Native Americans utilized wild sunflowers and began cultivating them perhaps even earlier than corn, beans, and squash—dating back to at least 2600 B.C. The Spanish colonizers introduced sunflowers to Europe from America in 1510, and crops proliferated on other continents.

These truly amazing, besides beautiful, plants do have a special relationship with the sun since the flower heads have motor cells enabling movement facing the sun—a phenomenon called heliotropism. So, the face of the sunflower follows the sun from east to west during the day and reverses direction at night, awaiting sunrise. But this remarkable functioning occurs only during the early stages of the plant's development. Once mature, with seeds formed in the head, sunflowers face eastward continuously.

North Dakota is presently the number one producer of sunflowers in the U.S., with about half of the nation's crops, and it also ranks high in the number of confection seed processing plants. Sunflower production, however, didn't become widespread in the U.S. until the 1970s, and the first commercial sunflower seed butter that I find delicious besides nutritious wasn't introduced until 2002. As I gazed at the sunflower sea, I felt a new connection with something that has nourished me. North Dakota is also a national leader in the production of thirteen other crops, including wheat, canola, flax, and sugar beets; and about ninety percent of the state's land and former prairie is used for crops and grazing. ND also has a large lead as the nation's biggest honey producer.

Ahead was Underwood—a community with 778 residents that

declined from 1,329 in 1980, which was established along the Soo line in 1903 and named after Fred D. Underwood—the vice-president of the railroad at the time. Around here was the Falkirk Mine that surface mines lignite coal and supplies the Coal Creek power plant just down the road—the largest lignite-fired plant in the country and also the largest power plant in North Dakota. *Road Trip USA* mentions the extensive strip-mined area being restored, and I didn't see visible damage from previous operations. So maybe the mining company minimized the environmental impact in this case. But when the two lofty smokestacks of the coal-fired plant came into view—belching clouds of smoke that mixed with the natural gray cloud cover—I saw effects of the mined lignite that didn't look pretty.

By the entrance of Coal Creek, the road went under an impressive, four-mile-long, tube-enclosed conveyor belt that feeds coal from the Falkirk Mine to the hungry furnaces of the plant. There were also plenty of high transmission lines branching out into the landscape from the generating station. My guidebook mentions this being one of the few coal plants in the country that's open for tours. Seeing it from about two miles away was enough proximity for me, though. I thought about the environmental necessity of replacing coal with cleaner technologies; but given the insatiable appetite for electrical power in the U.S., I might not live to see the day that the last polluting plant is closed. And of course, the industry wants to survive and thrive, which many still rely on for employment and boosting local economies. So, it comes down to another conflict of interests that can result in some of human life's greatest challenges. I just wish that the growing Earth Ethic would grow to the point where concern and actions for the health of the planet and its inhabitants decisively overpowers economic interests that there are potentially greener alternatives to.

My map showed the name Falkirk on the west side of 83—an unincorporated area along the same rail line where a depot was established in 1913 and a post office in 1916. Postal officials named it Falkirk after a town in Scotland, and it was the only place in the entire U.S. with that name at the time. About fifty people lived around there in 1920, which has been reduced to less than half that number; and the post office closed in 1955.

Some road construction was ahead that closed a lane for asphalt repaving. A few steamrollers were rolling on a Sunday, and both southbound lanes of the still four-lane highway had a rough, pre-paved surface that Wander rumbled through. Near the town of Washburn, I arrived at the exit for the Fort Mandan Historic Site, which commemorates where the Lewis and Clark expedition had their first winter refuge near the Mandan and Hidatsa villages, and right by the exit was the Lewis and Clark Interpretive Center. Like Fort Mandan, it's one of many designated sites along the 3,700-mile Lewis and Clark National Historic Trail established by the U.S. Congress in 1978, which approximates the route of the explorers and is part of the National Trails System. I pulled into the parking lot of the interpretive center, where a stretch of the Missouri River—the "highway" of Lewis and Clark—was visible well south of where it had re-emerged from Lake Sakakawea. The center was a large, modern, wooden building with some rustic character, which had recently closed for the day. I regretted that my timing was off to see the inside exhibits related to Lewis and Clark. However, I made a visit to an open restroom and picked up some flyers.

Outside were three larger-than-life-size steel statues representing the famed explorers having an encounter with the Mandan chief, Sheheke (translated White Coyote). The sculptures were created by a local artist, Tom Neary, and the historic meeting occurred in this vicinity in the autumn of 1804. An interpretive sign nearby was headed by a quotation that the chief addressed to Lewis and Clark that must have been recorded in their journals: "If we eat, you Shall eat. If we Starve, you must Starve also." The generosity of the first statement was fortunately realized for the expedition, which is why the sign had another statement: "If it were not for the goodwill and hospitality of the Mandan and Hidatsa Indians, the members of the Lewis and Clark Expedition may never have survived that first winter on the Frontier." I wondered if the Mandan chief would have been so hospitable if he had the foresight of the flood of other explorers, trappers, traders, and settlers that the expedition was a vanguard of, which eventually resulted in so much conflict, disease, death, and displacement for the Mandan and other tribes.

I drove a couple miles to the Fort Mandan site situated on the

Missouri River, and no other vehicles were parked in a large concrete lot. There was a nice, stone-sided visitor center that had also closed, but the grounds were open. Not far off was the reconstructed fort, which was a project of the McLean County Historical Society completed in 1972 and built according to the specs described in the journals of Lewis and Clark. The original fort is believed to have been about ten miles up the river at a site now submerged after changes in its course and the construction of the Garrison Dam. It was named Fort Mandan because of the local tribe's hospitality. I thought the reconstruction must draw plenty of Lewis and Clark buffs, since it represents a very significant chapter in what must be the most epic journey in American history.

A main objective of the "Corps of Discovery" was to navigate the Missouri River as far as possible into a then unknown region of the continent, and hopefully connect with other waterways that would lead to the Pacific Ocean—possibly finding the elusive Northwest Passage. This was a directive given by President Thomas Jefferson after the Louisiana Purchase of 1803 from Napoleon's France, which doubled the size of the U.S. and included the whole Missouri River basin. Other objectives were the pursuit of comprehensive knowledge—scientific, geographical, and cultural—of the vast new territory, and diplomacy with Native peoples encountered.

The Corps embarked from near St. Louis on May 14, 1804, with a 55-foot-long keelboat and two smaller boats called pirogues. Each had oars and sails, but bucking the upstream current limited the party of forty-four men to progressing only about five miles on some days. It was largely a military expedition because most of its members were U.S. Army enlisted men, and both Meriwether Lewis, close to age thirty, and William Clark, age thirty-three, had the rank of Captain. Lewis had been appointed to lead the expedition by Jefferson. There were also some backwoods types, a few French boatmen, and a Black man named York, who was Clark's slave whom he had known since boyhood in Virginia. The group possessed varied skills, and one of the civilians, George Drouillard, was an outstanding scout, hunter, and interpreter who spoke several Native languages. A strict military discipline was maintained that even included some harsh corporal punishment like flogging, and two men were court-martialed. Before the

Corps reached the Mandan and Hidatsa villages where the Knife River entered the Missouri, Sergeant Charles Floyd died near present-day Sioux City, Iowa, possibly from a burst appendix. Quite remarkably, he was the only one on the expedition to die.

Arriving at the Native villages, the party had plied 1,609 miles upstream on the Missouri, and on November 2, 1804, construction began on the original fort a little downstream. Cottonwoods were cut down for the lumber, and the men are said to have occupied the not yet completed structures on November 16, 1804—four days before the captains moved into them. Lewis and Clark shared the same quarters.

The winter of 1804-1805 is recorded to have been extremely frigid, with temperatures descending as low as minus forty-five degrees F. But the hardy group survived by hunting and trading with the nearby Natives and making clothing, and they engaged in preparations for resuming the journey in the spring. Lewis and Clark were also involved in their mission of diplomacy with the local tribes, which had their first official contact with the U.S. Government. It was at this time that the expedition was joined by Toussaint Charbonneau—a forty-four-year-old French-Canadian trapper and trader who had been living with the Hidatsa—and also his legendary wife Sacagawea (Sakakawea), who was just sixteen and a Shoshone from further west, who'd been captured by the Hidatsa when she was about twelve. Her name means "Bird Woman" in Hidatsa, as she is often referred to. The couple were recruited as interpreters for the expedition, and the captains' journals indicate they stayed at Fort Mandan during the brutal winter. On February 11, 1805, Sacagawea gave birth to a son, who was given the French name Jean Baptiste, after John the Baptist.

After the laborious process of freeing the three boats from the Missouri River's ice, The Corps of Discovery was ready for departure on April 7, 1805. The keelboat headed back to St. Louis with a dozen men and cargo of what had been collected so far, which included Native artifacts and live specimens, like four magpies, a sharp-tailed grouse, and a prairie dog—all considered exotic species at the time. There were also maps, letters, and reports, including a written record the captains had compiled on all their findings to this point, called the "Mandan Miscellany." The permanent party of thirty-three, with Charbonneau, Sacagawea, and their infant son, continued the journey upstream in the two pirogues and six dugout canoes the men had constructed. Up to the Mandan and Hidatsa villages, Lewis and Clark had been able to use maps from previous explorers, but from there on was a vast region basically unfamiliar to non-Natives. The leaders, however, got some information about what lay ahead from the Natives and traders around the villages, which Clark used to make a preliminary map.

The permanent party never found the long-sought Northwest Passage or continuous watercourse to the Pacific, which decades later was discovered as a convoluted, harrowing route through the Canadian Arctic. They had difficult portages, and the worst ordeal was crossing the Bitterroot Range of the Rockies with horses they had traded for with the Shoshone tribe. They were led by a Shoshone guide but came to the brink of starvation and had to resort to eating horse meat. Emerging from the Bitterroots, the emaciated party was luckily nurtured by the Nez Perce tribe. Afterwards, they connected with the Clearwater and Snake Rivers, which led to the Columbia River, and finally the Pacific Ocean in mid-November 1805.

For their second winter, the Corps built Fort Clatsop by the mouth of the Columbia River in what became Oregon, and this fort was also named after a local tribe. After a rainy and dreary Northwest winter, they began the long return journey on March 23, 1806, and later split into two groups to explore more territory, with Clark's group traveling down the Yellowstone River. There was a rendezvous on the Missouri on August 12, and two days later the whole party returned to the Mandan and Hidatsa villages. This meant parting with Sacagawea and her husband and son, and Charbonneau was paid the odd amount of $500.33. Sacagawea received nothing monetarily, but her name became renowned as a guide and interpreter on the epic journey. One replacement was Chief Sheheke, who was persuaded to join the returning party with a French interpreter to eventually meet the "Great Father," Thomas Jefferson. Fort Mandan was found to have burned to the ground, and the cause is unknown. A terrible fate awaited the Mandan and Hidatsa themselves, who would see their populations decimated by smallpox—having no immunity—after more contact with Whites in the coming years.

The rest of the journey was a relative express, where the Corps covered up to seventy miles a day going downstream; and they arrived in

St. Louis on September 23, 1806 and were greeted by the whole population of what was then just a frontier outpost. The most famous journey in American history had traveled about 8,000 miles in twenty-eight months and would have a profound effect on that history. This true story seems as dramatic as any fiction, and the expedition spent more time in what became North Dakota than any other future state.

I set out from the car to explore the grounds of the reconstructed fort, which I seemed to have to myself, and first walked toward the Missouri River. Near it was an over 1,400-pound steel sculpture honoring Seaman—the black Newfoundland dog that Meriwether Lewis brought on the expedition. The large canine is memorialized in a sitting position that's also the work of local artist Tim Neary, and it sits in a nicely landscaped section called Seaman's Overlook, with a picturesque view of the river.

I followed a riverbank trail east while appreciating the natural appearance of the Missouri. It looked quite wide with a strong flow, and thick rows of cottonwood trees lined both sides—perhaps descendants of trees that were here in Lewis and Clark's time. Tall grasses grew by shrubs near the shoreline. I was momentarily captivated by this great river of history, which is the nation's longest at 2,341 miles, and I again reflected on how rivers must have been the original highways.

One of the interpretive signs along the trail had the heading, "Current of Change," and a quote from William Clark's writing: "The River is a turbulent and muddy Stream." The sign mentioned the "Big Muddy" being an old moniker for the Missouri, and described the currents, snags, sandbars, ice, and other obstacles that the expedition had to navigate and how the present river is so different from the one Lewis and Clark experienced—given how dams constructed to stabilize the flow have tamed so much of a once wild and meandering course. But as I gazed toward the other shore and its sandy beach and nearby sandbar, with some autumn coloring in the background of trees, it wasn't hard to imagine the wooden boats of the Corps of Discovery passing through.

One thing Lewis and Clark never saw was a level road bridge visible downstream. Soon the trail led away from the river toward the reconstructed fort, which came into full view beyond a well-maintained grassy area with scattered cottonwood leaves. Its rusticity really evoked the past, and it had a triangular shape with tall, pointed palisades on each side. The front side facing the river had a gate that was locked after visiting hours. But I was able to peep into the interior and see different Spartan quarters representing how the men were housed and supplies stored, along with benches and an open central area with a short wooden flagpole. I later read there are replicated items inside the fort, such as muskets, the cannon from the keelboat, the captains' writing table, Clark's winter coat, and two fireplaces.

Outside the fort was an open-sided, small wooden structure with a flat roof representing the blacksmith shop that was situated away from the fort to lessen the danger of sparks igniting a fire. A sign titled "Men at Work" described how three privates manned the shop and did the blacksmithing that was very valuable for trading with the tribes. Mandan Chief Sheheke's promise of sharing available food was apparently not all about handouts, since the blacksmiths repaired tools and other items and crafted weapons like the "Missouri War Hatchet" that were traded for foodstuffs like buffalo meat, corn, beans, squash, and sunflowers.

The sense of history was heavy at Fort Mandan. Way back in 1976, I'd also visited the Fort Clatsop reconstruction on its original site in Oregon, where the Corps of Discovery spent their second winter. Decades later, I was very pleased to have made it to another very significant site along the fascinating trail of Lewis and Clark.

Driving off, 83 soon entered the small town of Washburn, which was once a busy river crossing with steamboats arriving from St. Louis in the 1800s, decades after Lewis and Clark. Now I found it to be a sleepy river town with about 1,200 people, which is the seat of McLean County and also the oldest town in the county, founded in 1882. Its name honors Cadwallader C. Washburn, who was a Union Army general, U.S. Congressman, governor of Wisconsin, and businessman who founded a mill that developed into the giant General Mills Company. An old Missouri River ferry called the Sioux Ferry operated in Washburn between 1952 and 1962 and was replaced by the bridge I'd seen from the trail at the Fort Mandan site, which didn't open until 1971. The old ferry is displayed at the local Riverside Park.

It was getting dark, and I was thinking more about where to spend the night and decided to make it to Bismarck—the state capital—which looked close enough on my map for some night driving.

Four-lane 83 ran near the east bank of the Missouri River ahead. On the west bank was Cross Ranch State Park—a very natural area along a remaining free-flowing stretch of the river in North Dakota. And adjacent to the park is the almost 6,000-acre Cross Ranch Preserve of the Nature Conservancy, which has a roaming bison herd. It rained lightly again after the last trace of daylight, and there were points of light in the flat landscape like ships on a dark sea.

I passed by Wilton—an interesting town with over 700 inhabitants, platted in 1899 when the railroad arrived. It was named after a town in Maine by the town's founder, William D. Washburn—a younger brother of Cadwallader—who was originally from Maine. Like his brother, William D. was a very wealthy businessman and prominent politician who served in both the U.S. House and Senate. Wilton was once a busy coal mining town that drew European immigrants in the early twentieth century. A reminder of this heritage is that one of the four churches in the community is Ukrainian Orthodox.

The signal for an AM Oldies station I'd been listening to became weaker, and I picked up an FM station playing Classic Rock and Bismarck-based commercials. Soon the lights of North Dakota's capital stretched in the distance, and 83 led into its outskirts. The light rain stopped again, continuing the day's intermittent precipitation.

It didn't take long to find another Walmart in a predictable outlying area. The behemoth retail chain was now a welcome sight to a carcamper, and this was another twenty-four-hour store that allowed overnight parking, where I picked a space in a far corner of the lot. Commercial neighbors included an America's Mattress store, a Super 8 motel, and some other motels that were again unable to entice me into paying for the comfort of a bed.

I walked into the Walmart to use the restroom and saw a Subway concession, and decided to eat there near its closing time when just one section was open. I sat at a small high table and was the only customer, while a young lady was working alone and cleaning up.

"I guess you're ready to head home," I remarked, to be a little engaging.

"I have to start again at 6:00 in the morning to do breakfast," she replied, without sounding too enthused about it.

Then I revealed I was traveling all of U.S. 83 and that this was my first time in Bismarck.

"So where are you from?"

"Fort Collins, Colorado, about an hour north of Denver."

"I spent some time in Denver."

"It's an exciting city," I added.

"It was alright," was her impression.

Then we got down to the business of my order, which I decided would be some leftover broccoli-cheddar soup that she microwaved, combined with a six-inch ham sub with selected veggie toppings. The soup wasn't home-made quality but was still tasty and warming after being out on a chilly day.

Seated near me, but outside the Subway area, were two women who I thought might be Native American at first and were speaking a language I didn't recognize—perhaps one of a local tribe. As I left, my curiosity compelled me to approach them and say, "Excuse me. I don't mean to interrupt, but could you tell me what language you're speaking?"—presuming they also spoke English.

Suddenly, they were attentive to me, and one of them answered, "Thai." I was surprised, and my reaction was to ask if there were any Thai restaurants in this area. The same woman said there weren't. But very coincidentally, she said they were just talking about the possibility of opening one in Bismarck! The English speaker said she lived in the city and that her companion was visiting. I told them I lived in a city in Colorado with quite a few Thai restaurants and was old enough to remember when about the only Asian restaurants in most towns in the country were Chinese.

"Thai food is better," the woman said and seemed to want me to agree.

I hesitated, then replied: "I love Thai food and appreciate its distinctiveness, but still enjoy good Chinese food. I hope you open a Thai restaurant in Bismarck."

They both smiled, and the same one said, "Maybe."

Signs in Spanish in the restroom were another indication of some ethnic diversity in this city, and I also saw a couple of Muslim women in the store wearing hijabs. One was Black and accompanied by a Black man. I thought Walmarts probably attract more diversity.

I walked around the parking lot, then down 83 quite a way before returning to Wander to catch up on journaling with the aid of my lamp again. Later I was back in the restroom to do some dental hygiene while two guys came in separately, who I thought might make a remark about my vagabond ways. But they just ignored me.

So, Day 6 started and ended in the parking lots of two Walmarts. When I got in my sleeping bag on Wander's back seat, a grubby feeling had returned from not showering for a couple of days. But I was coming to mind it less and mused on how the members of the Lewis and Clark expedition must have felt a lot grubbier.

DAY 7

Meeting more North Dakotans

When I awoke, two large camper vehicles had parked nearby, and I thought about RVs being a much more normal accommodation for travelers to sleep in—especially for my age group—than a car. But such homes-on-wheels are cumbersome on the road. I was quite proud of myself again for toughing it out in what I thought of as my "cramper," despite the temporary stiffness in my legs.

It was another overcast and chilly day, and a few ring-billed gulls were flitting around the lot. Then more flew in, probably from the Missouri River. I went into Walmart and saw the same young lady back at the Subway store serving breakfast, but I felt like having some hot oatmeal instead of a breakfast sandwich. Before I drove off to find it, I had an urge to clean up some of the repulsive amount of litter near my corner of the lot, which had attracted the scavenging gulls. Some slobby people had left their mark in Bismarck too, and I've often wondered about the demographics of littering. Is it mainly impulsive, immature teens? Or are some seniors also perpetrators? You see a lot more litter than litterers, so it's a little mysterious, like graffiti. Regardless of who made the mess, I cleaned up some of it using latex gloves and a plastic bag. After disposal in a trash bin by the store, I felt better knowing I'd left a bit of Bismarck looking better than before. I have hopes that a few people who notice a voluntary clean-up might be inspired to do the same thing, which could also inspire others. I like to imagine a mass movement where if enough people picked up even a little litter, it could result in a much cleaner America. A slogan for the cause: "If you love America, don't litter it. And pick up some of its litter."

U.S. 83 led down a long commercial strip on the north side of Bismarck, full of chain businesses and a mall. I was glad when I saw Kroll's Diner, which looked like a great place to have breakfast that was right before an intersection with I-94—the interstate I'd encountered back in Belfield, North Dakota. The front of the diner displayed a bold invitation—"Sit down and eat"—which I didn't hesitate to accept.

Inside, it was nice, clean, and uncrowded, probably after an earlier Monday morning work crowd. A small group of seniors were seated in a large dining area, but I decided to sit at a small empty counter and got prompt attention from a friendly, young male server, who brought me a little pot of hot water with some lemon for my green tea mix. The menu had a section with German breakfasts—indicating another ethnicity of many North Dakotans in this city with a very German name. But I still had a hankering for oatmeal instead of any cholesterol indulgence and ordered it. Soon a steamy large bowl arrived with a generous portion of raisins.

While enjoying the hot cereal, a young female server sat near me at the counter and started wrapping silverware in cloth napkins while watching a game show on a nearby screen. I tried engaging her by bringing up the weather.

"Excuse me, have you heard if the sun is supposed to reappear today?"

"I hope so, and I heard it's supposed to warm up to the sixties soon."

"That would be a step up from what it's been lately since I've been in the area."

"We had temperatures in the eighties last week after a cool summer."

"It got up to ninety-seven degrees when I was in western North Dakota then. So, when do you usually get the first snow?"

"Usually soon."

Then the young guy who'd served me and overheard the conversation commented: "The chilly temperatures now are normal for late September."

The lady added: "I've lived here long enough but don't pay a lot of attention to the weather around now because I don't like winter," which I took to mean she didn't like being reminded it was approaching. However, despite the very harsh winters that the northern plains are well known for, she and many others apparently continue to endure them for whatever reasons. I wondered if some of them have actually found something in North Dakota related to the "Discover the Spirit" slogan on its license plates, which might make it a good place to live even if the winters can be brutal. And I'd read that despite its climate, the state had a high rating in the Gallup-Healthways Well-Being Index in recent years. Maybe one factor was the state's current low unemployment rate because of the oil boom, since I suppose more people making money can have a positive effect on overall well-being.

When I left the counter, I said to the woman, "I hope the coming winter isn't too mean."

She replied, "Thanks."

At the crossroads of U.S. 83 and I-94, I thought this diner must attract plenty of travelers besides locals. While using the restroom, a radio station played Gordon Lightfoot's "Carefree Highway" over the sound system—an old traveling song that seemed appropriate for me and other travelers who "Sit down and eat" at Kroll's Diner.

U.S. 83 merged with I-94 at the intersection and would run concurrently with the interstate for about twenty-five miles east before resuming south. But I headed toward downtown Bismarck and took a turnoff for the state capitol area that I wanted to check out. Bismarck became the capital of the Dakota Territory in 1883, and of North Dakota in 1889, when it attained statehood. The city is also the seat of Burleigh County. Before it developed, its location on the Missouri River had been a steamboat port, and when the Northern Pacific Railway reached the east bank of the river in 1872, a community called Edwinton sprung up that was named after the railroad's chief engineer, Edwin Johnson. But it was renamed Bismarck the following year with the intention of impressing the then "Iron Chancellor" of Germany, Otto von Bismarck, with hopes it would encourage German investment in the railroad's construction, which was facing financial shortfalls. Money, however, didn't come from Germany, but the name stuck, making it the only state capital named after a foreign statesman. The railroad managed to get through bankruptcy and continue its construction. In its early years, Bismarck was another rowdy boomtown that got an economic boost from the 1874 Black Hills Gold Rush, and it became a freight shipping center. A railroad bridge across the Missouri was built and operating by 1882. However, development was set back by a catastrophic fire in 1898 that burned much of the city, including the downtown. But reconstruction followed the destruction, and largely with brick and concrete for greater fire resistance.

Bismarck continued to grow and even attracted some national businesses. In 1922, the region's first motor vehicle bridge across the Missouri River was completed and remained its only one until 1965. In late December 1930, another fire destroyed the state capitol building, which was replaced by a nineteen-story Art Deco structure completed in 1934. During World War II, the old army fort just south of the city became Fort Lincoln Internment Camp for POWs and German and Japanese-American civilians suspected of being national security risks. Over 4,000 prisoners were detained, which made it the largest of such camps in the U.S. during the war. The city was flooded by the Missouri River in 1952—the year before the Garrison Dam was completed to control its flooding.

Bismarck has had steady population growth throughout its whole history and is the second most populous city in North Dakota after Fargo, with 61,272 people in the last census. At the time, it was also rated as the seventh fastest-growing small city in the U.S., despite its winters. It's home to three colleges that include a two-year tribal school that hosts a huge pow-wow each September, and a university run by monastic Benedictine Sisters. Bismarck also has a busy municipal airport, and the railroad that played such a big role in the city's origin and development is now part of the giant BNSF Railway freight network.

I was able to park near the monolithic Capitol building, which at 241 feet is also the tallest building in North Dakota—known as the "Skyscraper on the Prairie"—with a light-colored limestone exterior and non-ornate Art Deco style. I wandered around the spacious, well-maintained grounds, where bright green lawns were bounded by rows of still green hardwoods, with a few starting to change color. In one far corner was the governor's mansion, and I came to a monument honoring "The Pioneer Family"—four personal family figures and a wagon wheel in bronze: "To honor the memory of the pioneers of the Great Northwest." When I heard the close sound of a train, it evoked what brought settlers here after the early pioneer wagons.

The autumn air was invigorating as I continued my stroll around the attractive Capitol area. There was also an interesting sculpture of a horse in stranded metal with the name "Cortes"—a symbol of the state's technological development with a caption reading: "From horsepower to contemporary power. Progress for the prairie." Near the capitol entrance was a statue of John Burke, who was governor of North Dakota from 1907 to 1913, a state supreme court justice and legislator, and a Treasurer of the United States who was known as "Honest John" for his personal integrity,

I climbed the capitol's front steps and found the building open to the public. I walked in and saw an elegant interior, where tall metallic columns lined the sides of a hall with handsome woodwork and marble floors. I wandered a little through this solemn seat of state government and saw signs for the legislative and judicial chambers, and even entered the empty Senate one. I also passed by the governor's office, where a state trooper stood in the hall. Otherwise, I was quite surprised by the lack of visible security. There were regular, free guided tours of the Capitol, but I was satisfied with a brief overview because I was more interested in the neighboring North Dakota Heritage Center.

By the center's entrance, I encountered Sakakawea of Lewis and Clark fame, with her name spelled like that of the giant reservoir that she's the namesake of, though better-known spellings are Sacagawea and Sacajawea. The first spelling is used in North Dakota because it's thought to be phonetically closest to her actual name. Here she was a twelve-foot bronze figure, bearing her infant son on her back as her face gazed west. This work of French-born sculptor Leonard Crunelle has been on the grounds since 1910, and in 2003 the state donated a replica of the statue that stands in the U.S. Capitol. It's been said there are more statues dedicated to Sakakawea than any other American woman, and most are not surprisingly along the Lewis and Clark National Historic Trail. Nearby was a more recently created steel sculpture of a bison similar to the Cortes horse and done by the same Native-American artist, Bennett Brien, who made a gift of this fitting symbol of North Dakota to its people for the state's centennial in 1989. I happened to be there the year that was the state's 125th anniversary. The state library was also nearby—a classical-looking structure with columns—whereas the Heritage Center was a large, modern complex that had recently been expanded and houses the State Museum, the State Historical Society, the State Archives, and the North Dakota Geological Survey.

I entered the spacious museum and was immediately impressed and somewhat overwhelmed by the wealth of artifacts, specimens, and information, with three main galleries hosting collections spanning 600 million years of North Dakota's natural and human history—from its geological beginnings to technological developments of the modern era. Everything from life-size skeletal casts of dinosaurs, including a T-Rex, which were denizens of ancient lands and seas here, to a hand-painted mural of a Native village on the Missouri River before the arrival of any non-Natives. I can get easily captivated by museums with a compulsion to want to see and read just about everything, which I'd need more hours for than I wanted to spend here. But I covered a lot of the place and developed a new appreciation of the state I was traveling through, and think I discovered some of its "spirit."

As I was leaving the museum, an elderly gentleman wearing a tie with dinosaur figures was at the reception desk, where I signed a guest book and left a donation—the excellent museum was even free—and a conversation started. He told me he'd been volunteering at the heritage center and Capitol for eighteen years since his retirement and revealed being ninety-three years old. He mentioned having worked on the Fort Berthold Indian Reservation that I'd passed through on the way to 83 as a practicing physician and had lived in New Town. My interest in this well-seasoned gentleman was further stimulated, and I started asking him a lot of questions that he answered graciously, which resulted in learning quite a bit about a long and interesting life. He was well-spoken, with a voice only slightly weakened by age, and displayed a mind that had maintained its sharpness.

His name was Herbert Wilson, MD, and he told me he originally hailed from Wellesley, Massachusetts, near Boston. "But I consider myself a North Dakotan," he said. However, despite many decades in

North Dakota, he had retained some of a New England accent.

"I was born in the village of Bethel, Vermont, in 1921 and was an only child, and my family left there when I was seven years old. My father was a World War I veteran who was disabled from exposure and trench fighting. Rheumatoid arthritis set in, and he wound up in a wheelchair. My father once shook hands with Franklin D. Roosevelt when he was campaigning somewhere and came over to him after seeing another wheelchair. And I once shook hands with Eleanor Roosevelt years later when she was hosting an event at a hotel in New York City."

Like so many of his generation, Herbert was a World War II veteran who had enlisted in the U.S. Army Air Force and was sent to Denver for training. He became a gun turret mechanic, but eventually a "flyboy" who flew thirty-one missions on B-24s over Europe from Shipdham, England, as a navigator and bombardier. When I mentioned that my deceased dad was also a World War II vet, Herbert was interested in where he'd been, and I told him he was in an anti-aircraft battalion in the U.S. First Army that was in the Normandy Invasion and the Battle of the Bulge. Herbert then told me about more of his experiences during the war years and the many ones afterwards.

"While in England, I met a British girl who was in an RAF division for women and did radar plotting, and we were married in January 1945. Eventually, we had six children, and two were twins. It was common to have large families back then. In the early years of our marriage, I finished undergrad work at Harvard, then attended Tufts Medical School on the GI Bill. After an internship in Massachusetts, I had a position with the U.S. Health Service in Tampa, Florida. But after sassing a superior, I was assigned to the Indian Reservation in North Dakota. It was supposed to be for just a year, but since 1952, I wound up spending forty-three more years there by choice. The Whites in the area needed doctors too, and the Native Americans were generally good patients. They did what you told them to do."

Through those decades, he was an old-fashioned GP and country doctor. "In the early years, New Town had no ambulance service," he said, "and I occasionally converted my own station wagon into one. One time a driver I had wasn't available, and I had to drive a woman in labor and her mother in a sleet storm over thirty miles to the nearest hospital because I was concerned about complications. On the way, we encountered an overturned car with two accident victims who were women—one with a broken arm and the other unconscious from a head injury. So, I had two more passengers that I tended to and managed to get into the vehicle. Then, while back in transit, a baby girl was born, and the umbilical cord was cut. But since the new grandmother was too nervous, and the others were unable to hold the newborn, I wound up having to with one arm while driving with the other through the slushy mess until we reached the hospital."

He had successfully been a doctor-driver, and I'm sure there were many other great stories he could have told.

"My old wartime bride who's a year younger than me also volunteers here"—which I thought was quite remarkable and realized they'd been together about seventy years.

"So, how have you both taken to the cold and harsh environment of North Dakota for so many years?"

"My wife especially missed the trees and greenery at first, but we both adapted eventually."

"So, I guess you plan to remain here."

"Despite the weather, we've put down roots here, and it's great having three of our six children nearby."

I thought that besides such roots, perhaps he had long ago discovered an intangible "spirit" in the state that might be another reason he continued to live here instead of packing up for the year-round warmth of Florida, where his career had started. If he felt exiled in North Dakota at first, it had truly become his home.

"A few of my kids have retired. That's when you know you're really getting on in years. Sometimes I wonder why God has kept me alive so long."

"Maybe one reason is to meet me," I answered half-seriously and did think there was something fateful about our paths crossing. I told him about my journey, and he liked what I was doing and knew a lot about U.S. 83 locally and its old moniker—The Border-to-Border Highway.

Before I left, Herbert showed me a book he was reading titled, *Encounters at the Heart of the World: A History of the Mandan People*, by Elizabeth A. Fenn—about the indigenous people of North Dakota that

Lewis and Clark had spent time with and who became one of the Three Affiliated Tribes on the Fort Berthold Reservation where Dr. Wilson had provided medical services for so long. Reading this book showed the keen interest he still had in these people and their culture.

Besides his reading, Herbert also mentioned being a writer who was working on memoirs about his eventful life, though not for commercial publication. An elderly woman stopped by who was about to relieve him after his shift, who I first thought might be his wife. But it turned out she was another volunteer and a very nice and perfectly spry older woman I found out was originally from Oregon. I didn't inquire, but wondered what kind of story she had about winding up in North Dakota from the opposite side of the country from where Herbert came from. I asked her to take a picture of him and me, and he put on a jacket with an old U.S. Army Air Force emblem that he was apparently still very proud of. I asked about its significance, and he said it represented the 44th Bomber Group 8th Air Division, known as "The Flying Eight-Balls." Before it was time to go our separate ways, we exchanged contacts. Then, feeling some emotion, I told him how great it was to meet someone like him left of what's become known as the Greatest Generation—the generation of my parents and so many others so influential in my life, now mostly gone. But I remember them being so numerous and so much younger and vigorous when we Baby Boomer offspring didn't always consider them so great. There were many child-parent and generational conflicts, and great clashes of values. But as our generation grew older and changed, so did many of our perspectives, and I told Herbert that I thought the description "greatest" for his generation was deserved in many ways.

"If I make it to ninety-three, I hope to be doing something like you are now," I said to him. He gave me a warm smile and handshake, and I departed with, "Stay well, and God bless you," despite my being an agnostic. He was a man who I thought was as interesting as anything I'd seen in the museum, and I felt very lucky to have met him.

I went into the museum store and bought two jars of jam made with wild North Dakota juneberries and chokeberries. A female employee with Native features helped me make the selection. At the checkout, I also conversed with a pleasant, elderly Caucasian woman who asked where I was from and going, and when I mentioned driving all of 83, she said she and her husband had traveled it as far as Liberal, Kansas.

"It was often a lonely road," she recalled.

"It's been called The Road to Nowhere," I replied, "which has a strange appeal to me."

An appetite drew me back to Kroll's Diner for a late lunch, and some different servers were there. This time I ordered a large bowl of cabbage soup that consisted of slivered cabbage, carrots, and small pieces of kielbasa, which had a hearty, home-made quality that reminded me of the delicious soups my Polish grandmothers made.

Ahead, I followed U.S. 83 South, where it merged with I-94 East. To the west, the interstate crossed the Missouri River into Mandan—a smaller city than Bismarck named after the indigenous tribe, which also has railroad origins. Seven miles south of this town is Fort Abraham Lincoln State Park, known for its reconstruction of the fort where Lt. Colonel George Armstrong Custer's Seventh Cavalry Regiment departed in route to their annihilation at the Battle of the Little Bighorn in Montana on June 25, 1876. There's also a replica of another Mandan village in the park, which I decided not to sidetrack to.

There are several stretches where 83 runs concurrently with interstates that are deviations from its essential two-lane character, and the approximately twenty-five-mile section of I-94 that I was cruising east on is the longest of these expressway stretches. U.S. 83's original route here is a very short distance south on what's now a county road along the historic railroad that passes through the tiny towns of Menoken and McKenzie. This had also been the route of U.S. 10—a once major east-west highway that ran from Detroit to Seattle but was shortened on both ends when interstates were built.

I passed some new housing developments on both sides of the super-highway that were signs of Bismarck's growth but was soon speeding through an open area with distant views, large, dried cornfields, sunflowers, wheat, and hay bales. The road had smooth new blacktop conducive to speed, with no shoulder lines painted yet.

U.S. 83 exited the interstate at the unincorporated community of Sterling, with a population of around 170. I didn't see much there besides a motel advertising "reasonable rates," and although I didn't intend to sleep in Wander again the coming night, I wanted to make it to Linton further south, with still quite a bit of daylight left. I was happy about 83 reverting to a two-laner for the first time since north of Minot, and Sterling is the original northern end of the highway, which in its earliest years also went only as far south as the border of South Dakota. It was in 1930 that U.S. 83 was commissioned to be a border-to-border highway, but it took years to complete and wasn't fully paved until 1959.

The pavement of the two-lane road I was now traveling had crushed pebbles and horizontal streaks of what looked like asphalt spaced apart, which gave it some older character; and the narrow shoulders were a contrast to those of the expressway I'd just left. I passed large, dry-looking sunflower fields with a dark appearance, and some cattle were scattered on the landscape. Traffic was light, and the sky was still gray to the south and west, with patches of blue appearing in the east.

Ahead was Moffit—another unincorporated community that didn't have much more than a post office and bar. The P.O. started operating in 1906, during the period a town was being established after a branch of the Northern Pacific Railroad came through in 1903. Presently, Moffit—the family name of some early settlers—had under fifty inhabitants. But it once was more populated and is a prime example of a once viable small Plains town that has steeply declined. It's ironic that the post office that was one of its first establishments—as in most towns—is also one of the last to survive.

Moffit is located at the western end of the eighteen-mile-long and aptly named Long Lake, which is surrounded by the 22,300-acre Long Lake National Wildlife Refuge, established in 1932 for migratory birds along the Central Flyway. The large, shallow lake also attracts many resident birds and other animals, and its avian significance is great enough for it to also have been designated a Globally Important Bird Area in 2001. Besides an abundance of waterfowl and shorebirds, the refuge is seasonally visited by sandhill cranes, whooping cranes, and bald eagles. I would have loved to make my own leisurely visit and hunt with my binoculars, but it was late in the day, and I had the momentum to do more miles.

A sign reminded me that 83 was also the Veterans of Foreign Wars

Memorial Highway. And another showed that this section had also become the Lawrence Welk Highway to honor one of North Dakota's favorite sons, whose birthplace and family farm lay a few towns ahead in Strasburg. Hazelton was the next little community also along the old railroad, which was founded in 1902 and named after a woman with the name Hazel. It wasn't as tiny as the last two settlements, with a population of 235; and in 1940, it had over double that number. To prevent further decline, there's been an unusual offer of free land and start-up money from town leaders to entice people to move there.

Ahead, my map showed Temvik on the east side of the highway—a place described as a ghost town on Wikipedia and another website. There was a farm, however, on the north side of what had been a real community and a cemetery on the west side of 83—appropriate for a ghost town. Some buildings were also reportedly left. The town came about in 1904 along the old branch of the Northern Pacific and had a few other names before it became Temvik in 1911, which was a combination of the names of the adjacent town of Templeton and its former name of Larvik that was given when the towns merged. In its early years, Temvik had several grain elevators where farmers hauled wheat to ship on the rails. There was also a school and about 200 residents, which had declined to about forty-five by 1960. In 2000, only four people were left in one census block at the town's location.

Daylight was dimming as I neared Linton, but I was able to see the increasingly familiar profile of another prairie town, with a big grain elevator, water tower, and an attractive, lighted church steeple. I came to a hospitable sign—"Welcome to Linton—90 businesses to serve you. Hunting and fishing at its best"—and thought there must be some lodgings in town. I turned off 83 by a sign for the business area and drove slowly up Broadway St., where I saw three bars, hardware and auto parts stores, a pharmacy, a bakery, a few eateries, a small Ford dealer, and a senior center. Some of these businesses had German names like Wagner and Schumacher. Toward the end of the quiet main street was the grain elevator, and before it, a bar with a Hamm's beer sign and the name Happy Hour under it. I stopped there, not to imbibe yet but to inquire about lodgings in town. Not having an omniscient smartphone can encourage a traveler to engage more with local people for information, which can result in some conversations and connections. In this case, I asked a woman tending the bar what was around, and she recommended a nearby motel on the highway. I thanked her and thought about returning to the Happy Hour Lounge for my own little happy hour.

On the way out, I noticed a poster advertising a German Heritage event: the "89th annual sauerkraut day" on October 8 in the town of Wishek to the east—featuring kraut, wieners, mashed potatoes, German music, and no doubt beer. It sounded like the kind of festive ethnic event I would have enjoyed attending if I were around at the time, and I would see a lot of the influence of this area's German population in the short time I was there.

The motel was easy to find and had a vacancy sign. It was an L-shaped, vinyl-sided place that looked respectable and independently owned. Some pumpkins outside the office added a seasonal touch. Inside, I found out the place had a reasonable rate and checked in with an older guy who was the owner, and I engaged him in some conversation by mentioning my journey down the whole length of 83.

"Is this a bucket list thing?" he asked.

"Sort of. I love driving old two-lane highways and have wanted to travel all of 83 for several years."

"I've been down 83 through a good part of Texas," he said, "though not all the way to Brownsville, when I worked in construction and drove trucks and heavy equipment. I worked in a lot of places before I left the business."

"So, I guess you're now settled in a very different kind of business along a road you drove a lot of."

"Yes."

Like at the motel in Westhope, I got an old-fashioned key instead of a key card for Room 30. The room was average sized with two double beds, and I was delighted there was a bathtub besides a shower that I could take a good soak in. But I decided to wait and started walking back to the Happy Hour Lounge.

It was now dark, chilly, and a little windy, and it felt good to arrive in a warm watering hole. There was a long bar where a small group of mostly baseball-capped guys were sitting and chatting toward the far end. The same lady tender was there, and I told her I'd checked into the motel. I found out the bar no longer served the advertised popular, old Midwestern Hamm's beer, and there were zero craft brews in their selection. So, I wound up sipping a pint of mass-produced Bud Light—the only draft beer there—which I'd heard had become the number one selling beer in the U.S. that I was finding to be very popular along the highway, even if it's a brand that beer snobs would regard as more like water than real beer. As much as I also appreciate good beer, I'm not such a snob and can drink any beer that doesn't taste bad.

Behind the bar was a small sign with a little play on the words of the bar's name: "Who said Happy is only an hour?" The woman working the bar looked about forty, and I was able to have some conversation with her since she wasn't too busy and hoped to learn more about small town prairie people and what keeps some of them in these towns. I mentioned my trip, then asked her how much of 83 she'd traveled.

"Not too far," she answered, "just some ways into South Dakota."

"Are you from Linton originally?"

"Yes."

"So, you like living in a small, quiet town?"

"Yes, but sometimes it seems too quiet."

"Have you ever left then?"

"I did. I lived in Minneapolis and Fargo. Minneapolis was too big, and I really didn't like its size. Fargo is a good size, but it's growing very fast."

She was another small-town native I met who'd left and returned, and I would hear this theme repeated.

"I was in Minot recently," I said, and saw all the growth there, which must have a downside. And I heard that the big oil boom around Dickinson has resulted in a lot more problems with crime.

"It's becoming more of a problem in Minot too," she added.

"Not surprising. But Linton must still be a very safe place."

"Lately there's been some riffraff around, though. They're getting down here too. This town doesn't seem as safe as before."

Wondering if her comments suggested anything racial in what seemed like a very Caucasian community, I asked, "Are these people White?"

"Yes"—indicating it wasn't racial.

"What do you think brought them here? Maybe some kind of work?"

"Not work. I think a lot of them aren't working and may be on public assistance."

She went over to serve the group of guys who were still conversing, with occasional expletives, then came back and we resumed our conversation. She didn't show much curiosity about me, but easily answered more of my questions.

"Are there many seniors in town? I did notice the senior center near here."

"There's quite a lot, and many are lifetime residents."

"So, besides Linton seeming too quiet here at times, are you glad to be back after living in the cities?"

"Sometimes. I like the lower rent here."

It seemed like she had some ambivalence about living here and that economics and roots were keeping her.

"Have you ever been to Colorado? That's where I live now."

"Just at the airport in Denver."

"Well, there's so much more there you really should see. You've got to go into the mountains. I moved to Colorado from New Jersey close to two years ago, and soon after the state's voters had decided to legalize recreational marijuana. I'm glad they did, though I haven't done pot in decades and still have no interest in it. I kid people that I moved to Colorado for the beer, not the pot, since it has such a great beer culture and so many breweries."

"I know about that and think that more states will follow Colorado in legalizing pot."

"Probably, but some will likely wait to see how the experiment with legalization works. So, where's the good hunting and fishing around here that I saw on a sign near town?"

"One area is Beaver Bay on the Missouri River that's about thirteen miles west and draws a lot of sportsmen."

When I got to the bottom of my pint, I could have continued the conversation with another round, but I was ready to eat something back at the motel and concluded with the words, "It was very nice talking to you."

"You too. And have a safe journey."

I forgot to check out her ring finger for a sign of marital status, but I got the impression she was single because she didn't mention a husband like married women usually do. It always feels good to make connections with strangers when traveling, even if superficial; and in this case, I heard another little story about the return of a native to a small town.

On the way out, I took a better look around the place, which had a linoleum floor, a usual pool table in a back area, a dart board near the bar, and electronic games up front, including two pull-tabs machines for a little legalized gambling. None of these were being used at the time, though.

Back in the motel room, I prepared a late supper of canned sardines packed in extra virgin olive oil, mixed in my plastic bowl with canned green beans, and some whole wheat bread on the side. The motel owner had informed me that the only place in town to get food after 8 p.m. was a convenience store nearby. But I preferred the food I had and found the combination tasty.

I turned on the TV and found a channel showing the classic movie, *Jurassic Park*, which reminded me of the dinosaur reconstructions I saw at the museum in Bismarck early in the day. I left the movie on as I took my first bath while on the road—indulging in the great pleasure of a long, hot soak, followed by a shower rinse, which gave me another "born again" feeling of cleanliness.

I finished the day writing in my journal until overcome by fatigue. Soon, under the covers of one of the double beds, I savored a very comfortable feeling again and was soon asleep. I hadn't traveled many miles on the seventh day of the journey and the end of the first week, but I had met more North Dakotans.

DAY 8

A Blachenda, Lawrence Welk, and South Dakota

I stayed in the motel close to checkout time. The last day of September was another gray, chilly, and blustery one. I drove to the small business area of Linton for a better look in daylight and to stop at the Model Bakery with German baked goods, which I'd read about in *Road Trip USA*.

On the way was the large, brick, two-story Emmons County Courthouse, which was built in 1934 as the first Works Progress Administration project of the New Deal era in North Dakota, and one of eight courthouses in the state with an Art Deco design. In 1985, this one was placed on the National Register of Historic Places. I parked near the bakery, which shared a building with a hair salon and florist, and there were signs in its window for blachendas, kuchen, and homemade soup noodles. A wonderful baking aroma wafting outside was a real enticement to go in, and inside the smell was even better. The counter area was rather small, but there were cases filled with a big selection of breads, pastries, and other goodies, including twelve varieties of kuchen—the German word for cake.

Soon a middle-aged woman with fair features came out to wait on me, who was very pleasant. I told her I was traveling 83 and had read some favorable things about the bakery in a guidebook and wanted to try something.

"Some blachendas have just come out of the oven," she said, "which are a crusty pastry with either apple or pumpkin filling and not too sweet. The pumpkin is like pumpkin pie."

"I'll go for one of those then, since I love pumpkin pie."

She wrapped it in a small, white bakery bag, and I also bought a loaf of whole wheat bread. We then eased into a conversation, and I found out the woman's name was Mary and that she and her husband have owned the bakery since 1975.

"I have a daughter in Denver," she said after I mentioned being from Colorado, "and another in Jacksonville, Florida. I have roots on my father's side in this part of North Dakota with Russian-German ancestry"—referring to the interesting group of ethnic Germans who had lived in Russia in the 1700s and 1800s before many emigrated to the U.S. and other countries—"my mother's side was Irish, though. My Russian-German great-grandfather arrived in North Dakota in the late 1890s, and he had a livery and some other businesses. My husband's background is fully German, and he speaks the language. His father didn't speak English until he went to school. I only know a little German, though, including some curse words."

What she said reminded me of the famous late musician-band leader Lawrence Welk, whose hometown of Strasburg was right down the road, and who also had a Russian-German background. I mentioned this to Mary.

"I once met Lawrence Welk when he returned to his home area and played golf at a local course," she said. "I liked his music, though it's partly local pride."

"I can't say I did," I replied honestly, "but his 'champagne music' was sure popular with a lot of the older generation at the time, including my dad, who was a big Welk fan. Linton sure seems like a peaceful little refuge after the bustle I saw in Minot and Bismarck."

"We like our quiet little town," she said, and made no mention of any invasive "riffraff" like the bar lady did the night before. "There's been a proposal, though, for a gas-powered plant near town that would bring in jobs and more people after there's been a decline in our population. There used to be five churches and five bars in town."

I chuckled a bit and replied: "I've already noticed a rather even number of churches and bars in these small towns along U.S. 83. So, I heard hunting and fishing are very popular around here."

"Yes, and it draws a lot of out-of-state people, especially from

Wisconsin. Neither me nor my husband are sportsmen, though."

"You're probably too busy baking," I kidded, "but do you know about different hunting seasons?"

"I don't know exactly, but I think it's deer season now, and the pheasant season starts soon, which is very popular."

Mary was unhurried enough to show me the much larger back working area where she practiced the art of baking.

"We plan on working quite a lot longer. I don't think anyone else would want to take over with all the work it involves, and this town needs a bakery."

"I admire that kind of community spirit, and an old-fashioned ethnic bakery like this is surely preferable to something like a Subway franchise moving in here. It's good to know that someone like you is carrying on a culinary tradition that was probably widespread in the area in past years."

She appreciated hearing that, then asked what I did for a living, and I told her about my old employment that I'd retired from. I had to get her take on the local winters, which was: "There is a lot of cold and snow that I really don't like."

But like many other long-time denizens of these plains, she still lived here regardless of the winters, apparently because of deep personal roots for the most part.

When it was time to leave and let Mary get back to work, she wished me a "great trip" and provided a cup of hot water for my morning tea. It was a good conversation with a woman who put out positive energy and seemed happy with her work and living in Linton. Perhaps when it was time to finally retire, she and her husband would remain there if they didn't opt for a much warmer place like Florida, where a daughter lived.

Back in Wander, I sipped my tea and savored every bite of the freshly baked blachenda, with its large and delectable, soft turnover-type crust and generous pumpkin filling. Long live the Model Bakery!

Besides this great business, my guidebook mentioned Linton having a very small bowling alley, which happened to be next door where a storefront stated Linton Cafe and Lanes. But both the cafe and miniature bowling alley were closed. When I started walking down Broadway St. again, I saw a small old theater that looked vacant when

I peered in—another sign of decline in the town. Demographics I later checked indicated that after reaching a peak population of 1,826 in 1960, Linton had a steady decrease to 1,097 in 2010. Yet among North Dakota's 356 municipalities, it's still in the top twelve percent numbers-wise. The median age of its residents has increased to fifty-four, and it's over ninety-eight percent White. Linton was established in 1899, and the branch of the Northern Pacific Railway had arrived in the area two years earlier. Its name was inspired by George W. Lynn—a settler, farmer, lawyer, and publisher—with an alteration of his surname.

While on foot, I noticed a sign for another German festival—the 5th Annual Oktoberfest on October 18 at the Linton Senior Center—and a festivity with a different ethnic flavor the week before—the 15th Annual Linton Chile Cook-Off, sponsored by the local chamber of commerce. I learned this event draws people from around the state and kicks off the pheasant season. So, this quiet and numerically declining town had some occasional vitality. While poking around and taking some photos, I wondered if anyone was watching me checking out the town.

I drove off for a look at another part of Linton and passed a small, one-story hospital, a Catholic Church with the steeple I'd seen illuminated the evening before, and a modern-looking Lutheran church that was close to a high school. I parked near some pines on a small hill by a residential area with one-story homes. Some grassy hills lie just to the east, and it was a nice, quiet spot to jot more in my journal, with the mood enhanced by the peaceful peel of church bells on the hour.

After I drove off and gassed up on the way out of town, it started raining. With the chill persisting, the hot and dry weather that had welcomed me to North Dakota had become a fond memory. I was very glad to be traveling south and was already looking forward to the subtropical weather in South Texas.

Soon I encountered the heaviest rain yet on the trip before Strasburg, which had Wander's wipers laboring. Despite poorer visibility, I could still see vast dried cornfields, hay, sunflowers, and some water bodies on both sides of the road that may have been prairie potholes. Some tiny hailstones were mixed in the downpour, but then it all let up, and the sky cleared dramatically in the west while still gray to the south and east.

I came to a circular sign—"1 Mile Turn Right, The Birthplace of Lawrence Welk"—which I decided to visit, despite having never been a fan of the late band leader's style of music. It was still local history, and Lawrence Welk happened to be the first inductee in the North Dakota Hall of Fame at the State Capitol in 1961. Before the turnoff, I pulled off the road for a photo of a spectacular prairie sky—with cloud formations and color contrasts that delighted my eyes in each direction. Across the broad fields to the south was the small skyline of Strasburg, with its grain elevator, church steeple, and spherical water tower above a line of trees. On the east side of the highway, a long row of power lines stretched toward the town.

After the turnoff was another sign for the "Welk Farmstead Historical Site," and I followed a ruler-straight unpaved road along vast fields of dried corn, tall sunflowers, sprawling wheat, and cattle grazing in open areas. When I reached the site, there was no one else around at a very isolated rural haven with a small, white, clapboard farmhouse, a few smaller structures, a barn, windmill, tractor, and bandstand. There were also shrubs and mixed types of trees, and in the background was a good-sized lake. I was immediately affected by the serene quality of this bucolic place.

Lawrence Welk was born in the farmhouse in 1903 to Russian-German parents who had immigrated in 1892 and became homesteaders. These "Germans from Russia," as they were also known, were a large population of ethnic Germans who had lived in Russia since the days of Czarina Catherine the Great, who was ethnically German herself, and who in 1763 began an open immigration policy. This was over a century before Germany became a unified country when unfavorable socio-economic conditions in some of the German-speaking states led to much of the population being driven to emigrate. In Russia, they were valued for their farming and other skills, and even granted certain privileges like exemption from military service. For over a century, these transplanted Germans lived in parts of Russia and Ukraine in separate communities, where they preserved their language and culture. But in the early 1870s, Czar Alexander II established policies that ended open immigration, and after 1874 the ethnic Germans were no longer exempt from military service. Later, they were also required to learn Russian in schools, and other privileges were lost. Many still remained in Russia, but large numbers emigrated to the U.S., Canada, and even South America. In the U.S., numerous Russian-Germans settled in the Dakotas, Nebraska, Kansas, and Colorado. The Great Plains were an attraction because of a similarity to the steppes of Eastern Europe, where so many of these also called Volga and Black Sea Germans had lived and farmed. In America, they were successful in a type of dryland farming that they'd done in Europe. The migration continued until the Russian Revolution of 1917, which restricted travel and emigration from Russia. Lawrence Welk's parents, Ludwig and Christina, had settled in Ukraine, and when they came to America in 1892, they were drawn to North Dakota by the Russian-German communities there and the prospect of farming and owning land made possible by the original Homestead Act of 1862. This landmark legislation really opened the West by making it possible even for immigrants who had applied for U.S. citizenship to own 160 acres of undeveloped land owned by the U.S. Government after living on it and developing it for five years. It's said that the Welks spent their first winter in the old homestead I was visiting in an upturned wagon covered with sod. And the clapboard house there now began as a sod house with mud walls.

Lawrence was the sixth of eight children, and he grew up speaking German, which resulted in his famous accent. His education was interrupted in the fourth grade when he left school to work full-time on the family farm. His father played the accordion, and during evenings gave the young Lawrence lessons. Eventually, he was playing his father's accordion at local dances and other social events. Then he purchased a couple of cheaply made instruments from a Sears and Roebuck catalog—the great mail-order resource that many rural people relied on that was sort of the Amazon of those days—which soon became dysfunctional and led to his persuading the senior Welk to buy him a high-quality accordion for the sum of $400—equivalent to over $4,000 today. In return, Lawrence promised to work on the family farm until he turned twenty-one and give any money he made from performing to the family. As soon as he came of age, with promises kept, he left the family farm to pursue a career in music, which had become his great ambition. Though his parents accepted it, his father was extremely skeptical about his prospects and disappointed that he'd turned his back on farming life.

In the 1920s, Lawrence managed to play in various bands and enrolled in a music school in Minneapolis. In the meantime, he learned to speak English and was able to lead bands in North and South Dakota. During the thirties, he broadened his range by leading a big band that traveled around the country by car. However, the band usually didn't make enough money to rent rooms, and they often changed clothing and slept in their vehicles. During a hotel gig in Pittsburgh, someone compared the band's light, sweet sound to champagne, which inspired the Welk "champagne music" moniker. They eventually drew bigger crowds during the Big Band era and did recordings, and from 1949 to 1951 the band had a national radio program on ABC. In 1951, Lawrence Welk settled in Los Angeles and began producing a TV show on KTLA—the first TV station in California—and the show became popular locally. Then, in 1955, it was picked up by ABC and became a national show. The rest, as they say, is history, and it became one of TV's longest-running shows that continued until 1982, the year Welk decided to retire. His orchestra also had a lot of recording success with a good number of high charting albums and a number one instrumental single, "Calcutta," in 1961.

After his retirement, Welk was involved in re-runs of his 1,065 shows, which became popular on public TV stations. He was also a very savvy businessman with investments in real estate and music publishing, who became the second wealthiest performer in show business after Bob Hope. All very amazing for a North Dakota farm boy and son of immigrant parents who had lived in a sod house. And there's probably no better example of someone with humble origins achieving what's considered the pinnacle of the American Dream. Lawrence Welk died in 1992 at the age of eighty-nine from natural causes, and he was married for sixty-one years to a woman named Fern Renner. They had three children and numerous grandchildren and great-grandchildren.

My own memories of the farm boy turned celebrity and his "musical family" are the Saturday nights at home while growing up, when my dad—always a music-lover—faithfully watched the Lawrence Welk Show, though my mom was rather indifferent to it. The "champagne music" that was a remnant of the Big Band era and the "wholesome" entertainment included in the variety show was aimed at an older White audience and didn't appeal to most of my generation. But millions apparently loved it, considering the show's decades-long run.

The old Welk farmhouse was closed at the time of my visit, but it's open for tours during the summer. I was content to just roam the grounds and look at and photograph the structures, though it would have been interesting to see the original accordion inside the house that Ludwig Welk bought for his young son that launched a famous career, along with other memorabilia and furnishings donated by the Welk family. Nearby was an outhouse—a reminder of the good old days before indoor plumbing—and I walked by the red barn where the young Lawrence is said to have practiced his accordion. Near the barn was the small, wooden Lawrence Welk Bandstand that was dedicated in 1989 and inscribed with a slogan of the bandleader: "Keep a song in your heart." Coincidentally, a private restoration of the farmstead was completed in 1992—the year Welk died, and it's actually a memorial to his parents and officially called the Ludwig and Christina Welk Farmstead. Neither of them lived long enough to see their son make the big time in the music business. In 1993, the site was placed on the National Register of Historic places, and I was there the year that the Welk family sold it to the State Historical Society of North Dakota.

I walked close to the prairie lake, where there were hovering gulls and floating waterfowl, with scattered hardwoods along the shoreline transitioning to autumn colors. The foreground had a carpet of bright green grasses, and golden fields stretched in the distance. The gray overcast created a gloomy beauty, and there was something idyllic about the isolation and peacefulness of this place that made it worth visiting, regardless of Lawrence Welk, which looked like it might not have changed much since the days of his youth here. My visit also revived memories of this personality and an old TV show that reminded me of my father and part of my own youth. I lingered longer than I thought I would at the site.

Back on 83, this section in Emmons County was designated the Lawrence Welk Highway in 1995. I also spotted a sign for the Welk Dam—a later name given to a Depression-era, WPA-sponsored water conservation project. A large sign where I entered Strasburg announced,

"Welcome to Strasburg—Birth Place of Lawrence Welk," and there was no doubt who the favorite son in these parts was. The name Strasburg was also on the town's spherical water tower, and I turned off the highway and parked on Main St. to begin another little foot tour. The town seemed smaller and sleepier than Linton, though the grain elevator operating near the other end of the street was noisy.

Strasburg is another prairie town with railroad origins that was founded in 1902. Its name came from a town in Ukraine where Russian-German settlers had lived and named after the historically German city in Alsace, and it's one of the North Dakota towns where German has been spoken. The last census showed 409 residents—after a steady decline from a population high of 994 in 1940—with a median age of 60.8, making it an "old" town.

Soon after I started walking, I heard a "Hello" from an older woman pedaling a bicycle, which sounded welcoming. I checked out the long and wide Blue Room Bar and Hall, which was largely blue on the outside, with a window sign advertising Bud Light. Peering in, I saw just a couple of customers. Nearby, a Harley-Triumph motorcycle dealer looked vacant. I also sauntered by a post office, senior center, hardware store, and the Strasburg State Bank in the small business section. A diminutive "city" hall shared a brick building with a food store and insurance company office that offered crop insurance for hail damage—a big nemesis of farming on the plains. Next door was the Time-Out Tavern that had a quaint storefront like some other businesses on Main St., and signs for several popular beers—including Bud Light, of course.

Near the end of the street and closer to the grain elevator was a well-landscaped veterans' memorial, with walkways, benches, a VFW-sponsored brick monument engraved with an image of the Iwo Jima flag-raising, an attractive gazebo with the name of the local American Legion Post, and a vintage army tank. I also wandered through some side streets shaded by mixed hardwoods and evergreens planted to create another small prairie oasis, where there were tidy homes of varied ages. I came to Saints Peter and Paul Roman Catholic Church—a large, handsome brick structure built in 1909-1910, which was Lawrence Welk's family's church. Lawrence himself was a devout Catholic and a daily communicant throughout his life. Presently, his old church had just two masses a week on Saturday and Sunday. There's a park named after Strasburg's favorite son in town, which he funded, but I didn't come across it on my walk.

Daylight was fading, and it was raining lightly when I was back on the highway and set on making it into nearby South Dakota for the night. Not far to the west across Lake Oahe, which is another expansive lake created by a dam on the Missouri River, was the Standing Rock Indian Reservation—an ethnic contrast to the Russian-German communities in the region. It extends into South Dakota and is the sixth largest reservation in the U.S. that's twice the size of the state of Delaware and home to over 6,000 Native people of different bands of what was once called the Great Sioux Nation. Fort Yates, almost due west of Strasburg, is the reservation's headquarters and close to where famed Chief Sitting Bull—a Hunkpapa Lakota Sioux who was a leader in the annihilation of Custer's force—was originally buried in 1890. Ironically, he was shot and killed by Native police on the reservation, who came to arrest him because of fears he would join the rebellious Ghost Dance movement, during a deadly scuffle with the chief and some of his supporters. In 1953, there was a controversial removal of the chief's remains to a re-burial site at a scenic location overlooking the Missouri River about fifty miles south on the Standing Rock Reservation near Mobridge, South Dakota, near his birthplace. And there's a huge granite bust of Sitting Bull by his grave that was sculpted by the late Korczak Ziolkowski—the originator of the still uncompleted, gigantic Crazy Horse Memorial in the Black Hills, which will dwarf nearby Mt. Rushmore when it's finally finished.

I passed a couple of small water bodies—perhaps more potholes—then crossed what looked more like a lake on both sides of the road that had a section with dead trees giving it a swampy appearance. Soon, sizable Rice Lake appeared just to the west, which attracts anglers. To the east was an intersection with ND Highway 11 that led to the town of Hague, a short distance from 83. I read that this hamlet with only about seventy inhabitants has a very beautiful Catholic church named St Mary's, which towers over the community. The huge brick structure with a 114-foot steeple was constructed by a Russian-German community in the early 1900s and was rebuilt after a destructive fire in 1929. This church is exceptional enough to have made the

National Register of Historic Places.

The light rain stopped, and I enjoyed the visual effects of the further diminishing daylight on the open landscape and some distinct, dark gray cloud patterns to the south. There were few other vehicles on the road, and I had a real Road to Nowhere feeling as 83 ran an arrow-straight course like so many Plains highways.

It was almost dark when I reached the South Dakota line, and *Road Trip USA* says there are 720 stone monuments spaced a half-mile apart that were erected along the entire border of the Dakotas in 1892. But if there was one close to the highway, I missed it. The border was set at the forty-sixth parallel, and all the borders of the stack of Plains states along U.S. 83 are such artificial latitude lines, with the numbers decreasing southward. South Dakota is the only state I re-entered on the journey, and this part seemed a long way from the Black Hills.

Unlike in North Dakota, the two-lane road had more than a sliver of shoulder and reflector posts, indicating some of the inconsistency in the design of the old federal highways. In South Dakota, 83 has been dedicated as the Vietnam Veterans Memorial Highway. Grassy embankments continued along the roadside.

I had the radio on for some audible company but reverted to silence, preferring a quiet, meditative state as I cruised through the early darkness, where little islands of lights glittered on the plains. Herreid was the first highway town in South Dakota—founded in 1901 when the Soo Railroad came through and named after the state's first governor, with a current population of not much over 400. It's another small town that's gotten smaller, and among the buildings in its quiet center were a Lutheran church and senior center. I also saw a sign for a city park—a designation I was finding more amusing in these miniature municipalities that were anything but cities in the usual sense.

Not far down the road was Mound City, with a name very ironic because of its mere seventy-one residents in the last census. "Mound" came from some remains of mound-like structures in the area left by an archaic Native culture. I saw a few Western storefronts and a well-lit "steakhouse and lounge" that looked very inviting. This tiny settlement that originated in 1884 and became the seat of Campbell County four years later has remained the seat despite its declining population and past efforts of Herreid to unseat it.

Further south and just north of Selby, I came to an intersection with U.S. 12, which I'd crossed paths with in Bowman, North Dakota, early in the journey while traveling U.S. 85; and it would run concurrently with 83 for a short distance. U.S. 12 is a long and original 1926 highway that extends 2,484 miles (3,998 km) from Detroit, Michigan, to Aberdeen, Washington, through ten states. Selby is larger than the last few towns I passed through, with its approximately 700 population. I wanted to check out the Berens Hotel in town described in *Road Trip USA*, since it seemed like the kind of old hotel I find very appealing.

I turned off the highway and easily found it on Selby's Main St. It was a two-story building that opened in 1949 and had a quaint character that made me want to stay there. Downstairs was a bar and the Cloverleaf Cafe. I walked into the bar to inquire about a room upstairs and found only an older man carrying a plate of food, and a woman. I asked the man about a vacancy upstairs, and his reply was, "We're already booked."

"So, you filled up early tonight?"

"There's a group of construction workers staying here."

"Could you tell me what the single occupancy rate is for a room? I'm just curious."

"$40 for a single."

"Is the cafe still open?"

"About five more minutes."

I headed right over to the cafe since I thought any other eateries in town might be closed already, and the only person there was a friendly, middle-aged female server who handed me a menu. The place was modest and unpretentious in appearance, with plain tables and linoleum floors; and the walls had some nice paintings of what looked like local, bucolic scenes. I ordered a chef salad, and the woman told me I had time to eat there while she prepared to close. But I decided on a take-out and had a short conversation with her before I left—mentioning my trip and that the guidebook I was using had some favorable things to say about this place. She said the hotel and cafe were under the same ownership and that the hotel rented to a lot of hunters this time of year—many from out of state and Canada—who were charged more when they brought dogs, which weren't accepted in some other places. "Pheasants and deer are popular game around here," she added.

I mentioned hearing that the hotel was full and asked if she knew of any safe and legal places to park overnight around town, and she told me to wait a minute while she asked someone who knew more. She went into the bar and returned with the older guy, who I made my intentions clear to about a place where I could sleep in my car; and he informed me that a nearby truck stop was a possibility besides a park in town. Then he gave me directions to both places before he went back to the bar. When I left, the woman said, "Stay safe," with some genuine concern, and I thanked her for being helpful.

I headed for the park and found it to be rather large for a small town, and I followed a gravel road that led to an area with a ballfield and shelter that looked like a good overnight haven. After parking, I sat at a table in the shelter and ate my chef salad along with some of the great whole wheat bread from the Model bakery while wearing my hooded sweatshirt with the hood up because it was quite blustery.

The night sky was clearer than the daytime one was, with some stars out along with wispy clouds drifting across a half-moon that had a great visual effect. Still way too early for me to sleep, I locked Wander and set out with my small backpack to do something I really enjoy—explore a strange town on foot and hopefully find a good, strange bar to meet and talk to some strangers.

I found the Time Out Lounge—close to the name of one of the bars back in Strasburg—which looked respectable and was roomy inside, with an arched bar, tables, electronic games that included a video lottery, and, of course, a pool table. It had the look of some recent improvements, and like the bar at the Berens Hotel, there was a crowd of two—a gray-haired bartender who was wearing a baseball cap and flannel shirt and a forty-something guy seated at the bar. I received a quiet reception as I sat at the bar a few seats from the other customer and again saw Bud Light as the only beer on tap. I asked the bartender what they had in bottles and if there were any craft beers or imports, which they didn't have, and I wound up trying a bottle of Michelob Golden Light that turned out to be a little darker colored light beer I didn't find distinctive otherwise. A baseball game was on one of the TVs that was an American League Wildcard game between the Oakland Athletics and Kansas City Royals at the Royals' home field. Another TV had a talk show on. The two men were attentive to the ball game and carried on a mixed conversation about the game and a couple of other things that showed a small-town familiarity between them. I haven't been much of a sports fan since my teenage years, but this was apparently a high stakes game that was very close, with the Athletics originally ahead and the home team Royals coming back, which resulted in extra innings. The bartender kidded the other guy: "We might have to stay here all night."

During a little break in the sporting drama, I started a conversation with the bartender by commenting: "I'm just in town for the night and glad to find a bar like this."

"So where are you from?"

"Fort Collins, Colorado," which aroused his interest.

"I lived in Longmont for years," he responded—which isn't far south of Fort Collins."

"I'm not a Colorado native, though," I said, "and lived most of my life in New Jersey. Maybe you notice my remaining accent."

"I'm not a Colorado native either, but from South Dakota, though not Selby originally. So where are you traveling?"

"I'm doing all of U.S. 83 from the Canadian border to the Mexican border in Brownsville, Texas."

He gave me a funny little look, then asked, "Why are you doing that?"

"I really enjoy traveling two-lane roads, and especially the old U.S. highways for the adventure."

"I wasn't sure 83 went as far as Brownsville. But I've done some of it in other parts of Texas. So how far do you go each day?"

"It varies. Lately I've had low mileage days checking out different places, and I don't have strict time constraints.

The other guy at the bar joined the conversation and asked if I was retired, and I told him I was, "but from employment, not work," to make a distinction. I asked if he'd traveled a lot of 83, and his answer was, "Not too much."

"Are you originally from Selby?" I inquired.

"Yes, I am."

"Have you lived anywhere else?"

"Bismarck."

"The big town," I said a little jokingly, "where I was recently. I guess you can get used to quiet small towns like this, and it seems like some people who leave them eventually come back."

And he seemed to agree.

"Has Selby's population stayed about the same?"

"There've been some new people and jobs at the elevator"—referring to the big grain depository in town—"but no big increase in numbers because there isn't much industry around here. I'm an auto mechanic with my own business. Sometimes I have to get disabled vehicles towed to dealers for special work."

"I'm driving an '06 Toyota Corolla, which I like for its known reliability and parts availability."

"There's a longer wait for some import parts," he informed me, "and it's actually easier to get parts for trucks and SUVs because of their popularity here."—which made me hope Wander would continue running reliably.

I bought another beer since a conversation had developed, which the bartender got back into, and he asked where I was staying for the night. I hesitated because of a concern about being perceived as a car tramp, and something made me blurt out, "In the hotel up the street."

"I'm surprised you found a room there," he said, and I felt uncomfortable about not telling him the truth.

The conversation continued intermittently when the ball game wasn't a big distraction. The bartender mentioned spending thirty years in Longmont, Colorado after following a friend there during a footloose period of his life, and that he had his own business there, which his son eventually took over. When I asked why he left Longmont, he replied: "It got a little too fast-paced for me, which I didn't mind when I was younger. I made a lot of friends in Colorado, though, and have stayed in touch with some."

"There's a lot of good people there who come from all over," I added, "and I've made quite a few friends in the less than two years that I've lived in the state."

The bartender seemed like another example of someone drawn back to a small-town lifestyle they'd known, after a long absence in his case. Meanwhile, the other guy, who was drinking bottled Coors

Light, offered to buy me another beer, which I gratefully declined, telling him I wanted to be bright-eyed and clear-headed the next day. He said he'd like to do a trip like mine some summer on his Harley motorcycle, and I told him I'd also been a touring biker for many years with an old BMW.

I left the bar before the extra innings Wildcard game ended with the departing words, "Good talking to you, gentlemen," and both wished me a safe trip. What had been a reticent reception for a stranger developed into some friendly conversation. Later, I found out the game went twelve innings, with the Athletics ahead at the top of the twelfth, and the home team Royals rallied to win a 9-8 squeaker that moved them on to the American League Division Series. For all those in Selby who watched the game, it might have been the most exciting thing happening that Tuesday evening in this kind of town.

While walking back to the park, I reflected on how the people who like living in these small towns must care less about excitement in the usual sense, and more about things like personal connections. They probably enjoy and appreciate the ordinary experiences of life more; and as I've gotten older, I've had a big realization of the "greatness of the ordinary."

Back at my car, I snacked on some peanuts and an apple and stayed up late journaling at a table in the quiet shelter using my lamp while wearing an added sweater on the chilly night. The air was stirred by light prairie winds, and the sky had completely cleared when I was ready for my backseat bed. There was an awesome multitude of stars, with the Milky Way visible again. And as I viewed Orion rising, I realized it was now October. I read a very fitting quote for the new month in the current Farmer's Almanac that was one of my literary companions:

"Winds! Are they winds?—or myriad ghosts, that shriek?"
(Paul Hamilton Hayne—nineteenth-century American poet.)

Some winds were audible, and it was now the month with Halloween at its end.

DAY 9

A Day in Selby

I awoke to see the park in the light of a clear day. Selby's water tower and grain elevator were also visible. Nearby were baseball and football fields, a swimming pool, a tennis court, and a kids' slide. A large, dried cornfield bordered the park. Two water fountains and faucets were by the shelter, so the place was vagabond-friendly except for not seeing a restroom around. Feeling a biological urge I didn't want to relieve behind some bushes, I drove the car hastily to the truck stop on 83.

I bought another small bag of unshelled sunflower seeds in the big convenience store there, produced by a company right up the road in Mound City. I opened the bag and started chewing on some of the crunchy shells to take the edge off my breakfast appetite before driving back to the park. I'd heard that this snack food is usually chewed whole with the shells for the salty flavor, then rather grossly spit out; though there's supposed to be a knack for cracking the shells with your teeth to extract the more palatable seeds. I definitely prefer a bag of just the tasty seeds.

On the drive back to Selby City Park, I noticed many well-kept homes and green lawns, and I passed an elementary school with a group of kids headed into a large, metal-sided Technology Education building, where these children of the Plains must have been getting the early technological training that us old folks never had—an example of what I consider the evolution of *Homo sapiens* into *Homo gadgetus* because of what used to be called "rampant technology" back in the Sixties—although what was around then was relatively primitive. Just behind the school was the blue and gray water tower proclaiming "Selby Lions"—apparently the name of the local school sports teams.

I parked where I'd spent the night and sat in the picnic shelter and had another raisin bran breakfast with peanuts and powdered milk. There was still no one else around until a maintenance guy came by the swimming pool area. In the peace of the park, I caught up more with my journal while mild breezes stirred the trees and the first day of October warmed up. Afterwards, I was ready to go back into town because I liked Selby and wasn't ready to leave until I got better acquainted with it.

The town came about with the arrival of the Chicago, Milwaukee, St. Paul, and Pacific Railroad in 1899 and is another one that was named after a railroad official. By 1909, Selby was incorporated, and it reached a population peak of 979 in 1960 that decreased to 642 in the 2010 census. The town was also about ninety-seven percent White then, with a median age over fifty. Selby is the seat of Walworth County, with the distinction of having been the home of the only father and son governors in South Dakota's history: George T. Mickelson, the state's eighteenth governor, and George S. Mickelson, the twenty-eighth. The railroad is still important in town and ships out five to six million bushels of grain a year. Selby also has the largest fertilizer plant in the region called the Northern Plains Co-op, Inc.

I drove back to the Cloverleaf Cafe and had a light lunch of Wisconsin cheese soup along with some of my bread. Two men and a woman were sitting rather quietly at another table, and the server was a sixtyish woman who was attentive but not too friendly, though I tried to engage her in some conversation anyway.

"How long have you lived in Selby?" I asked.

"Eighteen years."

"Are you from this area originally?"

"No," she replied, but didn't say where she came from, and I held back from asking.

"I guess you can get acclimated here."

"Somewhat," she responded, which sounded like she wasn't too happy about living here, and I didn't inquire any further about her story because I sensed she didn't really care about engaging. I did ask her about Hiddenwood State Park outside the town that I wanted to visit, and she gave me some directions. When I left the cafe, a young woman outside gave me a nice smile, which made me feel more welcome in town.

I got rid of some empty beer cans in a recycling facility behind the Cloverleaf that only accepted cans, then started walking down Main St. where a large group of young people appeared on the street with musical instruments, including a tuba, and started stepping and playing in what was apparently a marching band practice. Suddenly, there was more sound and energy in the otherwise quiet town center. After the band passed, a large truck making a haul to the nearby grain elevator rumbled down the street.

One of the first buildings that caught my attention was the two-story, brick-front opera house, built in 1908, which had a sign that it now housed the police department and city finance office. The opera house is a very interesting American cultural institution that had a heyday from the end of the Civil War through the 1920s, with roots that go much further back. They were never limited to opera, however, and many types of performances, entertainment, and community events took place in them. They sprang up around the country in towns and cities of all sizes, and the Plains states had a good share. I also found a small bowling alley near the opera house, but it had closed.

I stopped at a modern-looking post office with a nice stone facade to buy some post card stamps and asked a guy and gal behind the counter what they knew about the closed bowling alley. They told me I could find out more at a trucking company office in the same building as the old alley. So, I walked back and found a sixtyish woman with a small, cute, floppy-eared canine companion. She was very friendly after I expressed my interest in the old bowling alley, and we started chatting. Her name was Sandy, and she'd lived in Selby for eight years and came from a town in the Black Hills.

"I like Selby," she said. "The people are very nice, and they know and help each other. But I miss the Black Hills. There's something special about them. I've thought of going back, also because my kids are there. A marriage brought me here that I'm not in now."

"I was in the Black Hills exactly a week ago," I told her. "And they do have their own charm."

Sandy offered to show me the old bowling alley behind the small office where she worked. She thought it had closed several years before, and I was pleased to be able to see at least one of the miniature small-town alleys mentioned in *Road Trip USA*. This one had four lanes and its condition still looked good, except for a wet area from a leaking roof. Above the pins zone, where just one pin was lying, signs still advertised Miller Lite—not Bud Light—and lockers and some bowling balls and shoes remained in another area.

"If these walls could only talk," I said, in the now silent place where many weighty balls once rumbled and crashed, and local people recreated and socialized in what must have been a hot spot of Selby. I took a few pictures and asked what would be done with the place.

"I'm not sure what the building owner's plans are. I know all the wood is valuable but expensive to remove."

"I wish the alley would reopen," I said, "or at least be preserved as a piece of Americana."

An old counter from the bowling era was in the office, and Sandy said she used it on some of her lunch breaks. She told me a bit about her employer, which shipped grain and had ten trucks and drivers who kept the vehicles near their homes in different towns.

"They make pick-ups at local farms and deliver to grain elevators in the area, including the big one down the street."

"I've observed some big rigs coming and going along Main St.," I said. "Are there any organic farms in the area?"

"There's just a few, and a downside of organic is that it leaves more weeds in the transfer, which regulations require being cleaned out."

I thanked her for taking time away from her desk to talk and show me the old alley, and I was ready to move on and visit Lake Hiddenwood State Park, which is about five miles northeast of Selby.

I drove east a short distance on SD 130 toward the small town of Java, through open croplands where there were also some cattle; then turned off on a back road that was eventually unpaved. Across from a sea of dried corn stalks, I turned into the park and deposited an entrance fee in a slot. Just beyond a rim of rolling hills that rise from the plains was a verdant island of hardwoods, pines, and grassy meadows, surrounding a twenty-eight-acre lake. I followed the road near the lake and parked in a space with a good view.

The name Hiddenwood was appropriately given by early settlers because the heavy vegetation that's an anomaly on the Great Plains is hidden from view by the elevation around it. Native Americans had also been drawn to this wooded haven. The small valley was formed in prehistoric times by melting glaciers and a creek, and a lush area evolved. The creek would come to be called Hiddenwood Creek. The lake before my eyes was a work of man, however, created in 1926 by an earthen dam on the creek—one of the first of such dams used to develop an artificial lake. The mass of dirt required for the dam was extracted from the valley, which deepened the potential lakebed. The success of the project led to many similar lakes being developed in South Dakota.

I was ready for a little exploration of this oasis, where, unlike in towns and on farms on the Plains, trees had grown naturally. I grabbed my small backpack and followed a wide, grassy path that led to a narrow, dirt one, which drew closer to the lake through a very woodsy area. Leaves rustled as I stepped along the trail, and I became more impressed by all the heavy growth. Had it been in a heavily wooded region of the country, it would have been very ordinary. But here it seemed unusual. Tall, shaggy-barked cedars stood in the woods, and large cottonwoods were prominent near the lake, with their broad leaves turning gold. Other hardwoods had started their own autumn spectacle. Overhead, a turkey vulture was gliding gracefully, before others appeared and hovered. I also heard crows and spotted a belted kingfisher no doubt attracted to the water body's fishing opportunities, which perched briefly on a cottonwood branch before it flew off, rattling its familiar call. One thing I didn't see or hear, though, was other humans, and I enjoyed the solitude.

The path brought me to the shore of the lake lined with some cattails, and there was a swimming beach with a small shelter and two tables. Just a week before, it probably would have been hot enough to swim here. There were other facilities like a boat ramp, picnic areas, a playground, and a campground. So, the park must draw crowds at times.

I backtracked and came to a stone monument with a metal plaque that read: "Hiddenwood Park—built by Walworth County and The Works Progress Administration—WPA project number 3467—nineteen thirty-eight." The federally-run WPA employed millions of people in many projects from 1935 to 1943 during Franklin D. Roosevelt's administration, and what it did here were improvements after the early development of the lake. More were made in later years, and

Hiddenwood became a state park in 1951.

I got on the Blue Blanket Trail that crossed over Hiddenwood Creek on a small bridge near the dam and spillway that led back to where I'd parked. I stayed there awhile and savored the scene of the lake and woods, and a silence punctuated by the rustle of branches from prairie breezes.

With sunset near, I drove off and returned to the surrounding openness with expanses of corn, sunflowers, and other colorful crops. A few white-tailed deer darted across the unpaved road from a cornfield. Soon, the short skyline of Selby reappeared, and the dazzling light of a sinking sun radiated through some clouds in the west. I felt a fresh surge of love for this open country after visiting a woodland oasis in it.

I decided to spend another night at the city park. After returning, I walked to the downtown area again and was drawn to a bar called The Den with a "Welcome Pheasant Hunters" sign outside. Inside was a slightly sunken large back area with gaming machines, including electronic darts. Up front was a small bar that a middle-aged woman was tending, and the sole customer was a thirty-something guy wearing the common attire of a flannel shirt, jeans, and a brimmed cap. I got a friendly greeting from the woman and soon noticed Bud Light on tap, besides a Boulevard Wheat that I asked about, thinking I might have found a craft beer in town. And it was one from a brewery in Kansas City, Missouri. I was offered a sample of the unfiltered wheat beer, which seemed quite light with a refreshing quality, and I opted for a pint. Soon I was involved in a conversation with the two people and found out the bartender was originally from another part of South Dakota and had been in Selby for close to twenty years. The guy had grown up on a farm in the area and said he'd always lived around here.

"You must like the quiet life here," I said to him.

"Yes," he replied emphatically.

"I guess you get used to it. I met a couple of people who left here and came back."

"It often happens. They miss the quiet life, and I wouldn't want to live in a place where people don't know their neighbors."

"Have you ever been to a big city?"

"I've been to Sioux Falls"—apparently a small town and South Dakota farm boy's idea of a big city—"and I thought it was too big."

"I live in northern Colorado now, but I spent most of my life in New Jersey near New York City. I wonder what you'd think of a city that size."

"That's a real city," and he seemed negative about the idea of going there. "I've never been to any part of Colorado. I've had some good Colorado beers, though, like Fat Tire."

"That's the flagship beer of the New Belgium brewery in Fort Collins, where I'm from," and I pointed at the brimmed cap with an emblem of that brewery that I happened to be wearing.

"Not many craft beers are available in this area," the lady added, as I'd thought. "I once went to a bar in Phoenix that had a huge selection of beers, but not Bud Light like I'm used to drinking and wanted."

I thought of how tastes and habits can also travel.

"I really like this part of the country," I said, "despite what many outsiders think of it as flat and boring. To me, the plains and farmlands really have their own beauty, and I'm driving all the way down U.S. 83 to its end in Brownsville, Texas," which seemed to impress them. "I've noticed that most prairie towns I've been through seem to have about an even number of bars and churches, though I've seen just one church in Selby so far, and this is the third bar."

They both laughed, and I was informed that there were five churches in town. So maybe the bars were outnumbered here.

"This bar used to be a movie theater," the guy said, which explained the somewhat sunken back area.

"Do you know when the theater closed?" I asked him.

"It was before my time, but I think it was in the seventies."

"That wasn't before my time," the woman said.

"I was wondering about the small bowling alley that someone showed me earlier. Do you know why that closed?"

"It had gotten too expensive to maintain when business slumped," the guy replied, "but there's an open alley in another town in the area, which might have eight lanes,"—probably a big alley for these parts.

After another friendly conversation with a couple of strangers lubricated by a pint of beer, I bid them "Happy Trails" and headed over to the bar at the Berens Hotel. I took a seat there at a rather large, curved bar, where two elderly women sat at one end and an elderly man and woman near the other end. Some other customers were seated at upholstered booths. The bar had a glossy surface, and overhead was a cloverleaf design on the ceiling and some green lighting, which befitted the name of the bar and cafe. With the linoleum floors and unpretentious atmosphere, the place had a quaint character and seemed like it hadn't changed much since the 1950s. One thing that had, however, was Bud Light on tap, which doesn't have such a long history. And I wound up buying a pint of the extremely popular macrobrew that was poured by a fortyish woman who was working the bar alone. I asked for a menu and saw some good old meat and potato dishes I expected to see in an eatery like this, which was just what I felt like having. After a little deliberation, I ordered a six-ounce, boneless, grilled pork chop with a baked potato and salad. When the dinner arrived, I was very pleased with the perfectly grilled and very lean chop and a good-sized potato that I requested salsa for as a condiment. The salad had a lot of iceberg lettuce like the other one I'd ordered here.

Meanwhile, a group of young guys arrived that increased the age diversity in the place. Then came the familiar face of Sandy from the trucking company office, accompanied by a male companion. They sat at a booth and were soon conversing. The crowd enlarged with another group of young men that entered and took seats at the bar on my right side, and a young couple sat to the left. The guy closest to me on the right was imbibing a Guinness Stout, showing an import availability. He said he liked the look of my pork chop dinner, which inspired him to order the same. Two pork chop orders prompted the bartender—now really hustling to serve the larger bar crowd and also the tables—to pause and mention that she couldn't eat pork since she'd worked on a pig farm and had learned to "respect pigs." Her comment triggered some ambivalence I've had about whether I should be a vegetarian, but it didn't spoil my enjoyment of a very tasty pork chop that I hadn't indulged in for a long time.

A guy who had sat near me on the other side was toying with his phone a lot, and I tried to distract him back to his surroundings by asking if he was from Selby. He answered "No," then said he was working in the area, though, and lived in northeast South Dakota. Overall, the crowd was rather low key, with a little action at the pool table. It was a very homey bar and eatery that I was sure I'd frequent if I lived in Selby.

On the way out, I went over to Sandy to say "Hi" and mentioned my visit to Hiddenwood. "Nice, isn't it?" she remarked, and I certainly agreed.

It was dark when I was back on Main St., and I walked toward the railroad tracks and the big grain elevator and got close to the structure that rises over Selby. The prevalence of elevators in the region has earned them the moniker, "Sentinels of the Prairie." Their origins in North America go back to the second half of the 1800s when grain production increased greatly in the nation's heartland and created a need for local storage facilities before it was shipped to distant markets. Throughout their history, grain elevators have varied greatly in size, design, and building materials, and the early ones were largely iron-clad wood. After 1900, more were built of concrete and other non-wood materials. The one in Selby had multiple cylindrical structures of concrete and metal and seemed to be a "country elevator" that served the local area until the grain was shipped to much larger terminal elevators, and like most of these structures, it was along rails. I found out that this elevator and others in the area were owned by a farmers' cooperative called North Central Farmers Elevator. There were signs for an East Dump—for spring wheat and corn—and a West Dump—for winter wheat and soybeans.

Since the U.S. has been in the business of feeding much of the world for a long time, I wondered just how far some of the grains stored here might travel. The railroad by the elevator that essentially brought Selby into existence, like so many prairie towns, was still a big link to the outside world, for freight, anyway.

Walking closer to the truck stop I'd been at, I heard sounds from the highway. Then I wandered through some quiet side streets and saw a Lutheran church and a county highway department building. Back on Main St., I passed a grocery store and some other small-town staple businesses like a drug store and veterinary center, and the small downtown was just as quiet.

When I returned to the park, there was still no one else around my parking area. I did more writing in the shelter until I felt groggy after midnight. The sky wasn't as clear as the previous night, and some strange creature sounds had emerged from the wooded area and cornfields next to the park, which I thought might be coyotes. Before getting into my sleeping bag in Wander, I had a funny feeling about being watched. But it didn't prevent me from falling asleep rather easily at the end of Day 9 of my journey.

DAY 10

The Land of John Deere, and a night in "Peer"

It was a chilly forty-four degrees in the morning with lots of dew on the grass, and the car windows had fogged up. I added more layers of clothing and had another breakfast in the shelter. Then, while filling a water bottle at a nearby faucet, there suddenly appeared a man in blue who stepped out of a police SUV and walked toward me. My pulse quickened as what I was afraid was an inevitable encounter finally happened.

Anxiety prompted me to say, "Good Morning," as he approached, and his response was: "Is the car over there yours?"

"Yes, officer."

"I saw it during the night."

So, I'd been watched after all.

"Are you camping?"

"Not really. I heard you could park overnight in the park, and I didn't see any signs restricting it. I just slept in my car."

"You can stay here," he said to my relief. "But I wondered if there was a problem."

"There definitely isn't. I'm leery about parking overnight in some places where I'm alone, but this park and town seems safe."

"It is," he reassured me, then asked where I was heading.

"All the way to Brownsville, Texas, where U.S. 83 ends."

His facial reaction showed some interest, then he asked, "So when are you leaving?"

"Later today, but I had a good visit in this town and met some nice people.

"That's good to hear." He paused and concluded with, "So have a safe trip," and walked back to his vehicle without asking any more questions, or for an ID or anything else. This cop seemed more concerned and curious about me than suspicious. My anxiety subsided, and I had another positive impression of the people in Selby.

Before leaving the park, I picked up a little litter near my haven. As I was about to drive off, scattered flocks of red-winged blackbirds flew over that also seemed southbound. I stopped at Stoick's grocery store to buy some fruit and found a very friendly atmosphere. I heard it was the only grocery store in Selby and that the nearest supermarket was in Mobridge to the west on the Missouri River. When checking out a pint of slightly overripe grape tomatoes, a gentleman, who may have been the owner, said I could have it free since they were expecting a fresh shipment. I easily accepted the offer and thanked him. Assuming he knew something about local agriculture, I asked if dry farming, which is farming without irrigation during a dry season, was done in the area. And he said it was, except for corn by the Missouri River.

This brings up Selby's location just west of the hundredth meridian—the longitudinal measurement that very interestingly coincides with a natural division in climate on the continent. The mass of land west of this meridian is well known for its arid landscapes and lower rainfall compared to the more moist lands east of it, where irrigation is less necessary for agriculture. Moisture reaching from the Gulf of Mexico has a big effect on the greater amount of rain east of the meridian. So, Selby, being so close to it, probably has a mixture of the two basic climates. The hundredth meridian west—referring to its position 100 degrees west of Greenwich, England, which was designated the Prime Meridian or Longitude 0 degrees in 1884—has been a leading historical consideration of where the West begins, though there are many subjective impressions. John Wesley Powell—the great scientist-scholar-explorer who led scientific expeditions in the West after the Civil War—wrote much about the significance of the hundredth meridian in an 1878 report and discouraged farming west of it because of the arid conditions, which he deemed more suitable for ranching. For years, Powell's authoritative advice was not heeded, however, largely because the railroads heavily promoted homesteader settlement in the arid region for the sake of their profits, with a consequent abundance of failed homesteads. One of my maps showed that U.S 83 had been coursing quite close to the meridian on its west side since the Canadian border and extremely close since the border of the Dakotas. The highway would continue such proximity for a stretch past Selby before it would run further west of the meridian again. Then it would eventually cross it deep in Texas and remain on its east side for the rest of the road's route. U.S. 83's overall proximity to the hundredth meridian enables the highway to be considered another approximate divider of the country between East and West.

Back on the road, I felt a little sad about leaving Selby, which was a very memorable town along the highway. Ahead were stretches of corn and wheat, and U.S. 12 branched off and headed due east after its short concurrence. I stopped by a stone monument on the west side of the road by a cornfield that commemorated the location where the community of Bangor had existed, which was the seat of Walworth County from 1884 to 1909. Another previous county seat was marked on an engraved map on the monument, along with three ghost towns. I learned that Selby became the reason for Bangor's demise when Milwaukee Railroad officials decided to route an extension there instead of to Bangor. Selby also won a dispute over which town should be the county seat, and even buildings from Bangor were moved to Selby. It's a prime example of the importance of railroads in town development in the region.

I heard a distant train as I gazed toward the flat horizon to the north under an enormous sky, where the Selby grain elevator was visible. There was also a sign at the stop about this section of 83 being a Blue Star Memorial Highway—"A tribute to the Armed Forces that have defended the United States of America"—which there are many of around the country.

The highway continued its straight course south through more cultivated, colorful expanses, where a truck passing from the south carried a wide load of hay bales. Then the landscape became less agricultural and resembled a natural grassland again, with a few scattered trees in the distance. The day had warmed up, and I pulled over on a shoulder to remove a sweatshirt near a sign for the Swan Creek State Recreation Area to the west on Lake Oahe. Black and brown cattle were grazing not far from the road beyond some barbed wire, and a few of the bovines stared at me. Further on were bigger herds of cattle that included Herefords. There was also more truck traffic and eventually croplands again.

When I saw these agricultural stretches on the Plains, I sometimes wondered just who owned all the farmland. Much has been heard about the decline and struggles of the traditional family farm and a rise in corporate ownership. But, according to the 2012 Census of Agriculture conducted by a department of the USDA, just slightly over five percent of U.S. farms are corporate-owned, and the majority of these are family corporations that are very small with ten or fewer shareholders. However, foreign investment in American farmland from numerous countries has been rapidly increasing and becoming a greater concern for legislators and the public, though it's still a small percentage of the approximately 900 million acres of farmland in the country. It's been encouraged by the lack of restrictions in many states, and some struggling farmers have been enticed to sell out to foreign investors.

There are millions fewer farm owners and workers in the U.S. compared to the mid-twentieth century, and farm size has generally increased a lot since then. The percentage of farmland owners who are owner-operators who farm themselves has also increased, resulting in a decrease in the number of tenant or non-owner farmers renting the land they farm.

The road in the stretch I was driving had rumble strips, or horizontal grooves in the surface, along the edge of a rather narrow shoulder above an embankment. These cause wheels that stray on the grooves to make an alarming sound, in this case warning of an embankment. Back in North Dakota, I'd encountered such strips near center lines intended to prevent head-on collisions. I presume such safety features weren't around in the early years of U.S. 83 and other roads, which seem like a good idea until we're all using self-driving vehicles that are ingeniously safe—if that ever actually happens. There were also many unpaved turnoffs into the crop fields that must be used for farming operations.

Ahead was a junction with U.S. 212, which is considered a spur of U.S. 12 that it no longer connects with. The former road is a 1926 original U.S. highway that currently runs 949 miles (1,527 km) from Edina, Minnesota to Yellowstone National Park, through four states. What caught my attention was a sign for a town not far to the east on 212 with the historic name of Gettysburg—very associated with another part of the country. But some later googling informed me that this town, founded in 1884, was named to commemorate the decisive Civil War battle because many of its early settlers were Civil War veterans. To the west, U.S. 212 headed towards the Cheyenne River Indian Reservation across the Missouri River, resided by four bands of the Lakota Sioux. In land area, it's the fourth-largest reservation in the nation.

The landscape became flatter again, and abundant sunflowers were among the various crops in this area of great space and color. A sign of human controversy appeared on a roadside billboard regarding the very unsettled issue of abortion—"Choose Life"—expressing the social conservatism of the region.

Ahead was a miniature community called Agar, and I turned off the highway to take a closer look at it. Its population of seventy-six made Selby seem sizable, but it's nevertheless a farm and ranch service center. I was greeted by an attractive stone sign: "Welcome to Agar, Est. 1910," which was named after a county official. The town is not far from the acclaimed Sutton Bay eighteen-hole championship golf course, which opened in 2003 and overlooks Lake Oahe to the west. This panoramic course is part of a private club that also caters to wealthy hunters and fishermen. In the humble town, a turquoise water tower bearing Agar's name stood out, along with an annex-type grain elevator and two old wooden ones that were very similar in size and shape, though one looked extremely weathered, and the other appeared to have a fresh coat of white paint. Among the residences were a few trailers and a couple of mobile homes, and there was a United Methodist church, a post office, and a fire station. I also saw a rather drab, gray, windowless bar and cafe called The Bunkhouse, which displayed another "Welcome Pheasant Hunters" sign with a Miller Lite logo. The ring-necked pheasant, which is such a popular game bird in South Dakota, is native to Asia and was fully introduced in the state in 1908. But its non-native status didn't hinder it from becoming the official state bird in 1943.

I stopped at a small park with a little shelter, basketball court, playground, and a cinder block-sided restroom that was locked. I had the place to myself, and for a while just sat in the car and watched the leaves on some hardwood trees flutter in prairie breezes, while hearing sporadic sounds of traffic on 83. On the way back to the highway, some big, bright green John Deere machinery rolled by, which seemed like a common symbol of rural America, especially on the Plains.

The namesake of this very old and profitable American corporation famous for its agricultural equipment was indeed a real person who was born in Rutland, Vermont in 1804 and moved to Illinois in 1836, where he soon opened a blacksmith shop in the town of Grand Detour. John Deere began making commonplace tools like pitchforks and shovels, but he soon developed a new type of plow with steel blades that worked much more efficiently than the iron and wooden plows in use at the time, and his invention would have a big effect on the settlement of the Plains. At first, Deere produced new plows to meet the demand. Then, success led to increased production before orders that made the plows available immediately. As his business grew, Deere had different partnerships and factory locations, and his son Charles joined the enterprise. The company also began making other farming equipment, such as wagons, planters, and cultivators. Charles eventually assumed most of the management, but his father remained president until his death in 1886. Charles also greatly expanded sales nationally and established marketing centers and local retail dealers.

In 1907, Charles Deere died, and his son-in-law, William Butterworth, took over the business. The technological progress of the early twentieth century led to new production opportunities for the company, with gas-powered tractors becoming dominant; and in 1927, they produced the first combine harvester. Advances in farming equipment technology continued to the present day, and Deere & Company is the largest manufacturer of agricultural machinery in the world, with about half of its thousands of worldwide employees in the U.S. and Canada. The corporation's U.S. administrative center resides in Moline, Illinois—the town where John Deere lived for a good part of his life and died—and manufacturing plants hum in the central and southeastern U.S. Although best known for farming equipment, Deere also produces construction and forestry machinery, and even smaller products like home lawnmowers and snowmobiles. It's the farm machinery that flaunts the familiar bright green color with yellow trim. The company's slogan is "Nothing runs like a Deere," and the leaping deer logo with the familiar name underneath has been used for over 155 years, with some minor changes. What a history for an enterprise that began with a local blacksmith turning out shovels and other basic tools.

U.S. 83 continued its vertical course toward the flat southern horizon and crossed a prairie stream called Okobojo Creek. Soon the landscape was more rolling, then flattened again. My map showed 83 still running just west of the hundredth meridian. The water tower and grain elevators of Onida came into view, and before the town were vast cattail wetlands that had attracted large flocks of red-winged blackbirds. Like back in Selby, many were headed south in an undulating flight, as if also following 83. Then an expanse of cultivated sunflowers to the east suddenly burst with insect-like swarms of redwings that rose from the fields and created a visual "moment."

There was a "Welcome to Onida" sign with an image of a sunflower and cornstalk, and I turned off the highway by a sign for a business district to scope out another town. On the way was a huge number of metallic crop storage bins—about the most concentrated I'd seen yet—and two big grain elevators by railroad tracks. This town, with a current population under 700, was apparently a big agricultural center. It got started in 1880 and became official in 1883, with a name given by early settlers who came from Oneida, New York, but omitted one letter in the spelling, perhaps because they couldn't spell well. I liked the look and atmosphere of the small downtown right away, which had some street graffiti with several large personal names painted right on the main street. The focal point, however, was the attractive stone county courthouse building with a small dome capping a short clock tower, and two classical columns by its front entrance. Onida is the seat of Sully County.

I parked by the courthouse and snapped a few pictures of the photogenic structure. On the front grounds was a display of school spirit with two life-size images of football and girls soccer players, and a sign that exclaimed—"Tis the season to beat the Battlers and Patriots!"—decorated with two small haystacks, dried corn stalks, and pumpkins. No mention of the home team's name, though. I thought again about how school sports events probably provide some of the biggest excitement in these small towns. The silver, metallic water tower stood nearby, with colorful images of a sunflower, corn, and grain stalks.

Although there are thousands of these prominent structures with different shapes and sizes in towns and cities throughout the U.S., water towers stand out most on the Plains. But despite being so ubiquitous, probably few people really understand their purpose and how they function. Some googling informed me that storing water in elevated tanks provides the required pressure through gravity to distribute a community's water needs. And the higher the tower and tank, the greater the water pressure. The tank size is determined by the local water demand and is generally built to hold at least one day's water supply. As the supply drains, it's replenished through a big conduit called a riser that water is pumped through from the water main up to the tank. This continuous process keeps the water from freezing in cold climates. The average tower is about 165 feet high (50 meters), and the average lifespan is sixty years, although some have lasted close to a century. Modern water tower use began during the mid-nineteenth century. The older towers generally have simpler designs, and in small towns the structures are often located in the peak demand area in the center of town, like the one in Onida.

I walked over to a well-maintained, small park across from the courthouse that had another hospitable sign: "Onida welcomes you—a great place to call home—est.1883." Personally, I love visiting these small communities, but am much less enthused about the idea of living in one. I'm too accustomed to easy access to a lot more goods and services and culture, and I like the relative anonymity and privacy I have where I live compared to places where everyone probably knows just about everyone else and a lot of their business. But I certainly understand the upside of that kind of "community" where the people must be more inclined to help each other, and have a quieter and simpler life. Then there's the stereotyped political and social conservatism of small-town and rural America that I'd feel uncomfortable living in. Nevertheless, I'm glad that such places still have their populations and hope that more manage to arrest their decline.

I took a short walk down Onida's Main St., passing up Brewster's Tavern and Grill with another beer brand-sponsored "Welcome Hunters" sign. Church-wise, I'd seen a small Catholic one near the park. I went into Don's Food Center, which was like the store in Selby; and they let me use what looked like a non-public bathroom, and I bought a small bag of ice. This was another town that didn't seem sizable enough to have attracted a large chain grocery store. But it seems these smaller, local stores usually provide a small community's basic food needs so they don't become food deserts. This store didn't have any real take-out food, though, at a time when I wanted to eat something.

After driving off, I stopped at a small business by the intersection of 83 called The Corner, which advertised "pop, gas, groceries," to see if they had any takeouts. A young guy and two blonde girls were working there, and I was able to order a freshly made turkey sub. But when I asked about including some veggie toppings, one of the girls said, "We're not Subway," though not sarcastically. They had onions, though, which I requested, along with some mayo. And I had the tomatoes from the Selby store.

Back on the highway, it was early evening, and the low sun became radiant after emerging from overcast. The straight road continued through the level landscape, and I cruised through the biggest sea of sunflower crops I'd seen yet. Another roadside sign expressed more social conservatism on the same thorny issue as the last one: "God is Pro Life." Parallel power lines stretched toward the horizon, and ahead were also some dark clouds. By the intersection of 83 and U.S. 14, a well-arched rainbow appeared to the southeast, creating a splendid spectacle in the huge prairie sky. I pulled over on the road's shoulder and reached for my camera, and soon the words "Hi Mom!" sprang in my mind. For my mother, who passed away in 2009, liked the expression "Going over the rainbow" in relation to her own mortality, and I can never see a rainbow without thinking of her. This one arched beautifully above the open landscape with a distant island of trees and a few circular storage structures.

U.S. 83 veered southwest, further from the hundredth meridian, and ran in tandem with U.S. 14 on another straight, flat stretch toward the state capital city of Pierre. The latter road is another 1926 original, now 1,398 miles (2,250 km) in length through five states, between Chicago and the eastern entrance of Yellowstone National Park. There were more colorful fields and varied crops, billboards for businesses in Pierre, and some new homes on the outskirts of town where the terrain got hillier. I passed through an area strewn with hay bales near homes and thought more homes would probably replace all the hay eventually.

Entering the city limits, I was impressed by the hilly surroundings, and the highway descended somewhat as it headed through a residential area with shady streets before the domed state capitol building came into view. I strayed off the highway by mistake, backtracked after I realized it, and passed through a commercial area with quite a few chain businesses—the first I'd seen since Bismarck. A few were motels like Super 8 and Days Inn, but I stopped at an indie motel called Pierre Inn and Suites that advertised "clean, affordable, spacious rooms."

A man sat in the office who didn't greet me at first. Then a woman came in who was quite nice and said they had a single room for $50 and another for $40, which my frugality urged me to take. Sometimes I ask to see a room before I pay for it, but didn't this time. After using my credit card, I was handed another old key for room 108.

The room seemed fine with two double beds, a clean bathroom, and the usual TV and microwave. But I noticed a smell that seemed to indicate a dog had also been a guest. The AC was on, though it hadn't been that warm a day—probably to alleviate the odor that may have been the reason for the cheaper rate. I soon shut it off, though, then realized there was no chair for a small table, which I remedied by bringing in the small folding chair I had in the car trunk. As for the odor, it wasn't bad enough for me to make my own stink about it and ask to move to the other room.

I delighted in another hot, much needed shower, which was another temporary relief from the grubby feeling that was becoming more familiar. I was ready for an evening exploration of Pierre on foot, but first called my sister in Fort Collins and this time got through to my sibling, who was very glad to hear my voice. We did some catching up and gave each other assurances that things were OK on both ends. I told the woman in the office about the missing chair in the room and the odor, which she jotted down. And when I mentioned walking into town, she gave me a map of Pierre and some directions and said she'd heard it was supposed to get colder soon.

When I set out with my small backpack, it was already very chilly and somewhat windy, and I wore gloves and tightened the hood on my hoodie. The motel was right by the railroad that spurred the growth of Pierre in the 1880s. But the city's origins go further back, due to its location on the Missouri River—like North Dakota's capital, Bismarck—which I would soon reconnect with and again cross paths with my old heroes, Lewis and Clark.

The historic expedition had a dramatic experience near here in late September 1804 while navigating the Missouri upstream, when they encountered a large band of warriors of the Teton Sioux, who were known for harassing previous trading parties. At first, diplomacy went poorly, and violence almost erupted in the party's first tense situation with Natives. But both sides kept their cool, and eventually the captains partook in a peace pipe ceremony. The experience with this tribal group prompted Lewis and Clark to name a nearby tributary the Teton River, later renamed the Bad River.

In 1817, a man named Joseph LaFramboise—a French fur trader who worked for the American Fur Company—built a trading post and fort near the location that would become Pierre, which was the beginning of the oldest, continuous, non-Native settlement in South Dakota. Later, in 1832, Pierre Chouteau Jr.—a major figure of the same company, who was also French—built a fort nearby that replaced the original post and was named after himself, and it became the largest trading post on the northern plains that did plenty of business with Native tribes.

In 1855, the U.S. Army purchased Fort Pierre Chouteau and shortened the name to Fort Pierre—the first military fort on the upper Missouri. But they abandoned it just two years later and moved to nearby Fort Randall. However, some settlers remained around the site, and 1861 saw the establishment of the Dakota Territory. When the railroad arrived there over a decade later, it spurred what became known as the Great Dakota Boom that brought many more settlers and led to the development of a new town at a ferry landing by a rail terminal across the Missouri from the Fort Pierre site. The budding town was named Pierre, and it was founded in 1880 and designated the capital in 1889 when South Dakota became a state because of its central location. But anyone today who pronounces the name as two syllables would immediately be recognized as an outsider because South Dakotans pronounce their capital "Peer."

So, both the river and railroad shaped the history of the city and locality. Pierre is the smallest state capital after Montpelier, Vermont, with a 13,646 population in its last census. It's also one of only five state capitals not serviced by an interstate highway, and the only one without a nearby expressway. The city is also the seat of Hughes County.

I liked the uncongested, non-urban atmosphere around me as I walked toward the nearby downtown area on Pierre St., which wasn't big. A bar called Longbranch—"where good friends meet," according to a sign outside—beckoned me to go in. The inside was rather large, with different sections that included a good-sized table area, a dance floor, and a game area with two pool tables and darts. I sat at a bar in the back among about eight people, and I liked the atmosphere and vibes. A middle-aged guy was tending the bar, which had no draft beer—not even Bud Light. So, I bought a bottle of the regional Grain Belt beer from Minnesota, which I remembered having while traveling through the upper Midwest way back in the seventies. But this time I found it very light and without much character and wondered if it had been watered down. Not seeing a good opportunity to converse with anyone at the bar, who all seemed engaged in their own conversations, I moved over to a very comfortable-looking lounge chair by an aquarium and shifted into a meditative mood while watching the fish and sipping the mediocre beer. When my glass was empty, I decided to do a little barhopping.

Just around the next corner, I found Bob's Lounge in a small, separate brick building. It had a sign with a shamrock, and a slightly changed slogan from the previous place: "Where good friends are." And this watering hole had been here since 1951, according to the sign. There was also a green awning and big shamrock image on the sidewalk in front that indicated an Irish pub theme. Inside, it didn't look as Irish, but seemed like a small neighborhood bar with a lively crowd and two rather strange levels. I found a seat on the upper one and liked the elevated feeling where there was a better view of the place. I bought a round of Sam Adams Octoberfest that was on draft, which I'd had before and has a very satisfying seasonal quality. I asked the blonde, young woman bartender if Pierre had any microbreweries, and she replied, "I wish." A guy sitting on my left overheard and told me that there were only about four microbreweries in South Dakota at the time. I then bragged a little about living in the beer heaven of Colorado with its present bounty of breweries, and he recommended a place close by called The Crossing that had the best local beer selection. Then a conversation developed beyond the subject of beer.

He was an outgoing, cheerful, bearded, fortyish fellow who wore a brimmed cap with the name of an outdoor recreation business. His libation was a mixed drink, and he introduced himself as Ryan.

"I'm driving U.S. 83 all the way to Brownsville, Texas," I informed him, which aroused his interest.

"By yourself?"

"Yes. And it's the way I usually like to travel."

"I've been in Brownsville on business," he said, "and liked it down there. I was in sales for quite a while and traveled around a lot of the country, mainly selling veterinary products. Some of it was back East. I like the people in the West much better. Here you can talk to anybody."

"I lived most of my life in New Jersey, and there are lots of good people there. But I agree that it's not as friendly as out here."

"You don't sound like you came from New Jersey."

"That's what some say, but others notice an accent right away."

"I came from Nebraska and moved to South Dakota mainly for the hunting and fishing. This is a great state for sportsmen. It's number one in the U.S. for pheasants, and hunters come here from all over. The out-of-state fishermen are more from closer states like Minnesota and Wisconsin. This area has the best walleye fishing, and salmon are stocked in the Missouri River. I had a boat for a while, but it got too expensive to maintain."

"Is walleye a good fish to eat?"

"It sure is, and you should try it. You should also check out the

Oahe Dam near town that created Lake Oahe from the river."

"I'm sure Lewis and Clark wouldn't recognize most of the Missouri today," I said a little jokingly, and he agreed and went on to say a few things that showed some knowledge of the famous explorers and local history. Then we talked about the weather.

"The winters are very bad here," he said, which wasn't surprising. "It goes down to thirty-five below and often stays bitter cold for quite a while. The winds are terrible, but we usually don't get big snows. Eastern South Dakota gets more."

Ryan said his present occupation was a "freight broker" in the trucking business. He didn't mention a spouse, so may well have been single. Meanwhile, the rest of the bar crowd was still energetic, and a big group made an enthusiastic toast with shots of liquor. I thought this place might even draw a good crowd on frigid, sub-zero nights for those seeking the warmth of companionship. I bought another round—this time a Bud Light because I wanted something lighter and weaker so I'd feel normal enough the next day. I asked Ryan where there was a late eatery, now that it was nearly 11 p.m., and he recommended a taco place in the area.

We chatted some more before I said, "Great talking to you, and maybe I'll see you here tomorrow," since I was now thinking about spending another night in Pierre. On the way out, I thought that the Bob's Lounge slogan, "Where good friends are," might be quite true, as evidenced by the good conversation I just had with a total stranger. And I was reminded of a favorite saying I'd heard many years before: "There are really no strangers, just friends you haven't met yet."

Outside, the South Dakota wind had really picked up, and I walked against a stiff one back toward Sioux Avenue, which was also 83. It seemed like a harbinger of the severe winter season I'd just heard about. I didn't find the taco place but saw a McDonald's still open. Hunger drove me in, and it seemed like ages since I'd patronized the Golden Arches. There were no other customers inside, and an amiable, thirtyish guy behind the counter looked happy to see me. I wound up ordering a "sweet chili chicken combo" that included lettuce, tomatoes, and cucumbers—burrito style—with sweet chili sauce and some McDonald's famous fries on the side. My beer-enhanced appetite made even fast-food taste satisfying.

On the walk back to the motel, the wind howled along with a chill factor that propelled me to move very briskly toward the warmth of the room. I'd gotten the impression, though, that the people in Pierre were generally warm and friendly, in contrast to a lot of their weather. Back in the room, I stayed up a while journaling, and I could still hear the wind outside when I got into one of the double beds. It was no night to be sleeping in Wander.

DAY 11

A museum, the Capitol, more bar-hopping

The wind was still audible when I got up. While finishing a box of raisin bran, I had the TV on and heard the not-so-good news about the first Ebola case in the U.S. in Dallas, and ISIS capturing a city on the Syrian-Turkish border and possible escalation of the conflict. My mind gladly reverted to the world of traveling U.S. 83, but I was a little inert about leaving the comfort zone I was in. After a shave, it was near checkout time, however.

I dropped off the key in the motel office, and a fiftyish guy was at the desk. A conversation started, and he mentioned being from Pierre originally but had lived in Texas and Arkansas for twenty-five years before his recent return.

"I guess you're not back for the weather," I said kiddingly.

"Definitely not. It's to look after my ninety-six-year-old grandmother."

We talked a little about the weather, and he told me there had been a tornado just about a week before only about forty miles away, though it wasn't very destructive. "That's rather unusual for this time of year," he said, "and maybe it has something to do with global warming. When I lived in Texas, there were some very bad tornadoes there."

"That's where I'm bound, and I sure hope I don't encounter anything like that because of the warmer climate that I'm looking forward to otherwise."

He wished me a safe trip, and when I left it was sunny and still very blustery. My first stop was a state library I found in a larger building, where I thought I'd better check my emails for the first time on the trip. There were two computers there with no time limit, and after logging in on one, a not-surprising onslaught of messages was waiting for me. A few were from friends, which I replied to. Then I began to delete junk about dog food coupons, electronic cigarettes, dealing with toenail fungus, etc. For a while, I'd had a big influx of spam that I hadn't been successful in controlling, and I'm often nostalgic about the good old days when you could travel and do other things without the onus of such communications, which I've come to regard as The Electronic Plague. But what seems like such a pain in the ass to many of us older folks is probably taken for granted by young people who don't remember a much less techie world—a world that's led to the lunacy of things like texting while driving and other techno-zombie behavior. And I often think that modern technology has enslaved us more than it's liberated us—and turned most of us into unpaid secretaries with the amount of typing we have to do.

Next on my itinerary was a visit to the South Dakota Cultural Heritage Center, just north of the Capitol area. The road to it across from spacious Hilger's Park was hilly, and the center was an impressive, earthy, horizontal structure that was built into a grassy hillside to resemble a Native dwelling. It had opened in 1989—South Dakota's Centennial year—and replaced the original building at another location. When I arrived the wind was waving tall grasses on this piece of the prairie sea, which I found out had been landscaped with native plants and grasses.

Near the entrance of the building was the attention-grabbing Citadel statue. This golden metallic sculpture that features a female face above a tapered body with a winged angelic appearance was created by the sculptor Dale Claude Lamphere and dedicated to the pioneer women of South Dakota. A small sign had a quote from John Steinbeck's *Grapes of Wrath* about a woman character being "the citadel of the family." This artwork is just one example of the numerous outdoor sculptures that South Dakota has a reputation for. Monumental works like Mount Rushmore and the still incomplete Crazy Horse Memorial in the Black Hills are just the most famous. There have even been proposals that South Dakota be officially called "The Monument State" instead of merely "The Mount Rushmore State."

Inside the Center, I was immediately greeted by an elderly gentleman at a desk with a "Hi, how are you today?"—but in a warm and friendly manner that sounded sincere. I signed a guest book as he requested, and immediately a conversation started, reminiscent of the one I had with the retired doctor, Herbert Wilson, at the museum in Bismarck. This gentleman introduced himself as Marv Paulson, and he was also a volunteer who was upfront about his age—eighty-five in this case, making him eight years younger than Dr. Wilson at the other museum. And when I mentioned the other encounter to him, he quipped: "I don't mind second place age-wise." He'd also done a lot of volunteering in the twenty years since he retired from the insurance business.

"I really like it here because I meet people, and it's very different from my old job," he said. Like Herbert Wilson, his wife was also a volunteer, and he mentioned more about his life.

"I've been in Pierre since 1962 and doubt if I'll ever leave if I haven't by now. I came from the small town of Hayes, not far west of here, and grew up on a ranch. When I was thirty, I hurt my back baling hay, probably because I felt very strong at the time and overworked myself. That's what drove me into the insurance business. I have four children, fourteen grandchildren, and about fifteen great-grandchildren. I'm not sure about the exact numbers."

Marv wasn't quite old enough to be one of the "Greatest Generation" that were World War II veterans. But he mentioned being an Army vet who'd served during the Korean War period in Germany. When I mentioned my driving all of U.S. 83, he said he's been as far south on it as Liberal, Kansas, en route to visiting one of his kids in Albuquerque, New Mexico.

"I heard about some bikers doing all of 83," he said.

"I'm a biker too," I replied, "and have toured a lot of the U.S. and Canada on an old BMW. But this is a four-wheeled trip, and I'm glad it is most of the time."

Marv had some familiarity with northern Colorado and remembered having a "great enchilada" at a Mexican restaurant near Fort Collins during a trip there. Before our conversation ended, he got a little personal and mentioned having the age-related issue of macular degeneration, and that he also had a defibrillator. But neither obviously deterred this amicable gentleman from staying engaged and meeting people like he enjoyed. When our conversation ended, I found out I qualified for the $3.00 senior admission to the museum.

The sizable South Dakota Cultural Heritage Center is a counterpart of the museum in North Dakota and holds over 30,000 artifacts, besides housing the state's historical society and archives. I roamed slowly through its three main galleries and the feast of information about this land, its Native people, the arrival of White explorers, trappers, traders, and settlers, and all the developments that occurred into the twenty-first century.

In a glass case in the Proving Up Gallery, I gazed 271 years into the past at the original Vérendrye Plate—a small, 8.5 by 6.5 inch lead plate that was buried beneath a pile of stones on a hill near the future site of Pierre in 1743 by the French-Canadian brothers, Louis-Joseph and François Vérendrye, who are credited with being the first Whites to explore what became South Dakota. The plate was left to claim the region for France, and it was found partly exposed in 1913 by a group of local teenagers who weren't aware of its significance and brought it to a local print shop with the idea of selling it, since printers used lead. The printer, however, realized it was a big find and contacted the state historian, Doane Robinson, who preserved the plate. The relic has French inscriptions on one side and Latin on the other.

Another very valuable article was a Ghost Dance shirt that was worn by a Miniconjou Sioux man who believed in its protective power, but tragically fell at the Wounded Knee massacre on December 29, 1890. However, the museum's most acclaimed artifact—The Sioux Horse Effigy—wasn't present at the time, but on tour along with other Native art from the Great Plains that was being exhibited in museums in Kansas City, New York, and even Paris. On display, however, was an image of this sleek, three-foot-long wooden carving of a leaping horse mortally wounded in battle, which is considered an absolute masterpiece. Its creator isn't certain, but believed to be a Hunkpapa Lakota man named No Two Horns, who lived on the Standing Rock Reservation and was a cousin of Sitting Bull, and probably produced the effigy about 1875 to honor a horse that had fallen in battle. It was also used as a "dance stick" that was held like a club in ceremonial dances and in telling battle stories. Eventually, it wound up in the hands of missionaries on the reservations, who later donated it to the state historical society in 1920. Its image became the logo of that society, which administers the museum.

Upstairs was the Observation Gallery, which had changing exhibits, and the current one had the theme of past South Dakota environments in geological time. Here I learned that the largest fossil remains of a T Rex found anywhere were discovered near the small town of Faith, South Dakota, in August 1990, just outside the Cheyenne River Reservation northwest of Pierre. After a dispute over ownership was resolved and an auctioning, the extraordinary dinosaur specimen wound up reconstructed in the Field Museum of Natural History in Chicago.

After being absorbed by the different exhibits, I left by late afternoon. Outside, it was still windy, and I drove toward the Capitol building for a close look and parked nearby. The impressive structure has a dark dome topped by a cupola and was completed in 1910 and later restored for the state centennial in 1989. It's considered the best example of neoclassical architecture in South Dakota, with a very different appearance from North Dakota's Art Deco Capitol building. The interior was open to the public, and I entered through the door of a large annex on the north side of the original building that was constructed in 1932.

Like the other state Capitol, there was no security to go through. I picked up a booklet for a self-guided tour and strolled down a beautiful hallway with marble floor tiles and wall sections that were combined with attractive wood, which led to the original back entrance of the Capitol. I noticed a difference in the floor tiles that the tour booklet described, with Italian terrazzo tiles in the old part of the building. It's said that each of these tiles was hand-laid by sixty-six Italian artisans. Ahead was the Grand Staircase made of Vermont marble, and I walked down a hallway called the Governors Gallery, featuring portraits of all the South Dakota governors and state supreme court justices since statehood. Instead of ascending the marble staircase to the upper floors to see more of this seat of state government, I left the elegant building for a look at some outside attractions while there was still enough daylight.

On nearby grounds, the 125th anniversary of South Dakota's statehood during the present year was commemorated with a banner attached to a lamppost. From there, I moseyed toward the rather small and rounded Capitol Lake—a man-made artesian lake created in 1913. By its northwest corner were more examples of South Dakota's "monumental" reputation—six life-sized, bronze saluting figures that stood as a memorial to the 65,000 South Dakotans who served in World War II, with each figure representing a different service branch, and one appearing female. The 26,000 South Dakotans who fought in the Korean War, and 28,000 who served in Viet Nam were also honored nearby with other statues, and there was a memorial wall with the names of those who sacrificed their lives in these wars. The state's fallen law enforcement officers, firefighters, and EMTs also had memorials.

Amidst this grove of monuments was the Flaming Fountain Memorial, which honors all of South Dakota's veterans and is sourced by a 1,300-foot deep artesian well. The water that bubbles up under high pressure is ninety-two degrees F. and contains natural gas that's been used to light the fountain—hence the Flaming Fountain and Eternal Flame. However, the flames of recent years have been more intermittent than eternal, perhaps because of a decline in the underground gas supply. I observed a white crown of rushing water over a pool, without the dazzle of any flames.

I walked clockwise around Capitol Lake on a paved path near the rock-lined shoreline. The area grounds had well-maintained lawns and lush hardwood trees with mainly still green foliage. Groups of ring-billed gulls hovered above the water while others floated on the lake along with mallard ducks. Some strong gusts persisted. The Capitol building remained in good view, and I saw the sprawling, two-story Governor's Residence on the east shore.

I came to the Fighting Stallions Memorial that depicted two life-sized bronze equines in combat—dedicated to eight South Dakotans, including former governor George S. Mickelson, who were killed in a state plane crash on April 19, 1993. A sign read: "This sculpture was selected because it symbolically represents South Dakota's struggle to overcome adversity, desire for achievement, and courage to believe in the future."

The climax of my foot tour was the Capitol Grounds Arboretum Trail, which had about sixty different types of trees and shrubs, both native and non-native to South Dakota, and each specimen was identified. I moved slowly and read the markers through a pleasant grove where there had been no such vegetation when the Capitol was built, and there was even a belief that most trees couldn't grow on the prairie. This was disproved by Samuel H. Elrod—the state's fifth governor from 1905 to 1907—when he successfully planted some American elms by the Capitol. However, these beautiful trees were eventually infected by the Dutch Elm Disease that became so destructive in Europe and North America. The replacement trees fared much better, and Pierre itself became another oasis on the Plains.

After leaving the Capitol grounds, I stopped for a hearty bean soup takeout from the homey Country Kitchen Restaurant, then drove down to the nearby Missouri River when the sun was descending. I moved slowly along Island View Drive, following the shoreline toward Griffin Park, which my city map showed to have a campground. There were signs for the paved Lewis and Clark Trail along the river, where the Missouri has been significantly altered by Nature and humans since the explorers navigated it. I was enthused about being along the explorers' route again and the idea of camping by it after the winds had finally subsided, and it was a beautiful early evening.

I parked in a gravelly lot in the park adjacent to a larger paved one that looked like an RV area, with two large trailers and a motorhome. Tent camping was allowed nearby and even free, and I set up my tent and hoped the winds wouldn't resume. The park was very vagabond-friendly—with shelters, picnic tables, and a restroom—and it faced a narrow river channel with large and heavily wooded LaFramboise Island on the other side. The island was named after Joseph LaFramboise, who built the fort and fur trading post at the mouth of the nearby Bad River in 1817. I watched the sun sink behind the island as I set foot on the Lewis and Clark Trail, while again contemplating the mighty Missouri and its great role in the nation's history. A dirt road ran close to the river for fishing access, and I walked toward an angler near a parked truck—an elderly guy who had placed two standing poles—and asked him what kind of fish were running.

"Walleye, catfish, perch, and some northern pike," he replied.

"What's the best fish to eat?"

"Walleye," he answered without hesitation. "My wife cuts up little pieces of it for frying, but it can also be broiled. I throw catfish away."

That was more encouragement to find a walleye dinner while I was in the area.

The sunset left an afterglow over the island, and it was getting dark when I returned to my campsite. A more than half-moon was glowing quite high in the southern sky, and I was ready for another footloose night in "Peer." On the way out I noticed an old double telephone stand by a parking area, where the phones had been removed, but some wires still dangled. It sure seemed like a relic of another era that I remember so well when public phones were commonplace.

I walked up Sioux Ave. again toward the small downtown and found "The Crossing"—the bar that Ryan from Bob's Lounge had recommended for its beer variety. I went in and found it to be a small place with a crowd of five at two tables and no one at the bar, which seemed dead for a Friday night. I sat at the bar and was served by a young dark-haired woman with a reserved manner.

"What would you like?" she asked, and I said I needed a minute to ponder the fifteen draft beers. But if that was a lot for a Pierre bar, it was about average for Fort Collins.

"Do you have any South Dakota microbrews?"

"Two are from a brewery in Spearfish. Both are pretty light."

Since I felt like imbibing something heavier, I decided on a Shiner Bock from Texas, which was quite dark with a decent taste. I tried to get a conversation going with the young lady since she wasn't that busy.

"I heard Pierre doesn't have a microbrewery, which seems a little strange for a town that's the state's capital."

"This is a strange town."

"I like it anyway, even without a local brewery, though I'm from Fort Collins, Colorado, where there's an abundance of breweries and bars."

"I know, I've been there," she said nonchalantly, and afterwards seemed to have no curiosity about me or care to have much of a conversation. In a long past chapter of my life, I had a few bartending jobs and learned to sense when a customer was interested in conversing or not. And the same can apply to who's on the other side of the bar. Maybe it was this gal's mood, but it seemed more like her personality. I just drank my beer, then left since the overall energy of the place was so low at the time.

I walked back toward the river and found a much more energetic bar at the end of Pierre St. in a large log building that happened to be an American Legion post. The crowd had a lot of twenty-somethings, and I sat at the end of a long bar next to a guy who looked older than me. A short, young woman was working the bar, and I tried a Grain Belt draft from a limited variety of brews. This one was darker and more flavorful than the bottled one of that brand I drank the previous night. The place had some kind of bowling game and darts, and quite a few TVs playing that included the baseball playoffs. The older guy near me was sipping a bottle of Miller Lite, and I asked, "How are the playoffs going?"

"I'm not a fan."

"Neither am I really. I just wondered because I did see part of an exciting extra-inning game recently."

He was low key about a few other questions I asked, but still receptive. He told me he'd retired from the Air Force years ago and that his service had included being stationed in Minot. He'd been in Pierre since 1975 and hailed from Alabama originally, which I heard in his speech.

"So how have you handled the winters here? Someone told me about the bitter cold and winds but that it snows more in eastern South Dakota."

"They do get more snow, but there's still occasional blizzards here. The winters are rough, and it can be colder even this time of year."

"Have you considered moving to get away from the cold here?"

"Actually, I'm about to move soon, on November 8."

"To where?"

"Mississippi, near the Gulf, and not too far from where I lived in Alabama."

"Are you moving mainly for the warm weather?"

"That's part of it." But he didn't reveal more and had a reserve that discouraged me from being too inquisitive.

"I'm headed for the Gulf myself, traveling all the way down U.S. 83 to Brownsville, Texas, from the Canadian border. I live in northern Colorado now."

"Sounds like an interesting trip." But he wasn't interested enough to ask any questions about it. There was a lull in the conversation as I was almost done with my beer, and I decided to continue barhopping.

"Good luck with your move, and it looks like you'll dodge the real winter here," were my parting words.

"Yes, and I won't miss it. Have a safe trip."

I thought that besides being tired of a cold climate, perhaps he wanted to return late in life to the area where he lived in his youth.

The American Legion bar happened to be right off the Lewis and Clark path along the river. For a while I savored the reflections of moonlight on the Missouri and could discern its steady and timeless flow toward its confluence with the Mississippi and eventually with the Gulf of Mexico—that great body of water near the end of U.S. 83 where I was also bound.

I was drawn back to Bob's Lounge, and the small bar was quite crowded and lively like the night before. Before I found a seat on the upper level again, I discovered an interesting back room with tables, where the walls were decorated with a big collection of photos of hunters and anglers showing off their trophies. Some were even big game like caribou from outside South Dakota, and all a sign of the sportsmen's culture here.

I didn't see Ryan in the crowd, but again bought a Sam Adams Octoberfest, along with a small bag of salted peanuts. Sitting next to the empty seat on my left was a nice-looking woman who I thought might not have company, so I broke the ice with a "How are you doing tonight?"

"I'm doing OK," she responded in a friendly manner.

"I'm just passing through and happen to be traveling all of U.S. 83 to the Mexican border. This is my second night in Pierre, and I like the town."

Her face showed some interest, but just then a fairly young guy sat between us, and it became apparent they were together. At first, I felt a little awkward, but he was very friendly, and I wound up having a conversation with both of them and found out they lived in Pierre.

When the guy heard about my 83 adventure, he said he'd traveled a lot of the highway.

"Are you retired?" he asked—though some people didn't think I looked old enough to be.

"I like to say I'm retired from employment, but not work."

"So, what were you employed in?"

"My longest employment was driving for a paratransit service for the elderly and disabled."

"I'm in the construction business," he said. "We build roads and other things." And he indicated it may have been a family business.

"Have you always lived in Pierre?"

"Yes."

"And do you like it enough to want to stay?"

"Well, it's been my home, and I have the business here."

He and the woman were married.

"So how do you feel about the winters here?"

"Actually, I don't mind them since I had two six-month projects in Antarctica—the coldest, windiest, and stormiest place in the world. Even when I was there during the Southern Hemisphere's summer, temperature highs were usually only about forty degrees F."

Then he brought up the subject of the local Oahe Dam and asked if I'd seen it.

"No," I replied, "but someone else here last night told me I should see it, and I plan to."

"You really should." Then he showed me a Google Earth image of the dam on his phone and told an interesting story about it.

"In the spring of 2011, the dam release got out of control during a big snowmelt from Montana, which could have caused a serious flood in Pierre. Our company worked long trying to prevent it by building levees."

"I didn't see him for over a week," his wife added.

"The efforts helped save the town from a lot of damage," he said, then mentioned that now was a good time to see the dam because of another release that was very impressive. Apparently, things there were under control.

We finally made introductions, though I later forgot their names.

"Watch out for cops when you get to Nebraska," the guy warned.

"They're very tough on speeders. The South Dakota cops are easier."

"I'm looking forward to traveling through the Sandhills in Nebraska, which seem very interesting."

"The area is beautiful, but look out for snapping turtles crossing the road there. It's surprising how quick they can move, but they still get hit often."

"I'm surprised to hear about turtle crossings there. They must come from ponds in the Sandhills."

"Yes."

After finishing my beer, I was ready to leave and get something else to eat on the way back. I bid farewell to the friendly couple who both wished me well, and it seemed again like Bob's Lounge was "where good friends are," or at least where "good conversations are easy."

I found the late eatery, Taco John's, on Sioux Ave. and was the only customer inside at first, though a drive-thru was busy. For the second night in a row, I indulged in fast food with a Mexican flavor—this time a tasty combo of a decent-sized beef burrito with small, round fried potatoes, which weren't too greasy but still gave me a twinge of nutritional guilt.

Back at my overnight area called City Camp, I sat awhile at a table facing the river and again became enchanted by the moon's watery reflections, and wisps of clouds drifting across the lunar face. I had more thoughts about Lewis and Clark and how fitting it was that I was camping along the river that was their highway. When I got into my sleeping bag in the tent at a late hour—my night owl habits persisting—I felt comfortable where I was, even if it wasn't like the bed the night before in the Pierre Inn and Suites.

DAY 12

LaFramboise Island, the dam, and a walleye dinner

I had some breakfast at a picnic table while watching flying and floating gulls by the river, and some joggers were pounding the pavement of the Lewis and Clark Trail. On the way to the restroom, I talked to a guy with a trailer who lived in Rapid City, South Dakota, but was originally from Pierre.

"I make the trip here about twice a month to fish," he said, "and I have a boat. I also hunt, and the pheasant season starts soon."

"I'm driving all the way down U.S. 83 to the Mexican border,"— stating my purpose.

"Are you retired?" I was asked again, and this time I answered with a simple "Yes."

"I plan to retire in about ten years, but not fully because I'm in real estate, which is very easy to do part-time. So, what are you driving?"

"A Toyota Corolla over there that I often sleep in, though last night I used my tent.

"It sounds like you have a good, simple life."

"It's not always so simple. I stay in motels sometimes. Sleeping in a compact car sure isn't as comfortable as an RV, and that's why I call it my cramper, which he found amusing. "So, do you catch and eat walleye? I heard it's a tasty fish."

"I think it's the best," which really encouraged me to find a walleye dinner later that day. Then he cut the conversation short because he was probably anxious to pursue his catch of the day.

The restroom needed a cleaning but was functional. As I was doing my upper body wash cloth rinse with, unfortunately, cold water, an older guy came in and said, "Good morning," After I returned the greeting, I asked if he knew of a local restaurant that had walleye on the menu. He was from Pierre and recommended a place called McClelland's on the way to the Oahe dam, which was also on my agenda.

After taking down the tent and leaving the park campground, I made a stop at the vintage St. Charles Hotel on Capitol Ave. because of my interest in old hotels. This large, five-story, rectangular brick building, which has been renovated, presently housed a restaurant and lounge, with offices and apartments on the upper floors. Built in 1911, it once lodged South Dakota legislators when they were in town, and several of the state's governors also resided in the hotel before the first Governor's Residence was completed in the 1940s. The St. Charles also had famous guests like President Calvin Coolidge, Charles Lindbergh, Dale Carnegie, Bob Hope, and Clark Gable. It's all why the hotel's location has been called "Pierre's most prestigious address," and in May 1980, it made the National Register of Historic Places.

Later, I returned to the Country Kitchen for some lunch, and my parking space faced a single railroad track running through town. Although South Dakota's rails had brought many people to Pierre and throughout the state in its early years, the last regularly scheduled passenger train in the whole state stopped running in 1969. South Dakota is also the only state in the Lower Forty-Eight, besides Wyoming, without any Amtrak service. Plenty of freight moves through, however.

The neighborhood also had a tattoo and body-piercing shop, and I would have been surprised if I didn't see at least one of these surgical operations in Pierre or any sizable town these days. But to me, it's a very unappealing and prolonged fad that's resulted in the Branded Generation, which must be driven by a lot of peer pressure in "Peer" and elsewhere. Maybe I would have gotten tattooed myself if I were twenty-four and not sixty-four—though I like to think I wouldn't.

I headed to explore LaFramboise Island across from where I'd camped. On the way, I stopped at Steamboat Park just north of the island—with a name that evokes the steamboats that once plied the Missouri's waters. In a verdant environment of well-maintained grass and mixed trees, I saw Pierre's original one-room, fourteen by twenty-foot wooden schoolhouse, established in 1881, which had been moved from its original location. Its size indicated how small Pierre must have been in its early days. The park was just to the south of the U.S. 83-U.S. 14 bridge and the old, multi-spanned railroad bridge over the river. The latter was built by the Chicago and North Western Railway in 1907 and provided the first permanent crossing of the Missouri in central South Dakota. It has withstood the mighty river's flows and floods for well over a century and was placed on the National Register of Historic Places in 1998.

I drove across a causeway to the island constructed by the U.S. Army Corps of Engineers in the 1960s and parked where the road terminated. I was impressed by the heavily wooded environment, which is one reason I wanted to come here. Not since Hiddenwood State Park outside Selby had I been around so many trees. A nearby sign announced LaFramboise Island Nature Area and had a trail map with a description of the island, which was said to be typical of sandbar islands along the Missouri floodplain that existed before the upstream dams were built. Today, few remain. Sand deposits found on LaFramboise—which means "raspberry" in French—are a result of the natural flooding that occurred here that the dams now control. Consequently, the island has had big changes in vegetation since the flooding once removed old cottonwood trees and enabled their seeds to germinate and grow. But as the cottonwoods became less reproductive, species like cedar, ash, and invasive Russian olive have moved in. A flier I picked up said that most of the cottonwoods here are over sixty-five years old, and that they're not a long-lived tree. Eventually, the other species will become more dominant.

The sign also mentioned the wildlife and diversity of bird species sighted here, which includes bald eagles and the endangered least tern. The river is also home to the endangered pallid sturgeon—a large fish with origins in the Cretaceous period seventy million years ago that's remained relatively unchanged.

The island was described in the journals of Lewis and Clark, and it's near here where the expedition had its tense encounter with the Teton Sioux in September 1804, which led to the location being called "Good Humored Island."

I set out with a small map to hike some of the trails on the 580-acre island—first taking a wide dirt one with lots of gravel, then an offshoot that led to one of the well houses that supply some of Pierre's drinking water. I backtracked, trying to find another trail and encountered a thirtyish woman walking a leashed dog, and after greeting each other she gave me some directions to the Prairie Trail. This led to more of a conversation, and I found out she'd lived in Pierre for a year and a half and was drawn here from Wisconsin by a teaching job.

"So, how do you like it here?" I inquired.

"I love it."

"You don't mind the winters?"

"Not coming from Wisconsin. It's windier here, though, and for a while I did miss all the green trees."

"So, you're more acclimated to the prairie now?"

"You might say so."

"At least you can find some woods on this island."

"I come here a lot."

"I would too if I lived around here."

I mentioned my trip and where I'd started from, and that I really liked Pierre too. Then she recommended a restaurant outside town that had great steaks if that appealed to me.

"What I really want is a good walleye dinner tonight before I leave town, and someone told me about a place near the dam for that."

"Red Rossa in town might have walleye too," she informed me.

She seemed like a nice and smart young woman I would have enjoyed talking longer to, but her dog started getting restless. "I guess I should move on now," she said, and I thought maybe I should too, if I wanted to see enough of the island. Apparently, she was someone who came here for a job and seemed to have adapted very well.

I found the narrow trail I was looking for, which went through a heavily wooded area and eventually led to large open meadows with lots of tall, tawny grasses. Seasonal color had started in the bordering hardwoods, and it was a picturesque scene. I read a historical sign about the fur trade that played a role in the area's early development, which clarified the difference between the forts and trading posts involved in the business. The forts were larger and operated year-round and supplied the smaller seasonal posts. From Fort Pierre Chouteau, prized furs—with beaver pelts most in demand—obtained from Natives and trappers as the raw materials for hats and coats were shipped east on the rivers before the arrival of the railroads.

Ahead was a large field with more tall grasses that looked sizable enough to be considered a prairie, and the reason I supposed I was on the Prairie Trail. Some rolling and rather arid hills were in the distance. At this point, I headed back and was soon in the woods again with some mixed evergreens. I encountered four young men clad in camouflage with bows and arrows, and suddenly I thought I should be wearing orange and was surprised hunting was allowed in such a public place. One guy greeted me, and I found out their game was white-tailed deer, which was in season for their old weaponry.

"I better stay out of your way," I kidded, "but good luck."

"Thank you," one answered.

Then I wondered why I said that when killing a beautiful animal like a deer with a bow and arrow would not be my first choice if I had to be a predator. Of course, Native Americans once had no choice, and must have developed different sensibilities, as have some modern-day hunters, apparently.

I wound up back on the wide, dirt and gravel trail closer to the river, where I heard the distinctive calls of chickadees in the brush. The sun was descending, and it had gotten more overcast. Back at Wander, another car pulled in close to my space, and out stepped an elderly gentleman with white hair and a thin mustache, wearing a flannel shirt and brimmed cap that stated "U.S. Army" and was adorned with pins. He looked old enough to be a World War II veteran, which immediately aroused my interest.

We greeted each other, and I started a conversation by asking him about any problems caused by the different time zones on each side of the river that I'd heard about.

"Some things are pretty mixed up," he replied. "Some businesses in Fort Pierre like to stay on Central Time to coordinate with those in Pierre. But bars over there prefer Mountain Time to be able to close later."

"So do you live in Pierre, sir?"

"I do, but I came from Nebraska and have lived elsewhere in South

Dakota. I used to travel around the state and others to different Indian reservations to provide psychological testing services."

He was apparently a type of psychologist, and presumably retired. But I was most interested in his veteran status, proudly displayed on his cap, and asked if he was a World War II vet.

"Yes," he replied. "I was in the Army but stayed state-side. Somebody had to."

"I guess you consider yourself lucky, since that may well have saved your life or limbs."

"That's for sure. I had a few brothers who were also in the Army, and one of them was in ordinance and in a lot of combat in Europe and North Africa, and was even in the occupation of Japan. He always said, 'War is hell.' He lived through it but was very traumatized and died years ago of heart problems, which I think were affected by his psychological traumas."

We made introductions, and his name was Robert. I told him I was from Fort Collins, Colorado and slowly progressing toward the Mexican border on U.S. 83, and he seemed very interested.

"I've done a lot of driving but have never been south of Kansas on 83," he said. "I have kids that are scattered, though two are in Pierre. A daughter lives near Evergreen, Colorado, who I've visited quite a bit. She went to Colorado State University in your town and majored in music therapy. She's a special lady and excellent musician and singer who's in a small group called Dakota Blonde"—a name that sounded familiar to me from the Colorado music scene. "They've even performed for emotionally disturbed children and adults in institutions, and their music has been therapeutic for many people. I often come here to walk, which is good for me. But a few years ago, I had a real scare with pneumonia that I pulled through."

Being a World War II vet meant Robert had to be at least approaching ninety. He didn't mention anything about a wife, and I didn't ask if his spouse was still alive. Before leaving, he handed me a business card describing his background in special education, psychological service, and as a school psychologist. His psychologist's mind was still sharp, but I noticed his hearing aid, which must have worked well for our conversation. I told Robert I better head out since I wanted to see the Oahe Dam, and he said I should while there was still enough daylight.

Like Herbert Wilson, back in Bismarck, he seemed like another very nice gentleman from the Greatest Generation, and another look at his cap and pins inspired me to say: "You seem very proud of being a World War II veteran, and I'd like to personally thank you for your service. My father was also a veteran, and it's always great to meet some of you who are left."

He appreciated that, and we shook hands before he said, "Be careful."

The next time I got to a computer, I googled Dakota Blonde and read some very positive comments about Robert's daughter—whose name was Mary, and she was a blonde—and the two men who formed the acoustic group. Though based in Colorado, they had also performed nationally, and I was set on seeing them after I returned home. I had a better idea of why Robert seemed very proud of his daughter.

I drove across the Missouri on the bridge I'd seen, and was back on 83 and U.S. 14 briefly, then followed 14 where it split off to a quick connection with SD 1806 toward the Oahe dam. I was now in the huge region of South Dakota that I'd traveled through on the way to 83 known as West River—namely, all the land lying west of the Missouri River, which divides the state. The region east of the river is called East River, but the division is known to involve more than the river boundary. Like the hundredth meridian, West River is reputed as where the West begins, and the basic geological difference is that its terrain was shaped largely by erosion and not glaciation as in East River. The course of the Missouri River itself has been altered by glaciation.

I was now in bucolic surroundings, where some hay bales were scattered near the road. Arid bluffs stood out to the west, but the river corridor was lush with trees. The low sun had a dazzling brightness, and I was glad I wasn't driving into its glare. I passed McClelland's, where I looked forward to a walleye dinner after a good look at the dam.

Soon the long, grassy embankment of the downstream side of the massive structure came into view. I was looking at the second largest dam along the Missouri after the Garrison Dam, which is also an earth-fill type that's the fifteenth largest in the world, with grass cover to prevent erosion. I turned on a road that wound not far from the dam's base and saw some vehicles moving along an upper road. The road I was on led down to the power plant well below the summit of the structure, where I parked in a large lot and stepped out with my camera for some photos of the plant that provides hydroelectric power to both Dakotas, Nebraska, Minnesota, and Montana. Above the plant were fourteen large cylindrical structures called surge tanks in two rows, which control the flow of water from the intakes. And right in front of me was the tail race, or streaming channel of water that exits the dam and creates hydropower. Seven turbines were nearby, and a power substation. Numerous transmission towers stood at this great nexus of power production, and others stretched in the distance.

I drove up to Crest Drive and parked on its shoulder. It was aptly named for running across the top of the dam toward the bluffs to the west, and on the north side was the sprawling lower section of Lake Oahe—The fourth largest man-made reservoir in the U.S. determined by volume, which extends 231 miles north almost to Bismarck. For most of its course, however, it resembles a very wide river on the map, with numerous coves and inlets. The dam I was on that radically altered the Missouri River had origins with the federal government's Flood Control Act of 1944 and the Pick-Sloan Plan for the river's basin. Construction by the U.S. Army Corps of Engineers began in 1948; however, the dam wasn't fully completed until 1962, when electrical power generation began, and there was a dedication with President Kennedy on August 17. Though its construction began just a year after the Garrison Dam, the Oahe Dam took almost ten years longer to complete despite the Garrison being even larger.

Near the rock-covered shoreline was a pier-like concrete structure that I found out had the power plant's water intake control towers. These contain valves that regulate water flow into tunnels that carry the water under the dam to the power plant.

The sun had set beyond a clouded horizon, and before crossing the dam, I followed a sign for a visitor center that was closed when I arrived. But nearby was the photogenic, wooden Oahe Mission School and Chapel, with a historical sign I stepped out to read. I learned that a Congregational missionary named Thomas L. Riggs and his wife had established a mission among about 300 Sioux here in the mid-1870s, originally in a log building. Lumber to construct a school and church was later shipped up the Missouri by steamboat; and by September 1877, Riggs, a carpenter, and Native laborers had completed the structure that functioned as a church and school. It was given the name "Oahe"—meaning "a place to stand upon" in the Sioux language like "foundation"—and it became the religious center for a large area and the namesake of the dam and huge lake behind it. The building itself hasn't changed since its early days but was moved from its original location twelve miles upstream that's now under 150 feet of water.

Back on Crest Drive, I drove across the 9,300-foot-long dam. The remaining daylight was dim, and the landscape's forms grew darker. At the other end of the dam was the spillway, where I pulled off again. This was the emergency relief system that prevents water from going over the top of the dam during floods and directs it away from the power plant.

I left the scene with a greater appreciation of human engineering. But the "progress" it brought, in this case, had a usual downside, for Native Americans were again displaced, as with the Garrison Dam, through eminent domain claims by the Bureau of Reclamation. The Standing Rock Reservation lost 55,993 acres, and the Cheyenne River Reservation about 150,000; and most prime agricultural land was lost again. It's said that when a visitor came to these reservations years later, they asked why there seemed to be so few elders around and were told: "The old people had died of heartache." The Native groups did receive obligatory compensation for their losses, but additional claims for more fair amounts continued for years. Once again, a tragic conflict of interests.

Back on SD 1806, it was almost dark, and the tall streetlamps that lined Crest Drive were illuminated in the distance—creating a necklace of lights. Soon I arrived at McClelland's Restaurant with a big appetite for a walleye dinner. The large parking lot wasn't crowded, even on a Saturday evening. Inside, the first thing that caught my attention was a book on display titled *Walleye Troubleshooting—Answers 50 Of Your Toughest on the Water Questions,* by Mike McClelland. Apparently, the owner of the restaurant did more than just serve walleye. He was also an author and outstanding professional fisherman from Pierre, who was inducted into the National Freshwater Fishing Hall of Fame in 1993.

I sat at a small bar serviced by a pleasant young woman and announced I was here to dine on walleye, and she handed me a menu that showed three selections of the fish—fried, Cajun, and sauteed with black pepper dill sauce. The restaurant also touted itself as a steakhouse and offered other entrees. I bought a bottle of Coors Light and asked the lady what she thought was the best walleye choice, and her preference was the black pepper dill sauce. After a slight hesitation, I said, "I'll take your word for it," and ordered it. Soon, a salubrious salad came that included some good dark greens along with a warm roll.

Two young guys came in and sat close by at the bar, who were wearing brimmed caps and looked like anglers. I asked if they were walleye fishermen, and indeed they were. I told them I'd just ordered walleye for the first time, and they informed me that this restaurant would also cook fish that had been caught and cleaned. "We don't have our own catch today, though," one of them said.

When my walleye arrived, it was a substantial portion, along with a good-sized baked potato that I'd requested salsa for. I found it to be a non-fatty and mild-flavored fish with a distinctive sweetness. The slightly creamy sauce was delicious, and I had no reason to complain to the server for her recommendation. I savored a very satisfying dinner that was worth the price, especially if I might not have an opportunity to have walleye again. I asked the woman if the fish was locally sourced from the Missouri River, and though she wasn't sure about that, she said it was fresh and probably from South Dakota.

The young bartender was very poised and well-spoken, and I noticed her wedding ring. She said she lived in Pierre, and when I told her where I was from and traveling to, she said: "We're thinking of moving to Colorado, maybe around Fort Collins or Greeley. We've never been there but would like to check it out, including the school system for our kid."

"The area does have a lot going for it, but it's getting more expensive and crowded. So, are you tired of the winters here?"

"The winters here aren't that bad," she said to my surprise.

"That's not what I've heard from some others. Are you thinking of moving to a place with more amenities and more happening?"

"That's a big part of it."

She didn't mention Colorado's mountains, though, which are a magnet for so many. When I finished dinner, we had a little more conversation. Then, on my way out, she showed me owner Mike McClelland's office, with lots of plaques on the walls for his fishing feats, before going back to her job. And on a wall near the entrance of the restaurant was a big, mounted reproduction of a recent record-size walleye next to a deer head trophy. A close look showed a handsome fish with a greenish, gold coloration above a white belly. Now I could relate better to the fish I had just consumed, which is part of the local culture.

When I got to google "walleye" to learn more, I found out it's the largest member of the perch family that's native to rivers and lakes in most of Canada and the northern U.S. Not surprisingly, it's the state fish of South Dakota. Size-wise, they average about ten to eighteen inches and one to three pounds, but can be much larger, as I saw with the wall specimen. The current recorded maximum is a whopping forty-two inches and twenty-nine pounds. Walleyes are also a long-lived fish, known to live close to thirty years. The name "walleye" interestingly comes from the anatomy of the fish's eyes, which point outward as if looking at walls. That's a little of Walleye 101.

I decided to go back to the City Camp on the river for the night, sleep in the car, and leave Pierre the next day. On the way, I gassed up at a Sinclair station in town that had full service. A young Native-looking guy did the pumping while a Caucasian guy surprisingly cleaned my windshield—like back in the days we older folks remember. I stopped at a Dakota Market store down the street and picked up a few grocery items just before they closed, where I noticed a large sporting goods department, or perhaps a separate store, rather oddly located downstairs, with lots of guns in view. I took this as another sign of South Dakota's sportsmen's culture, since you could buy a rifle close to the groceries.

At City Camp, the same RVs were still parked, and I pulled into my previous space in the adjacent lot that was otherwise empty. I spent quite a bit of time journaling in the car by lamp light before I used the restroom, then got into my sleeping bag. Through the rear window, I could see part of the clear night sky, including Orion, which had risen quite high—a sign of winter drawing nearer and a reminder of the following season and its harshness on the northern plains. Hopefully, I would be far south if wintry weather arrived early.

DAY 13

Into West River

After breakfast, I drove off from the City Camp and felt a little sad about leaving Pierre. I crossed the river again into the West River region of South Dakota and Fort Pierre—the older but smaller sibling community of Pierre, with a population of about 2,100. However, it's rich in history, including its significance as the oldest continuous non-Native settlement in South Dakota. After the early trading posts and the military fort where its name came from, Fort Pierre evolved into a busy river port teeming with steamboats that brought settlers and gold seekers who made a rail connection there. There are no visible remains of the old fort after it was excavated through the years, but the site is commemorated as a National Historic Landmark with a stone monument about a mile north of the town off SD 1806.

After splitting from U.S. 14, U.S. 83 made a bend to the south into the center of Fort Pierre, where there was a "Welcome to Fort Pierre" sign by a sculpture of a cowboy on a bucking horse. The latter is a tribute to Casey Tibbs (1921-1990)—one of the area's favorite sons, who was a record-breaking rodeo champion who grew up on a horse ranch fifty miles northwest of Fort Pierre. In 1951, he made the cover of *Life* magazine, and after his great career in rodeo went on to become a stuntman, stunt coordinator, technical director, and actor. Tibbs had a long list of credits in film and TV, where he exhibited his varied talents. The local pride in him is also shown by the nearby Casey Tibbs South Dakota Rodeo Center—a museum dedicated to South Dakota's rodeo history.

I made a turn on Main St. where there was another museum—the small Verendrye Museum named after the brothers who are credited for being the region's earliest White explorers. It's in a former American Legion hall and has a collection of South Dakota historical artifacts, but it was closed this time of year. However, I was more interested in seeing the Verendrye Monument on a local hill, where the lead plate I'd seen encased in the South Dakota Cultural Heritage Center was buried by the Vérendrye brothers in 1743 to claim the region for France. I turned on another street and followed a sign for the monument, and the road wound uphill where there was a spectacle of the Missouri River.

At the crest of the hill was a bulky stone and mortar monument and a smaller stone one. After parking, my attention was just as much drawn by the river panorama that included LaFramboise Island, the city of Pierre, and Fort Pierre below. I walked over to the large monument, which had a viewing window for a replica of the 8.5 by 6.5-inch lead plate that was discovered here. Above it was a metal sign with translations of the plate's inscriptions on its front and back sides. The front was translated from Latin:

IN THE TWENTY-SIXTH YEAR OF THE REIGN
OF LOUIS XV, THE MOST ILLUSTRIOUS LORD,
THE LORD MARQUIS OF BEAUHARNOIS BEING VICEROY,
1741, PETER GAULTIER DE LA VERENDRYE PLACED THIS.

The back's translation was from French:

PLACED BY THE CHEVALIER VERENDRYE
(HIS BROTHER) LOUIS (AND) LALONDETTE AND
A. MIOTTI. 30 MARCH 1743.

The plate also had the seal of France, and nearby was a historical sign that included an old photo of three people from the group of teenagers, in their later years, who discovered the plate half buried on February 16, 1913. The other monument acknowledged the Vérendrye site's designation as a National Historic Landmark in 1991.

Much is unknown about the actual exploration of the Vérendrye brothers. Besides the lead plate, what is known is based on a journal found in the French archives in 1851 and another document there. It's said that the journal is difficult to interpret, and of four Vérendrye brothers, it's not certain which two made the journey, and two other Frenchmen accompanied them. The expedition of these first known Whites to have crossed the northern plains occurred sixty-one years before Lewis and Clark, whose journey is much less enigmatic. Like Lewis and Clark, the small Vérendrye party was seeking a water route to the Pacific, but they didn't navigate the Missouri River. They also had many contacts with different Native tribes; however, references like "Horse People" and "Snake People" make it difficult to positively identify certain tribes. The route of their over one-year journey is also uncertain, though it's believed they probably ventured as far west as the Big Horn Mountains in northern Wyoming and were the first known non-Natives to see part of the northern Rockies. It's known that they left Fort La Reine—a fur trading post at the southern end of Lake Manitoba in French Canada—on April 29, 1742, and trekked to what became North Dakota, where they had contact with the Mandan like Lewis and Clark decades later. From there, it's hypothesized they took a rather crooked course that went nowhere near the Pacific, but through parts of the future states of Montana, Wyoming, and Nebraska before they entered South Dakota and the Pierre area in March 1743 and claimed the whole upper region of the Missouri River drainage for France by burying the lead plate. The party went back to the Mandan on May 18 and returned to Fort La Reine by July 2.

Although they hadn't found the elusive water route or Northwest Passage, their expedition advanced French colonial ambitions. The huge region claimed for France became part of the Louisiana Territory, which was sold to the young United States in 1803 and set the stage for Lewis and Clark's great exploration.

Along with the flags of the U.S. and South Dakota that flapped on the overlook was a historic French flag with three "fleur-de-lis"—a reminder of the French role in history here. I lingered a while at the site, taken in by the panorama on a sunny and mild day with shifting clouds, until my connection with history and the landscape was interrupted by a young guy who drove in blasting Hip-Hop music from his vehicle. Fortunately, he soon left, and I enjoyed a little more peace and quiet until I thought it was time to head out and finally leave the Pierre area.

A sign by the Fort Pierre Motel that I passed had an amusing definition of a dietary orientation: "Vegetarian—Indian word for lousy hunter."

Just before leaving Fort Pierre, 83 crossed the narrow and dry-looking Bad River that connects with the Missouri, where Joseph LaFramboise established a trading post in 1817. Soon the highway expanded to four lanes and moved away from the great river that I had my last look at and final encounter with the route of Lewis and Clark.

It felt good to be really moving again, and this stretch of 83 had a dual dedication as the Pearl Harbor and Vietnam Memorial Highway. I entered a rolling grassland with the character of the West River region—appearing more Western than Midwestern. The highway coursed through the Fort Pierre National Grassland, where part of the movie *Dances with Wolves* was filmed. The designation of national grassland began with an act of the U.S. Congress in 1937, and the current twenty that have been established in the nation are managed by the U.S. Forest Service. Like the national forests, national grasslands may have multiple uses that include recreation, grazing, and mineral extraction. As an avid environmentalist, I just hope these grasslands have been less exploited commercially than many of the national forests are known to be. The Fort Pierre National Grassland covers parts of three South Dakota counties but is not contiguous.

Adjacent to the national grassland to the east is the Lower Brulé Indian Reservation—a haven for a sub-group of the Lakota division of the widespread Sioux nation. The name "Sioux" was first used by the British in the 1760s and was abbreviated from the French name "Nadouessioux," which was given by French explorers over a century earlier to the large tribal group. It's a very generic name for a complex family of Native people who have commonalities in history, language, and culture, which includes the use of ceremonial smoking pipes made from a type of clay called pipestone. Brûlé—meaning "burnt" in French—is the name French fur traders used for a group of Sioux called Sicangu, which divided into the Lower Brulé and Upper Brulé in the late eighteenth century.

The relatively small Lower Brulé Reservation has only about 1,300 inhabitants. But almost ten percent of the total population of South Dakota is Native American, and in West River it's over thirty percent, including those who live outside reservations. Since the 1960s, many Natives in general, inspired by a new pride in their heritage, have returned to the reservations, despite the impoverishment so many are known for.

There are some interesting differences between the early White settlers of East River and those of West River. Those who came to East River were largely homesteaders from states like Iowa and Minnesota, and immigrants from the East Coast with a high percentage of German and Scandinavian backgrounds. Whereas, West River was settled largely by gold seekers, with many coming from other gold rush destinations like Montana and Colorado. Ranchers arrived next from Colorado, Kansas, and Texas, and West River's non-Native population developed more ethnic diversity and a culture much like the Mountain states. But although West River has somewhat more than half of South Dakota's land area, it has just between one-quarter and one-third of the state's population. Politically, West River is more conservative and Republican than East River, yet ironically has had a long dependence on federal aid for its economy.

I passed some cultivated land to the east, and vast, flat grasslands sprawled to the south and west, with profiles of cattle, horses, and hay. More croplands alternated with undulating grasslands where dark cattle grazed where bison once did, and still did in my imagination.

An enormous dark cloud loomed to the south, and suddenly a double rainbow appeared in the east in another cloud formation. Neither was a full arch, but still a splendid sight. I pulled off the road for another photo op of the phenomenon with a Highway 83 sign in the foreground, and again thought about my deceased mother who had gone "over the rainbow." The colors soon faded, and a prairie wind began to whip.

The sky remained a changing spectacle as I continued south, with dark and light clouds, shades in between, and spout-like formations. On earth, prairie grasses waved furiously in the wind, and I thought about how much I loved this land even if I wouldn't want to live in the region—for its great space, power, color, and sense of freedom. I was still in the national grassland area, which resembled the plains of eastern Colorado here. Soon I was cruising through a sea of cultivated sunflowers, which I hadn't seen for many miles; then I was back in sprawling rangeland with scattered hay, followed by more cultivation that included wheat.

The highway was still four lanes, and ahead was a junction with mighty I-90—the longest interstate in the nation that I previously encountered briefly after coming out of the Black Hills early in the journey. I pulled into a Sinclair station to use the restroom, where I looked at my flat hair and whiskered face in a mirror and thought it was time to improve my appearance. There were $10 showers by a cafe and store at the gas stop, no doubt used by truckers; but I decided to wait since I intended to find a lodging that night. I've found out in my travels that some motels also offer just showers, with some reasonably priced and others rather pricey.

The picturesque village of Vivian was just to the east, set like an island on the prairie sea—with trees, assorted buildings, a grain elevator, and storage bins—amid surroundings of brown fields, huge sunflowers, and a hay-strewn hillside that all looked very bucolic. It lies along the Dakota Southern Railway and was named after Vivian Hunter—the wife of a railroad official. This community, with a populace not much over a hundred, had a significant event on July 23, 2010, when the world's largest measured hailstone descended on it during a ferocious storm. The melon-sized object was eight inches in diameter and weighed close to two pounds.

A colorful mixture of clouds was billowing over the landscape during my stop, and there was a brief sprinkling from a passing dark formation. A flock of noisy starlings also descended from above, which also appeared to be heading south.

My southbound direction was interrupted when 83 joined I-90 for a stretch that shot due west for about twenty miles toward the town of Murdo. This longest interstate courses 3,020 miles (4,860 km) through thirteen states and connects Boston with Seattle. While cruising at a higher speed, I didn't mind being on an interstate temporarily for a change of pace. Long before 83 became co-signed with I-90 here, it's old route ran further east on what's now two-lane U.S. 183—an auxiliary of the present U.S. 83. The worst thing about this interstate stretch was driving into a near blinding sunset. But I was able to see more rolling rangelands with cattle and hay, and a sign on the right side of the road boldly stated—"Jesus died for your sins"—

presumably intended more for skeptics since believers shouldn't have to be reminded. Some strong winds from the south started buffeting Wander, and a slew of billboards had appeared along the roadside—a lot for businesses in Murdo, which was my day's destination. The Dakota Southern Railway ran along the north side of the expressway, and I passed the tiny town of Draper—another settlement named after a railroad official. There was farmland close to Murdo with more hay, and the town's water tower appeared.

The brilliant sun was about to set when I pulled off the interstate where 83 made its exit. I stopped to buy ice at the Country Mart, and across the street was a bustling Pilot Travel Center teeming with truckers and other travelers. This is the largest travel plaza chain in North America. To the south were vast open spaces, where 83 rolled on as a two-lane road through the rest of South Dakota. I soon noticed six motels in this travelers' town—two big national chains and four indies that included the Sioux Motel. A sign by the Sioux boasted, "best rates, super clean," which enticed me to stop there.

The motel was a long, one-story building, and the office had some decor true to the Native theme—a bison skull, shield, and feathered artifacts. A woman in the office, who I found out was the owner, was a pleasant, fair-skinned blonde who looked late middle-aged and definitely not Native. The room rate was reasonable, and I also got a little discount for my AARP membership. Towns that have enough lodging competition must benefit the traveler-consumer. Once again, I was given a real key and not a key card for Room 26, which was as clean as claimed, and very tidy.

After two nights in my cramper, I had two double beds to choose from and a very desirable bathtub to soak in. The room also had a large, flat panel TV, refrigerator, microwave, coffeemaker, and a nice carpet. For a while, I reclined in a comfortable chair and imbibed a beer.

I decided to delay a hot soak in the tub and walk around Murdo and have another beer and a meal. Just across the street was the Rusty Spur Steakhouse, with its Old West Saloon that had a definite Western character but wasn't a real vintage place. Seeing no one at the bar encouraged me to move on, though. I came to a stone sign with the inscription "Welcome to Murdo," with an image of a cowboy on horseback and three longhorn cattle. Below, it read: "Head of the Northwest Cattle Trail, led by Murdo Mackenzie in 1880."

This town of under 500 people was named in honor of this great cattleman of the Old West, who lived from 1850 to 1939 and was a very enterprising and successful Scottish immigrant known for his determination and integrity. In a long career, he managed and partially owned different cattle companies that operated from Texas to the Canadian border, and later ran a company in Brazil. His years in the American West were still the era of gun-slinging, but Murdo never carried one and is known to have said: "A man who needs a gun is no man," and "for me to tote a six-shooter would be a provocation and an excuse to others..." This attitude worked even when he was threatened by armed men, which he handled with his wits. Mackenzie was also influential with the federal government's passage of the Hepburn Act in 1906, which regulated the excessive fares the railroads were charging Western cattle shippers. He also developed a friendship with Theodore Roosevelt and was appointed by the president to the National Conservation Commission in 1908. This small town's namesake was a remarkable man.

Murdo got its start in 1906 along the Chicago, Milwaukee, St. Paul and Pacific Railroad, and the rails still run through town as the Dakota Southern Railway. The cattle business is still big in the area, but Murdo's population, which was never large, has declined in recent years like most other small towns in the region. Nevertheless, the town is the seat of Jones County, and again, size didn't seem to matter in these parts for that distinction.

I soon found the old "business district" and Main St., and if the sidewalks didn't roll up by this hour, I was the only one walking them, and everything else looked closed. I passed by a Ford dealer, a bar and grill with a "pizza" sign, a post office, senior center, and an old, small hotel called The Gem, which looked like just the kind I would have loved to lodge in. But the front door was locked, and window curtains were probably a sign of long-term renters. Its era of transient guests was probably long gone. I also saw a small brick building with a stone storefront that housed "the Murdo Coyote newspaper—Serving the area since 1904," and a station of the Jones County ambulance service. The little business area looked so dead that I even wondered if the ambulance would run.

At the other end of the street was a grain elevator with the name, "Dakota Mill and Grain," and the water tower I'd seen also stood nearby displaying "Murdo" on its tank, with peeling turquoise paint noticeable in artificial light. I also wandered some residential side streets with numbering that didn't get very high in this small community. It was windy during the whole walk, though probably quite normal for these South Dakota plains.

Back near the motel, I saw the name Lost Souls Tavern on a ranch-like building that was also another motel. The name really enticed me, and when I peered through a window, I saw a woman behind the bar and a lone guy seated by it. A young lady was smoking outside the entrance who gave me a friendly greeting, and I told her how much I liked the name of the place because I'd known what it's like to feel like a lost soul. She responded, "We all have." The name evoked thoughts of a lost soul period earlier in my life before I finally found my way. So, my arrival here seemed belated.

I greeted the middle-aged woman tending a small bar and the guy who looked in his thirties at the bar, and again expressed my attraction to the name of this homey, little watering hole. I bought a bottle of PBR and eased into a conversation with the guy, who was sipping some kind of mixed drink. He spoke with a drawl unlike the local dialect and had dark hair, a thin beard, and wore eyeglasses and a bright green John Deere cap. I told him about my trip, and he'd also driven a lot of 83 because his business was harvesting—driving trucks, combines, and other heavy equipment—which made his John Deere cap a perfect fit.

"Right now, I'm in Murdo seasonally," he said, "probably through the winter. A local farmer is giving me a trailer to stay in for driving his truck, and maybe a motel room later."

When I mentioned being from Colorado, he said he'd worked and lived there too and was from Amarillo, Texas originally.

"I'll be driving from one end of Texas to another soon," I said, "and know that Abilene is one of the big towns 83 goes through."

"That's a real Christian town, with plenty of churches."

"I guess more churches than bars," I joked, "but I've noticed that a lot of the 83 towns seem to have a pretty even number of the two."

"There's three bars and five churches in Murdo," he informed me, "so the churches outnumber the bars here."

"That's not the first time I've seen the churches ahead," I said. "Maybe Murdo is a little Abilene."

"It's a good town. Now is between the tourist and hunting seasons."

After finishing his drink, he got up to leave, probably because he had to be up early for work the next day, and he introduced himself as Kyle. Sometimes introductions come at the end of conversations with friendly strangers. This one seemed like a very nice young guy, presumably single, who seemed to be content with his transient lifestyle and didn't seem like a lost soul if he was following the harvests.

I had a short conversation with the woman tending the bar and she thanked me for coming in. I told her I was glad I did and that I really liked the homey character of the place besides its name. Now very hungry, I left, and we exchanged friendly farewells.

Outside, I thought that maybe the place was given its name because there had been enough lost souls around here through the years—perhaps wandering U.S. 83 and I-90 rather aimlessly and hoping to find a prairie rainbow's end—who'd stopped and stayed in Murdo. I wasn't wandering in that sense now since I had a certain road to follow and guide me on this journey and for the rest of my life. Perhaps Lost Souls could also be a religious reference in a small town with five churches.

I stopped at the big Pilot Travel Center and found a Subway store still open, where I ordered a foot-long turkey sub with a heap of veggie toppings and Chipotle sauce. I learned that Subway's empire had expanded to well over 40,000 locations in 105 countries at the time, with over half in the U.S.—making it the largest such food chain in the world. And one thing I like about the business is that they offer some relatively healthy choices, and that a customer can pick and choose how a sandwich is put together, with all the ingredients in front of them.

Back in the room, I had a blissful soak in the tub. And after a rinse from the shower, I felt as squeaky clean as the room was. When exhaustion overcame me after recording more in my journal, I crawled into a good-sized bed and mused more about how experiencing some discomfort is the only way to really appreciate comfort like I now had.

DAY 14

The Big Show, Rosebud Reservation, a kiss in Valentine

Checking out of the Sioux Motel, I complimented the owner on the cleanliness of the room. A small sign in the office also related to cleanliness: "Politicians should be changed often like diapers, and for the same reason." The message resonated with me, but I didn't discuss any politics with the woman. She told me that she and her husband closed the motel and another they owned for the winter when there wasn't enough business, and that they were snowbirds in Apache Junction, Arizona, near Phoenix.

"Are you a snowbird?" she asked, after hearing I was traveling south on 83.

"No, but I am headed all the way to the Gulf Coast in Texas, where I know a lot of them spend the winter."

The woman mentioned being originally from about thirty-five miles east of Murdo and seemed like someone deeply rooted in South Dakota who now dealt with the winters by leaving them.

Before leaving Murdo, I wanted to check out its big tourist attraction—The Pioneer Auto Museum and Antique Town—which was located by the intersection where 83 leaves I-90.

Inside was a hospitable sign: "Hi! You're among friends," and almost immediately I was greeted by an older guy of about average height with a ruddy complexion, wearing a brimmed cap with the name "Pioneer Auto Show." He quickly offered me admission for half the usual price. "It's an anniversary special," he said, "since we're celebrating sixty years here. I really want you to see the place." The man had an enthusiastic and likable manner, and after paying him, I mentioned traveling the whole length of 83. He then handed me a small newspaper titled, *Canada to Mexico via Highway 83*, which I appreciated. His name was Dave Geisler, and he was the proprietor of the big complex. He escorted me into the first exhibit area that displayed 1950s cars and signs and turned on an oldie's soundtrack for the period. Then he left and returned to the entrance area, where I heard him greeting someone else.

I had a small map of the complex, which seemed quite overwhelming and had a lot more than vintage autos. Seeing everything would require a lot more time than I wanted to spend here, so I thought I'd go for more of an overview.

I roamed through most of the buildings, often taking a cursory look to avoid visual overload. Vehicle-wise, there were real antiques from the 1920s and 1930s—including a 1921 White Motorhome—classics from the '40s and '50s, and "muscle cars" from the '60s and '70s. The most vintage, though, went back to the early 1900s and included a black Auburn Touring model that had been used as a taxi to transport new settlers in the Murdo area from the town's railroad station. One building exhibited just Henry Ford productions from 1903 to 1932. A more recent model and big attraction was a bright red 1969 Dodge Charger with the big numbers 01 and the name "General Lee," which was used in the '80s TV series *The Dukes of Hazzard*. It's the only original car left from the show.

I also got a look at about forty vintage motorcycles—the standout being a 1976 1200cc, black and light blue Harley-Davidson Electra Glide that was owned by Elvis Presley, with the title still in his name. Another building had rows of tractors and other farm machinery, including old John Deere models, and even a very vintage steam-powered tractor. I eventually got to Prairie Town and its assortment of buildings, with a general store, barber shop, one-room schoolhouse, church, jailhouse, fire station, railroad depot, and others. Some of the structures, like the original Murdo Bank, had been moved from somewhere else in the area. A 1906 caboose that would interest any railroad buff was right by the belly tank of a World War II B-17 bomber.

By now, I had a better idea of why the whole place is called "The Big Show," and I could have poked around all afternoon. But I wanted to get back on the highway.

Before I left, I browsed in a gift shop and noticed a book with a title that jumped at me: *The Last American Highway—A Journey Through Time Down U.S. 83—The Dakotas*. The author, Stew Magnuson, is a Nebraska native who also set out to travel and explore all of 83, but on separate trips, and this publication was about his experiences in the Dakotas that was the first of his three-volume series about the highway. After skimming through the book, I bought it to learn more about this kindred traveler's experiences.

On the way out, I saw Dave Geisler again, and he asked how I liked the exhibits.

"I'm very impressed but also overwhelmed," I told him.

Then his mobile phone rang, and he had a brief conversation that sounded like it was about another purchase. When it ended, I commented: "I guess you're always wheeling and dealing."

He smiled, then said, "I'm glad you saw the place." Then he consented to posing for a picture with me, which someone else took.

"So, do you plan on keeping this great display going well past the sixtieth anniversary?" I asked.

"Will try, though we really don't make much money from the museum, but also own the diner next to it and another business. A lot of the back exhibit area is closed during the winter."

"How do you feel about the winters in South Dakota?"

"I don't mind them," he answered firmly, and didn't say anything about being a snowbird.

"It seems the people here are warm," I commented.

Dave also handed me a booklet about his amazing place and signed it. I thanked him, and he thanked me for coming. I soon read some of it and learned that it was Dave's father, A.J. "Dick" Geisler, who began the business in 1954. He was the son of German immigrants who first lived in Minnesota before he went off to California, got married, and settled in Pasadena. He and his wife had three children, and Dave was born in 1937. Though the senior Geisler owned a successful feed and hardware store, he bought a farm in Blunt, South Dakota, moved the family there, and also did well at farming. In 1945, his entrepreneurial nature led to investing in a John Deere and Chevrolet dealership in Murdo, and by 1950 he opened a Phillips 66 gas station at the intersection of 83 and then U.S. Highway 16, which remains there and is part of the Pioneer Auto Show complex. Dick Geisler bought and displayed several vintage vehicles at the station to attract more customers and later added more, which by 1954 was enough to lead him to construct a building to better exhibit his collection. And the rest, as they say, is history.

Both young Dave and his brother John were also active in the business. When their father died in 1973, John took over the management until 1979. Then Dave assumed the role which he still has today, and his brother continued as a scout and buyer. Dave also owned and ran a very successful Ford-Mercury dealership in Murdo from 1962 to 1980 and is known for his civic involvement with the local and state governments and love for South Dakota. Two of his four children are involved in the sixty-year-old business, which looks promising for its future. I hoped that the Big Show would be around for another sixty years and that Dave Geisler would live to be at least a hundred.

I went over to the diner that he mentioned for some lunch, which wasn't a classic metallic type but had 1950s features like rotating, round, red-upholstered stools. It's called The Diner and was built in 1994. I sat at a long counter and enjoyed a bowl of split pea soup with home-made quality. My server was a friendly, light-skinned African American woman who was probably the first non-Caucasian person I'd seen in South Dakota, other than some Native Americans.

I left Murdo feeling very glad I didn't pass up the small town's "Big Show." And if I ever return, who knows what other vehicles and curiosities might be displayed there.

Continuing south on back to two-lane 83, it looked like an older section with narrow shoulders, no rumble strips, and black streaks of asphalt that made the ride a little bumpy. The landscape was largely undulating grassland with occasional dots of distant grazing cattle, and some hay was about the only cultivation. Power lines, which frequently parallel the highway, were absent on this stretch.

On the lonesome prairie to the west, a neglected two-story house stood out beyond a barrier of barbed wire. I pulled over for a better look at the weathered structure, where a wooden section had partly collapsed. My binoculars revealed glass missing from the four windows in the main stone section, but a wooden corral still looked intact, along with a metal shed. I was reminded of other abandoned structures I've seen in the West left standing, perhaps because there's so much space around and the cost of demolition isn't considered worth it. This time-worn haven, which must have seen plenty of life in its time, had an odd aesthetic like many others like it, which can be another reason for just leaving them alone. And I captured the image with my camera.

The barbed wire at the site made me think about this innovation's significance after the Civil War, when a design by an Illinois farmer, Joseph Glidden, in 1874 made it practical for mass production. Gradually, barbed wire ended the open range and affected the main job of the American cowboy, which was to control the movement of cattle. Now, a nasty wire prevented bovines from straying, but also injured many, along with horses and some of the remaining bison and other animals. It's no wonder that the new and cheap fencing that was practical on the largely treeless plains, where wood was scarce for fencing, came to be called "the devil's rope" by cowboys, Natives, and others.

The highway went on through barren-looking grassland, with greater numbers of distant, dark cattle—more West River country. Descending from a rise, a much more fertile area appeared with large green fields and groves of cottonwoods and shrubs that marked the course of the White River. I stopped before a small bridge over the stream and saw that this tributary of the Missouri River has a strange, creamy color from a mixture of sand, clay, and volcanic ash from the badlands area to the west. Its source is an escarpment in northwestern Nebraska, and it has a meandering 580-mile course that reaches the Missouri near Chamberlain, South Dakota. I read that this river has arid stretches that occasionally have no flow, but it was moving here.

I entered Mellette County on the other side of the White River, and not far down the road made another stop for a photo of an eye-catching sign promoting the local beef industry—"Great BEEF begins in Mellette County"—with an image of two appetizing steaks on a grill, which made me think there probably weren't many vegetarians in these parts. Before I drove off, another car stopped in front of me with South Dakota plates, and I reacted with a little apprehension. Could there possibly be highway robbery or carjacking along 83?

However, a middle-aged woman stepped out, not to point a handgun at me or a camera at the sign, but to ask: "Do you need help?" Suddenly, any sense of alarm seemed very silly, and I told the woman I was fine and just wanted a picture of the sign, and I thanked her for stopping. When she drove off, I thought her helpfulness was probably quite typical of people on the Plains.

I passed through more big, open country, and the old highway undulated with the terrain. It crossed the Little White River—a tributary of the main one—with more large groups of trees typical of riparian areas in the region. Ahead was the town of White River, with a posted population of 595, which is the seat of Mellette County and was incorporated in 1912. I made a turn following a "business district" sign and stopped at a grocery store with the Native name Wig Wam to check it out and take a break. There were quite a few Native faces there, which wasn't surprising because the Rosebud Indian Reservation wasn't far down the road. Driving off, I passed a casino-lounge, then had a close call with a young guy on a bicycle who darted across the street just ahead. After blaring my horn, I hoped it encouraged him to peddle less recklessly.

An event this town is known for is a big, annual August celebration called White River Frontier Days, with festivities having a long tradition going back to 1912, when the town got started. It's said to even attract some international visitors, and includes rodeos in the local Frontier Arena, wild horse and 5K races, a parade, dances, and a Lakota Pow Wow, which must all be a big annual boost to the local economy.

Further on, a row of very "wide load" flatbed trucks passed me from the south, carrying giant circular structures. And soon came the sign—"Welcome to the Rosebud Indian Reservation"—which is home to the Rosebud Sioux Tribe, or Sicangu Lakota, one of the seven bands of the Lakota branch of the complex Sioux. The other two branches are the Dakota and Nakota. The three groups speak closely related languages that are a basis of the Sioux identity, and the different names mean "friend" or "ally" in each of their tongues. The Lakota, also known as the Teton Sioux, are the westernmost of the three groups, and the Dakota were the inspiration for the names of the two Plains states I'd traveled through so far. The Rosebud Reservation was established in 1889 after the Great Sioux Reservation created by the 1868

Treaty of Fort Laramie was broken up for the benefit of non-Native settlers, and it's the only reservation that U.S. 83 crosses. In previous travels I'd passed through numerous reservations, which are not like foreign countries where you have to deal with officials when entering. But they do have a complex sovereignty I'll describe later.

A lone butte stood out beyond a small lake near the road, and there was more open, rolling land. Cultivation reappeared with bright sunflower fields just before a junction of 83 with U.S. 18, and the two old federal highways merged briefly before the town of Mission. U.S. 18 runs east-west, and it's another 1926 original that's 1,043 miles (1,679 km) in length between downtown Milwaukee, Wisconsin, and an interchange with Interstate 25 by the tiny community of Orin in eastern Wyoming. I was greeted by a sign: "Welcome to Mission, est.1932." This reservation town of some 1,200 people was about eighty-five percent Native at last count and is the largest incorporated community in Todd County and its commercial center. The name came from the many Christian missions established in the area in the late 1800s. In 1971, Sinte Gleska University was founded here—a four-year, private Native tribal college with over 800 full and part-time students, which was named after the great nineteenth-century Lakota chief, whose name means Spotted Tail. Sinte Gleska was a great warrior who later became a great peacemaker and statesman for his people. There are other tribal colleges in about fifteen states, which, besides providing higher education for isolated Native populations, also teach and preserve tribal cultures and languages. This tribal autonomy in education is a huge contrast to the infamous boarding schools that developed from the early missions in the latter part of the 1800s, which were determined to "civilize" and "Christianize" many young Natives and purge them of their tribal identity and culture.

I stopped at a convenience store at a Cenex station and got a key for the restroom from a female employee who looked Native, then bought a bag of salted peanuts. Driving on, I noticed Lutheran, Episcopal, and Catholic churches in the town that must have been signs of the missionary influence. Overall, this reservation town looked pretty much like other small prairie towns I'd seen along the highway, but I noticed a few Native themes like a one-story building with the name Buffalo Jump and a bit of tribal-looking art on its colorful facade. A close look showed it was the Sicangu Lakota Youth Center, and when I later checked the town's demographics. I found out that forty percent of the population is under eighteen, with only about five percent over sixty-five, making Mission different from the many aging small towns along 83. Typical of a reservation, the town's median income showed to be only about half of South Dakota's. One local boy who did well financially after leaving town is Bob Barker—the old TV game show host whose background is one-eighth Sioux. He grew up in Mission, and his mother was a teacher on the reservation.

I passed Sinte Gleska University and a county middle school where 83 parted from U.S. 18 and shot south, and further down was another school. Then came a large, colorful sign with an arrow pointing toward the Soldier Woman Art and Gift Gallery, which was closed. The owner is a half Sicangu Lakota artist named Linda Szabo, who also has a Lakota name translated as "Soldier Woman." She's an accomplished and diversified artist who was raised on the reservation and comes from a long line of artistic Lakota women on her mother's side. Her gallery features the work of over 300 Native artists from the northern plains.

U.S. 83 continued further into the Rosebud Reservation as a straight, two-lane blacktop, with wide shoulders and rumble strips, and was back into open, grassy country often punctuated by trees that were sometimes in large groves and rows—signs of plantings. Power lines also stood along the right roadside. I passed some large hay fields and saw a sign about "Tribal Enterprises" that indicated a Native-run business.

The complex sovereignty of reservations, along with their organization and history, mainly began when the U.S. Congress passed the Indian Appropriations Act in 1851, which authorized the establishment of reservations in the Oklahoma Territory that later expanded to other areas. The Rosebud Reservation is one of 326 presently in the U.S. that vary greatly in size, and each is designated for certain tribal groups. A total of 574 tribes are recognized by the federal government, and some have their own reservations, while others share them with other tribes. The government recognizes reservations as "domestic dependent nations," and they're allowed to manage many of their own affairs through tribal councils and have laws that differ from the states they're in. However, tribal sovereignty is limited, and the federal government imposes most of the constraints. Some states have jurisdiction over crimes committed on tribal lands, which has caused some confusion because there are also tribal courts.

Native nations don't own their reservations' lands. Rather, it's held in trust for them by the federal government, which is the legal owner of all lands and assets in what's known as Indian Country and is required to manage it for the benefit of the inhabitants. There are federal agencies like the Bureau of Indian Affairs with a law enforcement division that polices reservations that don't have their own law enforcement and oversees ones that do. And the agency prefers hiring Native Americans as police officers.

U.S. Census Bureau figures from 2010 showed over five million people who identified as fully or partially Native American, and the numbers have been increasing rapidly because of more racial mixing. Of this large demographic, about seventy-eight percent live outside of reservations, according to one figure I came across on Google. There are different tribal requirements for reservation residence, and some allow non-Natives who work on reservations or marry tribal members, though their status may be different. The 14th Amendment to the U.S. Constitution in 1868, which gave automatic citizenship to anyone born within the U.S., wasn't applied to Native Americans; and most didn't become citizens until the Indian Citizen Act of 1924. This was encouraged by the approximately 12,000 Native Americans who voluntarily served in the U.S. military during World War I, who couldn't be drafted because they weren't citizens. Their ethnic group has had a continued high rate of enlistment in the military, and one apparent reason for this service—ironically for a government that had been the great oppressor of their ancestors—is for economic and educational opportunities that they've so often lacked. Another is perhaps the warrior culture heritage of many tribes, and many Native service people have distinguished themselves.

The widespread impoverishment on reservations has resulted in many residents needing public assistance from the federal government. There are still many third world conditions and hindrances to doing business in the modern, technological world, and the educational level among reservation residents is also generally low, with

Native youth having one of the lowest rates of even finishing high school. However, many residents own their homes but not the land they're on, which is tribally-owned. This has negative effects on home value and buildup of equity, and many substandard homes are another problem. High rates of alcoholism—despite alcohol prohibitions on many reservations—drug addiction, diabetes, and suicide also continue to plague many reservations,

Encouraging more private enterprises that originate on reservations has been promoted to keep more money circulating within them, and there have been some successful small businesses. The Native ownership of gambling casinos on many reservations in recent years has also had some success. But most Native entrepreneurs have operated outside reservations where there are more available resources.

There have been proposals to eliminate the whole reservation system, but with a lack of agreement on what would replace it. Since many tribes were forced onto lands that were considered undesirable to settlers and alien and confining to themselves, it seems the system had a very bad start. Although the majority of tribal members have exercised their freedom to live outside reservations and venture into mainstream society, it must be daunting for many still on them with little or no money, no marketable skills, facing the possibility of prejudice, and no social support in the outside world that they could at least have in a cultural community with communal values, which being less individualistic probably doesn't produce the best capitalists. And when you consider how ancient so many of these cultures are, it's no wonder that would continue to have a strong influence on numerous tribal members.

The Rosebud Reservation isn't as large as the Pine Ridge, Standing Rock, and Cheyenne Reservations in the region, but it covers close to 2,000 square miles and has over 20,000 inhabitants and twenty communities. The tribal capital isn't the largest town of Mission, but the unincorporated community of Rosebud that's well away from U.S. 83. The governing body is the Rosebud Sioux Tribal Council, which has representatives from each community.

I drove through some visually appealing fields with hay, scattered horses, and dried corn, where a bucolic charm was a distraction from the serious socio-economic problems said to exist on this reservation.

I stopped to look more closely at a modest but well-kept ranch house with a horse trailer on the property, which hardly looked third world. If this were a Lakota person's home, I wished they could all be like it on the reservation.

I drove back into big grasslands with far horizons, where I could easily imagine the ancestors of Rosebud's people hunting bison. I again saw great beauty in such spaces—beauty that was often a companion on the journey. Perhaps a love for these surroundings keeps many of the Sicangu Lakota on this reservation.

Further on, a water tower appeared to the south, and a lone wind turbine. Soon I arrived at what looked like a recent development of rather small, tidy, one-story, box-like homes, with no shade trees around. The tall, light-colored water tower was topped by a large sphere with a Native inscription and translation: "Sicangu Mni Wiconi"—"Water is Life," and "Rosebud Rural Water System." The name "Sicangu Village" was spelled out vertically beneath the sphere, which is the name of this residential development that was built by the tribe in the early 2000s.

Just down the road was the Rosebud Casino, where I parked at the rear of a large lot. The casino was in a long one-story building that also housed a Quality Inn, and right behind it was the wind turbine. I found out it's one of the first electricity-producing turbines in the country owned by a tribe, which partially powers the casino. Nearby was a 24/7 fuel plaza with a convenience store. The state line of South Dakota and Nebraska happened to run right through the lot, marked by a sign very close to where I'd parked on the South Dakota side.

I went into the casino for a look at the type of business that's been operating on many reservations for over twenty years since the U.S. Congress passed the Indian Gaming Regulatory Act in 1988. This enabled tribes to operate gambling enterprises even in states that restrict them, providing the states have some type of legal gaming. The Rosebud Casino is owned and operated by the Rosebud Sioux Tribe, and there were two restaurants on the premises beside the hotel. Inside was the noisy chatter of a mass of slot machines, and two large, connected rooms also had table games and bingo. Gambling has never been a vice of mine or had any real appeal, and I wasn't about to make an exception now, even to help support a tribe by probably losing some money. I did buy a bottle of light beer, though, and wandered around one of the big rooms.

The place was busy, especially for a Monday evening. All the employees looked Native, but most of the customers were Caucasian. A good number of them must have been truckers passing through since I saw quite a few parked rigs in the spacious lot. This casino was a 24/7 operation, so business must have been good for its isolation. After finishing my beer, I was ready to leave.

I read that despite some reservation casinos profits helping to decrease unemployment and increase tribal wealth for things like schools, housing, and health services, the results still haven't sufficiently improved conditions on many reservations. Some tribal leaders have also had cultural objections to the very idea of promoting gambling. I just hope that Rosebud and other reservations can find additional solutions for the maladies they've had to deal with for far too long.

The sun had set, leaving a gorgeous orange glow beneath a purplish cloud mass. And to the east, an almost full moon had risen over the plains—The October Hunter's Moon. After leaving the reservation and South Dakota, I snapped a picture of the sign: "NEBRASKA...the good life. Home of Arbor Day." Next was a sign indicating this stretch was another Blue Star Memorial Highway honoring the U.S. Armed Forces. A long streak of sunset afterglow and cloud reflections continued to awe me as the landscape seemed to flatten more with more trees appearing. Before the town of Valentine, the road entered an actual forested area that was a little hilly, with outlines of trees in the dim light.

A sign ahead said, "Valentine, population 2,820," and 83 soon entered the town's old and small business district. I saw a Comfort Inn, but didn't want to pay their price for comfort; so I checked out a nearby large lot behind a Shell station, where numerous trucks were parked and running and fouling the prairie air, which discouraged me from parking there overnight if it wasn't limited to truckers. However, across the street was a Super 8 motel, which also had a lot for trucks, but with fewer of them and less were idling. There was also a good corner away from the behemoths. I went into the motel office and got approval to park there from a young guy showing off heavily tattooed arms, who seemed to understand why I often like to avoid paying motel prices—the lowest here being $62 for truckers. I was pleased with the spot I'd found, especially with a restroom at the Shell station across the street that was open all night.

After some scribbling in my journal, I set out on foot into this town with a curious name and soon noticed a row of painted heart shapes all along a sidewalk—apparently related to the name Valentine—and these symbols led to two neighboring bars. I peeked into the Corner Bar and saw no one seated there but heard some conversation. Next door, at the Skylite Bar, a sign over the entrance announced, "Entertainment Tonight," which prompted me to go in, where I found a few guys wearing baseball caps seated at the bar, and a blondish young woman tending it. A small stage was near the bar, and close to it was a thirtyish woman with light brown hair who was very scantily clad—a dancer, no doubt, who must have been the entertainment, if not the kind I'd expect to find in a small town like Valentine. Bud and Bud Light were the draft beer choices, and I opted for the BL, which was probably very popular in Nebraska too.

"Are there any eating places in town open now?" I asked the bartender.

"Most closed earlier, but the McDonald's by the Shell station is open till 11:00."

"I did see it. I'm staying in town overnight and am driving all the way down 83 to its end in Brownsville, Texas."

"I didn't know it went that far," was her common reaction.

"It does, and I started where the highway begins at the Canadian border in North Dakota."

"There've been local people going up there for oil and gas jobs."

"Do you know if they plan on working there just temporarily?"

"Some went thinking they'd stay. I have a friend whose son recently found a job in the Dickinson area and a trailer to live in, but he's paying very high rent."

"I heard about price-gouging and inflation being one of the downsides of the energy boom there."

"Yeah, and it's supposed to be affecting the people who've lived there a long time too."

"Are they doing much fracking in Nebraska?"

"No."

"Well, I'm glad to hear that since they're sure doing enough elsewhere, including Colorado, where I'm from. It's such a mixed bag of pros and cons, including the environmental effects."

Suddenly, I was joined by the skimpy-dressed dancer, who sat next to me and said, "Hi" in a sweet tone, and another conversation started.

"Do you live in Valentine?" I asked.

"I've lived all over. I dance as a freelancer and have worked around the country.

"So, you don't have a manager or agent who gets you jobs?"

"No, I don't."

Her face was attractive, and she had a feathery, feminine voice and seductive manner that was stimulating.

"I'm surprised you found a job in this kind of town," I said a little kiddingly. "So, where are you from originally?"

"From Minnesota. And where are you from?"

"I live in Fort Collins, Colorado now, but came from New Jersey and lived there a long time."

"So, you're a Jersey Boy. I can tell from your accent."

"I guess I lived there too long to fully lose it. You must have known hard winters when you lived in Minnesota."

"Yes, and I hate the cold weather, even though I have Scandinavian background. I plan on working in Florida this winter."

"I'm heading south myself and driving U.S. 83 all the way to the Gulf coast of Texas, but I'm not a snowbird.

She didn't seem to know much about 83, and we got talking about some places where she'd danced for her living, like New York City and New Orleans.

"I was in the Big Easy once for Mardi Gras," I told her, "and loved it."

"It's sure an easy-going and fun place."

"This area might not be nearly as much fun and exciting, but I love all the open land, and the people who live in this part of the country seem very nice. Today, when I stopped along the road to take a photo, a woman who was a total stranger stopped to see if I had a problem and needed any help. I think a lot of the people on the plains are helpful like that. I might have another kind of problem, though, if

I lived in these parts and had to deal with some of the conservatism that the whole region is known for.

"I think the people around here are nice too. They're much friendlier in Nebraska than where I came from."

We finally made introductions, and her name was Lauren. I was ready for another round of Bud Light and offered to buy the outgoing young lady a libation too, and she chose the same rather watery but very popular beer. I inquired where she was staying, and she said at a local Economy Lodge. I began to wonder if this freelance dancer, who still wasn't dancing, might have the intention of seducing an older guy like me and perhaps was also a freelance hooker. My mind jumped to the possibility of her inviting me to her motel room later for that purpose. Whatever her motive, I was enjoying the conversation and was curious about what made this woman tick.

"So how long have you been dancing, Lauren?"

"A long time. Since my early twenties."

"Have you hit thirty yet?" I asked tactfully, since I thought she probably had.

"Yes," she said directly, "and I plan to keep on dancing."

Apparently, she didn't feel the early retirement pressures of her business yet. I next asked: "So, have you had other kinds of jobs?"

"I have, but can't make the money I do dancing."

I wondered what other occupations she'd tried but held back from asking.

"You're fun," she blurted to me, even though it wasn't how I perceived myself during the conversation.

Finally, she got down to business and said: "Could you give me two dollars and I'll dance?"

Though that was a very modest request, I said: "I'm enjoying just talking to you."

"I have to dance for my job," she reminded me.

"Sure, I understand," and I handed her three singles.

"Thank you." And she gave me a nice smile, then walked over to a sound machine to select some music for her performance on the small stage.

As I watched Lauren's body start moving to the rhythms, my mind flashed back to much younger days in my twenties and thirties—probably before she was born—when I frequented quite a few dance clubs back in New Jersey with old drinking buddies. It was a lot of fun at the time with the beer and erotic stimulation. But today it seemed like a real past chapter of my life and what I've come to regard as somewhat kid stuff, as much as I still appreciate the female body—though I've perhaps gotten more jaded about it.

Lauren moved her body in different positions around a metal pole like such dancers often do. Her anatomy was shapely, and much was revealed because of her skimpy top and bottom. Overall, her movements weren't too energetic, though, as if she was going through motions and doing a job that had become routine. And she didn't exactly rivet the attention of the few other men at the bar. I made sure I clapped after a couple of songs she danced to.

Finally, one of the other guys waved some bills at her, and she left the stage and let him stroke her arms and some of her upper body. For a few moments they even exchanged tender looks while holding hands. Then suddenly the contact stopped, and Lauren went back to dancing, and the guy got up and left. Maybe home to a wife, I thought. When she looked at me again, I threw her a kiss, and in response she briefly revealed her whole breasts; and I smiled to show appreciation.

Lauren took another break about the time I wanted to leave before the last open eatery in town closed. I went over to her and said I was leaving and that I'd enjoyed our conversation and her dancing.

"I'm glad to meet you," she said, followed by, "Love you."

The little flattery compelled me to respond, "Love ya back."

Then she moved forward and turned her cheek, and I took the cue and kissed her on it.

"Have a good, warm winter in the Sunshine State," I said.

"Maybe I'll see you there," she responded.

I smiled, and that's how the encounter ended. I left the bar in a very good mood after having a positive energy exchange with the dancer, besides a slightly amorous experience in a town named Valentine.

While walking toward the McDonald's, I thought there was something sad about Lauren, even if she didn't come across as negative or depressed. She seemed like a good-hearted, still young woman, with a sweet and sensitive side, and it was sad in a way that she was making a living doing something that many consider degrading, exhibitionistic, and even lewd. I wondered just what led her down that path. It probably wasn't all about money. Maybe she loved the freedom she could have as a freelance dancer to travel around the country and even find a job in a boondock town like Valentine, Nebraska. I wondered if she ever slept in a car, presuming she had one. She was another very memorable person I met on the journey, and there was a lot more I would have liked to know about her.

Again, I found myself in a McDonald's and ordered the same Sweet Chicken-Chile combo with fries that I had at the one back in Pierre, served in the same kind of awkward cardboard box—definitely not the best or healthiest meal I had on the journey, but it satisfied some hunger again.

Back in Wander, I wrote more in my journal as sprinkles fell and some clouds drifted across the face of the moon that had risen high. I could still hear some of the constantly running diesel engines at the truck stop across the street, with some rigs coming and going. But at least I had some distance from it. I was in my sleeping bag after midnight and had more thoughts about Lauren, and about Dave Geisler—two very interesting people I'd met that day who couldn't have been more different. I wondered what others I'd meet further down the long road that connects so many places and people.

DAY 15

The amazing Niobrara, sunset and moon rise in the Sandhills

I was back in the McDonald's for breakfast and tried their oatmeal for the first time, which was tasty if not as good as the kind I'd have at home. Sitting nearby were a few old guys wearing cowboy hats who looked like local ranch types and were hanging out. Outside, it was warming up, and I walked off again to see more of Valentine in daylight.

The busy truck stop across the street was at a junction where 83 is joined by U.S. 20 for a short stretch southward, and this highway has the big distinction of being the longest road in the U.S.—3,365 miles (5,415 km) from Kenmore Square in Boston to within a mile of the Pacific Ocean in Newport, Oregon. It's one of the original U.S. highways but wasn't first planned as a coast-to-coast route and ended at the east entrance of Yellowstone National Park. Its extension came in 1940, when it was expanded to run through twelve states, which is twice the number 83 does.

I walked up Main St. where I did the night before. Valentine was named not after a saint or because of anything to do with Cupid but for Edward K. Valentine, who was a prominent Nebraska politician who'd served in the U.S. Congress in the late 1800s. But the town has exploited the amorous association of the name by calling itself America's Heart City, and expresses it with painted sidewalk hearts, heart figures attached to lamp posts, and red street signs. The two weeks before Valentine's Day is a busy time for the local post office, which since 1941 has had a program for receiving Valentine cards addressed to other places if they include postage and are mailed in a larger envelope addressed to the Valentine postmaster. The cards are then re-mailed to their destinations with a special Valentine postmark and expression. It's amazing what can come out of a name.

The town came about when the Sioux City and Pacific Railroad arrived in 1883, and it's said to have been very rowdy and Wild West in its early years. Today, it's a very respectable and tidy community that's the seat of Cherry County—the largest county in Nebraska, which has more area than Connecticut. The surrounding area, and especially the wild Sandhills to the south, are prime grazing lands, and cattle ranching is a big part of Valentine's economy. The town is home to Sawyer's Sandhills Museum and the Cherry County Historical Museum, and it also attracts lots of outdoor enthusiasts because of the scenic and fascinating Niobrara River Valley in the area, which offers many recreational activities.

I sauntered by the First National Bank, where the exterior features Nebraska's largest brick mural, with striking figures of longhorn cattle and other figures. A big store called Young's Western Wear, that's been in business since 1950, also caught my attention, as did a banner proclaiming Old West Days and Cowboy Poetry—a type of poetry that originated with the folk heroes who work on the range. This referred to a big, annual weekend festival just a few days away that celebrates the area's Western heritage and present-day ranch culture, and I wished it had begun when I was in town.

I came to the Valentine Cowboy Trailhead Park, with a wooden building that had been the old train station by a cement pathway where the tracks were. I learned that this little park is the western end of a current 195-mile rail-to-trail conversion across much of northern Nebraska named the Cowboy Trail, which was previously the Cowboy Line when it was a route of the old Chicago and North Western Railway. The tracks were abandoned in 1992, and the right of way was bought by the Rails to Trails Conservancy, which donated it to the state of Nebraska. The state, in turn, has made it into a multiuse recreational trail. I think such "rail trails" that have developed in widespread places are fantastic, and there are plans for the Cowboy Trail to be extended further west for a total of 321 miles (516.5 km), which would make it the longest rail trail in the country. Behind the park was a small grain elevator that must have been serviced by the railroad back in the day.

I walked through more of the small and appealing downtown area, observing people and snapping photos of heart shapes. A few people looked Native, but that group makes up less than ten percent of Valentine's population. I presumed many residents of the Rosebud Reservation visit the town, though.

After driving off, I headed east away from 83 on the western end of Nebraska 12 to see the Fort Niobrara National Wildlife Refuge outside town. This 231-mile (371.7 km), two-lane state highway that runs near much of Nebraska's northern border has been designated the Outlaw Trail Scenic Byway—since among the colorful characters who roamed the region in the days of the Old West were those with a legendary defiance of the law.

The road led into grassy country, with pine-clad hills rising to the south and east that marked the course of the Niobrara River Valley. Soon I was in a hilly area with grass and trees and entered the wildlife refuge. The two-laner crossed Minnichaduza Creek before a turn-off that brought me to the Niobrara River and a bridge. I stopped by a canoe launch to photograph a beautiful stretch of the river, which appeared to have a healthy level and flow that would meet the mighty Missouri about 130 miles to the east. Its banks were heavily lined with pines and hardwoods, with the broad-leafed trees changing to autumn colors in a lush river oasis.

The Niobrara is a remarkable river for more than its beauty, with a name derived from the Ponca tribe that lived in eastern Nebraska—*Ni obhatha ke*—meaning "spreading water river." I'd traveled near its headwaters on the high plains of eastern Wyoming on the first day of the journey, and from there it streams east into Nebraska and flows 535 miles to the Missouri River. The source of most of the Niobrara's water is groundwater from the gigantic Ogallala Aquifer—one of the largest of such water tables in the world—which underlies parts of eight states. It has a Sioux-derived name that made it into geology. In the local area, the underground water seeps from 300-foot canyon walls that were slowly gouged by the river through several geological formations over the ages. An upper deposition called the Valentine Formation contains the aquifer, which is also known for an abundance of fossils that include prehistoric camels and mastodons. The deeper Pierre Formation contains much older fossils of sharks and giant marine reptiles, dating back 70 to 100 million years to the Cretaceous Period during the long era of the dinosaurs—when the Western Interior Seaway divided North America into two landmasses.

While the geology and paleontology of the Niobrara Valley are of great interest, the biology and ecology of what lives there today is perhaps the most fascinating. For lying near the center of the continent makes the valley a big convergence zone for many plant and animal species. The hundredth meridian also runs north-south, not far to the east through Nebraska, with its remarkable correlation to a natural transition between moist and arid areas. The refuge I'd just entered has examples of five different ecosystems that merge here—the mixed grass and tall grass prairies, the Rocky Mountain coniferous forest, the northern boreal forest, and the Eastern deciduous forest, which results in a large diversity of wildlife also.

In 1991, the seventy-six-mile stretch of the Niobrara River east of Valentine was designated a National Scenic River as part of the National Wild and Scenic Rivers System, and the Fort Niobrara National Wildlife Refuge was established way back in 1912 by an executive order of President Theodore Roosevelt. Like other such refuges, it's managed by the U.S. Fish and Wildlife Service, and its namesake is the military fort that preceded it at the location from 1879 to 1906. The fort's purpose was to maintain peace between the settlers and the indigenous Sioux, which must have been successful because, according to *Road Trip USA*, no battle was fought during those years.

I'd read about the Niobrara Valley's uniqueness years before and was excited about finally being there. On the other side of the bridge was a cattle guard, or metal grates on a road surface that deter livestock from straying there, and an unpaved road that led into open country, where there was a sense of being on the plains again. Soon I came to the refuge visitor center and parked there. A sign outside the building expressed the great biological significance of the location:

"Where it all comes together—Nowhere else in North America do the continent's major plant communities meet like they do on the refuge. Here, north, south, east, and west merge, creating an unrivaled abundance and diversity of plants and wildlife..."

Inside, the only other person was a young woman at a desk. I asked her some questions, especially about the bison I'd heard were on the refuge, and she informed me that the shaggy creatures had recently moved to a winter range on the other side of the river.

"We have a herd of over 350 here," she said, "which is over ninety-nine percent pure in their breeding. When the numbers get excessive, we have sell-offs because the refuge habitat has limits on how many it can support."

"When were the bison reintroduced here?"

"In 1912, not long after they were almost extinct and when the refuge was established."

I'd read that the herd that grew here played a leading role in re-establishing bison on other public and private lands, such as Theodore Roosevelt National Park that I'd visited in North Dakota. Presently, there were about 200,000 bison that have returned to North America—far short of the tens of millions that once roamed the continent, but quite a comeback for a noble animal that had been disseminated to less than 300 by 1900.

After looking around an interesting small exhibit in the center, I grabbed some maps and fliers and headed out to see more of the refuge. A 3.5-mile, self-guided auto tour started nearby, and the first stop was a prairie dog town, where I saw a couple of the squirrel-like critters basking on one of their low dirt mounds. It only took seconds for them to announce my presence to the rest of the colony with their shrill whistles, and other mounds in view produced more sounds, apparently because I was perceived as a potential predator. Prairie dogs have good reasons to act paranoid since they have numerous natural enemies with a taste for them. A flier said the local species is the black-tailed prairie dog, which is the most widespread of the five species in North America. These small communal creatures play a leading role in the ecology of the Plains, and a sign said that 140 species of wildlife have connections with prairie dog "towns"—making them a keystone species.

The tour continued through the big open area, with the river valley's hills and trees in the distance. Grasses waved in prairie breezes, and many tall ones lined the road that became narrower and rockier. Driving slowly was enough to flush a few meadowlarks from the grassy cover, and their straight flight displayed their white outer tail feathers. My flier said that both the eastern and nearly identical western meadowlark species reside here, which are more distinguishable by their songs. The western is Nebraska's state bird, but the very close relatives are known to interbreed.

The next stop was the site of an old shooting range that was part of Fort Niobrara, and remnants of ammunition are still found there and at the fort site, which has largely returned to Nature. To the south was a view of the northern edge of the sprawling Sandhills—another contradiction of the misconception that the Great Plains are all flat. The unpaved road made a bend, and to the east was the expansive bison range, but without the animals I'd been told had moved to the other range. I was now determined to see some bison wherever they were.

Ahead was a "buffalo wallow"—though true buffalo species are found only in Africa and Asia—referring to the habit bison have of rolling on the ground to help shed heavy winter hair when it's become uncomfortable and to rid their bulky bodies of pesky insects during the warm season. The wallows were said to look like depressions about fifteen feet wide, but I really couldn't make out any. Further on were corrals where the resident bison are annually rounded up in what looked like an elaborate system of temporary confinement for them to be counted, tested for diseases and genetics, and then sorted out. Test results determine which ones will be sold, and each year there's a public auction.

I passed by some ponds that attract waterfowl and fish-eating birds like ospreys and kingfishers. Then came a sign that presented interesting facts about elk, which, although considered a mountain species of the deer family today, were also denizens of the open spaces historically. Settlement on the plains eventually extirpated the native elk there, and the last wild one in Nebraska was killed in the early

1880s. So, their fate in this environment was similar to the bison's. Fortunately, elk have had their own recovery through reintroduction, such as the herd of about seventy on a range to the east of the tour route along a county road.

Ahead was the site of the Fort Niobrara parade grounds and historic flagpole, where you could only imagine the fort and the life that once went on there. Among those who served were a good number of African American troops, or Buffalo Soldiers as they became well known—a name presumably given by Native Americans who fought them during the Indian Wars.

A turkey vulture hovered as the route drew close to the hilly, timbered area by the Niobrara River. I drove to the Fort Falls parking lot and intended to walk a short trail down to a waterfall and the river. First, I had some lunch, and I saw just one other vehicle and person there that parked for just a short time before driving off. I set out on the trail with my backpack, binoculars, and Nikon Coolpix, about to enter the northern part of the refuge that was designated a wilderness area by the Federal government in 1976 under the Wilderness Act passed by Congress in 1964. 2014 happened to be the fiftieth anniversary of the historic legislation when five percent of all the land in the U.S. had received such wilderness designation, with all of it being on federally-owned land. Here's how the original act defined a wilderness:

> "A wilderness, in contrast with those areas where man and his own work dominate the landscape, is hereby recognized as an area where the earth and its community of life are untrammeled by man, where man himself is a visitor who does not remain."

The Fort Falls Trail descended into a very mixed pine-hardwood forest that was a big transition from the prairie. It was fascinating to see paper birch trees here—a species of the northern boreal forest—and this is their southernmost presence on the continent and a prime example of the unique convergence of different forest ecosystems in the refuge. Soon I was at the crest of the falls that the trail is named for, and I made a steep descent on a sixty-step grated metal structure with rails that led to the bottom of the cascade that flowed down a rocky slope. It's just one of over 200 falls along the western stretch of the Niobrara, mainly on north-facing slopes. All are from streams spring-fed by the giant Ogallala Aquifer, which often flow through small branch canyons into or toward the Niobrara. Not far east of the refuge along the river is Smith Falls in a state park named after the falls—the highest waterfall in Nebraska at sixty-three feet. Rather surprising that a Plains state like Nebraska has such waterfalls.

Below Fort Falls the stream was very narrow, and I followed it along a dirt path through a lush, woodsy area that led to a captivating spot along the river by the stream's foaming confluence with it. The Niobrara looked quite clear and fast-moving here, and again I reflected on rivers being great symbols of connection—this one flowing to meet the Missouri, and later the Mississippi—the Father of Waters that ultimately washes into the Gulf where I was also destined.

The National Scenic River section of the Niobrara is very popular for fishing, canoeing, kayaking, and tubing, and a lot of outfitters operate in the area. But I saw no one paddling or casting a line. Just downstream was a small canyon that the river's currents had carved through time, which exposed some rock formations rather dramatically. Upstream was a less rugged but more sylvan scene. The convergence of different ecosystems was very evident here, with ponderosa pines of the Rocky Mountains coniferous forest and hardwoods of the Eastern deciduous forest—each at their eastern and western extents.

As I was about to leave this idyllic place where I could have easily lingered, a bald eagle suddenly flew in from the east, soon followed by a smaller raptor that looked like a red-tailed hawk, which amazingly harassed the larger eagle. Then another eagle appeared that was probably a mate, which the hawk came at aggressively in what must have been a valiant territorial defense. It seemed to work when the second eagle flew further away on the other side of the river, and I watched it glide gracefully through my binoculars. But the other eagle had another and more intense skirmish with the hawk, which came closer to me. Then the second one returned and did a close flyby and headed west along the river, soon joined by its mate to the relief of the hawk. I reveled in seeing two magnificent specimens of the bird that's the national symbol in majestic flight, appropriately in a national wilderness area; and for a brief time, I had a strong sense of the primeval at this memorable location along the Niobrara River.

The Fort Niobrara National Wildlife Refuge also attracts much smaller avian life, like many neotropical warbler species that both nest and migrate through here along the Central Flyway of the continent. Altogether, over 230 different species have been identified at the refuge, drawn by its diverse habitats.

I ambled further on the Fort Falls Trail along the bank of the river to the west, which made a sharp turn and ascended a low bluff before returning to the parking lot. There, I encountered an older couple and shared my excitement about the bald eagle sightings.

On the final stretch of the auto tour I saw more prairie dogs than before, and a few crossed the road. The last site was the "hay shed"—the only building left here from Fort Niobrara. It's a long reddish structure that looked well-maintained and blended nicely into an open landscape, which had been used as a storehouse for the hay that nourished the horses at the historic fort. Originally, there were ninety buildings at the fort that accommodated over 800 soldiers. Some of the structures were moved after the fort closed, and a few remain in Cherry County. The one here was a visible link with the past.

Still hoping to see bison, I drove toward a Wilderness Overlook off Nebraska 12 that might offer a view of the winter range where the animals were supposed to be now. A dirt and gravel road led to the overlook, which offered a great panorama of a beautiful blending of grassy and wooded lands, where I could make out the course of the Niobrara River. Much of the view was in the wilderness area.

I kept scanning the open areas with my binoculars for the bison, with no luck. After a while I thought they might be under cover or somewhere else, and that this might be a day to see eagles but not bison. Then, just as I was ready to move on, I spotted a dark object on one of the grassy hillsides, which, at first, I thought might be a tree stump since it looked motionless. But after scanning more and coming back to the object, it appeared to have moved. My binoculars revealed a humpy appearance, and I realized it was indeed a bison grazing. I was quite thrilled to see even one at a distance and continued to watch it. Then another appeared, followed by others, to a total of eight. Their huge heads were usually down in a grazing position, and their profiles showed their distinctive back humps. There was more movement, and I could distinguish a calf in the group. The whole sighting really made my day, now that I'd seen the once King of the Plains soon after the King of the Skies.

I drove the short distance back to Valentine, and a sign at the re-entrance had the slogan, "small town, big adventures," which I could relate to now. I was soon on the stretch of 83 in tandem with U.S. 20 for a short distance toward the tree-clad ridge by the Niobrara River, which I hadn't seen the last of. Ahead were three bridges that crossed the river, and I saw a turnoff for the "historic bridge." But I stayed the course on 83 that went over the river on a long, high, level bridge with a good view of the older Bryan Bridge not far upstream. This structure was built in 1932 along a short, old section of 83 and 20 that's still in use. It's described as an arched, cantilever truss bridge, and is the only one of this type in the U.S. The designer was a Russian immigrant named Josef Sorkin, and it was named after the then governor of Nebraska, Charles W. Bryan. When completed, it was designated "Most Beautiful Steel Bridge" for its cost category by the American Institute of Steel Construction, and in 1988 it made the National Register of Historic Places.

The third bridge is the Valentine Railroad Bridge, not far on the downstream side, which is the oldest, dating back to 1909-10. It's a 140-foot-high steel structure with twelve towers that used lots of earth fill in its construction and was part of the old Cowboy Line that became the Cowboy Trail—now a great path for hikers, bicyclists, and horseback riders.

U.S. 83-U.S. 20 climbed into a hilly, piney area across the Niobrara, but was soon back in wide open country with grazing cattle and scattered trees. The two old U.S. highways diverged, with 20 branching off to the southeast to ultimately terminate near the Atlantic Ocean, and 83 continuing southward toward the Gulf. Ahead lie the sprawl of the Sandhills, and my map showed no towns ahead along the highway until Thedford, about sixty miles away. The road passed through farmland where some huge center pivot irrigators were watering crops, and also dried cornfields that were symbolic of the Cornhusker State I was now traveling through.

The Sandhills brought dramatic changes in the topography, which had a very bumpy appearance that looked like mini mountain ranges heavily coated with grass and sandy patches. Some of these elevated formations resembled large coastal sand dunes I'd seen. The Nebraska Sandhills are not just the largest area covered by sand dunes in North America, but the most sizable dune system in the Western Hemisphere. Their 20,000 square miles cover over a quarter of the state—extending 265 miles east to west—with dunes rising to 400 feet. The region also has the largest expanse of mixed-grass prairie that remains in North America.

The geological history began about 10,000 years ago at the end of the last Ice Age, when streams carried glacially deposited sands from the Rocky Mountains into present-day Nebraska, which were blown by winds and eventually created dunes that were stabilized by abundant grasses and other vegetation. Prolonged droughts have weakened the vegetation that holds the sandy formations in place, causing them to shift over time.

In the Sandhills, the Ogallala Aquifer is often close to the surface, and here it feeds shallow lakes, marshes, and streams in the valley-like depressions between the dunes. The enormous aquifer is located above the Ogallala Formation, which underlies eighty percent of the High Plains.

The sandy soil of the region makes it very unsuitable for farming, although attempts were made in the late 1800s and early 1900s that largely failed. Some agriculture has succeeded in much more recent years with center pivot irrigation systems, but most of the Sandhills have never been plowed. As a result, the ecosystem is more intact than elsewhere on the extremely-cultivated Great Plains, and with a great diversity of plant and animal life. An impressive ninety-three percent of the Sandhills' 720 plant species are native, which was a factor in the region's designation as a National Natural Landmark in 1984.

The Sandhills, however, turned out to be as fit for cattle ranching as unfit for farming, with an abundant variety of rich grasses and natural shelter provided by the dunes. Ranching began in the 1870s with Texas Longhorn cattle, and in the modern age, there are other types of bovines numbering over half a million in an area with a sparse human population that continues to decline. I saw groups of black Angus fattening up on grasses near a couple of sandy hillsides, and further on a sign for the Lovejoy Ranch.

A radiant sun was descending, and the golden light and shadows of early evening transformed the landscape into a gilded spectacle where dunes and grasses glowed. Some dark cloud cover to the east added a dramatic contrast in color, and I felt fortunate to have arrived here at such a visually stunning time of day. I came to a gorgeous lake lined with cattail marshes and stopped to gaze at the sandy hills blending with the sky, water, and green shoreline, which now looked magical. Some floating waterfowl became airborne, which were merely a few of the thousands of ducks and geese drawn to the abundant lakes and wetlands in the Sandhills during the fall migration. Many other feathered creatures fly through and rest in the rich habitats here in season, from huge sandhill cranes to tiny songbirds. And the outstanding ecosystem also has various nesting species.

I entered the Valentine National Wildlife Refuge that 83 slices through, which achieved recognition as a Globally Important Bird Area in 2001, with over 270 species sighted within it. The refuge includes almost 72,000 acres and was established in 1935 during the Great Depression. The highly-accomplished Civilian Conservation Corps had a camp here that was involved in constructing roads and buildings that are still used today.

I turned off the road for a look at North Marsh Lake to the east and followed an unpaved road to a viewing area with a captivating scene that included another large lake that was somewhat distant. A kiosk at the site had an informational sign about the decline of native prairies on the Great Plains due to the expansion of farmlands and towns. Another described the human presence in the Sandhills, going back to Native bison hunters. It also mentioned the Kinkaid Act of 1904, which was federal legislation introduced by a Nebraska congressman with that surname, which upgraded the Homestead Act of 1862 and enabled settlers only within the Sandhills to claim 640 acres of land instead of just 160 if the land was occupied and worked for five years. The settlers motivated by the act were called "Kinkaiders," and their attempts at farming generally failed because of the adverse conditions. However, many of the aspiring farmers sold out to ranchers, and the sign noted that most of the Sandhills land is owned by ranchers today. Interestingly, the Kinkaid Act wasn't repealed until October 21, 1976.

Another sign had an image and description of a very old inhabitant of the Sandhills—the Blanding's turtle, which lives in the wetlands but ventures onto drier ground to feed somewhat omnivorously. Unfortunately, many of these benign reptiles have become roadkill, and to reduce this cause of mortality, fences have been installed along 83 in the refuge to guide the turtles and other wildlife through culverts under the road. However effective this is, the Valentine refuge has the highest known Blanding's turtle population in the species' range. I wondered about the snapping turtles crossing the road that the friendly guy back at the bar in Pierre told me about, and perhaps he mistook which species it was. A wildlife checklist I picked up showed that snappers were also common in the Sandhills, though.

After a dazzling sunset, there was another great spectacle further on when a perfectly full moon rose in the east from a dark gray cloud mass above Middle Marsh Lake. Suddenly I was moon-struck and stopped quickly for a fantastic photo op. And in the west the sunset left a spectacular purple and orange glow on a long cloud bank above the horizon. Both spectacles continued for a while as I drove on, trying not to be too distracted by all the beauty. I now wanted to see and explore more of this magnificent area someday and felt encouraged by knowing that it's just several hours away from my home in northern Colorado—and free of crowds and commercialism, with a wonderful wildness and solitude.

The highway passed by some smaller lakes, and the over 1,500 varied-sized water bodies in the Sandhills are natural, which is unusual for the Great Plains along with the prairie potholes further north. The landscape was still alluring in the fading light as the hilly dunes darkened into silhouettes. After leaving the Valentine National Wildlife Refuge, the dunes I could still discern eventually appeared smaller. The road crossed the North Loup River—a sixty-eight-mile tributary of the Platte River with a French name meaning "wolf"—which glistened with the moon's reflections.

I drew closer to Thedford, where I planned on staying that night. Just outside the diminutive town, 83 intersected with Nebraska 2, which crosses a lot of the state's interior. I stopped at a Sinclair station Dino Mart, at a big truck stop where one rig was parked in a corner. Suddenly, I felt like I was back in civilization, however small the outpost. The store had food, and I bought a four-bean salad and some coleslaw for a takeout. A group of local teenagers came in with the vivacious energy of their age group, and a few more mature-looking guys were also in the store, wearing cowboy hats and other Western attire that looked like they might be local ranch hands. Before I left, I asked the guy at the checkout if it was OK to park my car and sleep in the truck lot overnight. His response was: "Absolutely, that's what it's for. It's what the truckers do." That made me feel very welcome in Thedford, and I found out the mart also had $5 showers, which were about to close, though.

Before having my takeout meal, I drove a short distance west, where the state highway joined 83, to check out the small community. A sign showed the current population to be 211, which was a decline from the 243 mentioned in *Road Trip USA*—apparently another small 83 town that's been losing some residents to larger towns and cities. But Thedford remains the seat of Thomas County and is believed to have been named after the Canadian town of Thedford, Ontario, which indicates a probable Canadian connection with one or more of its early settlers. The settlement began with the arrival of the Chicago, Burlington, and Quincy Railroad in 1887, and by 1914, Thedford was incorporated as a village. A recent census showed its population to be almost 100 percent White, with a median age of about forty-four.

I passed a restaurant with a sign boasting something about "best steaks," which in a big beef-producing area like the Sandhills were probably excellent for satisfying carnivorous appetites. Then I saw a Cenex station with a store and another big lot where some cars were parked, which looked like another possible overnight haven. Past an overpass and the turnoff sign for 83 south was a small residential area. I also saw a bar-cafe and a small park, but not much else. When I did some later googling, there were remarkably five churches listed for Thedford that I'd managed to miss somehow.

I drove back to the store at the Cenex station and asked the same question about overnight parking to a young, blonde female working there and got a very similar answer: "Sure, you're welcome to do it. Truckers park here all the time."

There were no trucks in the lot at the time, which made this lot seem more appealing; and I parked in a back area near some other cars that looked like they'd been left there for a garage service close by. Feeling good about my overnight accommodation, I imbibed a bottle of Miller High Life in my plastic glass in the driver's seat while the October Hunter's Moon rose higher in the clear autumn night. Then I consumed my takeout meal with some bread. The lot was right across from the Burlington Northern and Santa Fe Railroad, where the rails that brought Thedford into existence must have been laid. While catching up with my journal, a few long freights rumbled through from the east and west, blaring their horns as if trying to awaken the sleepy little community. Trucks also passed through intermittently, though none stopped in the lot. Thedford was a tiny town with a lot of movement through it.

I wrote until I was tired, then used the nearby restroom before getting into my sleeping bag. I reflected on what a great day it had been seeing two great natural areas—the unique Niobrara River Valley and the spectacular Sandhills—sighting bald eagles and bison, and ending with an enchanting full moon.

DAY 16

A forest in Nebraska, some company in North Platte

In the morning I was still the only one staying in the lot. Outside was a chilly forty-six degrees, and I had a bowl of cereal in the car. Then I drove off to the other truck stop to use their shower.

On the way, two long freight trains streamed nearby in both directions—one hauling oil and the other a long procession of coal cars that amounted to a huge supply of fossil fuels. Ownership of these rails has changed over the decades, and the current one is the BNSF, which was created by the merger of the Burlington Northern and the Santa Fe Railways at the end of 1996. Today, the BNSF is second only to the Union Pacific in size as a freight network in North America, with 32,500 miles of track in twenty-eight states.

The $5 shower at the Dino Mart included a towel along with a clean and good-sized shower stall. I also shaved and blow-dried my hair under a hand-dryer and went from feeling very grubby to Mr. Clean. The convenience store that was part of the Sinclair chain had a sense of place, with taxidermized heads of deer, elk, and bison on the walls. A local country music station was playing, and I heard a commercial about getting good prices from local beef producers. Some men who looked like truckers, with less friendly vibes than the locals, were coming and going in the store. The place also had a car wash, which Wander needed, but I decided to wait until I reached North Platte not too far down the road.

Before continuing south, I made a diversion from 83 by heading east on Nebraska 2 to see the largest of two districts of the Nebraska National Forest that looked close on my map, which is the largest man-made forest in North America that seemed very interesting for a state mainly known for its open spaces. About nine miles east of Thedford, I started seeing more trees, and there was a transition to an actual forest to the south. I took an exit for the Nebraska National Forest Recreation Area and spent a couple of hours there, including a drive to an old fire tower, which I climbed for a panoramic view of about 22,000 acres of pines and hardwoods that had amazingly grown from hand-planted seedlings that were cultivated in the nearby Charles E. Bessey Nursery in 1902—inspired by and named after a University of Nebraska botany professor. Dr. Bessey believed that the Sandhills had once been forested, and he was apparently right because the largely treeless grasslands of the Great Plains didn't evolve until 8,000 to 10,000 years ago when the glaciers receded further north along with the forests that had been much further south, including Nebraska.

In a much more recent time, there was another feat of tree growth in Nebraska when the first Arbor Day in the U.S. was celebrated on April 10, 1872, and about one million trees were planted in the state. Successful results encouraged the development of the Nebraska National Forest, and eventually Arbor Day caught on in other states.

I rejoined 83 in Thedford and resumed my southward direction. The second book in Stew Magnuson's well-researched *The Last American Highway* series that covers Nebraska, Kansas, and Oklahoma says that the last stretch of 83 to be paved was between here and the small town of Stapleton to the south, which is north of the regional center of North Platte. That didn't happen until 1959, and to celebrate the occasion, tiny Thedford had a big, free barbeque bash and dance that drew over 2,500 people on September 23 of that year. It was sponsored by the North Platte Chamber of Commerce, which expected the now paved road to greatly benefit businesses in their town. Magnuson also mentions that 83 originally ran west of its current route from Thedford to North Platte and that it later swapped numbers with auxiliary U.S. 183 from southern South Dakota through Nebraska into northern Kansas. These are other examples of how U.S. 83 has evolved, and it took thirty-three years to become completely paved.

A sign showed sixty-five miles to North Platte. I passed through more of the still impressive Sandhills and saw more cattle and occasional solitary windmill pumps that stood out in the undulating landscape. These vertical mechanisms draw water for livestock and irrigation from the vast Ogallala Aquifer, using an old, wind-powered technology that can pump water from wells without using electricity. If wind is deficient, the pumps can be operated manually. I find these old structures visually appealing, with landmark qualities like grain elevators and water towers on the Plains.

I crossed the rather narrow Dismal River, which flows about seventy-two miles through the Sandhills from its source to the west to its confluence with the Middle Loup River to the east. It's another spring-fed river nourished by the giant aquifer, with a strong flow through a scenic area that attracts canoeists and kayakers. *The Last American Highway* says the river got its unappealing name not from appearance but from the dangers early settlers faced in crossing it.

Further south the road crossed the South Loup River, which merges with the North and Middle Loup branches further east in Nebraska to form the Loup River. This French name meaning "wolf," pronounced "lup," was given by early French trappers because the Wolf People was the translated name of the indigenous Skidi band of the Pawnee tribe who lived along the river's banks,

Just ahead and west of the highway at the intersection of Nebraska 92 was Stapleton—the seat of Logan County with a population of around 300. Its numbers have been quite stable for years, and it never had much more than 400 people. An extension of the Union Pacific Railroad in 1911 led to the town's growth, and it was named for a partner of a promoter who made a big donation to develop the community. I didn't get off 83 to scope out Stapleton, but I did see its water tower and oasis of trees.

Not far east was Gandy, with a mere thirty-two residents. But this tiny community that was named after an early settler is older than Stapleton and was once larger and the original county seat. Founded in 1885, it was bypassed by the railroad spur that came through in 1911 and spawned the now larger town, which it lost business to, resulting in its decline—another example of the huge influence of railroads in the region. However, Gandy remained the county seat until a referendum changed it to Stapleton in 1929. Presently, these are the only two communities in Logan County, and *The Last American Highway* mentions that of the fifteen least populated counties in the U.S., seven are in the Sandhills.

The bumpy landforms went on for a while. Then, when descending from a rise, a much flatter terrain appeared ahead. I was soon in a sea of drying corn where big center pivot irrigators were parked in the fields. Some of the cornfields were empty and cut, and I also passed a more colorful brown crop and emerald-green fields. A rolling grassland was ahead, with cattle and windmills instead of crops. This continued till close to North Platte, where there were homes and trees, including evergreen windbreaks. The road descended into a broad, green plain where the town came into view with its big island of trees, and, of course, a water tower and prominent grain elevator.

I crossed a bridge over the North Platte River and turned into a park on the other side, with the intention of getting a photo of the river. It was named Cody Park after William Cody, otherwise known as Buffalo Bill, whose historic home is in North Platte. A few tents had been set up in the park, and I found out camping was allowed for just $5 a day. So, it looked like an ideal place to stay since I planned on spending some time in North Platte. I parked and snapped a few pictures and wondered just how far the downtown area was. To find out, I walked over to a car parked in a neighboring space, where a balding, middle-aged guy was seated behind the wheel. A younger-looking guy wearing a baseball cap was in the other front seat, and an older woman sat in the back. The three were drinking Bud Light from cans.

After "Excuse me," I asked about the distance to the downtown area.

"Maybe three miles," the guy in the driver's seat said.

"Are you traveling?" the other guy inquired.

"I sure am—driving all of U.S. 83 to the Mexican border," which aroused some interest and got a conversation going. The woman in the back also joined in.

Introductions were soon made, and the guy in the driver's seat was Tom, the other guy Chuck, and the woman Jane. I was offered a beer, which I accepted, and the conversation rolled on. Chuck was a North Platte native who had lived in California for quite a while before returning, and he still had family here. Tom lived in North

Platte too and had also spent time in Wyoming.

"I'd like to do a trip like yours if I get on disability," Chuck said. "I'm still in my thirties, but I had an injury on a job I did for almost twenty years that might qualify me."

Soon a guy who looked over forty and with strong Native features came by on a bicycle who knew the trio. They also offered him a beer and introduced him to me as "Chief"—a stereotypical nickname that I thought most Native American men would find offensive now, but he didn't seem to mind. He also lived in North Platte. All four of them smoked cigarettes.

It turned into one of those animated conversations you can ease into with sociable strangers while traveling until Tom and Chuck were ready to drive off. Jane remained because she was camping and had a dome tent set up, with a minivan parked by her site. I decided to pitch my tent nearby, and "Chief," who was still hanging around, offered to help. I said "OK" even though it was an easy set-up, and offered him a bottle of Miller High Life as I pulled one out of my cooler for myself. We found out that two people drinking and trying to get coordinated putting up a small tent can take a little longer than just one doing it.

I found out this Native American fellow's more proper name was Jim, which he not surprisingly preferred. He told me that his background was Lakota Sioux and that he was born on the Pine Ridge Reservation in South Dakota, just east of the Rosebud Reservation I'd been through.

"I was given up for adoption and adopted by a White family," he revealed after sipping more beer, "and my stepdad died a couple of years ago."

"Were you close to your stepdad?"

"I was very close to the man I considered my dad."

"I lost my dad over seven years ago," I told him, "and it's very sad and hard even when they're very elderly like my dad was. Do you know about your biological parents?"

"I never knew them," he replied with a tone of sadness. "Maybe someday I'll find out more about them."

His story sounded similar to one I heard from a Navajo woman I'd met the year before in Fort Collins, who was also born on a reservation and given up for adoption.

Meanwhile, my neighbor, Jane, came over and asked if we wanted grilled pork sandwiches with potatoes that she was cooking in a stone fireplace by her campsite, and both Jim and I put in an order. We continued our conversation, and he said he had a construction job, and that he was now living in a mobile home. He talked a little more about his Sioux background, and I mentioned driving through the Rosebud Reservation. He was familiar with the casino and asked if I went in.

"I did," I said, "but didn't gamble because that's never been my thing. I just bought a beer and looked around. It seemed like the tribal ownership was doing good business."

"One time a White guy asked what tribe I'm from, and I pronounced it 'Si-ox' just to confuse him."

"That would have confused me too."

Jane came back and invited us to her site for the meal. She also offered more beer, which I declined. The grilled pork chop sandwich was very tasty, along with some spiced potato wedges. I learned that Jane had arrived in North Platte during the summer and had camped in the park a lot of the time, but had also stayed in a motel awhile. She knew Jim and the other two guys from the park. I was very curious about her, but it took a while to find out more.

After we finished eating, Jane asked me if I'd drive her to a Walmart on the other side of town for some groceries because she had a little too much beer to drive her vehicle, and she offered to give me some gas money. Since I had just two lighter beers and now a full stomach, I said, "Sure, but don't worry about gas. That was a good meal."

Jim left soon after the meal, and later Jane got into Wander, and we headed for the Walmart. On the drive, this older woman who had aroused my curiosity, if not my libido, started opening up to me. She described herself as "a missionary and a healer," who claimed The Spirit had guided her here like everywhere else she'd been around the country; and she was originally from Ohio. She talked constantly on the way to the store with a fluency that seemed to indicate high intelligence. But her content was a lot of ramblings about the goddess Athena, Jesus, Mother Mary, and angels, which I couldn't make much sense of.

When we got to the Walmart, I waited in the car and did some journaling. She came back with a few bags of groceries and two 12-pack cans of Bud Light. She thanked me for waiting and not "taking off" but got irritated when I politely reminded her that she should move her shopping cart from the car area to the cart park.

"I'm not a maid!" she blurted. Then she moved it anyway. I thought her reaction wasn't too becoming for someone who claimed to be a spiritual healer, but she had been drinking, and I didn't say anything that might further agitate her. On the way back, she continued to talk almost non-stop and made the revelation that she'd had lung cancer, which she claimed to have healed herself. I had to bring up her smoking that I saw at the park, and her response was: "Smoking doesn't cause cancer. It's things like mold that I've been exposed to."

Her mentioning cancer made me think of an old and close friend of mine who'd been battling colon cancer for about five years, and his prognosis looked grim. I mentioned this to Jane to hear what she might have to say, and she said she would write up a treatment for my friend and give it to me later.

By now, my overall impression of her was that she was a good-hearted and smart woman who was nevertheless rather wacky. But instead of challenging some of her outrageous ideas, it seemed better to be more of a listener, and maybe ask a few questions to try and find out something about what made this woman tick.

I was glad to get back to the park after having my ears bent by Jane's chatter. It had gotten dark, and I decided to walk into town, partly for some exercise. I headed down Jeffers St.—a one-way main street that's also 83—and soon came to the intersection of east-west U.S. 30—the old coast-to-coast route that had been a major portion of the Lincoln Highway, which is considered the nation's first cross-country road that was dedicated in 1913. A little further was a bridge over nine tracks of the time-honored Union Pacific Railroad—a big part of the first transcontinental railroad. North Platte is a huge rail and highway hub, which I'll have a lot more to say about.

I walked by a biker-type bar, then saw the Depot Grill and Pub and went in to check it out. Inside, it looked like a nice place, but not very lively. Just next door in the same building was the Rail Bar, which was smaller and not any livelier, with just a few older women at the bar. But a nice-looking female bartender with strawberry blonde hair was working it, which drew me to sit at the bar apart from the other women. A sign read, "Get Railed at the Rail Bar," and there was another about this being Ladies Night. So, there I was, the sole male, in the company of four ladies, and perhaps the older ones were there mainly for cheaper drinks. The attractive bartender, who looked middle-aged, got some of my old juices flowing.

I bought a Coors Light draft and tried to get a conversation going by telling the woman about my trip and where I was from, and she reacted with some interest. Then she walked away from the bar area and wasn't back until I'd sipped a lot of my beer, and she talked to the other women awhile whom she seemed to know. I wondered if she could be focused enough to have a good conversation with me and thought maybe I should just move on after I finished the beer. But as I was nearing the bottom of the glass, she came over and asked if I was ready for another round, and I couldn't help saying "Yes." And knowing one more would give me a beer-induced appetite, I asked for a menu before the kitchen closed and ordered a grilled chicken sandwich with a side of baked beans.

Placing the order helped me get more of the woman's attention, and we resumed our conversation.

"Have you always lived in North Platte?" I asked.

"Since I was in elementary school."

"So, how is it living here?"

"It's a safe place and was great for raising kids when I was married. And I have grandkids here now."

So, I thought maybe she was single now and unattached, and she had a sincere and unpretentious quality I liked besides her looking very good for being a grandmother.

"Have you been to Colorado much?"

"Not too much, but I have been to Fort Collins and liked it."

"Did you make it to Rocky Mountain National Park?"

"I've never been there."—which I found rather hard to believe since it's a spectacular place just several hours from this part of Nebraska that even draws lots of international visitors.

After she served my order, she tended and talked to the women again. The pub grub was very good and reasonably priced, and I also had food for thought about the lady behind the bar that I was attracted to. Though I'd traveled far down 83, I was temporarily closer to home, with Fort Collins only about four hours away from North Platte. If this woman was now unattached, maybe I could see her again after my journey, and perhaps she could finally visit Rocky Mountain National Park—with me.

When I was finishing my eating and drinking, she came over again and asked: "Would you like anything else?"

I wished I could have been bold enough to say, "I'd like to get better acquainted with you," but instead said, "No thanks, I guess I'm ready for my tab," and while waiting for it thought about what I should say next. I knew I could give her one of the cards I carry with my contact information. But before that I wanted to confirm that she was single now.

After I paid with my credit card and left her a good tip, she thanked me and said: "Have a good, safe trip. It was nice talking to you."

"It was nice chatting with you too. And I hope you get to see more of Colorado, especially Rocky Mountain National Park, which isn't that far from here."

"Maybe I'll get there eventually."

Then I finally introduced myself and found out her name was Diana.

"Are you single now, Diana?"

"I am now but went through a divorce recently. I'm going through a readjustment now and not doing any dating, though—mainly enjoying my grandkids and being busy with this job and some other things."

It seemed like she sensed my intentions.

"I understand," I said. "I've certainly been through my own phases in life, including with relationships. But I think you're a nice lady, and here's a card with my contacts if you get to Colorado again and would like me to show you around. I love it there and will probably stay in Fort Collins for the rest of my life."

She took the card and at least seemed to appreciate the gesture and said, "I'll keep it in mind if I ever get around to going there." Then we exchanged "Good Nights." When I left, I read something about this building having been a fire station.

Though I really didn't expect to ever hear from Diana, I felt good about at least reaching out to her. Life can have some very pleasant surprises, though, and I thought of the possibility that when this woman was ready to expand her social and geographical horizons, I just might get a call, email, or even letter saying: "Do you remember me from the Rail Pub in North Platte in October 2014? I'm driving to Colorado and thought of meeting up with you." Very unlikely. But I thought stranger things have happened.

I wandered around part of North Platte's downtown with a good beer buzz, which looked familiar from a road trip I made in '07 when I stayed in a motel in this energetic traveler's town. Some streets had brick-surfaced sections, which I would see a lot more of in 83 towns further south.

Back at Cody Park, the camping area was very quiet, and there were restrooms near my tent site that were well-maintained. Inside the tent, I wrote for a while with the aid of my lamp until I started to fade. I again appreciated the relative comfort of the two-person tent compared to my cramper.

Before dozing off, I heard the rumbles of trains on the old Union Pacific—sounds that lulled me into sleep, and a reminder of all the movement through this town from different directions.

DAY 17

"We're friends forever," Buffalo Bill, and the Golden Spike Tower

It was good to be greeted by the sight of the strong-flowing North Platte River the next morning, with the cottonwoods lining its banks turning yellow. Four rounds of a pleasurable poison the day before left me a little hungover, though. While I was finishing some breakfast, Jane came over and handed me her cancer cure for my friend, which was hand-written on four small notebook pages. She even offered me a beer, and I said, "Thanks, but this time of day I'd rather have raisin bran." Beer wasn't part of her cure, though, which turned out to be a short, simple prayer or mantra and a vitamin regimen. The former read:

Say this out loud:
"LOVE COME, LOVE COME, LOVE COME, AMEN..."
Saying this out loud calls Spirits of LOVE into your body (temple). LOVE Spirits fight for your white and red cells fast...
White and Gold Tiny light beings enter you when saying this Prayer out loud.
Viruses, Bacteria, Bad cells are attacked, and killed by Angels of white and gold light...
LOVE is #1.
Bye – Dr. Jane L. Jackson

The vitamins included high doses of vitamins C, E, and some B vitamins along with pure orange juice, taken for six days. And there was the claim: "Cancers are cells from crude oil by-products... Healing requires Prayer #1."

It sure seemed like quackery, but I just listened to Jane talk more about her purported cures. She also mentioned more about her background and said she'd been married a couple of times and had adult children, had gone to college, and later worked in some trades. Then she got really interesting: "I myself was murdered by a woman voodoo practitioner in 1968, who ate my eyeballs and brains. There's a lot of voodoo people around looking for abductions, and many are illegal immigrants of color. Many illegals have also brought in exotic diseases like Ebola."

Apparently, she'd been reincarnated. Then she said something equally outrageous about a leading vaccine.

"The smallpox vaccine was derived from Adolf Hitler's cadaver. And Hitler didn't commit suicide. He was killed. Many who got the smallpox vaccine were contaminated by Hitler."

I tried to listen with a straight face, and she also had some bizarre things to say about sexually-transmitted diseases. Some racial slurs were next when she used the N-word in reference to then President Obama, and later said: "I'd never want an African, Mexican, or Indian in my bloodline."

Although I found such bigotry very distasteful, I thought any criticism of it would probably just trigger a verbal barrage and do nothing to change her apparently deep-seated prejudices that were likely influenced by something in her background. But despite this nasty side of her personality and her wackiness, there was something likable and good-hearted about this woman, and I'd seen her act nice and hospitable to the Native American guy, Jim, despite her bigotry.

I listened to some more of her ramblings and found out she'd been in Tucson, Arizona, before North Platte. She expressed some other very strange ideas, which all seemed part of an elaborate belief system, and I wondered how much was original and what had outside influences. Though so much of what she said was outrageous, she expressed it with passion and seeming conviction.

Finally, I needed a break from her chatter and had to use the restroom anyway. When I returned, she was back at her site, and I took my tent down since I didn't plan on staying in the park another night. When ready to leave, I walked over to her to say good-bye.

"So, where are you going?" she asked.

"To see more in North Platte, and I may leave town later. If not, I'll probably sleep in my car in the Walmart lot, which should be safe."

"I'll be grilling again in the evening, so come back if you're still around."

"Thanks for the invitation."

Then she handed me a small container of the McCormick seasoning she'd used on the pork and potatoes the evening before that I liked and said to keep it.

"Thank you," I said, but will you have some then?

"Don't worry, I have more."

I thought that was a nice little gesture, and to show some appreciation, I offered her what was left of the free grape tomatoes from the store back in Selby that still looked OK. She accepted it, gave me a hug, and said: "We're friends forever, and The Spirit led you to me."

I appreciated the sentiment, which seemed sincere, even if I didn't take what she said literally—though there was something fateful about our encounter, since I'd stopped at the park just to take some pictures of the river.

"How long do you think you'll stay in North Platte?" I asked.

"I really don't know. I like it here but am guided by The Spirit that could lead me anywhere."

"Happy Trails," were my concluding words before I walked back to my car, and I gave her the old peace sign. That's how I left one of the most interesting—and the strangest—person I encountered on the journey, and I wound up saving the small plastic container of the seasoning she gave me long after using up the contents as a little memento of the woman who said, "We're friends forever."

Before driving off, I walked closer to the North Platte River and watched its flow, which begins in the Rockies of north-central Colorado and courses about 716 winding miles before its fateful merging with the currents of the South Platte River just east of the town I was in to form the Platte River—more waters destined for the Gulf of Mexico after further mergers with the great Missouri and Mississippi Rivers.

The big park had somewhat of an outdoor zoo that I checked

out. Fenced enclosures contained a small group of bison, which didn't excite me like seeing them in the wild, and also deer, elk, and non-native llamas and peacocks. There were also a lot of recreational facilities that included a swimming pool and a small lake with an island that attracted gulls and waterfowl.

I came to a bright green lawn area with numerous international flags waving, with a brick monument that announced WILD WEST MEMORIAL, and another with a plaque that read: "Let it be known to all that NORTH PLATTE'S CODY PARK was the site of the 'OLD GLORY BLOWOUT' JULY 4, 1882." I read the whole content and learned that this celebratory event was organized by William "Buffalo Bill" Cody at a racetrack once here. It's considered the first "spectator rodeo" that resulted in then North Platte resident, Cody, being called the "father of rodeo." The Old Glory Blowout had cowboys of the Old West competing in events like bronc riding, steer roping, and horse racing, and its success was an inspiration for Cody to start his famous circus-like Wild West Show, which he added a lot of acts to through the years. These included Native Americans in traditional attire who sang, drummed, danced, and engaged in staged battles with cowboys and soldiers. The first public show took place on May 19, 1883, in Omaha, Nebraska, and it continued for three decades, well into the twentieth century, before millions of spectators across the U.S. and Canada, and many countries in Europe. It all started here in North Platte, where the rodeo tradition continues in the Wild West Arena in town, especially during the Nebraskaland Days in June with the Buffalo Bill Rodeo.

In the flag area was a life-size bronze statue of William Cody in a glass-enclosed gazebo, which was presented to North Platte and "All Americans" by the British artist, W. Bryan Mickleburgh in 1998. "Buffalo Bill," after all, is regarded as a quintessential American character. Behind the gazebo was another brick monument and plaque that gave "Honor and Recognition" to the Native Americans who were part of Cody's exhibition, and whom he credited with making it successful.

Another part of the park had a great relic of North Platte's illustrious railroad history, where the huge Union Pacific Challenger 3977 steam locomotive is permanently stationed. Built in 1943, and retired in 1961, it's over 121 feet long and is one of the largest steam engines ever manufactured. It hauled passengers and freight and is the only one in its class displayed in the world. There was also a smaller diesel locomotive. To call North Platte a railroad town is quite an understatement, since its Bailey Yard just west of town is the largest railroad classification yard in the world, and about ten percent of the town's population still works for the Union Pacific. So, it's no wonder there's a big annual Rail Fest here each September. But it's also an old crossroads community that I've traveled through numerous times on Interstate 80, and I've had a long fascination with it and think it's one of the most interesting towns in the country.

North Platte's origins go back to a construction camp for the Union Pacific that was part of the great ambition to build the first transcontinental railroad that was authorized by the U.S. Congress in 1862 during the Civil War. The railroad was thought to have strategic value for the Union, but the rails didn't reach here until after the war in 1866. The town that developed and was named after the North Platte River was originally one of the rowdy and vice-ridden "Hell on Wheels" towns that sprung up along the new railroad. The Union Pacific's chief construction engineer, Grenville Dodge—namesake of famed Dodge City, Kansas—liked the location because of its good water supply, and he established a division point here where the trains and crews were moved around, along with maintenance and repairs. The division point evolved into giant Bailey Yard.

But before the rails arrived, there was much other movement here. After the Natives, early trappers and traders followed the Platte River west, as did the covered wagons of many thousands of pioneer-emigrants on the Oregon, California, and Mormon Trails, and later the riders of the brief Pony Express period. This river route across the Plains came to be called the Great Platte River Road, which was a major route of westward expansion along with its North and South Platte tributaries. The Platte was never navigated like the Missouri, however, because of its shallow and muddy waters, many islands, and shifting sandbars. The first non-Natives to see it were French explorers and trappers in the early 1700s, and the name Platte is derived from the French name, "rivière plate," meaning "flat river." The Omaha tribe called the river "Ni Bthaska"—their name for "flat water"—which led to the region it flowed through being called Nebraska. The first transcontinental railroad was routed near the Platte. And when the automobile age arrived in the early 1900s, the largely crude, coast-to-coast Lincoln Highway coursed near much of the river, which became U.S. 30 in 1926 and was improved. The climax of this succession was Interstate 80—the most traveled interstate in the nation, and the second longest at 2,900 miles (4,666 km)—which came through in the 1960s and became the fastest overland route toward the setting sun and in the opposite direction.

Among all this historical movement through North Platte is the regional airport a few miles east of town that was built in 1921 to serve the young U.S. Air Mail Service. On February 22 of that year, what was then North Platte Field was the site of the first night air mail flight, which was a segment of an early transcontinental airmail feat, and it used the first lighted airfield that was illuminated by burning fuel in barrels. Present operations of the airport include daily shuttle flights to Denver.

I thought about my previous movements through North Platte, including my emigration to Colorado in December 2012, mentioned early in my story. Now I was traveling in a north-south direction in contrast to the historical east-west movement here. Among the innumerable travelers here was a young U.S. Army Captain named Dwight D. Eisenhower—future five-star general and U.S. President—who participated in an Army truck convoy that plodded along the rough-surfaced and still incomplete Lincoln Highway in two months and arrived in North Platte on August 5, 1919. And in the summer of 1947, Beat Generation writer, Jack Kerouac, stopped here while on a hitch-hiking adventure across the country on U.S. 30, which he described in his classic *On the Road*.

Besides all the travelers, over 24,000 people live in North Platte, and it never had much more. But it's a regional center for this part of Nebraska that's also the seat of Lincoln County.

Before leaving Cody Park, I headed south on Jeffers St. and stopped at a carwash where I stayed in the vehicle while it was conveyed through a soaping and rinsing process, after which I appreciated how much cleaner Wander's exterior looked. Then I made a turn on U.S. 30—the old Lincoln Highway—and headed west following a sign for the Golden Spike Tower, which is an observatory by the huge Bailey railyard that I was set on going to. But first I made another turn on Buffalo Bill Avenue toward the old home of William Cody in Buffalo Bill State Historical Park, and I passed the Lincoln County Historical Museum.

The Cody home is a handsome, white, three-story, eighteen-room Victorian mansion with green trimmings and topped by a cupola. And nearby is a long building that was originally the barn where Cody kept animals for his Wild West exhibition when he wasn't touring, with the name Scout's Rest Ranch painted boldly on the roof. This was the name given to the 4,000 acres that Cody once owned here, now reduced to the twenty-five that make up the state park that opened to the public in 1964 and was designated a National Historic Landmark in 1978. I'd been here before in 1976 on my thirty-six-state motorcycle odyssey to celebrate the nation's Bicentennial that year and toured the home with its Cody memorabilia. Now I just wanted to take a few digital images of the photogenic mansion to have in addition to the old slides I had of the place.

The famous personality first purchased land around North Platte in 1878 that was later expanded, and he developed a sizable working ranch where crops were also cultivated. The mansion was built in 1886 and was under Cody's ownership until 1913. He had a wife and four children who remained there when he was traveling with his show or on other business.

William Frederick Cody was a truly larger than life character who inspired many legends. What was exaggerated and fabricated was based on a very colorful life that embodied much of his times and the Old West. He was born on a farm near Le Claire, Iowa Territory, in 1846 and started working at age eleven after his father died. At fourteen, he was a Pony Express rider, according to popular accounts. In his late teens, he served the Union in a cavalry unit during the Civil War and later had a well-known role as a civilian scout for the U.S. Army during the Indian Wars. Cody also had a contract to supply workers on the Kansas Pacific railroad with buffalo meat, and it's said that he shot 4,282 of the animals in eighteen months during 1867 and 1868 and that he "earned" the name Buffalo Bill by beating another hunter in an eight-hour buffalo shooting competition. Ironically,

Cody became a conservationist in his later years when the great herds of bison dwindled—thanks to trigger-happy people like himself—and he came to oppose hide hunting and advocated regulations.

Buffalo Bill's fame and legend began at the young age of twenty-three when he met the writer, Ned Buntline, who would publish a story based on his adventures in a weekly publication that was highly fictionalized, and a successful dime novel titled, *Buffalo Bill, King of the Bordermen*. Sequels followed by Buntline and other writers who caught on to the character, which were published into the early years of the twentieth century. In the meantime, Cody started a stage acting career in 1872 in Chicago in a production called *The Scouts of the Prairie*, which was panned by critics but was a commercial success. Other productions followed on the same Indian Wars theme while the wars were still going on, and Cody played the role of the scout for part of the year, then returned to the prairies to work as a real one.

However, it was Buffalo Bill's Wild West extravaganza that brought him his greatest fame and celebrity status, and Cody resided in North Platte to be close to the railroad that transported it. Besides its performances throughout the U.S. and Canada, the show toured Europe eight times between 1887 and 1906, where it was extremely popular. Cody and company met many European luminaries, and some well-known personalities performed in the show, such as sharpshooter Annie Oakley. Cody was also able to recruit the great Hunkpapa Sioux chief, Sitting Bull, with a band of his braves for one season in 1885—five years before the chief's tragic death in 1890 at the hands of Indian police on the Standing Rock Reservation. In his later years, Sitting Bull, despite his role in the humiliating defeat of Custer's force at the Battle of the Little Bighorn in 1876, was on good terms with the man who had been an Army scout during the Indian Wars and claimed to have scalped a Cheyenne warrior during a skirmish. Despite a record of enmity, it's said that Cody always respected Native Americans and favored their civil rights. He referred to them as "the former foe, present friend, the American." He's also known to have supported women's rights, exemplified by his very progressive statement for his times: "What we want to do is give women even more liberty than they have. Let them do any kind of work they see fit, and if they do it as well as men, give them the same pay." Cody had an over fifty-year marriage to a woman named Louisa Frederici until his death in 1917, which was tumultuous; but the two had a reconciliation in their final years.

Another example of the dynamism and diversity of William Cody's life is his role in founding the town of Cody, Wyoming, near Yellowstone National Park in 1896 after being very impressed by the area's great scenic beauty and potential for agriculture and recreation. He was instrumental in getting the federal government to authorize the building of the Shoshone Dam near Cody to provide irrigation for the Bighorn Basin. When completed in 1910, it was the tallest dam in the world, and in 1946 was renamed the Buffalo Bill Dam and Reservoir by the U.S. Congress.

Some historians have said that Buffalo Bill was the most recognizable celebrity in the world at the turn of the twentieth century, which must have been aided by his distinctive appearance—with his wide-brimmed hat, mane of hair, thick, curled mustache, and long goatee that grayed with age. Perhaps he was also one of the first celebrities in the modern sense. His death came on January 10, 1917, at age seventy, from kidney failure while at his sister's house in Denver. More than 25,000 mourners came to see his open casket laid in state at the Colorado Capitol building in Denver. Tributes also arrived from President Woodrow Wilson and European leaders.

Cody's burial on Lookout Mountain, west of Denver, was delayed because of winter conditions, and his body was kept in a mortuary in Denver and repeatedly embalmed for almost five months before finally being buried on June 3, 1917, when over 20,000 people attended the event. However, a controversy developed because many people in Cody, Wyoming, wanted him buried near their town, and claims were made that it was Cody's real wishes. There's even a legend that his body was stolen from the Denver mortuary by a few overzealous Cody residents and replaced with a Cody local that died and was touched up to resemble Buffalo Bill, who was supposedly moved and buried on Cedar Mountain near Cody. Although there's no sound basis for this wild story, some residents of Cody are said to still believe it. North Platte could also have claimed Buffalo Bill.

When Cody's life began, the West was still wild, and a frontier beckoned a huge migration that was part of Manifest Destiny. During his lifetime, the West was gradually "won" and exploited, which he played a role in. And he lived to see the Old West gone. He'd achieved a lot of wealth from his enterprises, which declined, however, before his death. But it seems William Cody was richest in his legacy. His Wild West Show is said to have created an image and fascination with the American West that became the basis of many stories, movies, and later TV series, whether accurate or not. And so much has been written about him and the character he inspired—from comic books to an autobiography he published in 1879. He was surely a fascinating man with a greatness, who left an enormous legacy.

Right across the street from the Cody home was the Wild West Arena—the location of the annual Nebraskaland Days festival and Buffalo Bill Rodeo. After snapping a picture of a sign there, I drove toward the Golden Spike Tower through some outskirts of town with large, dry cornfields before reaching the parking area. The tower was a modern-looking, eight-story, white structure, topped by an enclosed observation deck, and below it an open-air deck with railing. It was opened in 2008 and replaced an old viewing platform that was deteriorating and greatly improved the view. Near the base was a visitor center with the design of a large train station, with NORTH PLATTE above the entrance. Nearby, an old railroad dining car looked permanently displayed, and on the other side of the center, twenty-three flags waved, representing each state served by the Union Pacific Railroad.

I walked into the visitor center, paid a reduced senior fee, bypassed an exhibit and gift shop, and took an elevator to the eighth-floor enclosed deck. There was a 360-degree view through all the windows, and the panorama of the world's largest railroad yard was very impressive. I gazed out at a huge grid of tracks with long lines of locomotives and freight cars and different service facilities. Inside, information was displayed with some statistics.

Bailey Yard covers 2,850 acres and is eight miles long, with 315 miles of track within. It has about 2,600 employees, and operations and repairs run 24/7. An on-site command center, with computerized controls, directs all train traffic coming through. The yard was named after a past Union Pacific president, Edd H. Bailey, who held the position from 1965 to 1971 and began his long career as a helper in a railroad car repair shop. The yard's location is strategically very central in the country, and the UP is the nation's busiest freight line. Like their main competitor, the BNSF, which they share a duopoly with, the UP has acquired many other lines over the years. From Bailey Yard, trains carrying all kinds of freight are bound for points throughout the country, and the yard has been described as "an economic barometer of America."

I walked around the circular top deck and read more information, and there was an older guy who was apparently a volunteer and talked a lot and answered questions about the yard. He'd worked over thirty-seven years for a locomotive parts supplier and had an enthusiasm that showed a real love for the rails.

"A lot of visitors spend hours here," he said, "and not all are serious railroad buffs."

I thought this place must be a Mecca for those who are.

I took photos from the lower open-air deck, then used my binoculars for a closer look at the humming operations of the rail yard that never sleeps—a huge symbol of all the movement through North Platte.

Down in the visitor center, there was an information panel about the well-known North Platte Canteen during World War II. This operation served multitudes of servicemen and was in the old passenger depot in downtown North Platte, and it may well be the most heart-warming example of ongoing kindness and generosity in the nation's history.

The story began on December 17, 1941—just ten days after the Pearl Harbor attack—when there was talk in North Platte that a Union Pacific train carrying a company of the Nebraska National Guard would be stopping at the depot in town, and a large group that included relatives and friends of local servicemen showed up to meet them. When the train arrived, it turned out to be a company from Kansas. But instead of reacting with disappointment, the crowd presented the Kansas company with food and gifts intended for the Nebraskans and gave them a warm send-off. A young woman and native of North Platte named Rae Wilson was there, and she was inspired enough by the event to organize a movement to meet and greet all the troop trains that stopped in North Platte and offer hospitality. The rest became history and one of the largest volunteer efforts of World War

II, when North Platte had about 12,000 people.

The Union Pacific company cooperated with the use of its depot and facilities and provided basic supplies. The movement kept growing and included fund-raising and volunteers from 125 different communities in the region, even into Colorado. The volunteers totaled over 55,000 during the over four years that the canteen operated, and most were women. As many as twenty-four trains a day stopped at the depot, and an average of 4,000 servicemen were greeted and treated daily with sandwiches, hard-boiled eggs, coffee, milk, fruit, home-baked goods, and many others—including cigarettes when smoking was much more fashionable—and all free and donated when there was national food rationing during the war. Even birthday cakes were presented, and "Happy Birthdays" sung to those having the occasion. Homemade popcorn balls were another treat, with some containing contacts for young single women who were willing to be pen pals. Some of the relationships that developed even resulted in later marriages and were called "popcorn ball marriages." The wonderful volunteers even did things like sending telegrams for time-pressed GIs and assisting with calling home. And when the hospital trains came through, the women boarded and tended to those who couldn't get off, also giving away magazines and decks of playing cards. By the time the canteen closed on April 1, 1946—some months after the war ended—over 6,000,000 service people had passed through and benefited from its great altruism, even though the stopover was often just about fifteen minutes.

In December 1943, the North Platte Canteen received the Meritorious Wartime Service Award from the War Department. One soldier referred to his experience at the canteen as "the warmest, friendliest, and most rewarding half-hour in my life." And I read another quote that put a real lump in my throat: "...We know you call us 'your boys.' but I wonder if you realize whom we saw in you? We saw our mothers, our wives, our sisters and daughters and sweethearts...above all this, we saw America."

These moving words made me reflect on how a lot of the "boys" had to be only eighteen or nineteen. Many had never been far from home until they wound up in uniform because of a global war, and from throughout the U.S., they stopped briefly in this railroad town in the middle of the country that they'd never heard of, usually not knowing where the hell they were going. Many must have been scared and homesick, and suddenly, a host of women who must have seemed like angels made them feel like they were at home with family and friends. Many of these boys never returned from the war, no doubt. But before their short lives ended, at least some must have had a shining memory of a short train stop in North Platte, Nebraska. And among those fortunate to have lived long, there must have been wonderful memories of the stop that were just as shining—all because of a kindness and generosity that became contagious. It's a chapter in North Platte's history that its people can be forever proud of.

The visitor center was closing when I left, and I drove back to the downtown area where I wanted to see just where the old passenger depot had been. It turned out to be on Front Street in the area I'd walked around the night before near the Rail Bar. The venerable building had been demolished by Union Pacific in late 1973 because the company had no real use for it after passenger service ended in North Platte over two years before. I learned that many local people were very disappointed and upset by the company's decision and rather hasty action, and that some resentment still lingers. What's there now is a small memorial park by the tracks, where an American flag and Union Pacific banner fly high over three brick monuments near some hardwood trees and shrubbery. Two of the monuments bear the red, white, and blue Union Pacific shield symbol. The larger one has these words engraved:

> SITE OF THE UNION PACIFIC RAILROAD DEPOT
> CONTAINING FAMOUS WORLD WAR II
> NORTH PLATTE CANTEEN
> SERVING MORE THAN SIX MILLION MEMBERS
> OF THE ARMED
> FORCES FROM DECEMBER 25, 1941, TO APRIL 1, 1946
> THE CANTEEN WAS SUPPORTED BY
> NORTH PLATTE CITIZENS
> AND NEBRASKA AND COLORADO COMMUNITIES.

I was happy to see this commemoration. But it would have been much better if the old depot had been preserved like so many less significant ones have. What was no longer here, I tried to imagine—thousands of trains that stopped to pick up and discharge countless passengers for decades, especially during a wartime when the very best qualities of human nature were splendidly displayed here.

From the memorial, I walked through more of the downtown along some of the brick-surfaced streets. I'd heard that the character of the area isn't what it used to be and that the depot isn't the only old building that's gone. But I saw two great vintage structures that evoked the past. One was the Fox Theater—a light brown brick building with a decorative corner and glowing marquee, which opened in October 1929 near the onset of the Great Depression. It originally had vaudeville shows before becoming a full-time movie theater that operated till 1979. But the following year it was donated by a family member of one of its builders to the North Platte Community Playhouse organization. A complete renovation was made with community support, and the theater reopened in 1983 and has featured live plays and other events. In 1985, the building was placed on the National Register of Historic Places.

Just across the street was the Hotel Pawnee—an eight-story Georgian Revival Style building of similar brick construction that also opened in 1929 and was designed and built by the same people as the Fox Theater. My attraction to old hotels led to my giving the place a good look, and its exterior appeared well-preserved, though a side sign looked weathered by the Nebraska climate. It was presently vacant, however, but had a real heyday when it held many events, including receptions in an elegant second-floor ballroom. Some celebrities and heads of state also stayed in the Hotel Pawnee. In more recent years it had been a residence for retirees, and later an assisted living facility. So, it seemed to have followed a pattern of old hotel decline, and I hoped this one managed to stay intact and find other uses and not go the way of the Union Pacific Depot.

The hotel's name was a recognition of the indigenous people that were originally the largest tribe that lived in Nebraska, and with the longest history there. The Pawnee were both farmers and hunters like the Mandan further north, who also lived in permanent earth lodges near their crops but lodged in tepees when on the hunt for bison and other game. They acquired the horse around the year 1700 by raiding tribes further south that were closer to the Spanish, who reintroduced the horse to the Americas; and the animal radically changed their way of life, as with many tribes. The Pawnee spoke what's called a Caddoan language, which was very different from what was spoken by other tribes in Nebraska. But they managed to communicate using the sign language of the Plains. They had many violent conflicts with neighboring tribes, especially the Lakota Sioux, who emerged from woodlands to the east and became nomadic hunters. Pawnee warriors were known to shave their heads like the Mohawks much further east.

There were Pawnee villages along the Platte River, besides the Loup River and its tributaries. By the early 1800s, their estimated numbers were over 10,000, which began to decline as American traders and settlers brought smallpox and other diseases that plagued different tribes. They were also more harassed by their old Lakota Sioux enemies and the Cheyenne. By 1860, the Pawnee population had plummeted to around 4,000, and in 1873 they were placed on a reservation in eastern Nebraska, where their numbers further declined from more disease, warfare, and crop failures. Then, in 1875, the tribe was forced onto a reservation in the Indian Territory of Oklahoma, where terrible conditions reduced its population to only around 600 by 1900—the tragic fate of another once proud Native people. It took many years, but their numbers rebounded and are presently around 5,600 in the Pawnee Nation of Oklahoma.

Historically, the Pawnee didn't resist American westward expansion like so many other tribes did. And bitter conflicts with enemy tribes led to large groups of Pawnees serving as scouts in the U.S. Army from 1864 to 1877 in campaigns against tribes that were old enemies. These Pawnee Scouts were an interesting chapter in the history of a very interesting people that once lived and thrived in Nebraska.

It was late in the day, and I found a laundromat to wash some clothes for the first time on the journey after giving Wander a wash earlier in the day. When I left it was dark, and I drove toward the Walmart where I'd driven Jane the evening before, assuming I could park there overnight, which turned out not to be restricted. One appeal of the location was that it was very close to the South Platte River, not far from where it converged with the North Platte River to form the Platte. However, a thick growth of trees blocked any view of the river from the lot. Just across the river was Interstate 80—"America's Most Traveled Highway."

I opened a bottle of Miller High Life in the car and got into one of my meditative moods. Afterwards, I was ready to eat something and went to a nearby Runza restaurant, which is part of a fast-food chain that's popular in Nebraska. Their specialty is "world famous" Runza sandwiches, which are rather small bread pockets filled with ground beef, onions, cabbage, and spices; and I learned that this combination originated with the Russian Germans who settled on the Plains in the late 1800s. I ordered a Runza Original and a side salad to get something green in my diet for the day. The sandwich, with daily baked bread, was very tasty and an interesting type of fast food.

Later googling revealed that the name runza is derived from the low German word "runsa," which translates as "bun shape." The Runza chain started back in 1949 in Lincoln, Nebraska and grew during the '50s, became franchised in the '60s, and currently had eighty locations, with seventy-five in Nebraska. Runzas are one of the foods served in the stands at Memorial Stadium in Lincoln, Nebraska—home of the Nebraska Cornhuskers—and thousands are sold during football games. And for those outside their region with a craving for them, these Nebraska specialties can be shipped frozen. The one I had was tasty enough to understand the demand.

After a short walk and more journaling, I got into my backseat sleeping bag, now "cramping" near the South Platte River, where I could hear the drone of traffic on I-80 instead of the trains of the Union Pacific in this town with so much movement.

DAY 18

McCook, in Kansas, a night in Oberlin

After having breakfast at the Subway store in Walmart, I walked to a little park right on the South Platte River by the Dewey St. bridge and took some photos of this other flow from the Rockies in Colorado, with headwaters southwest of Denver. Here the river looked quite wide, with some small, grassy sandbars scattered in its shallow waters. On the banks, a heavy growth of cottonwoods and other hardwoods displayed a seasonal mixture of green and pale orange.

It was time to leave North Platte, and on the way out I stopped at the touristy Fort Cody Trading Post just across the river. Outside was a large cutout likeness of Buffalo Bill Cody in Old West attire holding a rifle, and the trading post was within a wooden replica of an old fort stockade. Inside, the sizable store had merchandise ranging from moccasins and other attire to condiments, cookbooks, and books on Western history. There were also some museum-like displays that included a sergeant's uniform from the Indian Wars, an old U.S. Cavalry sword, a buffalo hide coat, and a bison skull dug up in the Sandhills. A gun display had a Winchester model/866.carbine—"The Gun that won the West"—which Native Americans named "Yellow Boy." What I thought most interesting was a miniature replication of Buffalo Bill's Wild West show, with its 20,000 hand-carved pieces of different figures, with Cody himself on horseback, along with mounted Natives, tepees, bull riders, and spectator stands—just to name a few. The ambitious project was done by artist Ernie Palmquist, and took twelve years to complete.

Outside, within the stockade, were a couple of small, covered wagons, a tepee, a cabin, a life-size bison replica, painted cowboy and Native figures, and large boards with openings for visitors' heads to pose for touristy photos. When I left the complex, the large image of Buffalo Bill was a final reminder of his heritage in North Platte.

I crossed a bridge over I-80, and just ahead on the east side of 83 made another stop at the 20th Century Veterans Memorial, which honors the branches of the U.S. Armed Forces and commemorates the five major conflicts of the twentieth century. I took photos of bronze statues and an impressive bar-relief mural. One of the statues was a likeness of Rae Wilson, who started the North Platte Canteen during World War II.

The highway had become four lanes with wide shoulders, and I passed car dealers and other businesses on the outskirts of North Platte. Soon there were cornfields, then a big housing development which had probably been cornfields. The road narrowed to two lanes by Lake Maloney to the west, which was created by an earthen dam in 1935 and is a popular state recreational area. Ahead was a rolling prairie with few homes and little farmland for a while, and it looked like I was out of the Sandhills.

There was a procession of power lines along the road, and I passed some oil or gas operations with tanks and a pipeline. Huge corn fields reappeared to the east along with more colorful crops, and future Nebraska beef grazed in grassy areas. A tree-studded ridge reminiscent of the Niobrara Valley became visible to the south and west, and the highway entered a hilly area around Medicine Creek and the village of Wellfleet, which had seventy-eight residents in the last count. It was oddly named in this very landlocked state after Wellfleet, Massachusetts—a summer resort town on Cape Cod—because its founder was a Massachusetts realtor named Carroll Hawkins, who had big plans for developing an industrial and agricultural community along a railroad that came through here in 1886, and he found investors.

The plans included a dam on Medicine Creek to develop a lake and hydropower for industry, and a town was platted in 1887 that grew to 400 people in a few years. However, a drought in the early 1890s was a big discouragement to an aspiring sugar beet industry, and the dam project was soon abandoned. The population declined, and the disillusioned promoters of Wellfleet abandoned the scene. Some buildings were even moved to North Platte. A determined group of residents stayed, however, and a smaller dam was eventually built in 1932 that created a lake for recreation and flood control. This town that experienced an early decline faced another in later years when more residents moved to larger towns and cities. But Wellfleet didn't become a ghost town and still has a post office and two churches. The rails that spurred its existence have remained and are now the Nebraska, Kansas, and Colorado Railway, which carries agricultural products and coal over 559 miles of tracks in those states. Wellfleet also has a Fall Festival in September with a parade, rodeo, and horse races down its unpaved main street that provide some annual excitement in what must ordinarily be a very quiet little community. Apparently, it would have been different if its founder's ambitions were realized, though I wouldn't be surprised if most of its present residents like it the way it is.

Further on, the road climbed into higher timbered ground, where many yellowish, changing hardwoods blended beautifully with dark evergreens, and there were also meadows. Then a panorama of green, level land appeared, with croplands speckled with trees—back to far horizons and resting irrigators in fields. Afterwards came a more rolling landscape again.

Closer to McCook—the first good-sized town since North Platte—83 had just been coated with new asphalt, and the going got sluggish because of a construction crew. There were many green cedars in the landscape, sometimes isolated, and sharp, pointed yucca in open areas. The road ascended another grassy ridge with scattered trees; then the land flattened again, and McCook appeared in the distance as another island of trees below two water towers. I passed a turnoff for the old McCook Army Airfield, which was a major flight training base during World War II for big old warbirds like B-17s and B-29s. It's nine miles west of town, and some of its buildings have survived but deteriorated. Eleven such airfields were in Nebraska during the war. Today, McCook has a regional airport closer to town.

A friendly sign proclaimed: "Welcome to McCook—the GO-TO city of southwest Nebraska!" And the town has long been a commercial center, besides the seat of Red Willow County. It was established in 1882 when rails arrived, with the location thought fitting for the nexus that the Chicago-Burlington and Quincy Railroad and the Lincoln Land Company—which developed a lot of Nebraska—wanted halfway between Denver and Omaha. Besides carrying freight, the present rails are shared by Amtrak. The community's namesake is Union army general Alexander McDowell McCook, who also fought in conflicts with Native tribes. Its present population was about 7,700, and it has some noteworthy history.

From 1890 to 1892, a fascinating man named Charles Jesse Jones—otherwise known as Buffalo Jones—had the largest surviving bison herd in the world northeast of McCook as part of his efforts to save the noble mammal from extinction. Like his contemporary, Buffalo Bill, he'd been a buffalo hunter earlier, and his life had other similarities to Cody's. I'll have more to say about Jones later. McCook was also home to three governors of Nebraska. But the town's favorite son is George W. Norris, who served forty years in the U.S. Congress from 1903 to 1943 as a representative and senator, and was a very highly regarded legislator. Norris lived in McCook from 1899 to 1944, and his restored home on namesake Norris Ave. is now a museum and a state historic site. Another significant residence in town is the Harvey P. Sutton House, which was designed by Frank Lloyd Wright in 1905-1907 and is now on the National Register of Historic Places. McCook has the distinction of having had the first two-year junior college in the state that was established in 1926 and first operated on the second floor of a YMCA. Decades later, in 1981, the reputable Heritage Hills Golf Course was opened in the west end of town. McCook also has an annual hot air balloon festival in August that draws pilots, balloons, and crowds from numerous states. Near the downtown area is the Museum of the High Plains next to a Carnegie Library built in 1907.

I was drawn to another Runza restaurant near some other chain places I passed and ordered another variety of their "world famous" sandwiches, which I liked as much as the one I had in North Platte. I also bought a cinnamon roll that the business is known for to have with my next breakfast.

Arriving at a junction with U.S. Highways 6 and 34, both joined 83 briefly through a nice, old downtown area. Then 83 did a ninety-degree turn south, and the other old two-laners continued together.

U.S. 6 has been given the appellation Grand Army of the Republic Highway, which commemorates an old organization of Union Civil War veterans that lasted until 1956 when its last member, Albert Henry Woolson, died at the age of 106. He was also the last confirmed Civil War veteran on either side to die, which occurred when I was six years old. It amazes me to think that in my earliest years there were still a few Civil War veterans alive.

U.S. 6 is a 1926 original that, from 1936 to 1964, was the nation's longest highway when it stretched from Provincetown, Massachusetts on Cape Cod, to Long Beach, California. When its western end was shortened to Bishop, California, it became second in length to U.S. 20 and now runs 3,198 miles (5,147 km) through fourteen states. U.S. 34—another original east-west highway—is much shorter at 1,122 miles (1,806 km) between Berwyn, Illinois and Granby, Colorado, through four states.

A grain elevator was in view, and I drove over tracks that are part of the huge BNSF rail network and Amtrak. Just past the city limits of McCook, I crossed a bridge over the Republican River—a stream with headwaters on the High Plains of northeastern Colorado, which flows eastward across a good part of southern Nebraska and close to the Kansas border for some distance. It was named Republican not after the political party with a big majority in this part of the country, but rather for a group of Pawnees who once had a village on the river and were known to early French traders as "the republicans"—perhaps because of how they governed themselves. South of McCook was the last stretch of Nebraska, where I was back in a lot of open space with little islands of trees and picturesque hay bales that I always find appealing.

I entered an area with vast fields of milo, which I'd seen before. This corn-like crop, which is a variety of sorghum, does much better than corn in hot, dry conditions and is commonly grown on the Great Plains. It's an ancient crop that originated in Africa some 4,000 years ago, was introduced to Asia, and eventually the Americas. Though it's grown for human consumption in much of the world, it's mainly a livestock feed in the U.S.—a practice I'm sure proponents of vegetarianism would like to change. I came to a big sea of milo, which was photogenic enough for me to stop and snap my camera. The crop had tawny stalks similar to corn in the autumn, and the cone-like heads of the plants were a bronze that stretched to the horizon.

It wasn't long before the landscape changed again as the road approached a ridge coated with trees. I entered Kansas without realizing it because I must have been distracted enough to miss a sign at the state line. The highway crossed Beaver Creek and railroad tracks, and on the west side of the road was a tiny, unincorporated community of about thirty-five people called Cedar Bluffs, which once had up to ten times that population and a post office, train depot, and about twenty businesses. Now there was only a grain company. The road wound uphill through an area with a heavy growth of cedars, and some gullies also came into view in rolling grassy areas more to the east. In the west, a bright sun was descending and radiating golden shades of light, and I cruised back into a more expansive landscape with large fields of corn and rows of windbreaker trees. Ahead on the east side was a huge stockyard with plenty of black and brown cattle, which made an impression on my olfactory sense.

Soon the water tower of Oberlin—the first good-sized town in Kansas—came into view, with its name visible on the tower. I passed a municipal airport on the way in, and 83 intersected with east-west U.S. 36 in town—another original federal highway about 1,414 miles (2,276 km) long that extends from Uhrichsville, Ohio to Rocky Mountain National Park in Colorado, covering six states. About a hundred miles east of here and close to 36 is the geographical center of the lower-forty-eight states near Lebanon, Kansas.

I saw two motels I intended to check out, but first followed a sign for a business district by a nice stone structure with the name "Oberlin" within a white circular design. Just down the street, I stopped at a statue monument with the name "Pioneer Family" on its pedestal, and above were back-to-back figures of a man, woman, and boy and girl with a nineteenth-century appearance. These were carved from local limestone by Kansas artist, Pete Felton Jr., to commemorate the area's pioneer heritage, and I suppose some of Oberlin's present residents are descended from pioneers and homesteaders of the latter part of the 1800s like in other Plains towns, where the roots put down by early settlers have grown deeper.

Soon, Wander was rumbling over a red brick surface, and I immediately found the town very attractive, with quaint brick buildings and storefronts that matched the colorful downtown streets; and the fading daylight had a special effect on the structures.

I drove back to the Frontier Motel on U.S. 36 and talked to a short, young guy in the office who looked Asian Indian—or true Indian, compared to the centuries-old misnomer that Native Americans have been subjected to. The appetizing smell of some kind of curry cooking in another area seemed to confirm his ethnicity, and I was aware of the many enterprising Indian families involved in the U.S. motel business for years—apparently even in small towns along the Road to Nowhere. At my request, the guy showed me a room for a $55 rate that looked nice, with a double bed, refrigerator, and microwave, and I took it without hesitation. He confirmed he was from India and spoke good, though heavily-accented English.

"So how did you wind up in Oberlin?" I inquired.

"My brother had bought another motel not too far from here."

"So, what led your brother there?"

"He found out it was for sale, and I followed him there."

The huge environmental and cultural differences between India and Kansas prompted me to ask: "So how do you like living here?"

He shrugged and replied: "It's nice, but very quiet and boring."

To possibly relieve a little of his boredom, I mentioned my border-to-border trip, and he seemed interested and had some knowledge about how long 83 is.

"I really like the people I've met along the highway so far," I said. "Most seem very nice, and I also like a lot of the small towns I've been through, like Oberlin. But if I lived in one, I think I'd find it too quiet too, since I live in northern Colorado now, where there's a lot more happening; and I originally lived in a very crowded part of New Jersey that's close to New York City. When you live in a place like this you must have to drive a good distance for some things."

"I go to Hays, where my brother's motel is for some things, and to Salina, which is further, but bigger and about a three-hour-drive."

"If this town is quiet and boring, at least it must be very safe." And he agreed. "But then there's the tornado danger," I added.

"Yes. About four years ago, before we owned this place, there was a big tornado warning in town, and I heard some people sheltered here. But it hit another town more."

"One of the reasons I'm making this trip this time of year is because there's less tornado danger than in the spring and summer."

We made introductions before our conversation ended, and his name was Raj. He also mentioned renting to quite a few hunters in season.

I settled in my room and showered before I walked out for a Friday night on the small town. My first stop was a Pizza Hut to find out how much longer it was open—a franchise I'd noticed in a lot of small towns in the region, which happens to be one of the largest food chain businesses in the world, with a presence on every continent except Antarctica. This pizza empire actually had humble origins in Kansas, where its first business opened in a small building in Wichita in 1958. It was run by two brothers, Dan and Frank Carney, who were Wichita State University students.

In the parking lot, a fairly young woman in an SUV told me the place was closing now. Then a little conversation started after I asked if she lived in Oberlin.

"I've been here three years and moved from near Greeley, Colorado."—which isn't far from Fort Collins.

"Really! I'm from Fort Collins. So, what brought you here?"

"My husband has family in town."

"Do you like living here?"

"It's OK, but there's a lot of small-town bullshit."

I thought she was probably referring to things like gossip. Then she asked why I was here, and I told her about my 83 odyssey.

"So why do you want to do that?" I was asked again.

"I guess because I'm a little crazy," I half joked. "But I'm also doing it for an adventure and because I love traveling old two-lane roads and visiting small towns. I also love the plains, even if I wouldn't want to live on them."

"I like living in the middle of nowhere," she said, "but I really miss the mountains."

So, she seemed to have some mixed feelings about where she wound up because of spousal influence—one of the consequences of marriage.

"Nice chatting with you," I concluded our little conversation with.

"Enjoy your adventure and be safe," she replied.

The downtown was very quiet, even on a Friday night, and I noticed red brick pavement also on side streets. A newer building with the name Sunflower on a brick facade caught my attention, which had a bowling alley and movie theater. My curiosity led me inside, and I saw that the alley had six lanes where some kids and teens were playing. I talked a bit to a woman who looked like she was with the kids, and she told me the place opened about three years ago and was the largest bowling alley in the area.

"One closed in another town," she said, "but another alley may reopen."

"I guess this is one of the hot spots of Oberlin."

She smiled a little and nodded.

"Have a good evening," I said.

I thought back to the old, closed four-lane alley I'd seen back in Selby, South Dakota, but bowling apparently lives on in some small Plains towns, especially for minors who can't go to bars. The theater next door was also very modest in size, with one screen with 3D capability. A present show and a coming one were posted.

I ambled down the main street, hoping to find another "hotspot," and came to a bar called the Re-Load in an older brick building with a sign that had a logo with two guns and the words: "Beer, Pizza, sandwiches, video games." Outside, it looked like the kind of place where you'd expect enough locals to be celebrating Friday night. Inside, it was spacious with high ceilings and nice wooden floors, but the only people were two women who worked there and were getting ready to close before 10 p.m. If there was any weekend spirit, it must have been earlier. There was the smell of cleaning fluid, and I asked one of the ladies if I could still get a beer, and she said, "Yes." So, I sat down at a squarish bar and chose a Coors Light over a Bud Light, and beer was really the only libation that was served. They seemed to have a good pub grub menu I was too late for.

"So, where is everybody on a Friday night?" I asked the young woman who served me.

"I don't know. Maybe they're at the American Legion club. It's open till 2:00 a.m. We close when we're not busy."

"So, do you live in Oberlin?"

"Yes."

"Have you always lived here?"

"Most of my life."

"I guess you get used to the slow pace here."

"Yes."

"I'm from Fort Collins, Colorado, which is so different. For one thing, I've lost track of all the bars there." Which made her laugh a little. Then I mentioned my journey down 83 to possibly arouse more of her interest.

"Why are you doing that?" I heard again.

"For the adventure," I replied again. I even sleep in my car a lot. It saves me a lot of money since motels are expensive, and even campgrounds can be a little pricey. It's good to have more to spend on necessities like food and gas—and beer, I joked.

"Where are you staying tonight?"

"I'm treating myself to a real bed at the Frontier Motel. Their rates aren't bad." Then I brought up one of my observations. "For over two weeks, I've traveled through a lot of small towns like Oberlin, and a lot smaller, and I've talked to some people in them who left and came back because they missed the slower pace. Has that happened much here?"

"There've been some kids here who couldn't wait to get out of this town after high school, who left and also came back. Sometimes in just a few years. They found out it's a whole different world out there."

"So do you like it enough here to want to stay?"

"It works for me," was her short, firm answer.

"Do you make some pretty long trips for necessities that aren't available locally?"

"I do go to Hays and sometimes Salina, but don't make special trips. I also visit someone out there. I've been to the Menards in North Platte, and Kearney, Nebraska is another shopping destination; but I haven't been there much."

"I suppose when you live in a small town that's pretty isolated where less is available, you might come to need less."

But she really didn't respond. The other woman, who could have joined the conversation, still said nothing and had a less friendly vibe. To keep it going, I asked the woman at the bar what the population of

Oberlin was, and to my surprise she didn't know, and neither did the other woman who she asked.

"We don't count our population here," the one who I'd been talking to jested.

The conversation lulled, and I noticed a sign on the wall near the bar with an old, serious message: "We reserve the right to refuse service to anyone." I presumed that in this age when racial discrimination is illegal, it applied to other things like someone who was intoxicated or obnoxious.

When I finished my beer, I asked the same woman where the American Legion place was. She said it was very close, then led me out the back and pointed in the direction. I thanked her and walked the short distance to it, where it seemed I'd found the liveliest spot in Oberlin that Friday night, even if it wasn't exactly jumping. Some men were at the bar—one with a bold neck tattoo—and a few others at a table. A mixed-aged group of women were at another table, and some others sat in an area that had dart boards. Two TVs were on with the baseball playoffs, which the guys at the bar seemed to be engrossed in. I also noticed an Internet Jukebox that could play thousands of songs but was silent, supposedly because the high stakes ball game was on, which probably had greater interest because a regional team—the Kansas City Royals—were playing against the Baltimore Orioles. I was indifferent to the game, however, and would have preferred music.

I sat at the bar also tended by a young woman, and went for a Michelob Amber Bock on tap, which was served in a good-sized mug. This place also served liquor that probably drew some customers from the beer-only Re Load. Soon the two ladies from the latter place came in and sat nearby at the bar without acknowledging me, which didn't inspire me to greet them. After they both got their drinks, they moved to the table behind me and joined the other women there, who they obviously knew. To try and make some more contact with the locals, I asked an older woman standing by the bar close to me and holding a beer, "So how are you tonight?" but got no real response. Soon, she sat next to me when an older guy wearing a cowboy hat arrived, who she'd apparently been waiting for. The bartender seemed pleasant, and I tried conversing a little with her when she didn't look too busy.

I mentioned my just passing through on a long trip down 83, but she didn't ask why I was doing that or any other questions. Maybe she was still too busy to show much interest in a new face. At an appropriate moment I asked her if the place ever had live music.

"Sometimes we have a DJ," she answered.

"How about Karaoke?"

"We have it occasionally,"

If that were the entertainment tonight, I might have had enough nerve after a couple of beers to perform for an audience of strangers, whether they liked it or not. The bartender became distracted by her mobile phone during some short down time, and the group of young women at the table behind me looked captivated by their own devices even while together—another example of what I've come to regard as *Homo gadgetus*—that next step in human evolution with addiction to gadgetry, which pervades small towns in Kansas too.

If not the friendliest bar I visited while on the road, the place did have a comfortable atmosphere and unpretentious appearance you'd expect in an American Legion club, with fixtures like an American flag and an image of the famous Iwo-Jima flag-raising on a wall, with the caption: "God Bless Our Soldiers." Behind the bar was a humorous message: "Every man should marry. Happiness isn't the only thing in the world."

After finishing my beer, I was ready to eat something, but it was too late for any open eateries in this kind of town. I snacked on some peanuts I carried in my backpack and left the bar for the motel, where I could have some food stored in the car.

The night air was very chilly on the walk back, and plenty of stars were out. The charming downtown was illuminated by globe lights along the main street near the old storefronts. I also saw a Methodist church and later found out there were ten churches in Oberlin, which must greatly outnumber the bars. I sauntered on a wide sidewalk under a metal canopy that each side of the street had. There was no one else around, but the quiet was broken by the sounds of continuous oldies music playing from speakers, which was interesting. When the classic hit, "Cara Mia," started playing with the sound of Jay Black's great tenor voice, I paused at a bench and was loosened up enough after a couple of beers to sing along in a lower range—like

Karaoke without an audience—which brought a little vitality to the deserted streets.

Back in the motel room, I heated the contents of a can of minestrone soup in the microwave and consumed it with some whole grain bread, followed by more peanuts—soup to nuts. With enough hunger satisfied, I sat at a small desk and got back to my journal, then read for a while before I was tired enough to call it a night. It felt great to be under warm covers in a bed again, and sleep came easily that night in Oberlin.

DAY 19

Monument Rocks, and the smell of money

Before leaving the motel, I talked to Raj again, met his parents, and found out the motel was a real family business where they all worked on the upkeep. I also learned that this industrious Indian immigrant family had owned the place for a year and had lived in Dallas for two and a half years previously. They hailed from the city of Surat in India, which was over four hours from Mumbai. Raj mentioned his brother's motel in Hays again and said they planned to stay in Oberlin for about two more years. "Then, we'll see," he added.

"Good-bye and good luck," I said as I left the office and wondered if they'd get more accustomed to American small-town life after living in a big city in India and Dallas. Again, there was the pungent aroma of Indian cooking.

It was a sparkling autumn day with a brisk fifty-two degrees. I stopped at a liquor store for some beer and ice and recognized a mature-looking woman working there as the one who didn't respond to a friendly question I'd asked the night before at the American Legion club. But she was friendlier now and mentioned seeing me there. "I guess it's easy to remember new faces around here," I said. And in a little conversation that ensued, she told me she'd been in Oberlin three years and came from Sheridan, Wyoming.

"I came to help a close friend living here who had health problems and decided to stay longer. The people in Oberlin are awesome."

That was a significant statement, and she didn't mention anything about "small town bullshit" like the woman the evening before. So, I heard another reason someone had moved here.

The town's history goes back to the early 1870s when settlers arrived, and an early community was named Westfield. In 1878 the name was changed to Oberlin after Oberlin, Ohio, and a town was platted, and a post office opened. The Burlington and Missouri River Railroad arrived in 1885, and Oberlin became incorporated. Passenger service continued until the 1950s, and I'd seen tracks by a grain elevator near the downtown where the station had been, which was moved to a local museum's grounds in 1985. In 1980, the town had a population close to 2,400, which slowly declined to 1,788 in the 2010 census—so someone counts its numbers, despite what the bar lady said. Nevertheless, Oberlin is the most populous town in Decatur County and the county seat. It's located on a meandering tributary of the Republican River called Sappa Creek, and there's a city-owned park called Sappa Park a couple miles east of town that was originally a state park. A lake created by the Works Progress Administration in the 1930s was there that became degraded by silt build up, which was drained and developed into wetlands. Today, the park has Nature trails, camping, a disc golf course and other facilities, with a nine-hole golf course adjacent to it. An annual event that draws crowds to Oberlin is the long-running Home-owned Carnival the first week in August at the Decatur County Fairgrounds during the annual county fair.

I took another walk around the charming downtown area for a good look in the bright daylight, and speakers were still playing oldies continuously along South Penn Avenue from a local radio station. The quaint buildings with some interesting shops and wide, red brick streets seemed to glow in the autumn sun.

I came to the Decatur County Last Indian Raid Museum, which appealed to me as a history buff. It was about to close for an hour, though, and I picked up some flyers and thought of returning. The museum has fifteen historic structures, including the local train depot that had been moved. Some of the others were moved from elsewhere in the county. There are also plenty of artifacts related to the area's pioneer heritage. But a lot is focused on an exhibit on what's considered the last Indian raid in Kansas, which occurred on September 29, 1878, near Oberlin when the town was getting started. That's when nineteen early settlers were killed by a band of Northern Cheyenne, who were being pursued by numerically superior U.S. Army forces determined to return them to a reservation in the Indian Territory of Oklahoma, which they'd fled because of deplorable conditions. There's a memorial near Oberlin to the victims of the local raid in the cemetery where they're buried, and the tragedy is also commemorated less somberly each early October with Mini-Sappa Days at the museum, which includes some festivities. Apparently, it took place the weekend before my visit.

The long flight of the over 300 Northern Cheyenne men, women, and children—led by Chiefs Dull Knife and Little Wolf—from their hated reservation in Oklahoma with the purpose of reaching their old homeland on the northern plains has been called the Northern Cheyenne Exodus. It was the subject of a 1950s best-selling book, *Cheyenne Autumn*, by Mari Sandoz, which inspired a movie with the same name with a cast of old stars that was directed by John Ford. The Cheyenne were amazingly elusive in their flight. But their killing of innocent settlers near Oberlin, not hostile to them, left a black mark on an otherwise heroic story—raising questions about what motivated the killings. One explanation is a rage that built up among the Natives from their mistreatment by the U.S. authorities that became directed toward the settlers. It seems that in the Indian Wars, like in all wars, there were some atrocities on both sides. Many Northern Cheyenne were also killed before the long episode ended. However, there was a positive outcome for the survivors who finally surrendered to the U.S. Army further north, who were assigned to their own reservation in southeastern Montana and not forced to return to the alien and dreadful one in Oklahoma.

I walked further down South Penn Avenue and heard more rumbling traffic over the main street's brick surfaces. I paused and admired the largely red brick Decatur County Courthouse with six white classical columns, and on the return, I encountered a small group of older people in a gazebo, where a sign read:

PRAYING THE ROSARY FOR AMERICA. PLEASE JOIN US!
As human efforts fail to solve America's key problems, we turn to God, through His Holy Mother, asking His urgent help.

The sign had a small image of the Holy Mother, and my mind flashed way back to my Roman Catholic school days when I also uttered the repetitions of the rosary. But that now seemed like a distant past life, and I had evolved very different beliefs. Seeing this little public display of faith in the downtown area was a reminder of the religious conservatism that Kansas is known for, and Oberlin is supposed to have ten churches.

I decided to skip the museum when it reopened, knowing I'd probably dally there; and I didn't want to spend too much time in Oberlin, as nice a town as it is. As I drove off, a little small-town friendliness was expressed by a nice-looking woman who waved to me from the sidewalk as Wander's wheels rumbled on the bricks.

I stopped at Rayes Grocery for a few items—a good-sized store where I got another smile from an older woman I briefly glanced at. A very world-traveled friend of mine once told me that in some cultures it's not considered polite to smile at strangers, which probably applies to enough places in the U.S. too. But apparently not in this part of Kansas.

Before leaving town, I thought I better check my emails again, and I found the local library and logged on to a computer. I deleted much of the usual junk from the Electronic Plague, sorted the worthwhile messages and responded to a few, besides googling some places I'd been through. I also engaged in a short, quiet conversation with a very nice young lady seated nearby, who was a local high school senior. She told me she'd lived in Oberlin for a good part of her life and had moved there with her family from Arizona when her father got an administrative job in the Kansas prison system. She said she didn't like the winters there, not surprisingly, and didn't seem so happy about some other things. I typed her as one of the young people eager to leave the small town after high school for college or wherever, but perhaps to eventually return like some others I'd heard about.

My last stop in Oberlin was a Cenex station, where I ordered a tasty vegan burrito at a concession called the Green Chile Grill. As I pulled out of the lot, a truck with a big trailer load of square hay bales pulled in—no doubt cargo that was cultivated on the plains I was about to set out on again. When departing from one of the most attractive towns I'd seen along 83, I saw another residential area with nice homes of different styles and ages along pleasantly shaded streets.

I was soon back in wide spaces with crops and colors quite typical of Kansas. The state's name comes from the Kansa tribe—their name meaning "the people of the south wind." They were also known as the Kanza or Kaw, which by the mid-eighteenth century had become a dominant tribe in the territory that became Kansas. The Kansa spoke a Siouan (related to the Sioux) language, and today their descendants have a tribal jurisdictional area in Oklahoma that grants some additional authority to tribal courts. Kansas was the home of many tribes historically, and the one the state was named after was forced to live in neighboring Oklahoma in 1872.

The highway had wider, paved shoulders on the next stretch. I passed plowed areas and bright green fields of grassy-looking winter wheat that's planted before the winter and harvested the following summer. Brown milo and green alfalfa were also part of the cultivated landscape, and occasional black Angus grazed in open areas with scattered hardwood trees. I crossed Prairie Dog Creek—one of numerous meandering creeks in northwestern Kansas. Farmlands alternated with rangelands with more grazing cattle.

At the intersection of KS 383, U.S. 83 headed southwestward for some distance, running close to rails on the west side of the road, and the landscape had a flatter appearance. I soon entered the little town of Selden that was established in 1888 and named for one of its founders, Selden G. Hopkins. Its most recent census figure of 219 is a decline from a population high of 438 in 1950. Nevertheless, I read about a strong sense of community here that's kept the place viable with basic amenities through volunteer efforts and monetary contributions. It has a Main Street and some businesses that include a small motel and fitness center. There's also an elementary school, volunteer-run library, Catholic and Methodist churches, and four bars that I saw listed—so perhaps twice as much drinking as worshiping.

I stopped at the town's small city park along the railroad tracks and was again amused by the word "city" in connection to a community this size. I sat at a table and snacked on some nuts and fruit while prairie breezes stirred the air. A big grain elevator was near the tracks. Sadly, there was quite a bit of litter around the park, and perhaps the culprits were more travelers than locals. Again, I did a little voluntary cleanup that left one corner of Selden looking a little better.

Further ahead, the elevator and water tower of Rexford were in view. This town dates to 1887—close to Selden—and lies along the same tracks. The name Rexford commemorates a member of the Rexford family who died in a fire that destroyed the family home of these early settlers. A more amusing tidbit about the town from Wikipedia is that in 1923, a three-year-old boy was elected mayor and held office for five months before his incompetence was finally realized. Even if the child was an absolute prodigy or no one else wanted the job, it's hard to imagine such a bizarre thing happening. Rexford's population was 232 in the last tally—about the same as it was in 1920, with some fluctuations through the decades. Set off from where 83 turned and shot due south again, there was once a town called Gem with about 200 people and some basic businesses. But it's now considered a ghost town on a website I checked out.

The landscape leveled even more and was close to the flat and monotonous stereotype of the Plains. But this flatness, with huge, colorful croplands, big sky and far horizons, still had a visual appeal.

Soon, 83 intersected with U.S. 24—another original east-west U.S. highway that courses 1,540 miles (2,478 km) between Independence Township, Michigan, and Minturn, Colorado, through seven states. I again thought of how "border to border" U.S. 83 crosses paths with all the long east-west roads in the country, regardless of their status.

Just past U.S. 24, I crossed the North Fork Solomon River and further on the South Fork. Both of these sluggish prairie streams flow completely in Kansas before they join to form the Solomon River.

The junction with I-70—an east-west interstate that's the fifth longest in the country—was now ahead as I approached the town of Oakley, and I stopped for gas at a Phillips 66 station. Oakley is the seat of Logan County, with a recent population of 2,045 that's been quite stable through the years. Settlement started in the 1870s, and the town was founded in 1884—close to the development of other communities in the area. The name Oakley is said to have come from the middle name of the mother of one of the town's founders. An east-west branch of what was originally the Kansas Pacific Railway that's long been part of Union Pacific's vast network runs through town, and the railroad was very significant in early settlement here too.

Highway-wise, Oakley is a crossroads town where 83 also connects with U.S. 40. But it's even more of a cowtown because its outskirts include the big nationally recognized Pioneer Feedyard that provides about 1.3 million pounds of feed daily to 53,000 head of cattle, which greatly outnumber the humans in Oakley.

U.S. 83 ran along the west side of town, where I had another encounter with Buffalo Bill. This time it was the Buffalo Bill Cultural Center, which is a large, modern travel information center with a gift shop and event facilities. But "above all" was a large, striking sculpture on a hill of Cody on horseback shooting a bison at close range. The impressive work is sixteen feet high and was sculpted from 9,000 pounds of bronze by Kansas artist, Charlie Norton, and dedicated in May 2004. It has the distinction of being voted one of the 8 Wonders of Kansas Art and is historically accurate down to the saddle and type of Cody's firearm. The Buffalo Bill connection here is that about ten miles west of Oakley is where the legendary character claimed in his 1879 autobiography to have won a day-long bison shooting contest with William (another Bill) Comstock in 1868 to determine which of them deserved to be called Buffalo Bill. Cody was a contract buffalo hunter for feeding crews constructing the Kansas-Pacific Railway, and Comstock hunted to provide meat for soldiers at Fort Wallace. Cody's claim was sixty-nine kills for himself and forty-six for his opponent. But there are no conclusive confirmations of the contest, and Cody was great at self-promotion.

Road Trip USA mentions the Fick Fossil Museum in Oakley in this fossil-rich state, which sounded interesting, but I was anxious to move on and see the Monument Rocks not far south, where abundant fossils have been discovered. U.S. 83 came to the intersection with U.S. 40 and joined it briefly along the southern edge of Oakley before continuing a straight course south. East-west 40 is also a 1926 original that currently stretches 2,286 miles (3,678 km) and connects Atlantic City, New Jersey, to Silver Summit, Utah, outside Salt Lake City, across twelve states. It's been called the Main Street of America because of its central route through most of the country, and it once reached all the way to San Francisco. Now it runs concurrently with or parallel to a number of interstates for long distances, such as I-70, which it joins just east of Oakley and crosses most of Kansas.

South of Oakley, 83 passed the town's municipal airport, which I was finding a lot of the larger towns along the highway have. It was back into more flat croplands with milo and other cultivations, and later a transition to rangeland strewn with yucca that looked more Western. I came to an oil extraction area with scattered, see-sawing pump jacks and storage tanks and a sign with the name of a Kansas oil company.

Ahead was a prominent sign for a turnoff for Monument Rocks, also called the Chalk Pyramids. This geological phenomenon is less than ten miles east of 83 and seemed worth a short side trip. The turnoff road was paved at first but had long streaks of hard, bumpy dirt stuck to it. I passed more pump jacks and tanks, a range with tall, wild grasses, and a verdant cropland. Wander's movement stirred lots of meadowlarks from the grasses that darted ahead, and I was soon in an area that started to feel remote, despite the proximity to the highway. There was still no sight of the rocks, and I started thinking that this would be an awful place to break down or get stuck, not seeing another soul around and in a region where my cell phone didn't have coverage.

I arrived in an area with tawny grasses and yucca where the road came to a T, and a sign stated two miles to the rocks. I turned right on a dirt road, and all I still saw were far and largely empty horizons that made everything seem more remote. A raptor hovered to the east over tall grasses in the gilded light of late day, which made me stop and grab my binoculars. I identified it as a Swainson's hawk, and as it receded it added to a sense of the primeval on these plains.

After crossing a grated cattle guard, the road got rougher. But the surface soon improved and led to my first view of a rock "monument" to the east—a rather small, light-colored protrusion in the landscape that was just a preview. Soon, other similar-colored formations appeared in different shapes and sizes scattered around the terrain. Some groups had a resemblance to ruins of ancient buildings. I stepped out with my camera and binoculars and observed the unusual forms that included buttes, arches, and sedimentary layers, often dark-colored on top. I'd certainly seen more spectacular and colorful formations elsewhere in the West, but what was unique about this place was how the rocky monoliths rose from the grassy plains as if they'd been placed there.

It was all the work of Mother Nature, however, which began about eighty million years ago during the late Cretaceous Period—and late in the long era of the dinosaurs—back when what's now a prairie sea was the seafloor of the expansive Western Interior Seaway that divided North America. The formations are composed of chalk—a soft limestone formed from ancient underwater deposits that became exposed and eroded over time. As a result, the layers contain an abundance of fossils from marine creatures that once inhabited the relatively shallow seaway. These include sharks and swimming reptiles like mosasaurs and plesiosaurs. However, fossil hunting is prohibited here, as is climbing the rocks which rise to seventy feet. In 1968, Monument Rocks became the first National Natural landmark designated by the U.S. Department of the Interior and was later named one of the 8 Wonders of Kansas. The spectacle is on private rangelands, though, often bordered by barbed wire; but the owners have allowed public access.

No other humans appeared on the scene, and I felt I was in the most remote place on the journey so far. The late daylight was as glowing as it had been in the Nebraska Sandhills, creating golden shades on the rocks and other features of the landscape. I drove further, then stopped again to gaze at "monuments" to the south, smaller ones near the road, and a more isolated rounded formation toward the east. To the north was a long mesa-like formation. I reflected on the forces of geological evolution that had transformed the watery sea of eons past to the prairie sea of the present in this now very landlocked region.

A meditative moment was distracted by the sweet song of a western meadowlark, and as the sun sank lower, I thought I'd better get back to the highway since I'd wildly imagined what it might be like getting stranded here in the dark. On the drive out, a pickup truck appeared, kicking up dust in the distance. Then came some four-legged company with a group of cattle moping along the road. The low sun was blinding as I drove toward it, followed by a stunning sunset over a sprawling, flat horizon. The side trip to Monument Rocks was absolutely worth it.

U.S. 83 crossed the Smoky Hill River—another stream with a source on the High Plains of eastern Colorado that flows 575 miles eastward across much of Kansas. Its connection with the Kansas River, which flows into the Missouri, makes the Smoky Hill another tributary in the gigantic Missouri-Mississippi watershed that sprawls over the continent. Though presently a shallow and not very wide river in western Kansas, the Smoky Hill was once a powerful, erosive force that over thousands of years shaped a lot of the chalk formations in the region known as the Kansas Badlands, including Monument Rocks. Its name came from the Smoky Hills of north-central Kansas that it flows through, which got its name from a misty or smoky appearance that early westbound travelers saw.

I passed the Keystone Gallery, located in one of the remaining native limestone buildings in this part of Logan County. It's a gift shop–fossil museum–art gallery that I would have checked out if I hadn't arrived at another interesting place when it was closed.

I did stop just ahead in the fading light at a kiosk with information on local history and learned about the Smoky Hill Trail that coursed near the river and became "...one of the nation's most important overland routes..." and "played a central role in America's expansion westward..."—which sounded like the Great Platte River Road in Nebraska. The main traffic began with the start of the Pike's Peak Gold Rush to Colorado in 1858, and the Smoky Hill Trail extended from Atchison, Kansas, on the Missouri River to Denver. It was said to be the most direct, but also the most dangerous route across the Kansas plains toward the Rockies. Despite the dangers that included attacks by hostile Natives, pioneers bound for settlement in the West also traveled the trail. In 1865, it was used by the Butterfield Overland Dispatch for stage and freight service. Stage stations, settlements, and military forts were established along the trail. But the construction of the Kansas Pacific Railway pushed west in the region and was completed in 1870—a year after the first transcontinental railroad further north was—and it also replaced an old trail.

A panel mentioned the indigenous peoples that had inhabited the Smoky Hill River Valley for centuries before the arrival of prospectors and settlers—tribes like the Cheyenne, Arapaho, Kiowa, Prairie Apache, and Sioux, who were all drawn by the vast bison hunting grounds. The valley was also an ancient trade route for the tribes.

Driving off in the dusky remnant of light, there appeared a long, dark form on the western horizon that resembled mountains. But I knew it had to be a cloud formation and not the Rockies at this distance. Nevertheless, I knew that the eastern plains of Colorado lie beyond that horizon, and the mountains further beyond. It reminded me of an elderly guy I'd met in Fort Collins who grew up further east on a farm in Iowa, who told me that as a child he would imagine similar distant cloud formations to be the Rockies. I guess some Plains people long to see mountains, which must be why many of them migrate to places like Colorado, like the old Iowa farm boy I knew.

I later regretted I didn't take the turnoff for Lake Scott State Park and camp there, which I'd read is a scenic place with a spring-fed lake, rugged canyon terrain, an oasis of trees, and historical sites. But I was distracted by Scott City being my day's destination and thoughts of many other places ahead to visit.

I did stop up the road at a state historical sign about El Cuartelejo (The Barracks in Spanish) and learned about a group of Taos Pueblo Natives who left their homeland in New Mexico in 1664 to escape the Spanish colonial power and settled in this part of Kansas. Here they lived peacefully with the Prairie Apache, hunting and raising crops with irrigation into the 1680s. But a Spanish military expedition eventually arrived and forced them back to their old territory. Then, in 1696, another group of Pueblos, known as the Picuris, also fled from New Mexico and arrived in the same area and joined the Apache. However, this group was also coerced to return by the Spaniards in 1706. I wondered why the colonizers couldn't just accept some Native people wanting to live freely in another region, but I suppose they had a domination mindset. The Pueblo groups left a multi-room pueblo ("village" in Spanish) structure of rock and adobe that's the trademark of their culture, and its ruins are in Lake Scott State Park. What's really significant is that no other Pueblo sites have been found this far north and east. This one was discovered in 1898, and the foundation was rebuilt in 1970. El Cuartelejo is on the National Register of Historic Places and is also a National Historic Landmark.

Darkness descended on the plains, and Scott City appeared as a string of lights. As I drove closer, my nostrils picked up the strong smell of a livestock feedlot. In town, I saw quite a few businesses that included a John Deere dealership. The feedlot smell persisted, which I didn't envy the locals for having to live with, though perhaps many had gotten desensitized. I stopped at a convenience store and asked a young woman inside if she knew a safe and legal place in town to park overnight, and she told me there was a city park right up the road and a truck stop just past it.

I checked out the park, where a sign about video surveillance discouraged me, so I moved on to the truck stop. There was another convenience store there that was open twenty-four hours, and quite a few trucks were parked in the back area. I saw a space near a parked pickup and a propane tank that was away from the trucks and not too close to the store, so I pulled in and went into the store for permission to stay here.

"Should be OK," a female employee said, "as long as I can get my pickup out."

"Thanks," I replied, then bought two small packs of shelled sunflower seeds to give the store a little more business. Conveniently, there was a Pizza Hut and some other eateries around. But before heading to one of them, I quaffed a PBR in the car while jotting in my journal, then walked to the Pizza Hut in the state where the giant international chain had very humble beginnings.

There weren't many other customers inside, even on a Saturday evening. My server was a friendly and energetic young woman with red hair that looked very artificial. I ordered a small personal pizza along with the salad bar and chatted a little with the genial lady who I felt comfortable enough with to mention her obviously colored hair. She said she wished she was a real redhead, not surprisingly. When I left, I talked to another young lady at the checkout, who was also very pleasant and with similarly colored hair, which I didn't comment on, but assumed she also had a thing about being a redhead. I did mention traveling all of 83 and asked if she knew it ran all the way to the bottom of Texas.

"I didn't know that, and I've never been to Texas. The furthest I've traveled is Oregon, which was beautiful."

"You look very young, with plenty of years ahead to travel," I responded. Then I asked about living here with the pervasive livestock odor, and she said she "did get used to it," like I thought many locals probably had. Outside, I thought that the two upbeat, unnatural redheads might indicate this was a town with quite a bit of contentment despite the feedlot smell. And for those in the livestock business, it must be the smell of money.

I walked down Main St., which was also 83, and it was a bit of a distance to the real business area of the fairly good-sized downtown. In front of a bank was a life-size bronze statue of a cowboy carrying a calf, with the description "Cattleman's harvest"—a symbol of a big local industry. I noticed some signs in Spanish around that indicated a Hispanic presence. The town was quiet, except for a bar I saw on the east side of the street but didn't notice a name. I went in and found it to be quite lively, with a largely young crowd and some scattered older faces. A few people had Hispanic features, but overall the crowd looked Anglo. Not surprisingly, there were some cowboy hats in this cowtown bar. A few pool tables in the back were busy, and a CD jukebox was playing. Bud Light looked popular here too, and I also bought one to imbibe something light. At first, I had a sense of being looked at as a stranger. But it was probably just some self-consciousness. Whatever, I didn't get any bad vibes while I sipped my beer, but still left after one round.

Further up the street was a bar-restaurant that was quiet and might have been closed already. Saturday night in Scott City wasn't much more swinging than Friday night in Oberlin. And there were no oldies or other music playing in this downtown area. I walked down to a big grain elevator by railroad tracks where I thought plenty of livestock, besides grain, must have moved over the years. But I've learned that cattle or stock cars are almost completely a thing of the past in the U.S.—long replaced by trucking captive animals in special trailers over shorter distances to more local "processors."

Walking back, I wandered some side streets of a quiet residential area that had some nice neighborhoods with trees. On a street heading east, I saw Orion rising earlier than the last time, with winter drawing nearer. The air was very chilly, and I wore my ski hat and gloves along with some warm layers.

Back at the truck stop, the pickup near my space was gone, and some big rigs were still parked in the rear. Two soon pulled out and passed my space, and one of the trucks still parked was idling.

Once in my sleeping bag, I did a little soul-searching before dozing off—wondering why I was still doing things like sleeping in a small car on a chilly night at a truck stop near a propane tank—at age sixty-four—instead of staying in a motel or RV like I presumed most travelers my age would. It wasn't just to "sleep cheap," I thought, but also to be adventurous in a way more common with young people, who generally care less about comfort. Being able to deal with some discomfort from such vagabond ways seemed like one way of feeling young at heart, at least for me.

"Wander" near the U.S.-Canada border and the northern end of U.S. 83

Replica of Gol Stave Church in Oslo, Norway, Scandinavian Heritage Park, Minot, North Dakota

Sea of sunflower crops, south of Minot, North Dakota

Sculptures of Lewis and Clark meeting Mandan chief, Sheheke, Lewis and Clark Interpretive Center, Washburn, North Dakota

Reconstruction of Lewis and Clark's Fort Mandan, near Washburn, North Dakota

Herbert Wilson, MD, volunteer at North Dakota Heritage Center, Bismarck

Model Bakery, Linton, North Dakota

Lawrence Welk's birthplace, outside Strasburg, North Dakota

Grain elevator, Selby, South Dakota

Vacant four-lane bowling alley, Sandy Wellman and pet dog, Selby, South Dakota

South Dakota prairie, south of Agar

Water tower, Onida, South Dakota

Marv Paulson, volunteer at South Dakota Cultural Heritage Center, Pierre, South Dakota

South Dakota State Capitol building, Pierre

Missouri River, across from LaFramboise Island, Pierre, South Dakota

A memorable bar and name, Murdo, South Dakota

Elvis Presley's motorcycle, Pioneer Auto Show and Museum, Murdo, South Dakota

Author (on right) with Dave Geisler, owner of Pioneer Auto Show and Museum, Murdo, South Dakota

Niobrara River, Fort Niobrara National Wildlife Refuge, near Valentine, Nebraska

Wetlands in Valentine National Wildlife Refuge, Nebraska Sandhills

Nebraska National Forest, east of Thedford, Nebraska

Captive bison, once "King of the Plains," Cody Park, North Platte, Nebraska

Buffalo Bill's mansion, North Platte, Nebraska

Part of Bailey Yard from the Golden Spike Tower, the world's largest classification railroad yard, North Platte, Nebraska

Indian family owners of Frontier Motel, Oberlin, Kansas

Red brick main street, Oberlin, Kansas

Monument Rocks, south of Oakley, Kansas

Rainbow over
Liberal, Kansas

The Yellow Brick
Road, by Dorothy's
House and
the Land of Oz,
Liberal, Kansas

Entering the giant
Lone Star State,
top of Texas
Panhandle

Restored Tower Building, intersection of U.S. 83 and Historic Route 66, Shamrock, Texas

Mesquite country, north of Menard, Texas

Remains of Presidio de San Saba, Spanish colonial fort, outside Menard, Texas

Inside Burnham Brothers, the nation's oldest game-calling device store; owner's son, Steve Roberson, Menard, Texas

Old general store, Mountain Home, Texas

Rio Frio in Garner State Park, Texas Hill Country

Popeye statue, Crystal City, Texas

Rio Grande, Roma, Texas (Mexico on left side)

"Wander" before the U.S.-Mexico border, and the southern end of U.S. 83

Author at the Gulf of Mexico,
South Padre Island, Texas

DAY 20

More of Kansas, the Land of OZ, two state panhandles

In the morning I felt cold and grubby, but the feedlot odor had faded. I went to a Subway store across the street and ordered a breakfast sandwich of predictable quality.

At first, I was the only customer and talked to an outgoing young lady working there, who told me that she'd always lived in Scott City and liked the town, but lately had an "itch" to move and have her own Subway somewhere else.

"I'm sure your experience here would help a lot," I said.

"So, where are you from?" she inquired.

"Fort Collins, Colorado, and now I'm driving all of U.S. 83 down to the Mexican border."

"I've been to the Denver area but didn't make it to Rocky Mountain National Park like I wanted to."

"Well, make sure you get there. It's absolutely spectacular and not that far from here. So do you have deep roots in this area?"

"They do go back far."—like I supposed it was with many locals who probably had pioneer-homesteader ancestry.

"Does that smell from the feedlots bother you? It was pretty bad last night but seems to have lifted this morning."

"The feedlots close to town do smell worse at night and after rains. I'm used to it."

"So, it's not what's given you the itch to move now," I kidded.

"No," and she giggled.

A tall, thirty-something guy with a shaved head and dark goatee came in for a takeout. We exchanged greetings, and another little conversation started as I was sipping my green tea formula in a cup of hot water.

"I'm traveling the whole length of U.S. 83," I mentioned to him. "Do you know that it runs from the Canadian to the Mexican border?"

"Yes, I do, and that's quite a trip. So where are you from?"

"Fort Collins, Colorado."

"Really! I lived in Windsor awhile"—a nearby town—"and worked in Greeley. I loved the mountains but moved back here because of family."

"It's great to have the mountains and plains in Colorado."

"Yes, it is. Nice talking to you, and enjoy your trip."

When I got up to leave, the young lady wished me a "good, safe trip."

"Thanks, and I hope you get to have your own Subway where you want."

It felt good to have exchanged some positive energy in this one, but I was ready to leave Scott City, especially before the smell returned. The town's founder was a very dynamic woman named Maria DeGeer, who came from Chicago with one of her daughters and claimed a homestead and built a cabin in the center of Scott County in October 1884. Later they teamed with three men and formed a town development company. DeGeer was a leader in the Temperance movement and had the goal of founding a model community free of vices like drinking and gambling. Kansas had already become the first state to establish an alcohol prohibition with a referendum in 1880, which lasted until 1948. More settlers arrived in the new community, and it and the county were named after the illustrious nineteenth-century U.S. Army general Winfield Scott. In 1886, the town already had three weekly newspapers, four banks, and fifty other businesses, and it became Scott County's largest town and seat. Scott City's present population was 3,927, and it had been fairly stable since a peak of 4,154 in 1980.

As I was driving out of town, I glanced at a spherical, light blue water tower that proclaimed, "Scott City," and then watched it recede in my mirror as I continued southward. To the east was the town's municipal airport, and just to the south was an area marked White Woman Basin on my map. Here lies a large, low bottomland area of rich alluvial deposits, where the clear running White Woman Creek, with a source in eastern Colorado, flows and suddenly sinks to become a subterranean stream that's said to be heard running during the flood season. There are stories about the origin of the stream's name, including a legend about a White woman's ghost that haunts the area.

My map also showed a tiny, unincorporated settlement on the west side of the highway called Shallow Water, where the listed population that included the surrounding area was eighty-nine. The community once had a post office that was established in 1913 and closed in 1957, and a school that closed due to consolidation. I presumed its name had something to do with the nearby creek and bottomland area.

I entered totally flat agricultural land with milo and sprawling green winter wheat. There were also what looked like scattered corn stalks in a dry brown field, which I'd seen before and found out had grown from stray seeds. Then came a large field of cultivated sunflowers in "The Sunflower State," though Kansas was fifth nationally in production according to the latest statistics, with the Dakotas having a big lead. What Kansas really leads is in wheat, and it produces nearly one-fifth of all that's grown in the U.S., which is why it's also called "The Wheat State," and "Breadbasket of the World." About 20,000 of the state's approximately 60,000 farmers grow wheat, and Kansas is also in the lead in wheat storage and the amount of wheat and wheat products exported, which is half of the crops grown. Not surprisingly, agriculture is the largest industry and employer in Kansas, making up nineteen percent of the state's GDP and employing seventeen percent of its labor force.

The flat farmlands continued, occupied by some metallic storage structures and large irrigators necessary in this semi-arid region still west of the hundredth meridian. Small islands of trees punctuated the openness, and cedars planted as windbreakers lined the road. I passed another minuscule place along the nearby rails called Friend on my map, which is unincorporated and with no census figures. It was originally named McCue after a railroad official, then changed to Friend when another railroad company took over the line between Scott City and Garden City. It also had a post office that operated until 1992. There was a sign for the Friend Terminal, which probably referred to two oil tanks I saw along the tracks where some railroad cars were parked. A grain elevator was in view to the southwest, and there was also a sign and a turnoff for Friend "via county road."

I hadn't played the car radio or one of my CDs in a while because I was driving in a more observational and meditative mode. But closer to Garden City, I turned the radio on and picked up an FM station that was part of the National Public Radio network that I'm an avid listener of. At first, I was serenaded by some classical guitar music, then came the syndicated *Prairie Home Companion*, with host Garrison Keeler's wit working as usual.

Approaching Garden City, I was less than ten miles from the small community of Holcombe to the west, which was extremely obscure until a day in November 1959 when it became the location of a heinous crime that shocked the nation. That was when four members of the highly respected Clutter family, who had a very successful farm outside town, were savagely murdered by two young ex-convicts on parole from the Kansas State Penitentiary, named Richard Hickock and Perry Smith. The tragedy, of course, was brilliantly depicted in Truman Capote's best-selling "non-fiction novel," *In Cold Blood*, first published in 1965, and a great film with the same title in 1967.

The motive of the murderers was based on a false tip given to Hickock by a prison-mate and former employee of Herb Clutter, who believed that the farm owner had a safe in his home with a huge stash of cash. Hickock conceived a scheme to burglarize the house, steal the safe, and run off to Mexico to start a new life. He then enticed his former jail cellmate, Smith, to be his accomplice.

The pair drove across Kansas and found the Clutter home. They were armed and entered the unlocked house in the early morning hours of November 15, 1959, while the family slept. But they found no safe, which wasn't there, and woke up the family and had them bound and gagged. After a decision to leave no witnesses to their break-in, the two failed thieves became brutal murderers who blasted Herb and Bonnie Clutter and their teenage son and daughter, Kenyon and Nancy, in their heads with a shotgun. They made off with less than $50 in cash, a portable radio, and a pair of binoculars.

Six weeks later, they were caught and arrested in Las Vegas and extradited to the authorities in Kansas. Eventually they confessed to the murders, and their trial was the following March in the Finney County Courthouse in Garden City, where they were quickly convicted and faced the mandatory sentence of death by hanging. However, they spent five years on death row in the Kansas State Penitentiary during several appeals, and their execution didn't come until April 14, 1965.

The gallows are in the collection of the Kansas State Historical Society, and the old Clutter home is still privately owned and not open to the public. I would bet both still attract curiosity seekers. A community park in Holcombe is dedicated to the Clutter family, where a monument with a tribute to them was erected for the fiftieth anniversary of the murders in 2009. I wasn't inclined to make a short trip to Holcombe to see it. But having read *In Cold Blood* and seen the movie many years before, I was very reminded of a tragedy that had effects way beyond the small town.

Garden City's profile included a grain elevator and two water towers. At the junction where 83 joined U.S. 50, which was concurrent with U.S. 400, I turned east where the three highways ran together and avoided the business route through town, and the road widened to four lanes for a short distance. U.S. 50 is a long and significant east-west original U.S. highway that sprawls 3,017 miles (4,855 km) and nearly coast to coast—from Ocean City, Maryland, to West Sacramento, California. It courses through thirteen states and includes a lot of mountainous and desert areas in the West, and the lengthy stretch through Nevada has a reputation for being "The Loneliest Road in America." U.S. 400 is a much shorter and newer east-west road that wasn't commissioned until 1994 and was extended in 1996. Almost all of its 481 miles (774 km) are in Kansas, with the eastern end just about a mile past the Missouri line and the western terminus a short distance into Colorado.

U.S. 83 ran along the east side of Garden City through a modern section with newer homes and a sizable commercial area with big box stores like Home Depot and Sam's Club. *Road Trip USA* describes an old but still viable downtown that's apparently along the business route I didn't take.

The guidebook also mentions two popular attractions in the city—one being a giant outdoor public swimming pool that's longer than a football field and holds over two million gallons of water. It's known as the Big Pool and was originally hand dug in 1922 and later enlarged by horse-drawn soil scrapers. For decades the pool was free until a fee became necessary to cover improvements. Another attraction is the Lee Richardson Zoo near the pool, which brought big mammals like elephants, rhinos, and giraffes to the plains of Kansas, even if confined.

Garden City's population has had steady growth throughout its history and was 26,658 in the most recent census—down somewhat, though, from the previous count. It's the seat of Finney County and dates to 1878 when two brothers from Ohio—William and James R. Fulton—homesteaded here along the Santa Fe Railroad. They had the ambition of developing a town and recruited some capable people to assist them, including C.J. "Buffalo" Jones, who arrived early in 1879 and became a co-founder and promoter of the town. A railroad station was constructed and also the Garden City Ditch, which brought irrigation to the area and contributed to an agricultural boom in this part of Kansas, and a land rush by the mid-1880s. It's said that Garden City's name was inspired by the suggestion of an itinerant who admired the garden of Mrs. W.D. Fulton—the wife of one of the founders. By 1900, the town had over 1,500 people and was fully incorporated.

During World War II, there was a U.S. Army airfield southeast of town, which was one of fifteen in Kansas for training pilots and crews of bombers and fighters. Like Nebraska, Kansas was chosen for such bases because of a more secure location in the heartland of the country, good flying conditions, and sparsely populated areas that were suitable for operations. After the war, the Garden City airfield developed into the city-owned regional airport there today—similar to what became of many other old military airfields.

In the 1970s, a big transformation began when Garden City's council allowed a huge meatpacking plant to be built, and another came along in 1983. These brought in many new residents that included large numbers of immigrants from various countries—especially Mexico and other parts of Latin America. By 2010, nearly forty-eight percent of the population was Hispanic. Other immigrants arrived from distant countries like Vietnam, Laos, and Somalia, and Garden City has been called the most ethnically diverse city in Kansas, where well over twenty different languages are spoken. Many of the diverse immigrants, including illegal ones, were intentionally recruited by the meat packing companies for cheap labor. According to a Wikipedia article, the huge numbers of immigrants have been well-received by the community overall, which is a big accomplishment if it's true.

There are also huge cattle feedlots in and near the city—though I didn't see or smell any on the route I took—where bovines spend their final months fattening up on an unnatural diet of grains and additives before being "processed" at local meatpacking plants, which I suppose used to be called slaughterhouses. The biggest plant is owned by the behemoth corporation, Tyson Foods, and it's the city's largest employer with over 2,200 employees, according to the most recent report.

A few years before my journey, an erudite and perceptive British gentleman close to my age named David Reynolds also traveled all of 83, including the Canadian section, and wrote and published his own narrative called *Slow Road to Brownsville*. He spent some time in Garden City and learned about sordid conditions in the feedlots and meatpacking plants, which motivated him to write a very unflattering description of the modern American beef industry, which has certainly received enough criticism. Despite such ugly downsides, the beef industry in Garden City led to an economic boom there.

U.S. 50 and 400 soon split off from 83 and continued east in tandem toward Dodge City—that legendary town of the Old West about fifty miles away that's close in size to Garden City. Besides being a crossroads for three U.S. highways, Garden City was once on the National Old Trails Road, also called the Ocean-to-Ocean Highway, which was one of the very early auto trails that was established in 1912 just prior to the Lincoln Highway and incorporated in the National Auto Trail system in the U.S. This one extended 3,096 miles (4,982 km) through twelve states, from Baltimore to Los Angeles, with branches to New York City and San Francisco. It challenges the claim that the Lincoln Highway was the first transcontinental road.

Ahead, 83 crossed railroad tracks that are part of Amtrak's Southwest

Chief line, and there's an old depot in downtown Garden City that's been restored. Like North Platte, Garden City has long been a place with a lot of movement.

Past the city limit, I crossed a bridge over the Arkansas River that has historically been related to this movement. However, the riverbed looked dried up—with sand and shrubs and no visible water. I learned that this desiccation was due to water siphoned for irrigation more than drought, which began when the Garden City Ditch was completed in 1879. But *The Last American Highway* edition, covering Nebraska, Kansas, and Oklahoma, refers to a long-running conflict over water rights between Kansas and Colorado that's gone to the U.S. Supreme Court, which made a ruling in 2001 that required Colorado to pay Kansas for diverting excessive upstream water from the Arkansas River that deprived its neighboring state. That compensation apparently didn't help the flow of the river in this part of Kansas years later, and I wondered just how often it looked so dry here.

It's an ironic condition for a river that's the sixth longest in the nation, which, like the Platte, originates from snows in the Colorado Rockies, in this case near the town of Leadville. The Arkansas River courses 1,469 miles eastward through parts of Colorado, Kansas, Oklahoma, and the state of Arkansas before emptying into the Mississippi. Also, like the Platte, the Arkansas has played a major role in the drama of westward expansion. Before that, numerous Native tribes had lived near the river for millennia.

A very significant early expedition that followed the Arkansas River was led by Zebulon Pike, from July 15, 1806 to July 1, 1807, which overlapped the last part of Lewis and Clark's epic journey. Like Lewis and Clark, Pike was a U.S. Army officer who led a small military group of twenty-three men with the purpose of exploring the southern portion of the newly acquired Louisiana Territory. Pike's party also started near St. Louis and went on to contact different Native tribes for diplomatic purposes. Another of Pike's objectives was to find the headwaters of the Arkansas and Red Rivers. When the expedition reached the Arkansas River, they navigated upstream in canoes they constructed across the Plains toward the Rockies and into what became Colorado. There they sighted a prominent peak that would later be named after Pike. Several members of the party, including

Pike, even attempted to climb the mountain, but without success. Pike split the group, and a smaller one returned to St. Louis. He then led the other to seek out the Red River and discover its source.

This party wandered into Spanish Territory in present-day southern Colorado, where they built a small fort along the Rio Grande River for the winter. In February 1807, they were apprehended by a Spanish military force and taken to Santa Fe, and later to colonial authorities in Chihuahua, Mexico, to be interrogated. Pike said he believed they'd been exploring American territory. The Americans were treated well while captive, and since the U.S. and Spain were not at war, they were released and escorted on a long trek back to the Louisiana Territory through Mexico and Texas.

Pike's expedition didn't become as renowned as Lewis and Clark's, but an intrigue developed over its true motives that resulted in some uncertainties that persist to this day. For it has long been contended that the real purpose of the mission was espionage of the Spanish colonial territory, since Spain was considered a rival power at the time, and that the capture of Pike's party could have been planned to provide intelligence about conditions in the territory.

Pike was later promoted to brigadier general but was killed in the War of 1812. Before his death, he'd published an account about his expedition that became very popular and stimulated a lot of interest in the region he'd explored, which influenced later trade and settlement there, including the opening of the Santa Fe Trail that followed much of the Arkansas River.

In 1821, another War of 1812 veteran and businessman named William Becknell was instrumental in developing the Santa Fe Trail that Pike's expedition had somewhat pioneered, which became a trade route between Independence, Missouri, and Santa Fe. The latter city had come under the control of Mexico, which had just won its independence from Spain. Mexico removed trade barriers that the Spanish had imposed, and the old provincial capital was a big potential market for many commodities. The close to 900-mile Santa Fe Trail followed the Arkansas River through much of Kansas and into Colorado, across a vast, untamed land. But despite great hardships and dangers, the trade route that used oxen and mule-drawn freight wagons became successful. Later, gold seekers bound for the California and Colorado gold fields traveled the trail, and the U.S. military used it as an invasion route into New Mexico during the Mexican-American War that started in 1846. When the war ended in 1848, the U.S. won control of the Southwest, which became open for settlement. But unlike the Oregon and California Trails, the Santa Fe Trail continued to be used more by traders and the military than emigrants.

Like the trails further north, it was the railroad that resulted in the demise of the Santa Fe Trail, and by 1880 the Atchison, Topeka and Santa Fe Railway was completed. The National Park Service has established the Santa Fe National Historic Trail, with an auto tour route that courses near the original trail. In this part of Kansas, the historic route is on the north side of the Arkansas River, and U.S. 50-400 runs near it, as does the Amtrak route—all very reminiscent of the Great Platte River Road in Nebraska.

South of the Arkansas River bridge was a merger with the 83 business route, and the highway continued as a single road. I was looking out for the State Buffalo Preserve, which has bison descended from a small herd that was captured for preservation by C.J. Buffalo Jones when the species was threatened by extinction.

Charles Jesse Jones (1844-1919), like his contemporary, William Cody, was a larger-than-life character of the Old West whose experiences and achievements were also much like Cody's. He was a farm boy from Illinois who headed west to Kansas at age twenty-two, where he operated a fruit tree nursery, married, had four children, and moved to central Kansas. He lived there in a sod house and started hunting bison as part of his livelihood, and his skill in killing the great animal for hides and meat also earned him the honorific of his times—"Buffalo" before his surname.

Jones also had business skills that led to his becoming one of Garden City's founders in 1879, where, like the other three, he homesteaded the standard 160 acres. He was elected the first mayor of Garden City and ventured into some real estate development. He also donated land for the first courthouse and was influential in getting the railroad to construct a depot in town, and in Garden City becoming the county seat. He organized four irrigation companies that channeled water 100 miles from the Arkansas River for the cultivation of farmland, and even served two terms in the Kansas House of Representatives. Perhaps the greatest legacy of Buffalo Jones is his ironic role as one of the "preservers of the bison," as recognized in the National Archives. By the mid-1880s, the former bison hunter, like Buffalo Bill, had become very dismayed by the mammal's dramatic decline, and over the next few years he used his roping rather than shooting skills to gather a herd from different places in a preservation effort—selling animals to zoos, parks, ranches, and even a wealthy purchaser from England. Like Cody, Jones also made ranching ventures, which included experiments with producing cattle-bison hybrids that he named "cattalo," which failed, however, because they couldn't reproduce. In 1897-1898, Jones spent time with a group in Alaska and other parts of the Far North trying to capture musk ox, but without success. At that time he also published an autobiography.

In 1902, Jones was appointed by President Theodore Roosevelt as the first game warden of Yellowstone National Park, where he helped to strengthen the small holdout bison herd there that eventually grew into the large, well-known present one. Buffalo Jones also had a big influence on Western novelist Zane Grey after a trip he made with the author to the Southwest in 1907, and Grey used him as a model for several of his characters.

Jones later organized two game-catching expeditions to Africa, which captured large mammals like zebras and rhinos that were sold to zoos. On the second expedition Jones became infected with malaria and was evacuated, but he never fully recovered. He lived another five years, which were spent back in the American West, and his last projects included patenting an irrigation device that he tried to find financial backing for, and ideas about cross-breeding bighorn sheep with domestic sheep.

Jones died in 1919 at the home of a daughter in Topeka, Kansas, and he's interred with family members at the Valley View Cemetery in Garden City. He's been honored with a large bronze statue in front of the Finney County Courthouse, which he donated land for, and a permanent exhibit devoted to him at the Finney County Historical Museum in town. There's also a Buffalo Jones Elementary School in Garden City.

Perhaps the greatest honor to Charles Jesse Jones came forty years after his death in 1959 when he was inducted into the Hall of Great

Westerners of the National Cowboy Hall of Fame in Oklahoma City. I doubt if there's anyone more deserving, even Buffalo Bill. And if Buffalo Jones isn't as famous, maybe he should be.

The local preserve I wanted to see is now called the Sandsage Bison Range and Wildlife Area, which, besides having native fauna, is also a remnant of what's called the sandsage prairie—a unique ecosystem of this part of the High Plains that's been almost totally converted to irrigated croplands. It's associated with sandy soils and a mixture of tall, mid, and short grasses in a region where the shortgrass prairie, or steppe, dominates, along with sand sagebrush. In the early 1900s, the Kansas National Forest was established near Garden City in this ecosystem, which expanded to over 270,000 acres as far as the Colorado border—an experiment that planted more than 800,000 trees of varied species to determine which ones were most suitable for the High Plains. But unlike the Nebraska National Forest I saw, this experiment failed, and the national forest ambition ended in 1915. But it remained federal land that was available for homesteaders and eventually developed into the croplands there today.

The local bison refuge was established in 1916, when 3,021 acres of the former national forest were granted to the state of Kansas to become a game preserve, which was later expanded. Presently, there are over forty bison there that are the oldest publicly-owned herd in Kansas. Other native wildlife on the preserve include mule deer, coyotes, black-tailed prairie dogs, and prairie chickens.

As I drove south, I was looking for a sign for the preserve on the west side of the road and did pass some rolling terrain with tall grasses, scattered yucca, and the largest amount of sagebrush I remembered seeing since the Dakotas, which I assumed was a remnant of the sandsage prairie that was never put to the plow here. However, I saw no sign and came to a rise in the road where a table flat panorama appeared, and soon drove by see-sawing pump jacks extracting oil out in cropland. I'd apparently missed the preserve somehow and pulled off the highway to take a closer look at my map.

Within minutes, a pickup truck stopped, and a middle-aged woman sprang out and asked, "Are you lost?"

"Not really," I replied. "I'm just checking my map because I wanted to see the bison range near Garden City, and I think I passed it."

"You did. You have to head back toward town and bear left at the business route of 83 to get to it."

"I took the other route, which must be how I missed it then."

"If you want to see the bison, you need a guided tour to their pasture for safety reasons. The animals can be dangerous. You also need a reservation, and access is limited."

I thanked the helpful stranger before she drove off after being another Good Samaritan on the Great Plains. I decided not to backtrack to see the preserve, especially since I needed a reservation to see the bison; and I continued my progress southward, satisfied to know that there was another small herd of the animal that had reclaimed a small piece of the immense region where their species had once reigned supreme. The bison is the official state animal of Kansas, besides the national mammal of the U.S.

The level landscape stretched on, with expanses of corn, spring wheat, milo, and large center pivot irrigators—some the size of short freight trains. I crossed what my map indicated was the course of the Cimarron Route, or Cutoff, of the Santa Fe Trail, which split off from the main Mountain Route west of Dodge City and the town of Cimarron—meaning "wild" in Spanish. This route shortened the distance for the supply wagons to Santa Fe by about a hundred miles and was also less rugged and more suitable for wagons. But the downside was being the "dry route" with no water along its first sixty miles across the Cimarron Desert between the Arkansas and Cimarron Rivers—a formidable challenge for wagon travel that often did only about twelve to twenty miles a day. And during frequent droughts, the distance to the next water source could be further. Most of the oxen and mules used as draft animals couldn't endure a prolonged dry stretch, and there are accounts of dead animals and abandoned wagons. Attacks from hostile Comanches and Apaches were also common in the area. These tribes didn't tolerate trespassers on their lands and would often drive off the livestock.

In 1831, the famed trapper-explorer Jedediah Smith was killed by a band of Comanches near Wagon Bed Springs along the Cimarron River—not far from my present location—when he went off alone to search for desperately needed water for a large trading party he was with that had gotten disoriented. But despite its hazards, the

Cimarron Route was still the favored one, except during droughts and when danger of attacks was highest.

I reached an intersection with U.S. 160, which joined 83 from the west and would run a straight course with it for some distance before turning east. This east-west U.S. highway dates to 1930 and runs 1,465 miles (2,358 km) from near Poplar Bluff, Missouri to five miles west of Tuba City, Arizona, through five states. As its three digits indicate, 160 is considered an auxiliary route, in this case of U.S. 60—a much longer road that intersects 83 further south.

Right by the current intersection was a huge feedlot with different breeds of bovines and the accompanying stench. Nevertheless, I stopped and stepped out for a closer look and saw cattle crowded behind a short concrete barrier with a metal railing, and some structures stood in the background. As I approached closer with my small Nikon, trying to tolerate the smell, some camera-shy cows backed away. I thought about how these animals were literally being fattened for their slaughter, with the next stop one of the meat-packing plants in Garden City or Liberal down the road. Cattle typically spend about the first year of their now shorter lives in a healthier environment, grazing on grass that's their natural diet—like the many I'd seen on the ranges and pastures along the highway. Then, except for the minority that are totally grass-fed for a certain market, they end up in a big feedlot for an average of about six months where they're fed a corn and grain-based diet that enables them to reach a marketable weight faster. I have less of a problem with slaughtering animals for food if done in a way that mitigates their trauma than with creatures being subjected beforehand to squalid, captive conditions like the crowded, manure-saturated environment I was seeing up close. These cattle might not have looked like they were suffering at the time, but I wondered what was going on in their minds, which must have some sentience. When I saw some eyes in the feedlot looking back at me, any thoughts about eating hamburgers were much less appealing. Perhaps someday, the moral and environmental objections to eating beef and other meat will win out in me. But in the meantime, I still intend to indulge moderately and selectively. One of my justifications, or perhaps rationalizations, is that most of these animals exist and are raised only because so many people want to eat them. But that doesn't justify a miserable, captive existence before they meet their fate.

Figures I checked showed Kansas having a cattle population over six million, which is a little over twice its human one. This number ranks very high nationally, and the state is also way up in the number of the animals processed (to put it politely) annually, total red meat products and fed cattle marketed—more than twenty-two percent of all cattle fed in the U.S. in 2012. One answer to the old catchphrase "Where's the beef?" could be "Kansas."

I came to the small town of Sublette, where U.S. 56 crossed 83–160. This is a relatively short highway that was commissioned in 1957 and has a run of 640 miles (1,030 km) through four states, and generally east-west between Kansas City, Missouri and Springer, New Mexico. A significant feature is this route's proximity to the historic Santa Fe Trail and its Cimarron Cutoff. Sublette has under 1,500 residents and is the seat of Haskell County. It was established in 1912 and named for William Sublette—a leading fur trapper, trader, and historic figure of the West of the early 1800s, who pioneered trails through this and other regions. As a result, his name also appears in other places, such as Sublette County, Wyoming, the Sublette Range in Idaho, and a Sublette Ave. in St. Louis, where he retired from the fur-trading business after having been a co-owner of the Rocky Mountain Fur Company. I didn't turn off 83 for a good look at the town of Sublette, but I couldn't miss a huge grain elevator and water tower. The highway crossed the tracks of the Cimarron Valley Railroad, which must have played a role in the town's development.

More pump jacks appeared in big open areas with winter wheat and some other crops, and the sky had gotten quite overcast. Before U.S. 160 made a ninety-degree turn off 83 and shot due east, a huge, dark, mushroom-shaped cloud loomed in the southwest with sparks of lightning. I knew it wasn't Armageddon from an atomic blast, but I suddenly had some anxious thoughts about encountering a severe thunderstorm with hail or even a tornado possibly developing. The cloud expanded and looked massive and malevolent, darkening more than half the sky, and I was headed right under it. In the meantime, I crossed the Cimarron River—a tributary of the Arkansas River—which looked as dry as the Arkansas had. The Cimarron Cutoff of the Santa

Fe Trail had followed this river further west.

Part of the ominous, dark gray cloud mass was now overhead, and there was a bolt of lightning ahead, and a sprinkle started on my windshield. My anxiety increased as I remembered reading that the biggest tornado danger is in the late afternoon, and it was now about 3 p.m. I also knew that one of the most dangerous places to be when a tornado develops is in a vehicle, which the violent forces could easily turn into scrap metal. If caught driving in the open, one is supposed to evacuate the vehicle and lie flat somewhere, preferably in a ditch if possible. With such frightful thoughts, I watched for an infamous funnel forming over the landscape. Someone had also told me that if a stormy sky turns yellow, it's a sign of a tornado coming.

After passing a turn for the Cimarron National Grassland to the west—the largest public land area in Kansas—the rain fell harder, and I wondered if some hail might descend next, which storms on the Plains are notorious for. Fortunately, I saw signs showing I was getting close to the large town of Liberal, where I might be able to find shelter in a worst-case scenario.

When I arrived there, it was raining heavily, and by the crossroads of 83 and U.S. 54, I spotted the Economy Motel advertising the "best rates in town," which I headed for, though not to check in but because I saw an overhanging roof by the office that I could park under if it hailed heavily. And just as I neared it, small hailstones started pelting Wander. The office driveway had enough space to park in to wait out the storm.

Pretty soon the precipitation let up, and a biker pulled in on a Harley with quite a bit of gear, wearing a big bandana instead of a helmet that looked soaked. He dismounted and went into the office, and when he was back, I asked how he'd fared in the storm.

"You can see I'm a little wet," he joked.

"Did you run into much hail?"

"It wasn't bad."

"I have an old bike back home," I said, "and lightning scares me the most when I'm caught in a storm." The biker seemed familiar, and suddenly I realized he was a guy I actually met a couple of months before!—at a bar-restaurant in the historic Virginian Hotel in the little town of Medicine Bow, Wyoming, where I'd ridden my old BMW with a couple of biker friends from Fort Collins; and we had a conversation with the same guy.

"This is strange, but I know we met before in August," I said, "in Medicine Bow, Wyoming."

He reacted a little puzzled and asked, "Just where?"

"At the Virginian."

Then he quickly remembered me and seemed just as surprised by the coincidence.

"It must still be a small world," I said, though I wondered what the odds of our crossing paths again were. We introduced ourselves, which we didn't do the first time, and he was Brad from Pocatello, Idaho, where he'd mentioned being from before. He had a business buying motorcycles—often in distant states—which he'd pick up and ride back home and resell, often on the overseas market. The first time we met he was returning to Idaho on a machine he'd purchased in faraway Maine, and now he was heading back from somewhere in Texas. This was a sideline business, and he'd recently retired from his main one.

"So, I'm traveling in my four-wheeler now," I told him. "Going all the way down U.S. 83 to the Mexican border after having started at the Canadian border."

"Sounds like an interesting and different kind of trip," he replied.

"Suddenly we were both stunned by the appearance of a fully arched rainbow to the east. I pulled out my camera and took multiple shots, then got a couple of Brad and his bike before he left for his room to dry off. We both joked about running into each other somewhere else down the road of life, and I was still amazed that it happened here.

The perfectly arched rainbow continued to wow me after the precipitation stopped completely and it started clearing, and I had more thoughts about my mother's affinity for rainbows and her having gone "over the rainbow." Another coincidence is that this splendid spectacle happened in a town that has a connection with the *Wizard of Oz* story, where in the classic movie version, the beloved song "Somewhere Over the Rainbow" was introduced to the world. The story, of course, begins and ends in Kansas, and although no specific town is mentioned, Liberal has asserted itself with a re-creation of the character Dorothy's house and the Yellow Brick Road from the Oz fantasy that's described in *Road Trip USA*. This was a tourist attraction I couldn't pass up, and it was very close to where I'd stopped.

The street I turned on to get to Dorothy's House was named Yellow Brick Road, and I came to a sign saying, "Welcome to DOROTHY'S HOUSE," with colorful images of the story's four main characters. I parked in a lot, then walked back to the sign area where there was also a bronze statue of Dorothy holding a book with some familiar words on the cover: "There's no place like home." And to further enhance the fantasy theme, a large mailbox near the road had the name Dorothy Gale painted on it.

I was ready for my own little flight into fantasy that you're never too old for and walked over to the house. It turned out to be a small, white, clapboard cottage with a brown, shingled roof and a picket fence, which was originally a farmhouse outside of Liberal that was built in 1907 and moved here in 1981. It was dedicated as Dorothy's House because of some resemblance to the one in the movie. Inside, it displays early twentieth-century furnishings and appliances that can be seen on tours led by young girls in Dorothy attire; however, the house was closed now. Near the front entrance were cut-out figures of Dorothy and her famous little black canine, "Toto," by a Yellow Brick Road that started from the house and wound through the grounds. Most of the embedded yellow slabs had names of individuals, families, and organizations that were apparently donors. Among them, I learned, were Ronald and Nancy Reagan.

Behind Dorothy's house was a large metal building marked Land of Oz, which was also closed. In it were lots of Oz-related exhibits and memorabilia, including the miniature house that was used for the tornado sequence in the movie, and an imitation of Dorothy's renowned ruby slippers. It's said that four pairs were used in the movie, and one has been in the Smithsonian Institution for decades. Adjacent to the Land of Oz was a "Munchkin's Playground," with a slide and swings for munchkin-sized kids. I didn't feel too old to "Follow the Yellow Brick Road," where, like young Dorothy Gale, I encountered the Scarecrow and Lion as wooden cutouts, and a metallic Tin Man. And there was another bronze, life-size likeness of Dorothy holding Toto.

An older woman also following the fanciful path commented to me: "Isn't all this really cute?"

"I find it very charming, and it does bring out the kid in you."

"I agree."

The Yellow Brick Road led to a white, two-story building with a touch of elegance that was once a private home constructed in 1918 and now houses "Dorothy's Gift Shop" and the Seward County Museum. It was still open, and I went in and found out from a costumed young lady who worked in the downstairs shop that an annual "Ozfest" was just the day before, which includes games, prizes, entertainment, and Dorothy look-alike contests. "We had visitors from as far as Alaska and England," she said, which said something about the appeal of the timeless fantasy.

The gift shop was full of Oz wares like ruby slippers and doormats with "There's no place like home," and "You're not in Kansas anymore!" And, of course, L. Frank Baum's original book titled *The Wonderful Wizard of Oz*, first published in 1900, was there in paperback.

The classic movie was playing continuously on a screen in the downstairs area, and I happened to catch the early scene of the young Judy Garland as Dorothy singing her inimitable, original version of "Somewhere Over the Rainbow," which had more of an effect on me after recently seeing a perfect rainbow in the land where the story starts and ends. I also mused about the movie's famous final line: "... there's no place like home." For some people I'd met or heard about in small towns along U.S. 83 were driven to escape at some point in their lives to somewhere else with more excitement and opportunity—only to eventually return with a new perspective and appreciation of "home." And the character Dorothy was a Great Plains girl who expressed a deep longing to escape from her ordinary and often troubled environment to a fancied land of glowing happiness. But after her surreal escape, she had an epiphany about the importance of home and the people there, and what I've come to see as the "greatness of the ordinary"—which took me much longer to realize in my own life than the very young character in a great story.

Upstairs was the Seward County Museum, which exhibited history in contrast to the fantasy downstairs. It's also called the Coronado Museum because one of its exhibits is about the famous expedition of

Spanish Conquistador Francisco Coronado from 1540 to 1542, which is believed to have passed through this part of Kansas. A few of its artifacts that have been discovered are in the museum, including an old Spanish bridle bit. There were also exhibits on Native Americans, and the more recent history of the early decades of Liberal and Seward County, with lots of vintage photos.

Outside was a bronze creation of Coronado, erect on a pedestal. Nearby, a historical sign summarized the experience of his contingent that came through this area close to five centuries ago:

WHEN CORONADO CAME TO KANSAS

> Francisco Vásquez de Coronado, with 36 soldiers and Father Juan de Padilla, marched north from the Rio Grande Valley in the spring of 1541. Coronado's objective was the land of Quivira, described to the Spaniards as a fabulously wealthy kingdom where gold was commonplace. In June, the expedition entered present Kansas, presumably near here, and moved on northeastward across the Arkansas River to what are now Rice and McPherson Counties. The Spaniards found no gold, only the grass lodges of the Quiviran Indians, and the guide who misled Coronado was killed.
>
> After more than a month searching central Kansas, the expedition returned to the Southwest, disappointed in the quest for riches but favorably impressed by the land itself. Juan Jaramillo, Coronado's lieutenant, wrote: "It is not a hilly country, but has tablelands, plains, and charming rivers... I am of the belief that it will be very productive of all sorts of commodities."

The last statement turned out to be very prophetic. The Conquistadors who came to future Kansas were a small part of a much larger army that had split up for different reasons. It originally included over 300 Spaniards with several friars, perhaps over 1,000 Native allies, some Native and African slaves, and hundreds of horses, mules, and livestock. The force started moving in February 1540 from the Pacific coast, west of Mexico City, and advanced up the coast before turning inland and marching further north. Coronado, with an aristocratic background, was chosen to lead by Antonio de Mendoza—the viceroy of New Spain, which became Mexico. From the beginning, the expedition's purpose was to seek and plunder transferable riches, especially gold, like other Conquistadors had done much further south with the Aztec and Inca empires. But Coronado's expedition found out reports of such riches in the north were exaggerations and fabrications, and when it returned to Mexico in the summer of 1542, it was regarded as a failure for not having achieved its primary purpose. It was, however, a monumental feat of exploration that covered parts of five future states, and some of the Spaniards were the first non-Natives to see the Grand Canyon and the Great Plains, with enormous herds of bison. They were brutal to some tribal groups in many encounters but had better relations with others. The army had its chroniclers, who left big clues to the route, along with the artifacts that were discovered. But the exact route is still quite a mystery.

I imagine there are many Coronado history buffs, especially in the expedition's region, as there are Lewis and Clark buffs. While standing by the commemoration of Coronado, which I'm sure has its detractors because of his mission's exploitative purpose and cruel treatment of many Native people, I thought of how that purpose contrasted with the exploration and diplomacy of Lewis and Clark centuries later, and also later Spanish colonial policies. The large expedition that advanced under the flag of Spain in the western interior of the continent was decades before England began its colonial ventures along the continent's east coast.

I got back on 83 where it intersected with U.S. 54—another 1926 original that extends 1,197 miles (1,926 km) between Griggsville, Illinois and El Paso, Texas, covering six states. Locally, 54 is also known as Pancake Boulevard because of a quirky tradition that links Liberal, Kansas, with the town of Olney in England, where the tradition originated around the year 1445.

According to legend, way back then on Shrove Tuesday—the old English name for the day preceding the start of the Lenten season—a woman in Olney who was frying pancakes, which were among the rich foods prohibited during Lent, was suddenly interrupted by the ringing of church bells announcing a pre-Lent service. This compelled her to run off in her apron while still holding the frying pan to try and make the start of the church service. The story inspired other women in the community in later years to have a race to the church with frying pans every Shrove Tuesday for the prize of the "Kiss of Peace" from the church bellringer.

The tradition came to Liberal in 1950 after the president of a local Jaycees organization happened to see a magazine picture of the race in Olney, and he got the idea not only to organize such an event in Liberal but to propose a friendly competition with the British women for the fastest time. The event materialized and has taken place on both sides of the Atlantic, hours apart, as International Pancake Day on Shrove Tuesday. The race involves a 415-yard course, where the women runners are required to wear aprons and head scarves while holding a frying pan to toss a cooked pancake at the beginning and end of the race. The fastest time is usually just under a minute, and when I checked the results, Liberal has been ahead of Olney—thirty-seven wins to twenty-nine through the years. The "Kiss of Peace" is also a prize for the winner in Liberal, where there's also a church service. It's said to be the only race of its kind in the world, and though it may all seem very silly, it's a harmless tradition that sounds like a lot of fun.

The intersection of 83 and 54 was also a terminus of U.S. 270, which dates to 1930 and runs 643 miles (1,035 km) southeast from this point to White Hall, Arkansas, through three states, and joins 83 for a short distance into Oklahoma. It's considered an auxiliary of U.S. 70 that runs further south.

The Oklahoma line was just a few miles ahead, but I can't leave Liberal without mentioning more about this very interesting town, which is the seat of Seward County and has a population of over 20,000. Its ironic name in a state known for being the opposite of liberal politically is said to have originated with an early settler named Seymour S. Rogers, who was very generous in sharing his well water, which many thought was "mighty liberal." Rogers also named the post office that opened in 1885, Liberal. But it was the arrival of the Rock Island Railroad that led to planning a town, which was incorporated in 1888.

Early in the town's history, drought on the High Plains pressured many local farmers to leave and seek better luck in less arid areas. Later decades would see growth spurred by discoveries of oil and natural gas near the town. And in 1963, the largest helium plant in the world, called National Helium, opened here. But the biggest employer is the National Beef Company, which has about 3,500 employees—another huge beef processing plant in the region. Modern irrigation methods have also made farming in the area successful. Liberal's young median age of twenty-eight would seem to be linked to employment opportunities and a community college in town. I also read about the relatively low cost of living here.

Right next to the city's regional airport is the Mid-America Air Museum, which is the largest aviation museum in Kansas, and also one of the nation's largest with over a hundred military and civilian aircraft from every period of aviation history. The museum and airport are on the site of another World War II U.S. Army airfield.

I left Liberal and Kansas behind under a gray sky that looked somewhat threatening again in my direction. A sign in the pancake-flat landscape said, "Welcome to Oklahoma–Native America"—a state known for its large Native population that was originally "Indian Territory." I stopped for a photo of the sign as gusts blew over the border area, then drove into another state, hoping that more dark clouds ahead didn't mean real trouble. This was Oklahoma's only thirty-four-mile-wide panhandle between Kansas and Texas.

Oklahoma has a rather complicated history and became a state in 1907 by combining the Indian Territory with the Oklahoma Territory that had been established in 1890. Before then, the Indian Territory had been much larger and was first designated in 1834 for the relocation of southeastern tribes west of the Mississippi River after the oppressive Indian Removal Act of 1830 during President Andrew Jackson's administration. The name Oklahoma is derived from a combination of the Choctaw words "ukla" (person) and "huma" (red)—meaning "red person"—and between 1830 and 1850, about 100,000 Native Americans were forcefully moved there, with the most infamous displacement being that of about 16,000 Cherokees from the southern Appalachians along the tragic Trail of Tears. Reservations were established in the Indian Territory for the new arrivals who joined those indigenous to the area. Oklahoma's statehood brought the end of any Indian Territory, but the state's current Native population is over 321,000, and only California has a larger one. It's also fourth among the states in percentage of Native Americans at 8.5 percent.

The Oklahoma Panhandle has a complicated history of its own since it wasn't part of the Louisiana Purchase from France like the rest of Oklahoma because it was Spanish territory, which became part of Mexico when that country gained its independence. Later the area was included in the short-lived Republic of Texas that became independent from Mexico. To further complicate matters, when Texas joined the Union as a slave state at the end of 1845, it had to exclude the future Oklahoma Panhandle area because the 1820 Missouri Compromise prohibited slavery north of a certain latitude that was the southern border of the panhandle area. This strip of land consequently remained a strange, neutral area of the U.S. that was never incorporated into the large Indian Territory or any other jurisdiction between 1850 and 1890 and was known as the Public Land Strip, and especially No Man's Land. Not surprisingly, it was a largely lawless and rowdy region. Then, in the late 1880s, its settlers organized the Cimarron Territory, which was never officially recognized in Washington, however. There was a big development in 1890 when the territory became part of the new Oklahoma Territory, which was followed by statehood in 1907. So, the panhandle wasn't really called that until it joined the rest of Oklahoma and created a panhandle-like configuration.

As I moved on, a wall of dark clouds had formed to the south, and it started raining lightly. U.S 83 expanded to four lanes briefly, then back to two that became somewhat bumpy. More bobbing pump jacks appeared on the flat landscape, which were signs of the oil wealth that Oklahoma has long been known for. I also passed irrigated, cultivated areas with corn and milo.

There was a time when this area became an agricultural wasteland when the panhandle was the nexus of the region that came to be called the Dust Bowl in the 1930s. After these lands were opened to settlers by the first Homestead Act of 1862, decades of poor farming practices removed deep-rooted grasses that held the soil in place. This had catastrophic consequences when a series of severe droughts started in 1930, and High Plains winds blasted tons of unanchored topsoil away that created massive dust storms—the worst sending dark clouds of dust as far as New York City and Washington, D.C. One storm that struck on April 14, 1935, which came to be called Black

Sunday, had started in the Oklahoma Panhandle and spread east, blowing an estimated three million tons of topsoil off the Plains. This prompted Associated Press reporter Robert Geiger to coin the name "Dust Bowl." Well known are the massive relocations of farmers and other residents of the six states in the Dust Bowl region after disaster struck, which is said to have been the largest migration in American history and involved about 2.5 million people during the 1930s. Huge numbers went to California, and since many were from Oklahoma, the migrants came to be called "Okies." Their ordeals and spirit were famously depicted in John Steinbeck's novel, *The Grapes of Wrath*, and the classic movie based on it.

The long drought was finally relieved by the end of the 1930s, but the economic effects persisted, and population decline in the worst affected areas continued into the 1950s. But as I was seeing, plenty of agriculture had long come back from the desolation of the Dust Bowl years, with much better farming methods and modern irrigation. Some of the devastated areas became National Grasslands after being purchased by the federal government.

I came to a junction with U.S. 64, where U.S. 70 left 83 to run east with it, and 64 joined 83 for a brief stretch south. U.S. 64 is a long, original, east-west highway that has a rather straight course for 2,326 miles (3,743 km) in six states—from the Outer Banks of North Carolina to the Four Corners area of northeast Arizona. Soon I passed through Turpin—the first town on my Oklahoma map—where 64 turned west from 83. It's a small, unincorporated community that had 467 inhabitants in the last census, which got started when a post office opened in 1925. The community's namesake is Carl J. Turpin, who was general manager of the local Beaver, Meade, and Englewood Railroad. There was a school and grain elevator there, with the latter on the National Register of Historic Places for some reason. About all I noticed was a gas station and a sign for Perryton, Texas, which was thirty-two miles south and now my day's destination.

The rainfall increased, and there were occasional flashes in the clouds to the south as daylight faded. I passed a feedlot on the east side of the road, and soon there was a transition to a more rolling landscape with sagebrush. I crossed the North Canadian River, also known as the Beaver River, here, which is a 441-mile tributary of the longer Canadian River—one of Oklahoma's main rivers. The area looked very shrubby, and the rain was lighter again as daylight further decreased. Then there were more grassy spaces, and some of Nature's fireworks continued flashing in the clouds. I didn't notice anything where Boyd was marked on my map, and further on was Bryan's Corner at the intersection of U.S. 412—also OK 3—where there was a Cenex station, a store, a few homes, a short grain elevator, and a couple of storage tanks. Just up the road, east on 412, was the unincorporated community of Balko, which had 623 residents in a past count.

East-west U.S. 412 is a relatively new federal highway first commissioned in 1982, and it runs 1,130 miles (1,820 km) through five states between Columbia, Tennessee, and Springer, New Mexico. A quirk is that although it's another three-digit auxiliary highway, it has no proximity to U.S. 12, much further north, which would be considered its parent highway in the system.

The last stretch of Oklahoma was flat and grassy with some cultivation. My map showed the final name of Gray along the road where I saw no signs of a community. As daylight faded, a sign ahead proclaimed the "Texas State Line," and an adjacent one said, "Entering Ochiltree County." The light rain seemed to stop at this boundary, but winds were picking up. A little further was a prominent "Welcome to Texas" sign with the Lone Star flag and "Drive Friendly—The Texas Way." I'd entered the last state along The Road to Nowhere that's a dramatic contrast to the thirty-four miles of Oklahoma I'd just driven, since 906 miles of gigantic Texas were ahead of me, from one end to the other. That's close to half of the total driving distance of U.S. 83, and almost the distance between New York City and Jacksonville, Florida, for an East Coast perspective.

The terrain at this top of the wide Texas Panhandle looked as flat as that in most of the thin Oklahoma Panhandle. Soon the lights of Perryton became visible to the south, and some lightning still flashed in the distance. At the city limit, a sign stated an 8,802 population. I passed a spherical water tower, then crossed some tracks near a tall grain elevator, and 83 led into the business area and became another Main St. It was a nice downtown with a movie theater with a large marquee that glowed in the darkness that had fallen. No rain had resumed, but some winds persisted, and a gust socked Wander at a stop light. I recalled the Texas Panhandle having a reputation for winds, which seemed to be greeting me.

I still thought I could tough it out in the car another night, though the Great Plains Motel I passed was tempting. Before looking for an overnight parking haven, I stopped at a grocery store called Lowes to buy some bread, where a lot of the customers had Mexican features. Now in Texas, I expected to see a lot more of this ethnicity. After all, Texas was originally part of Mexico. The name Texas has complex Spanish and Native origins, with some uncertainties. However, it's generally believed to be derived from the tribal Caddo word "tayshas," which means "friends," or "allies." This led to "Friendship" becoming the state's motto.

I found a nearby truck stop that had a large store with the appropriate name Waterhole 83. There were some empty spaces away from the trucks, and since it wasn't too noisy or reeking of fumes from running engines, I pulled into one of the back spaces then went into the store for an OK to stay.

"It should be alright," said a woman store associate, "as long as you don't get in the way of the trucks," I heard again.

Before eating, I poured a PBR into my plastic glass in the car and got back to my journal, using my lamp again. Then I walked over to a restaurant I'd seen. But when I arrived, it was closed, as was the grill at Waterhole 83, though other facilities there were open 24/7. Luckily, there was a good old Subway store still open next door, where hunger led me to order a foot-long grilled chicken sandwich with avocado and selected veggies, which was my second Subway meal of the day after starting with the breakfast sandwich back in Scott City.

I wanted to walk around downtown Perryton, but almost right after I returned to the car, the rain resumed quite heavily, and the winds got stronger. Inside my cramper, it felt raw and quite miserable, and it was one of those low points where I wondered what the hell I was doing. Thoughts of home comforts shot through my mind again, besides considering a late check-in at the motel I saw. But I felt inert, and situated, if not comfortable where I was. I would tough it out again at a truck stop and again said to myself: "The only way to really appreciate comfort is to experience some discomfort."

The car's gauge showed forty-eight degrees, and I put on another sweater. I managed to write more for quite a while, and the rain eventually stopped, but not the winds. When I was ready to sleep, I left a window open a crack for a little ventilation as usual, then removed some layers of clothing before getting snug in my old mummy bag again. As my consciousness faded, the audible gusts of the Texas Panhandle continued. It had been a long day traveling in three states, through changing landscapes and a lot of history along The Road to Nowhere.

DAY 21

Down the Texas Panhandle

It rained again during the night. But by morning the sky was largely blue with drifting clouds, though some strong winds persisted. After a cereal breakfast in the car, I went into the Waterhole 83 store and paid for a shower that the truckers use.

I asked an employee if it was usually so windy around here, and she laughed and said: "Maybe one out of seven days isn't. That's why we have wind farms in the area."

"I'm headed south on 83 and sure hope the winds weaken."

"They should eventually."

Some gusts blew from the north as I was leaving Perryton, and I thought I might have some tailwinds to help propel me south. The town is the seat of Ochiltree County, and its population has increased moderately in recent years. Its beginnings are linked to a small farming and ranching community named Ochiltree, which was once about eight miles to the south. In the early 1900s, this town needed a railroad, as did the small town of Gray almost twenty miles north in the Oklahoma Panhandle. The Panhandle and Santa Fe Railway responded by building a new line across the grasslands between the towns, and in 1919, both Ochiltree and Gray were amazingly moved to the railroad by steam-powered tractors hauling buildings off foundations. This technical accomplishment received some national attention with a cover story in the February 1920 issue of *Popular Mechanics* magazine, and it created the consolidated town of Perryton. The new name came from county judge George M. Perry. Some of the original buildings that were moved still stand in Perryton, and the only remnant of Ochiltree at its original location is a schoolhouse that wasn't moved. This big move is why there was no sign of Gray, Oklahoma, when I passed through where it had been.

Perryton came to be called the "Wheatheart of the Nation" because of the area's abundant grain production, and it also sits in a part of the Texas Panhandle with many oil and gas resources. The gas also contains some relatively rare helium. There's a Museum of the Plains right in town that I didn't visit, but *The Last American Highway* edition that covers Texas says some favorable things about it, and also mentions that for a time Perryton was the headquarters of the U.S. & Canada Highway 83 Association—originally the Great Plains Highway Association (referring to another old name for U.S. 83)—which consisted of chamber of commerce members from different highway communities that promoted travel on 83 for decades, but the association folded some years ago.

The landscape south of Perryton was totally flat, with large fields of wheat, corn, and milo, where some oil wells also appeared. The sky was enormous, with puffy cumulus clouds, and 83 had a good surface with large, paved shoulders. Soon the landscape transformed to a more undulating and grassy High Plains look, where sharp-pointed soapweed yucca reappeared along with some blowing tumbleweed, scattered trees, and rocky outcrops. Ian Frazier's very informative book, *Great Plains*, says that the abundant tumbleweed in much of the West is non-native and came from the steppes of southern Russia, which have many similarities to the High Plains in North America. The most common species is known as Russian thistle and is thought to have arrived in 1873, along with Russian-German immigrants in the Dakotas. It became one of the fastest-spreading invasives—from seeds scattered when the large weeds tumble after being naturally severed from stalks that grounded the plants—and is just one of numerous invasives from the Russian steppes, which I was surprised to learn.

Ahead was Wolf Creek, which eventually feeds into the North Canadian River that 83 had crossed back in the Oklahoma Panhandle. On its south bank near here is a concentrated archeological area known as the Buried City, once thought to be the stone ruins of an ancient city but now regarded as the remains of a smaller settlement of the Plains Village culture that flourished in the region between 1200 and 1400 A.D. It was a culture that practiced farming in addition to hunting and favored settling and sheltering in more lush riparian areas instead of living on the dry, open plains. The creek is fed by groundwater of the Ogallala Formation, which, however immense, is being dangerously depleted largely because of agricultural demands. I stopped by a sign for an oil and gas company lease near a white tank and some other small structures, with a caveat for the operators: "Please respect landowners, stay on lease roads."

There were more rolling rangelands and rocky outcrops—some large and chalky in color that were often in gullies or creek beds. Strong gusts still whipped from the north, and when I stopped for a photo of an appealing landscape, one blew Wander's driver side door wide open and made it difficult to close. Watching prairie grasses wave frantically, I thought the Texas Panhandle must be one of the windiest places in the country.

At a crest in the road, a panorama appeared that looked almost Southwestern and included a mesa, buttes, and a ridge-like formation. These must have been features of the 200-mile-long Caprock escarpment that *Road Trip USA* refers to. The road crossed the West Fork of Horse Creek twice, which looked dry within its low banks, then drew closer to the buttes and ridge, with lots of trees in the foreground. Hardwoods appeared again along the road and a warning sign for deer. Soon I was cruising through a heavy grove with orange flashes of autumn color as the landscape kept changing.

Ahead was the Canadian River and the town of Canadian, where two water towers stood with a few buttes in the background. Just before the river was a junction with U.S. 60 that would join 83 for a short distance. This highway is another major 1926 original that, despite ending in 0, which usually indicates a transcontinental route, originally had an eastern terminus in Springfield, Missouri. But that became extended to Virginia Beach, Virginia, and the western end that used to be in Los Angeles was shortened to near Brenda, Arizona, in 1964 after Interstate 10 was completed and largely replaced U.S. 60 as a route to the West Coast. The old federal highway's current distance is 2,670 miles (4,297 km), through nine states, and it has an origin as an early auto trail that was one of the first marked ones called the Midland Trail, which was established in 1912 and considered for the route of the Lincoln Highway, but rejected.

I crossed the Canadian River—the longest tributary of the Arkansas River—on a long concrete bridge, and its flow was also low. Nearby was the original twenty-one-span truss bridge known as the Wagon Bridge, constructed in 1916, and at that time it was the largest steel structure west of the Mississippi. A restoration was completed in 2000, and its wooden deck is now used by pedestrians and bicyclists. The origin of the rather odd name for a river this far from Canada is uncertain. One explanation is that it could go back to early French-Canadian explorers, or perhaps the Spaniards, since "cañada" is a Spanish word for "glen." Like other major rivers of the Plains, the Canadian was followed by indigenous peoples, explorers, traders, and gold seekers during the 1849 California Gold Rush. One of the explorations was a scientific expedition in 1820 led by U.S. Army Major Stephen H. Long, who originated the name "The Great American Desert" for the High Plains. Sections of the Canadian River have also been designated as territorial boundaries historically. A long stretch of the river west of the Caprock escarpment is considered the northern boundary of the Llano Estacado—"staked plains" in Spanish—which is the sprawling and most southern area of the High Plains in part of northern Texas and eastern New Mexico that's larger than the state of Indiana.

A sign said "Welcome to Canadian"—the community with a 2,649 population that's named after the river, which has also been called the "Oasis of the High Plains" because of the abundant vegetation along the river. Coronado's expedition is believed to have wandered through the area in 1541, and its overall history has been very colorful. The early and middle years of the 1800s brought the traders and gold seekers bound for far horizons, and after 1870, hunters, cattlemen, and settlers were drawn to this part of the Texas Panhandle. Canadian was originally known as Hogtown for its opposite of elegant appearance—a tent city for railroad workers building the Southern Kansas line—and the area was very much the Wild West. Hogtown had thirteen saloons—but no churches—and drew its share of gamblers and prostitutes. The legendary Texas Rangers, which had been organized officially in 1835, were the only lawmen in the region at the time. There is still a small, modern-day Ranger force in Texas, which is a statewide investigative law enforcement agency that evolved out of a checkered past that included violent racist behavior along with commendable accomplishments.

The Southern Kansas Railroad—a subsidiary of the Atchison, Topeka, and Santa Fe—arrived in the area in 1887, and the following year Hogtown was renamed Canadian and moved to the south side of the river and became the seat of Hemphill County. On July 4, 1888, Canadian's first celebration included a rodeo with newspaper coverage that made it the first recorded public rodeo exactly six years after Buffalo Bill's original rodeo in North Platte. This also started a tradition that's continued every July 4 since then in the local arena. The Women's Christian Temperance Union established a center in this town that had so many saloons, and they were apparently successful because Canadian became a dry town in 1903. A railroad depot was completed in 1907, and farming had begun in the area. Canadian went on to become a thriving marketing and railroad center.

The Great Depression and Dust Bowl years of the 1930s were a big setback for the town's economic progress that resulted in substantial population loss, but eventually it came back, with cattle ranching and the development of the area's very rich oil and gas resources. During a boom in the 1970s, Hemphill County was one of the top ten producers of natural gas in the U.S. By the new century, that boom had declined, but was revived by fracking, with its mixed blessings. Canadian is said to be a place with a lot of community pride and spirit, which seems determined to survive and thrive in its rather isolated location through the ups and downs of time.

Trees lined the road as it led into this "Oasis of the High Plains." I saw the attractive, Spanish-style River Valley Museum and parked further ahead in Canadian's quaint, small business center on its red brick Main St. Some of the well-preserved buildings were also red brick—like the old, restored Palace movie theater that now had shows. Regarding movies, the closing scenes of 2000's *Cast Away* with Tom Hanks were filmed near Canadian. On a slightly elevated part of Main St. was a view of arid plains to the north and verdant vegetation along the river—set below a blue sky with lots of puffy white clouds.

I ambled down Main St. with my camera, where small banners attached to lampposts proclaimed, "Welcome to Canadian." But when I walked by a parked pickup, a cowboy-hat-clad older guy seated inside seemed to look at me suspiciously, perhaps because of my unfamiliar face and tourist manner in this kind of community. Some side streets also had red brick surfaces, and when I came to the back side of the museum I passed before, I saw a colorful and photogenic long mural with the words, "CANADIAN—Texas Best...Past, Present, Future," and local images like the river, old bridge, county courthouse, and rodeo. On the walk back, I heard the approach of a train in another old railroad town. The Panhandle winds had persisted and discouraged me from taking a longer walk. Perhaps locals get used to it the way others get used to the smell in towns near feedlots.

The Texas Panhandle has a history of alcohol prohibition that's loosened up in recent years. However, of its twenty-six counties, four—including Hemphill—were still completely dry at the time. Canadian became an exception in the county by being allowed to open a couple of bars. But they were way outnumbered by the thirteen churches in town—the same as the number of saloons said to have been in the original community when there were no churches.

Heading south from Canadian, U.S. 83-60 was four lanes for a stretch with a rather wide median, though the road got quite bumpy. It ascended into the elevated area I'd seen from a distance, and ahead was a huge reproduction of a brontosaurus of all things atop a bluff on the east side of the road. This quirky, unnatural landmark is a concrete and steel sculpture created in 1992 by local artist Gene Corkrell. His dinosaur is fifty feet long, seventeen feet tall, weighs a ton, and was painted black and gold—the colors of Canadian's high school football team—and named "Aud" after his long-time wife, Audrey. You never know what you might see along The Road to Nowhere.

I passed the Hemphill County airport and entered scrubby country, where I might have seen the first mesquite shrub that would soon dominate the landscape. Some hardwood trees were near the road, and there were more outcrops, creek beds, and some grazing black Angus in the rocky, hilly terrain. The highway descended, and four lanes narrowed back to two where U.S. 60 branched off toward the southwest and the city of Amarillo, and 83 continued south into big, open rangeland. Wind turbines finally appeared in the distance, utilizing one of the Texas Panhandle's great natural resources. There were also oil and gas wells extracting the dirty energy sources. Windmill pumps were also in the sprawling terrain, where small tumbleweed occasionally rolled across the road. It all looked quintessentially Texas here.

The road crossed the Washita River—a 295-mile tributary of the Red River that had some flow and is said to carry an extreme amount of silt. Hay bales were scattered to the west of the road, but what appeared in abundance were natural gas wells with light brown cylindrical tanks. It was no wonder, since I was amid the 50,000 square miles of Anadarko Basin, which contains one of the largest gas reserves in North America, besides about 495 million barrels of oil. More wind turbines also towered not far from the road, displaying Texas' prodigious production of energy—clean and dirty.

As I entered Wheeler County, the somewhat rugged and rolling land became quite flat again, with cultivated fields with light green hay. Just east of 83 along a county road was the small community of Briscoe, which was established in 1929 and named after an official of the Panhandle and Santa Fe Railroad. Its most recent population figure was 135, and once had twice that number in the early 1960s. The changing Panhandle landscape soon reverted to looking bumpy again, with scrubby, open areas with sagebrush, tall grasses, and scattered trees. There were a lot more trees, especially cottonwoods, where 83 crossed dried-up Sweetwater Creek. The banks of this creek that connects with the North Fork of the Red River were the location of bison hunting camps for tribes like the Comanche and Kiowa. After 1870, American hide hunters were also drawn to the area, and it became a scene of the great bison slaughter of that decade. This led to conflicts with the Natives that were a factor in the Red River War of 1874 between the U.S. Army and an alliance of the Comanche, Kiowa, Southern Cheyenne, and Arapahoe. Almost all the engagements occurred in the Texas Panhandle, where the U.S. military's superior firepower, equipment, and numbers defeated the Native alliance, who were forced on or back to reservations in the Indian Territory. This marked the end of the Indian Wars in Texas and fully opened the Panhandle for settlement.

A water tower and heavy growth of trees in the distance was

Wheeler. A green, leafy crop appeared that looked like cotton, which Texas has a long history of cultivating. Apparently, I was now south enough to see it. A sign showed Wheeler's population to be 1,592, and it's the seat of Wheeler County, with the name commemorating the nineteenth-century Texas Supreme Court Justice, Royall T. Wheeler. Ahead was the attractive and imposing, largely red brick county courthouse, with four white columns. It was constructed in 1925 and replaced the original frame-built courthouse that had been moved here in 1908 from the original county seat in Mobeetie.

I parked behind the large building, and now the winds were even worse. So, I stayed in Wander and ate a couple of peanut butter and sliced banana sandwiches. When the winds subsided, I ventured out for a short walk and crossed paths with two women who looked like a mother and daughter, and after greeting each other, I asked, "Are these winds pretty normal here?"

"This is higher than usual," the older one answered in a Texas drawl that would become more familiar, "but it happens enough and usually lasts about twenty-four hours."

We made a few other comments about the weather before we each moved on.

Suddenly, a walloping gust blew a bucket-style hat I was wearing off my head, and I ran after and retrieved it. I was getting more annoyed by these Panhandle winds, still blowing mainly from the north. But at least it was blowing in my direction of travel, which sure beat having to buck strong headwinds or crosswinds.

I refueled at a Shell station in Wheeler, then went inside to use their restroom. Once again, I commented on the winds to a middle-aged guy working at the station, who responded in a heavy drawl: "It gets even windier here. We had a storm yesterday, and part of I-40 down the road was closed for a while because some trucks flipped over. I hate the winds around here."

"Have you always lived here?"

"No. I came from the Austin area."

"So, what brought you to the Panhandle?"

"I came after a divorce because I have family in the area. It sure wasn't for the weather. Besides the winds, we get everything here—tornados, heat, snowstorms."

I mentioned my 83 adventure, and he knew how long the highway was. I left the station saying, "Good talking to you," which he repeated, adding, "buddy." I didn't envy him for having to deal with the Panhandle climate a lot longer than I did.

Wheeler had an appealing, small downtown near the courthouse. The town's history goes back to the early 1880s when ranchers settled in the area. Two enterprising ones named Robert B. Rodgers and J.E. Stanley were instrumental in establishing the town and getting the county seat relocated there in 1906. Rogers also became the town's first postmaster. Unlike so many towns along 83, Wheeler never had a railroad, but it still managed to develop into a commercial center. The discovery of the "black gold" of oil in the 1920s brought an industry in addition to ranching and farming and increased the town's population.

Wheeler has ties with the fourth man to walk on the moon in November 1969—U.S. astronaut Alan Bean, who was part of the Apollo 12 second moon landing mission. Bean was born in this small community in 1932 and spent his early years here. He's honored with U.S. 83 being named Alan Bean St. within the city limits. Before leaving town, I saw a sign for a city park, along with well-kept homes on shaded streets that looked quite like residential areas of some other highway towns further north.

Progressing south, the road had a somewhat rougher, chip-sealed surface, and it ran a little closer to the hundredth meridian not far to the east, which was used to establish the eastern boundary of the Texas Panhandle with the main body of Oklahoma, excluding its panhandle. The landscape ahead was a mixture of rangeland dotted with dark cattle and farmland with green winter wheat. Scattered trees and shrubs added to the diversity, as did more cotton fields further ahead.

The winds kicked up again with renewed intensity. I passed through a tiny, unincorporated community at the intersection of a local road with the peculiar name of Twitty, which was the surname of an early settler and store owner. It once had a cotton gin and over a hundred inhabitants, but declined to a mere twelve by 2000, according to state historical association records.

I crossed a long bridge over the North Fork of the Red River that looked like a trickle in an otherwise arid riverbed, along which there were grasses, scrubby trees, and red rocky outcrops to the east. This 271-mile-long stream with a source in neighboring Gray County is a tributary of the Red River, and the latter forms much of the boundary between Texas and Oklahoma. After the Adams-Onis Treaty of 1819 established the Red River as the border between the U.S. and New Spain shortly before Mexico's independence, the North Fork was also part of a border between the two countries.

I arrived at the junction with Interstate 40 in the north end of the town of Shamrock. This east-west superhighway that has a southern route across most of the U.S. is the third longest interstate after I-90 and I-80—sprawling 2,555 miles (4,112 km) between Wilmington, North Carolina, and Barstow, California. Between its western end and Oklahoma City, I-40 largely replaced legendary U.S. 66—best known as Route 66.

U.S. 83 became Main St., and just before the downtown area was its intersection with Historic Route 66—an actual, short stretch of the original highway that's now the Business Loop of I-40 through Shamrock. This meeting of two great old U.S. highways running in different directions, along with nearby I-40, is appropriately called the "Crossroads of America," which was displayed on banners by the intersection.

Most attention-grabbing, though, was one of the big relics of old Route 66—The Art Deco-style Conoco Tower and U Drop Inn at the northeast corner of the intersection. This impressive structure was built in 1936 and had the only cafe within a hundred miles of Shamrock when it opened. After the decades of Route 66's heyday, when the highway's traffic was greatly reduced by the opening of I-40, the Tower was headed toward disrepair, and eventually the business closed. Its saving grace came from the First National Bank of Shamrock, which in May 1999 purchased the old landmark and generously donated it to the City of Shamrock. The city was able to receive a 1.7 million-dollar grant from the federal government to hire a company that did historical restorations, and the result was the attractive building that must look very close to how it did back in the 1930s, and now contains a museum, gift shop, and Chamber of Commerce information center. I parked to get a closer look at the landmark structure that made the National Register of Historic Places, and being quite late in the day, everything inside was closed. However, the early evening light of a clear day enhanced the visual appeal of this great example of Art Deco architecture, with its geometric forms and light, earthy colors. Below the Conoco Tower were two vintage gas pumps, and the old, attached U Drop Inn had a shorter tower with the word CAFE. "If those walls could talk, what travelers' tales they could tell," I mused.

Across the street was a steakhouse displaying the well-known Route 66 U.S. highway shield symbol—another reminder of the legendary highway that was a 1926 original and once ran 2,448 miles (3,940 km) from Chicago, Illinois, to Santa Monica, California, across eight states, and was completely paved by 1937. Though certainly not the longest of the old U.S. highways, coast to coast, or necessarily the most scenic, Route 66 still became by far the most famous and with the greatest mystique. One reason must be the many references to the highway in John Steinbeck's *The Grapes of Wrath*, which he called "The Mother Road," since it transported thousands of migrants to California from the Dust Bowl states during the 1930s; and the book inspired the movie. Then, in 1946, the very popular song, "Get your kicks on Route 66," was released—written by Bobby Troup and first recorded by Nat King Cole. And 1960-1964 saw the running of the popular TV series *Route 66*. But I also think that a highway bound for sunny and balmy southern California from cold and gray Chicago drew more travelers and contributed to the mystique, along with its general east-west direction that's the main direction of movement in the American psyche. Even the sound of the road's name with double sixes probably made a difference, and two men who were involved in planning the old highways made a case for 66 over 60 or 62 for this route because they thought it sounded better. Early on, there was also a U.S. 66 Highway Association that promoted traveling the road.

The building of the interstates had an especially big effect on the decline of the old Mother Road, and I-40 drew much of its traffic, with depressing effects on many businesses and communities along the old route. Many fought to prevent being bypassed to keep their economies alive, but time wasn't always on their side.

On June 26, 1985, U.S. 66 was decommissioned as a U.S. highway. Some sections were abandoned and not maintained, and many were re-designated in different ways, such as frontage roads for nearby interstates or business loops like in Shamrock. Others became state or local roads that often retained 66 in their numbering, and some were given the designation "Historic Route 66." Though it's no longer possible to drive the entire old route, about eighty-five percent of its original alignment can still be traveled.

Perhaps the mystique of Route 66 has even been enhanced by its loss of status as a U.S. highway, and it attracts many enthusiasts from around the country and even internationally who explore what they can of it. Route 66 associations have formed in states along the route, beside preservation groups attempting to save many of the full of character highway landmarks and old motels and restaurants.

Although U.S. 83 may never have the fame and mystique of the former U.S. 66, I think it's just as fascinating a road in its own way, and it should at least be better known. Of all the old and long federal highways, 83 is probably the most intact and closest to its early route, despite some re-alignments of its own. And as Route 66 has also been called "The Main Street of America," I think 83 can be called "The Spine of America" because of its vertical route and location near the center of the country.

The next stop in Shamrock was to check out the quirky attraction of an actual piece of the Blarney Stone from Blarney Castle in Ireland. I found the rectangular fragment in Elmore Park, embedded on top of a hefty concrete cylinder, appropriately painted green. Kissing the parent stone in Ireland is supposed to bestow the gift of gab that the Irish call "blarney," and this fragment was imported from the Emerald Isle in 1959 because of the Irish association of the town's name.

This Irish connection began in 1890 when an early settler with Irish background named George Nickel, and his wife, Dora, accepted to run the community's first post office in their dugout dwelling—a type of early shelter constructed by many settlers on the Plains along with sod structures. George named the post office Shamrock after the Irish symbol of luck and courage. However, he didn't have the luck of the Irish when a mysterious fire soon ravaged his humble abode before the post office opened, and the latter was moved to another home. But after the Chicago, Rock Island, and Gulf Railway came through in 1902, the name Shamrock was retained for the burgeoning community. The town became more Irish when an annual St. Patrick's Day celebration started in 1938, which grew a lot and attracted thousands more people than lived in Shamrock. It even developed into multi-day festivities that drew many prominent people and included crowning a "Miss Irish Rose." In 2013, the state of Texas declared it the official St. Patrick's Day celebration for the state. Another example of how much can develop from just a name.

Since I'd never kissed the Blarney Stone across the Atlantic, I thought, why not do the same with the fragment here while I had the chance? But I can't say it gave me any more blarney.

I followed 83 down Main St. through Shamrock's business district, which I found to be not the most attractive old downtown I'd seen, with some weathered buildings. But it still had some charm with vintage storefronts and green banners attached to tall lamp posts announcing, "Welcome to Shamrock." There were also green fire hydrants and a nearby tall, white, water tower with a round tank displaying "Shamrock" in green letters. Shamrock seemed as green as Valentine, Nebraska was red, and looked like it was always St. Patrick's Day here.

After spotting another large, colorful mural on the side of a brick building, I parked to get a closer look and photo. The wall art had colorful images of the city's water tower, the Tower Building, the railroad, and a map of the U.S. showing the Crossroads of America here. There was also a likeness of Bill Mack—a well-known personality and talent in country music for decades, who was born in Shamrock in 1932 and grew up there.

After its beginnings in the early 1890s, Shamrock became incorporated in 1911, and after the railroad arrived, it developed into a local trade center that continued to grow. The discovery of the area's oil resources in 1926 and operation of natural gas wells led to further growth, and the town hit a population peak of 3,780 in 1930. But the cycles of the industry led to some drop in the town's numbers, followed by a comeback and stabilization from a stronger local economy that benefited from the increased traffic on Route 66. When the highway lost traffic to the interstate, Shamrock's numbers dropped again. Nevertheless, it remained the largest town in Wheeler County, with industries that included oil and gas processing plants. The most recent population figure was 1,910.

The sun was getting low as I headed south of the Crossroads of America. It had remained clear and cloudless, and the fierce winds had finally faded. I cruised through grassy, open country again with some groves of trees. To the west, the sun radiated a brilliant orange glow over what was probably part of the Caprock escarpment. The road still had a rougher surface and soon rose, then later descended to a lush area with trees by Elm Creek, where the creek bed was concealed by heavy growth. The open country ahead appeared different from the High Plains to the north, with shrubby mesquite starting to dominate. I saw some foraging Angus, but no cultivation since Shamrock.

Then it reappeared with huge cotton fields on both sides of the road. The sun was sinking, and there was a sign for Childress—forty-four miles away—which had become my destination for the day. The highway was back in a very level landscape before the road and terrain became more rolling again.

Just west of 83 was a place on the map named Samnorwood—a community with fifty-one inhabitants that had about double that number in 1940. It was established in 1931 when a line of the Fort Worth and Denver Northern Railway came through, and it became a shipping center for local agriculture and ranching. Interestingly, its appellation is a combination of the first name and surname of one of the area's pioneers—Sam W. Norwood.

Down the road was an even smaller habitation called Lutie, which came from the first name of the wife of the Collingsworth County attorney in 1909. Before 1890, the townsite was part of the sprawling Rocking Horse Ranch that covered most of the area, and the little community that developed there reached its population high of 125 in 1941. It declined to 35 by 1990 when all its businesses had closed, and a 2009 record showed an estimated ten souls. I noticed a few homes and buildings that looked occupied, but others appeared vacant. Lutie was called a "ghost town" on one website I checked out.

The highway expanded to four-lanes, with a wide, grassy median. I was finally on smooth asphalt again with good, paved shoulders bordered by reflector posts. This expressway section crossed the Salt Fork of the Red River—a 193-mile tributary that winds across half of the Texas Panhandle into Oklahoma. Next to the concrete bridge that carries 83 across the river was an old steel truss bridge, built in 1939, which had a predecessor that played a role in an episode of the infamous outlaws Bonnie and Clyde. For on June 10, 1933, they were driving north on 83 in a stolen, high-powered Ford, and plunged into a dry riverbed after missing a detour for the bridge being out. Along with Clyde Barrow's young accomplice, W.D. Jones, they were rescued by members of a local farm family named Pritchard, who witnessed the accident and took them to their nearby home for assistance. Bonnie Parker had a seriously burned leg from battery acid, but when she refused medical service and guns were retrieved from the wrecked vehicle, a family member became suspicious and drove to Wellington down the road to alert the authorities. Later the local police chief and sheriff arrived. However, in a strange twist, the outlaws managed to disarm and capture the lawmen, and then sped off in the sheriff's car with him and the other officer as hostages toward the Oklahoma border not far to the east. There, they had a rendezvous with Clyde's brother and his wife near the state line, where the lawmen were tied to a tree by the side of the road, and the outlaws sped off in their accomplices' car. Later, the captives managed to escape. It's no wonder this bizarre series of events became legendary in the area.

The highway narrowed back to two lanes as I neared Wellington, and in the fading light, the familiar figure of a water tower and some other vertical structures stood beyond fields with grazing cattle. A city limit sign showed there were 2,189 residents.

Wellington was proposed as a town in 1890 and elected to be the seat of newly organized Collingsworth County. The community was platted the following year, and one of its promoters was Ernest T. O'Neill, who owned land where the town would develop. It was named Wellington, not after any local figure, but to honor the British Duke of Wellington, who defeated Napoleon at the Battle of Waterloo. One explanation for this namesake is that the wife of O'Neill was an admirer of the British hero and influenced her husband with the naming. He remained involved in the town and county's growth and was also a postmaster from 1895 to 1897. Wellington grew more in the early 1900s, and the cotton industry became as important as cattle. Two railroads reached the town in the coming years, and by 1931 its population had grown to over 3,500. Since 1980, the numbers have declined, but Wellington has remained a place of industry that still has cotton gins that service the area's crops. With over two-thirds of the county's population, it's no wonder that the town has remained the seat.

Wellington's downtown has a concrete obelisk marking the route of the Ozark Trail—one of the early twentieth-century auto trails that predated the U, S. highway system, which was organized by the Ozark Trails Association as a network of local roads. It had different branches that ran from St. Louis, Missouri, to El Paso, Texas, and Santa Fe, New Mexico, and some sections became parts of Route 66. Numerous obelisks were erected along its route, but only seven remain.

South of Wellington, I was back on another rougher, chip-sealed surface. The sunset left a blended afterglow of pale orange and blue with a rainbow-like effect. Also visually appealing were the forms of power lines along the road, with taller ones to the west appearing as silhouettes in the last light of day. I was also looking for an outline of the Rocking Chair Mountains to the west that are not real mountains but a range of mesas named after the sprawling 1880s ranch that covered parts of Collingsworth and Wheeler Counties and was owned largely by British aristocrats. But I couldn't make out any elevations, perhaps because of the dim light.

Large cottonfields were ahead, and further on some tall bare trees stood prominently to the west as spooky silhouettes in the foreground of some lingering afterglow. I crossed the line into Childress County, and beyond a grassy area to the east was a heavily wooded one that seemed to mark the course of a tributary of a big fork of the Red River to the south that I noticed on my map. I crossed a bridge over what must have been the stream amid a cluster of trees and shrubs; then the road widened to four-lanes again for a very short distance, with bright reflectors dividing the lanes.

When 83 reverted to two lanes, it was joined by U.S. 62 coming in from the east, which would run with it well past Childress. U.S. 62 is a significant federal highway that's the only east-west one connecting Canada and Mexico, as 83 does north-south. That's because of its rather diagonal route across a good swath of the U.S.—from Niagara Falls, New York, to El Paso, Texas—2,248 miles (3,618 km) across ten states. It's an early but not original federal highway dating to 1930, and parts of it follow the older Ozark Trail. U.S. 83-62 crossed the Prairie Dog Town Fork Red River, and in the darkness I could still make out some channels reduced to a trickle. When it flows, this 160-mile-long stream is the more southern of the two major tributaries that merge to form the main Red River to the east.

The lights of Childress glittered in the distance—a city with a 6,105 population as posted at its city limits. Soon I arrived at an intersection with U.S. 287, which is a direct connection with home for me, since this long, three-numbered auxiliary highway that runs 1,791 miles (2,882 km) passes through the center of Fort Collins between its northern end in Choteau, Montana and southern one in Port Arthur, Texas. However, its route through five states is split by Yellowstone National Park.

At the junction of 83-62 and 287, I pulled into a truck stop with a Valero station and convenience store. Earlier I was set on sleeping in a bed after the uncomfortable night at the last truck stop with the wind and rain, But the weather was a lot better now, and I felt recovered enough from the discomfort to check out this truck stop. I found a suitable space in a corner of the lot close to the restrooms and got permission from a store manager to stay there—"But we're not responsible for any losses," he said, which I wasn't concerned about.

The intersection was bustling with truck traffic, and there was a big commercial area as there often are at crossroads. Back in the car. I sipped a PBR while jotting in my journal, then set out on foot to find an eatery. A short way up 287 was another truck stop with a big Pilot gas station-store complex. Outside the store I asked a thirtyish guy wearing a brimmed cap how far the downtown area was, which according to *Road Trip USA* has had a big decline; but I wondered what might be open there.

"The downtown is about a mile," he answered with the local drawl, "but it's not a place to eat this late or for nightlife."

"I heard it's declined."

"It has, though some businesses are open during the day. One reason for the decline is that the old people who had businesses for years passed away or moved on."

"So, have you always lived here?"

"I am a native of Childress," he said, pronouncing the first syllable like "chill" and not "child" like I might have at first and sounded more like an outsider. "So, where are you from?"

"Fort Collins, Colorado, and I'm traveling the whole length of U.S. 83 from the Canadian border in North Dakota to Brownsville."

"Wow! I didn't know the road went that far north to Canada. It must be great to take a trip like that and take your time. Are you going to the Coast too?"—which is what I would hear Texans call the large area of the state along the Gulf of Mexico.

"I'm planning on a visit to South Padre Island after making it to Brownsville, since it's so close."

"It's a really nice place—and warm."

"That's a big part of the appeal for me. So is Childress a dry town?"—referring to its alcohol laws.

"No, it's wet."—An example of the diversity in Texas drinking laws.

He was a friendly young guy, and our encounter ended with a handshake and good wishes from him. I wound up eating in a cafeteria section in the store complex, where there were some Black employees around who were the first Afro Americans I'd seen for many miles. A girl working there wished me a "safe trip"—assuming I was another traveler at this big crossroads.

It was a clear night with a half-moon on the wane. Back at the truck stop, there were a lot of idling engines, but at least they were away from my space. I wondered again why so many are kept running, even overnight, and why so many places allow it, considering the noxious nature of diesel fumes. I would later find out that one old reason for prolonged idling is to avoid difficulty in starting cold diesel engines, especially in cold weather. But that's supposed to be less of a problem with modern diesel technology. Another reason is to keep the electrical system charged for heating, air-conditioning, and other accessories used by truckers. However, a website I came across called "Smart Trucking," with advice for truckers, expressed an opinion that idling is done much more than necessary. I also learned that engine idling regulations vary widely around the country, and that there was currently "no policy" among most of the states along 83, which is apparently why I came across so much idling. Hopefully, that policy will change.

I walked near a few of the running rigs for a closer look at the bunk compartments behind the cabs where the drivers might have been sleeping. These "sleepers" have a range of sizes, and I'm sure that even the most compact ones offer more comfort than the cramped accommodation I had. Back in my cramper, I did more writing until it was late and I was overcome by fatigue. Besides the idling engines in the lot, there was also the sound of moving ones through what might have been the busiest crossroads I encountered on the journey.

Before I fell asleep, a little melancholy set in that might have been triggered by being so close to U.S. 287, which could take me home and back to the comforts, security, and familiar people there. Momentarily, I felt anxious to finish the trip. But I tried to regard this feeling as just a passing mood and part of a cycle in the traveler's psyche. My enthusiasm for the journey would return, I felt sure. That was my state of mind at the end of Day 21 at another truck stop.

DAY 22

A walk in Childress, mesquite, cotton, an unfriendly cop

Rest relieved my mind from most of the little episode of traveler's blues, and the new day was perfectly clear and not windy. After checking Wander's tire pressures and a few other things, I drove to a nearby McDonald's and ordered their oatmeal again. While sipping my tea afterwards, I started a conversation with a middle-aged guy seated near me, who was from Amarillo to the northwest and working in this area for a termite company.

"I had to deal with a lot of fierce winds further north," I told him, "and I'm sure glad they stopped."

"In my area the spring winds are the worst, and often blow seventy miles an hour," he said with another drawl.

"How about tornadoes? Do you ever get them this time of year?"

"They can happen now. But we haven't had a bad tornado in the Amarillo area in fifteen years."

"I'm traveling the whole length of 83, and tornadoes are one of my concerns, even if it's not the most dangerous season. I had a little scare near Liberal, Kansas, but the storm didn't turn into anything serious, and there was a beautiful rainbow afterwards."

"That sounds nice. So, are you going all the way to the Coast?"

"Yes. After Brownsville, I plan on spending some time on South Padre Island and am looking very forward to the warm climate there."

"It is much warmer close to the Coast. I used to have jobs down there." Then his present job beckoned, and he got up and said, "Good talking to you. I have to get to work. Have a good trip."

"Have a good workday." And I preferred whatever rigors my trip had to having to deal with termites daily.

Before leaving the McDonald's, I watched some TV news for a little update on some happenings in the outside world, then brushed my teeth in the men's room. While heading out, I saw two camouflage-clad hunters at a table and asked them what the main game in the area was, and they informed me it was deer, wild hogs, and quail this season.

A good mile away off U.S. 287 was the old downtown of Childress that I wanted a look at, and I turned by another sizable Texas county courthouse—a white stone structure built in 1939—on to red brick Main St. The surroundings were quaint, and I was ready for a little walking tour and parked in front of a furniture store. The clear day had warmed up to seventy-one degrees. Quite a few other vehicles were parked, and some traffic rumbled over the red bricks. A banner along Main St. announced, "Childress Historic Downtown," and there were enough well-preserved buildings—also largely brick—and signs of business life besides closed storefronts and vacant structures. Another old Palace theater, like the one in Canadian, caught my attention with its largely white facade. It looked vacant but still photogenic.

After aiming my camera at the theater, I was approached with a friendly greeting by a couple that looked in their thirties with a young boy. They asked where I was from, and after mentioning my trip and how I liked the old downtown, I found out both were very active in its restoration. Their names were John and Shelly, with their five-year-old son, Jared.

"The restoration started about three years ago, mainly with private funds," John said. He had a heavy Texas accent, as did his wife. "We even hope to re-open the theater eventually. In the meantime, movies have been shown outside on Main St., with the street closed off. We've made some real progress, and downtown is more vital than it was before the project."

"Have you always lived in Childress?" I asked, making sure I pronounced it correctly.

"My roots go deep here. I'm descended from homesteaders who came here about 1890. We did live in Plano near Dallas for a while, but it's great to be back here and we plan on staying."

"I have deep roots in the area too," Shelly added, "not far from Childress."

Then I brought up something I'd been wondering about: "Why are so many of the rivers and streams I've seen from the road so dry? Is there a lot of depletion due to irrigation?"

"It's really because of drought," John replied.

"Well, I hope you get all of the rain you need, but after I'm well south of here." And they both smiled.

I got the family to pose for a picture in front of the theater. Then John recommended I visit the Childress County Heritage Museum. He also handed me two business cards—one with his name as an archaeology steward for the Texas Historical Commission, and the other for an insurance agency he owned in town. He also wrote down the website for the Palace Theater restoration project in case I was interested.

I admired this couple's attachment and service to their community, and I commended them for their efforts in revitalizing the old downtown. When I asked about a good local lunch spot, they recommended a place that's locally owned and had been around a long time.

"It was great meeting you folks," I said, "and you too," to the little guy, and we parted with mutually warm regards.

This town's history started with two small townsites—Childress City and another called Henry—which were about four miles apart on the old OX Ranch. One was named after George C. Childress, who was the principal author of the Texas Declaration of Independence from Mexico, which was signed on March 2, 1836, during the famed siege and battle at the Alamo. When the Fort Worth and Denver City Railway arrived in February 1887, Childress County was established, and both nascent communities vied for the county seat. Henry was eventually chosen but changed its name to Childress and became consolidated with the other community. A boom was spurred by the railroad, which built a depot and the Dwight Hotel, and the town was incorporated in 1890. In the early 1900s, Childress also became a diversion point for the railroad with service facilities for the trains, which led to more employment and population growth. Walter P.

Chrysler—the future founder of the Chrysler Motor Corporation—happened to be the general foreman of the Childress railroad shops in 1905-1906. For decades, the railroad was the main industrial presence in the town, but eventually the shops were closed and torn down. Some other industries moved in, and the area's first productive oil well was drilled in 1961. Then, in 1991, a state penitentiary for men was established outside town.

The population of Childress has fluctuated through the years and reached a high of 7,619 in 1950. It presently was a little over 6,000, and the town was a local center for agri-business, with grain elevators and cotton gins. An annual event held every July with remarkable consistency since 1888 is the Old Settlers Reunion, which features a rodeo and other festivities. Such themed reunions are common in Texas communities.

Continuing my walk, I also had a little conversation with a local chiropractor by his office—a friendly, fortyish guy who was originally from north-central Kansas and had previously lived in Dallas, which he thought was "too big and crowded."

"There was a big need for a chiropractor in Childress," he said, "and I really like the town and people here, who are very nice."

It didn't take long to see a couple of churches that didn't appear to need aid from the preservation effort, and I came to a large mural on the side of a long brick building dedicated to the Childress Army Airfield that operated outside town during World War II from 1942 to 1945, which specialized in bombardier training. Among the mural's images were a bomber, a male bombardier, and a female Wasp—Woman Airforce Service Pilot—of which there were over 1,000 during the war who flew in non-combat operations. Like many of the old Army airfields, the one near Childress became a civilian airport after the war.

Close to some railroad tracks was a big symbol of the town's rail history—a very vintage steam locomotive of the Pacific-4-6-2 Class—on display on a segment of track inside an open-sided shelter in a grassy area. It was manufactured in 1911 and had accumulated 2,500,000 miles in its service life on the Fort Worth and Denver Railway. Nearby was the rectangular, block-shaped, five-story Hotel Childress. This brick structure opened in 1929 and was currently vacant, but aroused my interest the way old hotels always do. Outside, it didn't appear to be in great disrepair. At the time it was built, Childress also had other hotels, with most near the rail depot as these old lodgings often were.

Behind the hotel was the Childress County Heritage Museum that John had recommended, which was a well-preserved brick building on another red brick street that had been the old post office. My sauntering led to another old building mural with the heading, "Childress 1902"—depicting the downtown streets of that year with horse-drawn carts, people in period dress, and buildings that were probably still largely standing. When I returned to Wander, the outside temperature read seventy-eight degrees, and I changed to a tee-shirt, feeling delighted that the weather in Texas had become a lot more benevolent than the way I'd been welcomed in the state by the fierce winds.

I drove to JT's Drive-In for lunch, which the friendly couple had recommended, and found it to be a small, roadside type of place with a couple of outside tables. Inside, it had a lot of Texas character, with images of cowboys on the walls that included John Wayne, along with mounted guns and farm implements. A sign over the counter read: "I spent most of my money on beer and women, the rest I just wasted." When I saw that the menu included burgers from fresh Texas Angus, I put any compunctions about eating beef aside and ordered one embellished with lettuce, tomato, onions, a pickle, and the mustard that was the standard condiment here, and it was a very good burger. A guy was working in the kitchen, and I talked to a middle-aged woman who happened to be the owner and told her I was traveling 83.

"The business has been in the family for forty-five years," she said in her drawl. "Before that it was a carhop with a different name. "

"So why the name JT's?"

"That was my dad's initials."

"Well, I hope your place keeps going another forty-five years. It's great to see small, family-run eateries like this doing so well. There's too many McDonald's and Burger Kings."

"Thank you, sir. You're right about that. Before you leave town, you should see Fair Park near here." And she gave me directions.

I decided to stop there next and found it to be a very nice and well-maintained municipal park with typical facilities, plus a swimming pool and small zoo. What I found most interesting was a small lake that had been a watering hole for cattle on the Goodnight Trail.

The namesake of this historic cattle trail was Charles Goodnight—a very prominent early Texas cattleman who's been called the "father of the Texas Panhandle." A historical marker commemorated the cattle drives that came through here between 1866 and 1871, bound for New Mexico and Colorado before Childress existed, and when many bison still roamed the plains.

I returned to the busy crossroads with all the commercial development and traffic, and it felt like I'd made a little trip back in time to the old, slow-paced downtown that I hoped would make a comeback. Childress has been called the "Gateway to the Panhandle." If that's accepted, I was about to leave that well-known part of Texas. However, *The Last American Highway—Texas* mentions a general agreement that the southern border of Cottle County, further south, marked the southern boundary of the region.

The landscape south of Childress changed from flat to rolling, and I cruised by cotton fields, grasslands, green cultivations, and groups of trees. A few low ridges lie ahead, with blankets of green timber and bare spots. Then came a very scenic stretch with red, rocky outcrops and cedar-clad hillsides, where the highway sliced through a solid rock formation to the east. Light green mesquite appeared again—some of it small tree-sized.

I crossed the sixty-mile-long North Pease River, reduced to puddles, and not far ahead was the slightly longer Middle Pease, which looked completely dry. Both "rivers" merge not far to the east and form the Pease River—another tributary of the Red River. The highway had passing lanes on uphill sections, and its surface was still somewhat rumbly.

The sun was descending, and a water tower loomed ahead in the town of Paducah. On the approach, there were grazing black Angus and white speckled cotton fields. The highway ran near the water tower, and I was greeted by a "Welcome to Paducah" sign indicating a population of 1,186. I passed an old brick train station that looked very interesting, though vacant, by a small rail remnant. U.S. 83 became the red brick Main St. of Paducah, and I parked in front of a monumental, four-story brick and terra cotta county courthouse that was the most impressive building in an old, run-down business center.

There was an atmosphere of deterioration here way beyond the old Childress downtown. I started another walk and saw lots of vacant buildings and closed businesses up close in what amounted to the first real dying town of some size that I'd seen along the highway. There was another Palace theater in a tile-roofed, brick building that appeared in decent condition on the outside but looked long closed. Through its fogged windows I could make out the lobby, and the marquee displayed the name of the very old Western movie, *Red River*, with John Wayne. A much sadder sight was the Cottle Hotel—a vintage, three-story brick structure with a boarded up bottom floor and upper ones marred by broken windows, torn shades, and bent blinds. A very weathered "Hotel Cafe" sign added to the appearance of total neglect, which was especially sad because of my fondness for such hotels. I mused about all the life that must have pulsed there for decades.

I walked by a row of vacant brick buildings on the north side of the courthouse, and one had been demolished. On another side a store was open, but about every other building there was vacant. I saw no one else walking, just some parked vehicles and occasional traffic rumbling down 83-Main St. One was a passing pickup, and the driver waved to me. The late light of day left golden shades and shadows on run-down buildings, giving a glow to the deterioration.

I walked down red brick side streets and saw an open restaurant and a First Baptist church that still had a nice appearance across from a vacant lot. On 11th Street, I came to an elegant two-story brick structure with front columns called Hunters Lodge Motel, which looked more like a small hotel that appeared as well-kept as the Cottle Hotel was decrepit. This was turning out to be a town with some sharp contrasts that I also saw in a residential area I wandered through—from weathered and boarded up old dwellings to viable Craftsmen and ranch-style homes and some nice lawns.

Back near the courthouse was a historical sign with the heading, "The Gray and the Blue," about how around the year 1885 the western part of Texas was settled by many Civil War veterans, including some who had fought for the Union. Not surprisingly, eighty-five percent of the early pioneers in Cottle County had been Confederates. The sign said veterans of both sides "verbally refought the war on the courthouse square, but lived peacefully together to build a great country."

There was another little history lesson right in front of the courthouse about its construction in 1929 that referred to it as "one of the premier Art Deco style courthouses in the state." The sign also mentioned the building's design being compared to an Egyptian temple, and its listing on the National Register of Historic Places along with the surrounding square. The grounds around the still functioning courthouse also looked well-maintained amid the deterioration.

Cottle County was established in 1876 and named in honor of George Washington Cottle—one of the defenders of the Alamo who died at the iconic battle in 1836—but it wasn't really organized until 1892. Paducah was chosen as the county seat because of its central location, and it was named by the early settler, R. Potts, who had arrived about 1850 from Paducah, Kentucky and was determined to name a new Texas town after the one he came from. He even offered later settlers free land if they voted for his chosen name, which succeeded in 1892. The name Paducah has a Native origin from a large tribal group that was known as the Padouca.

The town grew slowly and had 151 residents by 1903. Then, on Christmas Day in 1909, the Quanah, Acme, and Pacific Railroad arrived, and Paducah was incorporated the following year, with the population increasing to 1,350. A rather steady growth followed, reaching a peak near 3,000 in 1950. There's been a steady decrease since 1980, when there were 2,216 people and the town still had a prosperous economy as a farming and ranching center with thriving businesses. Then things happened that led to the decay before my eyes.

An online article I read attributed a lot of Paducah's plight to a big demise in the area's agriculture combined with bad economies and faulty government programs that reduced farmland production. And it seemed that the decline in local agriculture had a domino effect that led to more people leaving Paducah and shrinking its tax base. Also, the oil and gas industry, which brought an economic boom to much of Texas, hasn't operated in the area, and efforts to attract other industries failed. Nevertheless, the article also quoted a Paducah resident with a positive outlook that praised the people still left in the town. Where there's life, there's still hope, as they say. Perhaps someday this town's decline will be reversed.

U.S. 62 branched off 83 at an intersection in Paducah and shot west along with U.S. 70, which came in from the east. The junction of these three federal highways is why Paducah is another town that calls itself the "Crossroads of America." U.S. 70 is a long 1926 original that stretches 2,385 miles (3,838 km) across seven states—from Atlantic, North Carolina, to Globe, Arizona. However, it once ran coast to coast and was known as the "Broadway of America," before the interstate era, when it was a major east-west route.

I passed a Chevrolet dealer on the way out of town that looked like it was still in business, and a small RV park. It was just after sunset, which left another striking afterglow as daylight faded. Cotton fields reappeared to the west, and then I was back into very brushy country with tall mesquite on both sides of the road. Soon I was cruising through a very open and flat area with cotton fields to the east and cattle grazing on the grassy west side in what was still ranch country.

The light was dim, but the gorgeous glow lingered over the horizon of a vast plain. The road crossed the North Wichita River, which I couldn't see, but was probably dry. When it flows, it's one of three branches that form the Wichita River to the east that's yet another tributary of the Red River. Wichita is another indigenous name of a people who once inhabited parts of Texas, Oklahoma, and Kansas, which is why their name appears in the region—another example of ironically commemorating a Native people after they were displaced.

I had entered King County, and soon came a stretch with mesquite so thick and tall that it appeared forest-like. This abundant deciduous growth has roots as deep as seventy feet that absorb groundwater and deprive the grasses cattle feed on, which is why ranchers have great animosity toward it. Though native, mesquite's range has expanded tremendously since settlement because natural fires that once kept it under control became suppressed. Also, prairie dogs, which eat its seeds that also controlled the shrub's spread, have been exterminated in many places, largely by ranchers, ironically. Bovine overgrazing has also favored mesquite in the conflict between trees and grasses on these southern plains. So, ranching has contributed to its proliferation.

The landscape became more open again to the west in the last bit of daylight, and bright yellow reflectors in the center of the road strung far ahead. There was hardly any traffic, and it was one of those stretches when I almost felt like I owned the road.

It was completely dark when I entered Guthrie, and I didn't see much of this very small, unincorporated community of about 160 people. It happens to be a company town where few homes are privately owned, and most are provided by two local ranches, including the huge, historic 6666 or Four Sixes Ranch, or the school district. Despite its miniature size, Guthrie is the seat of King County, which contains only one other community that's even smaller. The county is the second least populated in Texas and the third least in the whole country. But there's still a courthouse in Guthrie, built in 1982, that's the fourth in the town's history. The first one was a two-story frame structure that was destroyed by a tornado in 1905. The town was named after W.H. Guthrie, who was a leading stockholder of the Louisville Land and Cattle Company based in Kentucky, which in 1883 purchased several hundred acres where the town would develop. A townsite was platted in 1891 on the South Wichita River, and Guthrie opened a post office later that year. By 1904, it had 104 residents, and the following year was the scene of a bizarre shootout between the only doctor in town and a hotel manager, in which seven shots were fired but all missed. But that didn't stop the local sheriff from charging the two men with attempted murder, though both were acquitted.

Guthrie got through the Great Depression and Dust Bowl of the 1930s and reached a population high of 200 in 1963. It was a ranch supply center, especially for the Four Sixes Ranch, whose founder, Samuel Burk Burnett, had purchased the old Louisville Land and Cattle Company in 1900. In 1975, the ranch's headquarters in Guthrie was a location for a Western movie set in the modern era that starred the famous Roy Rogers in his last feature film, *Mackintosh and TJ*.

I crossed a bridge over the South Wichita River, then drove under an overpass for U.S. 82. This 1931 east-west federal highway originally ran across central Mississippi and southern Arkansas and became expanded to 1,625 miles (2,615 km) through six states—from Brunswick, Georgia, to Alamogordo, New Mexico. On the return route of my motorcycle odyssey in 1976 to celebrate the nation's Bicentennial, I'd ridden 82 east from New Mexico into Texas, then across the state below the Panhandle all the way to Wichita Falls, passing through Guthrie. So, I'd been here before on another kind of journey. Further back in 1950—the year I was born—Beat Generation author Jack Kerouac had also passed through with a couple of companions while traveling 83 south for a stretch in a 1937 Ford Sedan bound for Mexico, and he briefly mentioned Guthrie in his classic tale of wanderlust, *On the Road*.

A sign said it was fifty-two miles to Hamlin—a larger town I wanted to reach and probably spend the night even if it meant driving longer in the dark. I could still make out a couple of mound-like landforms to the west, with tall mesquite in the foreground. Stars were shining in the southwest, and I again enjoyed the calm feeling of cruising the highway at night, especially with so little traffic; and the road's center reflectors glittered for miles.

Further on, I crossed a bridge over the Salt Fork of the Brazos River. This meandering, approximately 150-miles-long stream, with a source near the edge of the Llano Estacado, merges with the Double Mountain Fork Brazos River not too far east of 83 to form the Brazos River—a major Texas River that flows 840 miles toward the Gulf of Mexico. Both tributaries are said to often be dry and braided with sand.

A line of lights appeared that was the community of Aspermont, with over 900 inhabitants. North of town, U.S. 380 came in from the west and merged with 83 for a very short distance before it continued east. This three-digit auxiliary highway, commissioned in 1931, is 673 miles (1,080 km) long between Greenville, Texas, and San Antonio, New Mexico—not to be confused with the big city in Texas—and runs in only two states. The parent highway, U.S. 80, runs further south, which 380 had a connection with until 1971 before some re-routing.

In Aspermont I saw two motels and a truck stop, but I was still intent on making it to Hamlin, now twenty-two miles away. I did stop, though, to put on a jacket in the chilly night air and also snacked on half of a ripe avocado that I cut and spooned out and had with a slice of bread to satisfy some hunger.

Aspermont got started in 1889 when it was platted and provided land by a man of Swiss-Austrian descent named A.L. Rhomberg, who also named the town, which means "rough mountain" in Latin and is thought to refer to the local Double Mountains. In 1898 Aspermont replaced the town of Rayner as the seat of Stonewall County, which was contested by Rayner. But Aspermont won the litigation in 1900 in this often contentious matter in some counties, and a new courthouse was constructed. The town was incorporated in 1909, and the Stamford and Northwestern Railway extension also arrived that year. By 1910, Aspermont had 600 people, which was reduced by the time of World War I, but the numbers rebounded. Oil was discovered in the area in the 1930s, and along with ranching is still the basis of the local economy. However, there's been a steady decline in population since a peak of 1,357 in 1980.

I discerned a lot more mesquite in the dark landscape ahead. Another bridge crossed the Double Mountain Fork Brazos River, which would converge with the other fork I'd crossed. Hamlin was soon visible as another string of lights in the distance. At the city limits, a sign posted 2,124 residents, and I could see a few lofty grain elevators. After passing a couple of gas stations, a Subway store, and Dairy Queen, 83 led into a downtown area and became South Central Avenue. The old business district looked viable but quiet now.

I gassed up at a Conoco station, then went into a convenience store and asked a fiftyish woman if there were any motels around.

"There's only one, and it's not far from here," she said.

"Only one? Then it's probably expensive if there's no competition."

"I heard it is on the expensive side. There's also motels in Anson, the next town south, and a lot in Abilene, which is about forty-five miles."

"I'd rather not travel further tonight. Are there any truck stops in town? Or a Walmart, or other places to park legally and safely overnight?"

"There's no truck stop or Walmart, and I can't think of any other places."

"Well, thanks anyway. I'll find something. Have a good night."

I went back to the car to think about what I should do and looked at my map. The lady soon stepped outside, and when she noticed my Colorado plate, she asked where I was from in the state. When I said "Fort Collins," she told me she had relatives living there that she'd visited.

"I know the town's really growing," she added, "I originally lived in Denver but eventually wanted to move to get away from all the snow. I haven't been here that long, but I lived in Alabama before in an even smaller town."

It seemed that for years, more people have been moving to Denver than leaving it. So this woman was in the minority of emigrants.

"So, what brought you here? And do you like Hamlin?"

She made a face that expressed some negative feelings, then replied: "I'm here to be near my grandkids, daughter, and son-in-law. He got a job in the oil industry, which is about the only good work around here, though I heard the town used to have more industry. A dog food plant is still here that was a big employer but has fewer employees now."

"How about agriculture?" I asked, remembering the grain elevators I saw.

"They do raise wheat in the area," she replied. Then she got into describing some rather shocking results from people leaving Hamlin. "A lot of people who've left this town left a lot of belongings in their homes—even cars."

"That's hard to believe."

"In Alabama, all the stuff would have been grabbed. But it's not like that here. You could get one of the abandoned homes and belongings cheaply," which sounded like a lot of foreclosures. "Some of the homes are OK, but not others."

We conversed a little more before she went back into the store to check out a customer, and I went in to ask if she knew if the Subway I saw was still open, or if there were any other late eateries.

"They're all closed now, but there's an Allsup's store near here that has some things they'll heat up, and they're open all night."

A very young woman entered the store with a baby in a stroller that happened to be the woman's daughter and grandchild. She told her daughter I was from Fort Collins, and the young lady reacted favorably, then mentioned growing up in Alabama. We all chatted a little more before I thanked the older woman for informing me about a few things and concluded with: "It was really nice meeting you."

I found the store the woman recommended to check out what kind of food they had. There was a tractor-trailer parked in a small lot between the store and a Dollar General, and I wondered if I could park there overnight. Outside the store, I got a friendly greeting from a heavy young woman, and the same amiability from another woman inside who worked there. A sign touted one of the prepped foods: "Celebrating forty years of the world-famous beef and bean burrito." The hype led to my ordering two burritos, since they were small, and continuing some beef consumption in this beefy state. Then I asked if I could park overnight and sleep in my vehicle in the lot, and the woman serving me said, "It's OK," as did another who might have been the manager. I was also offered an option of parking on the side of the store, and one of the ladies even said, "I hope you sleep well."

I decided on the lot further from the store, which seemed to offer more privacy, and parked away from the truck there that wasn't idling. It seemed like I'd found another vagabond-friendly place, and I quaffed a Miller High Life in the car before eating another half of an avocado along with the burritos, which were tasty if not deserving of "world famous." Then I got back to catching up with my journal.

After midnight I was ready to sleep, and first walked to the store to use the restroom. On the way back I was faced with the sight of an SUV police vehicle parked by Wander, and a fairly young cop checking it out.

"That's my car, officer," I said as I approached, "and I got permission from the store people to park overnight."

"So where are you going? And I'd like to see your driver's license and registration."

I'm traveling south on 83," I said as I got out my credentials, and after looking at them he started asking me more questions.

"So, just where are you headed?"

"The Coast. I'm driving 83 all the way to Brownsville, then plan on spending some time on South Padre Island before I head back to Colorado. I'm actually driving all of 83 and started at the northern end in North Dakota a few weeks ago."

He reacted to my explanation with a somewhat puzzled look and asked, "Why would you want to do that?"

I gave a similar reply to what I had before to the now familiar question: "For the adventure. I really like long road trips."

But he didn't seem satisfied with my answer. "Just wait here," he said before getting into his vehicle to use his radio to presumably get a background check on me, which my having a clean record made me think things would be fine from there on. But after he came out, the next thing he said was, "Mind if I look in your car?"

I thought if I asked, "Why?" or said, "Yes, I mind," he would get more suspicious and could easily get a search warrant. So, I said: "Go right ahead, I have nothing to hide."

He then started going through the car, and more than once told me to keep some distance from him—"for the safety of both of us"—and that he wanted to be able to see my hands. He wasn't really nasty or arrogant, but seemed very suspicious and somewhat anxious that I could be a danger to him, even though I thought I looked pretty harmless and not at all criminal.

As he went through what seemed like everything, he also asked me a slew of questions: "Where are you headed next? Where were you last night? When do you plan to leave Hamlin? What will you do when you get to the Coast?"—and what must have been his biggest concerns—"Do you have any weapons? Were you ever in trouble with the law?" which he repeated. After giving him truthful answers that were negative to the last two questions that I thought should finally satisfy him, he still asked more questions: "What do you do for a living? Are you married? Do you travel a lot?" And when he came across a plastic bag with some empty beer bottles and cans I was saving to recycle, he said, "You should get rid of these."

There were more questions about the small bottles of nutritional supplements in the trunk, and I reassured the officer that they were only vitamins and other supplements. Then he asked, "What kind do you take?" and "Are you healthy?" The interrogation continued when he noticed a window sticker for a Colorado police organization that I'd donated to: "Do you support Colorado police?"

"I've made a donation."

"How much did you give?" He was intrusive enough to ask. And when he saw my binoculars on the front passenger seat, his reaction was, "Why do you have these?"

"I like to look at birds and other wildlife and scenery," which I thought pretty obvious reasons.

And when he went into my glove compartment and saw my

large fit-over sunglasses, he made the remark, "These look like ladies' glasses."

I continued to bite my tongue, though I was tempted to sarcastically say that I had them because I was a cross-dresser. But instead, I made my masculinity clear by explaining these were men's and women's sunglasses that fit over prescription glasses.

By this time one of the women from the store was outside watching the police–suspect drama. Finally, the cop said: "Everything looks OK, and I'll let another officer who's out know so you won't be bothered again."

"I'd appreciate that, officer. So, there's no problem parking here overnight and sleeping in the car? I heard there's one motel in town but it's expensive."

"They are, and it's OK to stay here. Do you know of anyone else who's driven all of 83?"

"Yes, and I have a book with a chapter about doing it that inspired me to do it. I could show it to you."

He wasn't interested in seeing it, though, and I didn't care because he finally left, which is all I really cared about. What a difference between him and the few women I'd met previously, who made me feel very welcomed in Hamlin. The cop incident shook me up, and I thought about the unique way such an encounter with law enforcement can make you feel controlled and oddly guilty, even if you've done nothing wrong.

So, the encounter that I had some anxiety about happening all along happened again, which was so different from the benevolent attitude of the officer back in Selby, South Dakota. The irony was that what I thought would be the reason for it—sleeping in the car where there might be an ordinance against it—wasn't the issue here. I supposed this small-town cop, whose job was probably usually boring, was suspicious of an out-of-state person traveling alone on a trip he regarded as strange. And my being from Colorado, which had recently legalized recreational marijuana, might also have provoked suspicion that I had possession or even intended to sell the substance. Or maybe the cop thought that even an older guy like me could be on the lam from the law and headed down 83 for Mexico, which undoubtedly has been a route for fugitives besides bootleggers through the years.

I realized he was just doing his job in a way, and that he might have even been told by a superior to search my car. But I still thought he was overzealous and that a lot of the questions and comments were inappropriate and even silly. It seemed that he and/or some higher-up did a lot to try and bust me for something, and I was so glad I didn't provide a reason. The search of my vehicle made a mess, which to a neatnik like me was especially annoying. But for now, I just cleared out the back seat and was ready to sleep after the ordeal.

Outside, the sky was clear and starry. Before falling asleep I heard a lot of barking and yelping from a distance that must have been coyotes. After all, this was another town on the Texas plains where the creatures lived long before there were any towns.

DAY 23

Anson, Abilene, a bed in Ballinger

After reorganizing the mess the cop made, I walked over to a nearby place called The Piper to have breakfast, which was in another convenience store and had plastic tables and seats, and no real character. At the counter, I ordered two scrambled eggs with hash browns, a side of salsa, and whole wheat toast. While waiting for it to be served, I tried having a conversation with an older guy wearing a brimmed cap at the next table. He answered a few questions I asked about Hamlin in a thick drawl but said he didn't know a lot about the town because he'd lived there less than a year. He also didn't seem eager to have much conversation.

The breakfast was good and included a large portion of potatoes that weren't too greasy. But a few flies were also drawn to the food that urged me to move to another table, where I was followed and shooed the pests when necessary. Another older guy was seated in front of me wearing work clothes with a label on his shirt. He was friendlier than the other one and told me he'd lived in Hamlin most of his life.

"I saw the grain elevators in town," I said. "So just what do they farm around here?

"Some wheat and milo, also cotton. Some farmers also let cattle graze on winter wheat till a certain point. I've known a lot of farmers through the years."

"Someone told me that the local economy isn't good overall, and that a lot of people have moved and even left a lot of belongings in some homes."

"The economy here has declined, and many people have moved because they had to commute too far to work. Some have left stuff. The town has been steadily losing population, but I still like living here."

He seemed like another rooted small-town person.

I drove to the downtown area and parked to take another stroll with my camera, and the day had warmed up close to seventy degrees. Banners attached to tall lamp posts along the main street had the hospitable words, "Welcome to HAMLIN—Home of The Pied Pipers," which I assumed was a reference to a school sports team. There were also green and white images of the legendary Pied Piper—the Medieval character whose legend originated in the German town of Hamelin. However, Hamlin, Texas, with its slightly different spelling, was not named after a European town, but for a railroad executive—W.H. Hamlin. So, this is another example of what can come out of a name.

The town got its start in 1902 when an early settler named R.D. Moore conveyed 320 acres of land for a town site along the Kansas City, Mexico, and Orient Railway that was in the works. It was organized and named after the railroad man in 1905, and the tracks arrived in 1906. Hamlin was incorporated the following year, and by 1910 had almost 2,000 residents when two more railroads reached the area. As a result, it became a big shipping point where various businesses and institutions developed, and the discovery of oil in 1928 brought more economic growth. The population peaked at 3,791 in 1960 and has slowly decreased since.

As I strolled around the old business area, I did see vitality, however, although there were some vacant stores. After the walk, I drove to a recycling facility that I found out about to dispose of the empty beer bottles and cans that the cop advised I get rid of, and it happened to be right by the City Hall where three police SUVs were parked. One of them could have been at the scene of my interrogation the night before, and it aroused some anxiety about seeing the same cop again. The recycling bins turned out to be for newspapers only, and I grudgingly made an exception to my ingrained habit of recycling cans and bottles and threw what I had in a trash bin—not knowing if I'd find a better facility in a region that probably didn't offer much recycling.

To satisfy some curiosity about the abandoned homes I'd heard about, I drove around some residential streets and saw a lot of weathered and neglected dwellings, and some did look vacant. Many others looked well-maintained, showing a contrast like Paducah. But instead of red brick, there were some side streets with dirt surfaces.

I came to a modern-looking post office where I could mail a few postcards I'd bought, and I parked and finished writing the cards and jotted in my journal. Before I stepped out to mail the cards, an attractive, middle-aged woman came out of the building and walked toward the car.

"Is everything OK?" she asked in a friendly manner.

My initial reaction was a little anxious because of the recent cop episode, and I replied: "Everything is fine. I just wrote some postcards I'm about to mail."

"I saw you out here with the Colorado plate and thought you might be lost."

"Thanks for your concern, but I'm OK."

"I was in Colorado recently," she said, "to Durango, where we took the popular train ride to Silverton. I really loved the area, and it's too bad it's so far from here."

"It is truly awesome, and I've been there a couple of times. I now live in Fort Collins in the northern part of the state."

"How far is that from Denver?"

"About sixty-five miles north. So do you work for the post office?"—since it was obvious now she wasn't a cop.

"I'm the postmaster and was also the postmaster in Anson before I came here. I have twenty-one years of service altogether."

"So did you work your way up from the ranks?"

"Yes. I started as a carrier."

"Well, we have something in common because I was a carrier for six years back in the seventies in New Jersey, where I'm originally from. If I worked longer maybe I would have become a postmaster," I kidded. "When I started in 1970, it was about the time women carriers were coming around, back when Women's Lib really got going."

"Times have sure changed," she remarked.

Our conversation continued a little longer, and I told her about my trip. She didn't know about 83 being a border-to-border highway like a lot of people who live near it, but she had been south on it all the way to "the Coast." Before returning to her postal duties, I received another wish for a "safe trip." Although this was a very friendly encounter, I suppose it was an example of how outsiders are often conspicuous in these small towns. But at least I aroused concern rather than suspicion this time.

Before leaving Hamlin, I stopped at a good-sized grocery store called Lawrence Brothers, which I found out was a chain in Texas. It had a sizable produce section and some not surprisingly high prices, which is often the case in small towns further from shipping centers. Of course, the inhabitants of these towns usually pay substantially less for big expenses like homes, rents, and property taxes. I bought bread, avocados, and a small Greek yogurt, and when leaving the store, a couple of Black customers walked in, which indicated some racial diversity in this community, or perhaps they were also travelers.

At the southern edge of town along 83, I stopped at a pull-off by a nice grassy area with some tables and shelters and had a light lunch. There was also a white stone arch with the words WELCOME TO HAMLIN on one side and COME BACK SOON on the other, and suspended by cables in the middle of the arch was another green image of the Pied Piper. Driving off, I had a good view of the town's tall, white water tower in the distance with the name "Hamlin."

The highway turned southeastward toward Anson and was back in a lot of mesquite and some open fields. The road surface looked quite old, but with wide, paved shoulders. Ahead were huge cotton fields to the east and grassy stretches to the west. I pulled over by the expanse of cotton for a photo and took a closer look at what's the number one cash crop in Texas. Besides the innumerable, fibrous white balls was a forest of dark green leaves, which up close had some resemblance to maple leaves. The crop looked full grown and ready for harvest, which varies in timing in the different Texas climates where it's cultivated. I couldn't see this much cotton without being reminded of the fortunately bygone days when Black slaves and later sharecroppers toiled in the tedious and backbreaking work of hand-picking it before harvesting became mechanized.

Between Hamlin and Anson, 83 crossed the invisible hundredth meridian and would run to the east of it for the rest of the highway's route, after having stayed on the west side of the meridian since the Canadian border. My map showed the name Radium on this stretch, but I didn't notice many signs of a settlement. A website described Radium as a tiny, unincorporated community that started with a store in 1910 and never had more than twenty-six people because of its proximity to Anson—the seat of Jones County—which discouraged its development. Nevertheless, the "town" was said to be a trading center for ranchers and farmers, but the origin of its name wasn't mentioned.

In the 1880s, there was a successful rancher in this area named William Lawrence Chittenden, who hailed from Montclair, New Jersey—not far from where I grew up. He also wrote poetry based on his experiences in Texas and became known as the "poet-rancher," who's best known poem is "The Cowboys' Christmas Ball," which is considered an excellent example of Cowboy Poetry that was first published in 1890. Chittenden was inspired by attending a traditional Christmas season dance with cowboys and their ladies at the Star Hotel in Anson.

Just before Anson, U.S. 277 came in from the northeast with four-lanes and joined 83 as a two-laner for a short stretch. This federal highway is a 633-mile (1,019 km) north-south route commissioned in 1930 that's an auxiliary of U.S. 77 and runs through just two states—from Newcastle, Oklahoma, to Carrizo Springs, Texas—further south along 83—and it would now be co-signed with 83 until Abilene.

I entered Anson and passed homes, a tractor dealer showing off bright green John Deere models, a First Baptist church, followed by what looked like a classic roadside eatery with a bold DINER sign. It touted "Chicken Fried Steak"—a very popular culinary tradition in Texas—and I stopped, not to indulge in a fatty, greasy meal, but for a photo op of a small establishment with lots of local character. Some sizable mesquite trees grew in town, and I saw both weathered and well-maintained homes. I came to a stately and handsome county courthouse with a clock tower and sculptured figure on the summit of a small dome. The courthouse was in a central square, like in Paducah, but this downtown area had some vitality. U.S. 83 was again the main street, and there were more red brick side streets.

I parked near the courthouse and started another walk in a town where I was a lot less anxious about cops, though I was amused by the thought of the Hamlin police possibly alerting the department in Anson about a mysterious solo traveler from Colorado headed south on 83. Though appearing generally viable, this town had some elements of decline, such as an old boarded-up Palace Theater and a partially collapsed brick building adjacent to it, along with some vacant stores. As impressive as the courthouse was a large brick opera house behind it that looked occupied. It dates to 1907 and has had many uses through the decades, and it's now on the National Register of Historic Places.

I found a verdant refuge among the vintage buildings called the Mays Botanical Memorial Garden, with lush, green vegetation and a charming wooden gazebo; and on the wall of an old building across from the town library was a long mural with the words—A TRIBUTE TO FARMING–ANSON, TEXAS 1905, with historical images. A small section acknowledged the importance of cotton in the local history: "At one time, Jones County led the state in the production of cotton."

Beneath an awning on another building was a small sign with another kind of message: "Jesus...Be Lord over Anson–2 Chron 7:14."—another example of the big influence of Christianity here and in the whole region. But in Anson, overzealous Christian Fundamentalism even resulted in a ban on public dancing that began in 1933, with the exception of the traditional Cowboys' Christmas Ball that was revived in 1934. History, however, wasn't on the side of the puritanical policy that regarded a lot of dancing as too sensual and leading to sins of sexual transgression. In the 1980s, a group of locals who largely came from elsewhere formed an organization called the Footloose Club to fight for change. Their name was inspired by the popular 1984 movie *Footloose*, about a fictional town much like Anson that had also banned dancing, until an exuberant male teen from Chicago moved there and started a movement that defeated the ban. After some setbacks, the real life ban eventually ended in 1987 through the efforts of the Footloose Club, but only after they resorted to getting the ACLU involved that threatened to sue the town; and the town couldn't afford costly litigation. From then on, young people could dance at proms and other events if they were supervised. Interestingly, Anson is the hometown of Country singer Jeannie C. Riley, who's big 1968 pop-country hit, "Harper Valley PTA," had a theme about a small town's puritanism and hypocrisy.

Though the powers that be in Anson became more tolerant of natural body movement, the town had a prohibition of alcohol at the time of my visit. So no bars. But I saw six churches listed for a community of about 2,400 people, and it seemed the balance was getting lopsided in favor of churches in Texas.

Anson sprung up at a location where an early promoter anticipated the Texas and Pacific Railroad to arrive. However, it was routed further south through Abilene, which didn't stop Anson's development, though. Its original name was Jones City, which became the seat of Jones County in 1881. The following year it was renamed Anson, but after the same person—Anson Jones—who was the last president of the Republic of Texas, which existed from 1836 to 1845 as an independent nation before it joined the U.S. The attractive county courthouse was completed in 1910.

In 1926, oil was discovered in Jones County, and the industry grew with Anson as a supply center. Along with agriculture, the town had some other thriving businesses, and its populace peaked at 2,890 in 1960. Since 1980, it's decreased, but not as much as in many other small towns along 83. Anson continues its big tradition of the Texas Cowboys' Christmas Ball on the weekend before Christmas, which draws a crowd from around the country. The event has a throwback dress code that requires women to wear dresses, and the men must remove their hats on the dance floor as a sign of respect for the ladies. It's been held at one of the numerous, traditional Texas dance halls, named Pioneer Hall, since 1940, and for years the acclaimed Country-Western singer-songwriter Michael Martin Murphey has performed with his band. The year I was in town was the Ball's 80th consecutive year, and I love that kind of continuity.

Before leaving Anson, I came to a crossroads with U.S. 180—an east-west federal highway commissioned in 1943. Its eastern end is Hudson City, Texas, but Wikipedia said the western terminus in northern Arizona is "unclear," though a total length of 1,092 miles (1,757 km) was given that's in three states. It also mentioned that, like many subordinate, three-digit highways, 180 is no longer connected to the main route—in this case U.S. 80

South of Anson, 83-277 became four lanes with a grassy median. It was back into broad fields with some cultivation and also wooded areas. The next community was Hawley on the east side of the road along the Clear Fork of the Brazos River, which had a small water tower. I passed a Shell station, a Subway, and another Dollar General store among its small number of businesses. The current population was a little over 600, and the history goes back to 1890 with typical farmer and rancher settlers. The Wichita Valley Railroad arrived in 1907, and I found conflicting information about the town's name origin—with one source claiming it was a railroad official named C.W. Hawley, and another U.S. Congressman Robert B. Hawley. Maybe it was named for both. Though the town prospered for its small size, it wasn't incorporated until 1970. In 1988 its population reached a high of 884.

The bridge over the Clear Fork of the Brazos had barriers that blocked a good view of the 180-mile-long river that's the longest of the three main tributaries of the Brazos River. It was seventy-seven degrees, even late in the day, and I was starting to feel more like I was in a warm region. Closer to Abilene, the highway ran through a flat stretch with big, brown fields, and a huge wind farm with spinning turbines stood to the east beyond a heavily wooded area. There was more mesquite and an open agricultural landscape before I reached an industrial area on the outskirts of Abilene, with what looked like a small oil refinery. I came to a sign for the Business 83 route that led into the busy downtown area, but I took the 83 and 277 expressway that runs down the west side of the city. Although Abilene has attractions like museums, a zoo, and a Discovery Center with Nature-themed exhibits, I decided to continue cruising through this city with well over 100,000 people that I wasn't inclined to explore.

Ahead was an intersection with Interstate 20, where I saw a sign for distant El Paso to the west, and soon another for Fort Worth in the opposite direction. The skyline of Abilene appeared to the east with some standout buildings, and I felt like I was in the first good-sized city I'd seen along 83. I passed a big Hyundai dealer and a modern residential area with an abundance of ranch-style homes, but also lots of trees and mesquite. Then came a long commercial strip with more car dealers and chain restaurants, and the expressway expanded to six lanes. U.S. 84 joined 83 and 277 from the west, which is a 1926 east-west original that in its early years was just a Georgia-Alabama route that became extended through seven states—stretching 1,919 miles (3,088 km) from near Midway, Georgia, to Pagosa Springs, Colorado.

U.S. 277 soon branched off southwestward, and just to the west was Dyess Air Force Base—currently Abilene's largest employer. There's also a regional airport on the east side of the city. I passed more big commercial strips in what was a dramatic change from the sleepy towns I'd seen for hundreds of miles that I was now anxious to get back to, and the congestion was exacerbated by it being a mid-week early evening rush hour. Though late in the day, the temperature had risen to eighty-five degrees, and Abilene is situated at the edge of the humid, subtropical climate zone I was heading into.

This bustling city originated in 1881 when a group of enterprising cattlemen succeeded in convincing a planner of the Texas and Pacific Railway to route the new line through their land and develop a town for shipping cattle. A landowner named Claiborne Merchant was the most influential, who also encouraged the railroad to name the new town after Abilene, Kansas, which ten years before was at the end of the old Chisholm Trail used for early cattle drives and had been the first real center for the shipment of cattle east on the rails. As a result, Merchant became known as the "Father of Abilene." The name Abilene actually has a Hebrew origin—meaning "grassy plain"—which was a territory near Damascus that was referred to in the Book of Luke in the New Testament. Abilene, Texas, was quickly incorporated in 1881 and became the seat of Taylor County two years later. The railroad had bypassed the earlier seat at Buffalo Gap, which arrested that town's development.

Like Abilene, Kansas, the Texas one was a rowdy Wild West town in its early days, but it eventually tamed and promoted business and population growth beyond being a cowtown. In 1891, Simmons College—the first of three future universities in the city—was established. Today, Abilene has seven institutions of higher education, with three not surprisingly Christian schools; and its public education system has been highly rated. Besides the schools, there are over 160 churches in the city—the friendly guy back at the bar in Murdo,

SD was right about it being very churchy—which helped it earn the nickname "The Buckle of the Bible Belt," although this distinction isn't unique to Abilene. I'd been in what's generally considered the Bible Belt since I entered the Oklahoma Panhandle—that large southern region of the country where evangelical Protestantism has a dominant presence and influence. I didn't find out how many bars are in Abilene, but I'd bet they're heavily outnumbered by the churches; and Abilene had a long "dry" spell until 1978. I read in David Reynolds' *Slow Road to Brownsville* that Abilene isn't known for excitement, and that T-shirts are even sold saying "Keep Abilene Boring."

The Last American Highway—Texas mentions Abilene having the largest number of African Americans of any town along U.S. 83—approximately 9,500. Except for a slight decline in the 1960s, the city's total population had steadily increased through its history and had reached about 120,000 when I passed through. This follows a growth pattern of many Texas cities in contrast to the decline of so many of the giant state's small towns.

Close to Abilene's southern boundary, the highway ran straight along the west side of Kirby Lake—a man-made reservoir. It was back to four lanes and still co-signed with close in number U.S. 84. There were now wooded areas along the road, including lots of mesquite. To the south was a prominent dark ridge stretching west that the highway was headed for, which appeared heavily wooded. The elevation was the Callahan Divide, named after a neighboring county, which lies between the Brazos River to the north and the Colorado River to the south—the latter having no connection with the famous river of the same name further west. The road started a moderate climb and coursed through a large gap in the ridge, where a big solitary house was perched. The close-cropped trees looked like junipers. Some unidentified roadkill lay rotting in the lane I was in, which wasn't surprising since traffic on the four-laner was still quite heavy.

On the other side of the ridge, 84 parted from 83 at a fork where the four lanes ended, beginning a course that would swing eastward; while 83, back to two lanes and a rumbly, chip-sealed surface, veered southwestward for a short stretch. Some wind turbines appeared with the descending sun in the background as the road headed toward another ridge that had a north-south direction. A water tower stood by the small community of Tuscola, with 742 inhabitants according to a sign. This settlement dates back to the mid-1890s, when a landowner named John L Graham donated land for establishing a school, church, and a couple of businesses. Clarence M. Cash was an influential settler who arrived in 1898 and named the burgeoning community after his hometown of Tuscola, Illinois. The name became more official the following year when the U.S. Post Office Department recognized it. Two railroads—the Abilene and Southern, and the Gulf, Colorado, and Santa Fe—arrived in the area in 1907 and 1910, resulting in growth for the community. By 1927, Tuscola had about 500 people, and after a few small decreases, it grew slowly to its present numbers, avoiding typical decline.

Just down the road was the smaller, unincorporated community of Ovalo, spawned by the Abilene and Southern Railroad that had owned townsite property and sold lots. A new town was given the Spanish name for "oval" because of the shape of the valley that had been camping grounds for bison hunters and a stopover for trail drivers. Ovalo grew rapidly, and by 1930 there were 600 residents and over forty businesses. But unlike Tuscola, this town declined, with its population reduced to 225 in 2000, and many old businesses and buildings were gone. I didn't see much besides the old post office, and it's puzzling why Ovalo fared so differently from its neighbor.

The next name along the road was Bradshaw, which has a story of perhaps sharper decline. It was another offspring of the railroad that came through in 1909 and was named after C.M. Bradshaw—a local landowner who's thought to have donated some of his holdings for the railroad's right of way and to develop a town. Rapid growth occurred here too, and Bradshaw became a local commercial center that had 450 people in 1929. But in the following years, U.S. 83 had the negative effect of providing easier access to Abilene, which hurt local businesses. Eventually, even the town's school and post office closed. By 2000, there were eight remaining businesses and merely sixty-one residents. I didn't find a more recent population figure, but Bradshaw is mentioned in a book titled *More Ghost Towns of Texas* by T. Lindsay Baker. Passing through, I did see a few vital signs, though, besides closed stores and other evidence of a dying town.

I drove through a varied terrain with grasses, more juniper-covered hills, and mesquite groves often mixed with prickly pear cactus. There were also clumps of interesting, light green vegetation I hadn't seen before. A sign about a historic cattle trail that came through was ahead, and soon I saw some future beef grazing in an open field. Further on, numerous Angus foraged around mesquite.

A spherical water tower loomed ahead in Winters—the largest town since Abilene with over 2,500 denizens—at a crossroads with Texas Highway 153. I saw a sign for the Winters Rodeo Arena and passed through a residential area with ranch-style homes called "Lone Star Estates." The town's name was inspired by John N. Winters—a local rancher and land agent in the late 1800s who donated land for the first school here. The first settlers had arrived in 1880, and by 1891 Winters had a post office. Before the town was incorporated in 1909—the year the Abilene and Southern Railway connected Winters to Abilene—a brass band was formed here that traveled around West Texas for years. Some manufacturing came to town, and the population grew to 3,266 in 1960. Since then, it's decreased rather slowly, but actually had more businesses in 2000 than it did in 1970, when the population was a little higher.

I passed some businesses, an older residential area, and two churches— one a First Baptist proclaiming: "Jesus is your most trusted friend." Then came a "Welcome to Winters" sign as I entered the downtown. Every first Saturday in September there's a tradition called the Dove Fest, which celebrates the start of the dove hunting season and draws more people to this community. Also noteworthy is that Winters produced the great baseball Hall of Famer, Rogers Hornsby, who was born in the town and spent his earliest years here. Hornsby had the highest batting average of all time after Ty Cobb.

Ahead was more cotton and mesquite, and a one-horse town called Hatchel—named after the first postmaster of the office established there in 1904. But there's been no post office since the 1970s. The Abilene and Southern Railway arrived in 1909, and Hatchel once had a depot and over eight businesses. However, its number of residents dropped from fifty in 1940 to just sixteen by 1990.

Soon a water tower and island of trees appeared, as a brilliant sun was sinking, in the much larger town of Ballinger, where I planned on staying. U.S. 83 hooked-up with U.S. 67 and ran with it shortly into Ballinger. The other highway also dates to 1926 and follows an officially north-south route from Sabula, Iowa, to Presidio, Texas, on the

Rio Grande border. U.S. 67 is 1,560 miles (2,510 km) long and has a rather crescent-shaped pattern through five states that makes its long stretch in Texas also somewhat of an east-west road.

I crossed Elm Creek and was soon in a very nice downtown with well-preserved buildings, which was probably the most attractive one I'd seen since Oberlin, Kansas. There was another stately stone courthouse, since Ballinger is the seat of Runnels County, on what is one of the largest courthouse squares in the state. The structure was completed in 1889 and had major remodeling in 1941.

Ahead was an intersection where U.S. 67 parted and crossed a bridge over the Colorado River, which had some flow. The 862-mile-long waterway can easily be confused with the much better known Colorado River with headwaters in my home state. But apparently someone in Texas also liked the name, which means "colored red" in Spanish. The Texas Colorado is the eighteenth longest river in the U.S., with a source south of Lubbock on the vast Llano Estacado or "Staked Plain." From there it flows largely southeast to the Gulf of Mexico near the town of Matagorda, and it's the longest river in Texas with a source and mouth within the state. Along its lengthy course are eleven major reservoirs, and like its famous counterpart, it's a huge water source for agriculture, cities, and electrical generation.

I pulled into a gas station with a Stripes store—a very popular convenience store chain in Texas I'd be seeing more of—to find out where any motels were, and a woman was very helpful and told me about three in the area. I followed her directions and backtracked to what she said was probably the cheapest one, called the Budget Inn, which I found on a side street. It was an older place built with the same light-colored stone that was common in town. The office, like the one at the motel in Oberlin, was permeated by aromatic Indian cooking and occupied by an older man with South Asian features. His English wasn't too good, but we were able to communicate. He told me the single rate was $50, and I took it after he showed it to me. Then I had a brief conversation with the man.

He confirmed he was from India and had owned the motel for a year. I told him I liked the smell coming from the kitchen and asked where he got some of the exotic ingredients in an area like this.

"Trom Dallas," he replied.

"So, are there any Indian restaurants in this area?"

"One just opened in San Angelo, and it's the only one around."

Again, I was given a real key and not a key card for Room 112. While moving a few things in, I had the company of a friendly feline with a reddish-white fur pattern that had been hanging around outside and was now drawn to me and being very communicative in its meowing way. I got the impression it wanted to be a roommate, but I stuck to the single occupancy I paid for. I did pick up the cute creature after it let me stroke it and thought maybe it belonged to the owner. The cat stayed near the door outside when I closed it.

I poured a brew into a glass and just relaxed in a reclining chair, followed by another round. Afterwards, a hot shower felt wonderful again, and I was ready to set out on foot in another strange town to find an eatery. My feline friend was gone when I stepped out in the dark, and it was still warm enough to dress lightly.

The motel was right by the tracks of the historic Santa Fe Railroad and an old station, which now housed the City Hall and a Chamber of Commerce office. Curious if there were any bars in town, I asked a young guy in the parking lot of a Shopping Basket grocery store, who informed me that there weren't any, but that beer was sold in liquor and grocery stores. I wandered down the main street and some side streets among many attractive stone and brick buildings, where I saw some Mexican restaurants and a Chinese one in an old stone structure. After some indecision about where I should eat, I decided to just go back to my room and have a sardine sandwich from my canned supply since I was splurging on a motel. On the return, I stopped back at the grocery store and bought a tomato and small onion for the meal.

Back in the room, I made the sandwich and opened a small can of green beans and had a simple, healthy meal. Afterwards, I stayed up late writing and reading, and when I finally got between the sheets, I really appreciated the comfort of a bed again. Some rumblings of freight trains on the nearby old Santa Fe tracks helped lull me into a very sound sleep at the end of Day 23.

DAY 24

"The Greatest Little Town in Texas," in Eden, Motel 83

It was another time comfort made it easy to stay in bed, and after some breakfast in the room I left the motel close to check-out time. On the way out, I had some conversation with a young Indian woman in the office who was the older man's daughter and spoke better English.

"So do you like Ballinger?" I asked

"No," she quickly replied, "but the town is nice, quiet, and safe, and we plan to keep the business after being here a year." So, maybe she thought Ballinger was boring, like the other Indian motel owner thought about Oberlin. Whatever, the family apparently thought the livelihood they found in this Texas town made it worth staying there.

"How long has your family been in the U.S.?" I inquired next.

"About four years."

"And where did you live in India?"

"In the city of Gudra, not too far from Mumbai."

We chatted a little more about the weather, and she said it had snowed in town during the past winter, which must be less common this far south, and stranger for someone from a hot country like India. I told her how erratic the weather in Colorado is and that Fort Collins has had snow in May since I lived there.

Before I left, an older Indian woman walked in, who was the younger one's mother, and this was another family business where the owners did most of the work, which is typical for such immigrant motel businesses. I've learned that Indian families have come to own about half of the motels in the U.S. and that the majority come from the state of Gujarat, with most from there having the surname Patel. This has been called the "Patel Motel Cartel" in jest. And since independent, non-chain motels in the U.S. have become a minority, the Indian presence must also be in enough big company franchises. It's an amazing business phenomenon for a certain ethnic group.

I stopped at the old railroad station along a single track—a very photogenic, long stone building with a red tile roof. After taking some photos, I went into the Chamber of Commerce office there next to the City Hall and wound up talking to a very pleasant, young female employee who had a charming Texas accent that stretched out vowels in words like "right." I commented that Ballinger looked like a very nice town, and she said, "Thanks."

"And it looks like your economy may be doing well," I added.

"It's doing better than many other towns because of the oil fields about thirty to a hundred miles away. Driving that distance isn't a big deal here, and the rails here are busy with freight, which also helps the economy."

"Do you know when the last passenger service was?"

"Not since 1963. The station was on the old Santa Fe line and was built by the old railroad company in 1911. It was donated to Ballinger in 1984 and now has our City Hall too."

"I noticed that and am glad they preserved the old building and found other uses. I really like the downtown area too."

"It's better than it was a few years ago when there were more vacant stores. The preservation has involved community effort. A place that's really booming is the city of San Angelo not far to the west, also because of the oil industry. But that's caused a lot of prices there to really shoot up. Even modest motels are charging $200 a night."

"I'm driving all of U.S. 83, and such inflation reminds me of what I heard about the big oil boom area in North Dakota that I passed through early on my trip."

Before I left, I picked up a couple of fliers on Ballinger, which touts itself as "The Greatest Little Town in Texas," and I did sense a lot of community pride here. The flier mentioned its old limestone buildings, which the well-preserved station appeared to be one of.

I drove to Ballinger's City Park—a delightful, shaded, twenty-acre refuge right along Elm Creek, which looked more like a river and is a tributary of the Colorado River. Its banks were lush with green, deciduous vegetation, including mesquite. There was no fall color, and on a bright day with the temperature now well over eighty degrees, it seemed like I'd gone back to summer. I changed into shorts, which was the first time I wore them since the early heat on the trip, then took a walk along the riverside.

Above a short flight of steps, standing tall on a stone pedestal, was a bronze statue of a Native American male with a feathered headband and braided hair over a scantily clad body, with the right arm raised in a friendly gesture. Engraved on the pedestal were the words: "A Friend." Known as "Friend the Indian," this sculpture was done by a local artist, Hugh Campbell, and has been here since April 2012. It's a replacement for a similar statue that was erected at the site in 1937 and later damaged. It certainly presents a more benevolent image of a Native American than the fierce warrior—though both must be historically accurate. Whatever the image, it's a good thing to see the original Native presence acknowledged.

Back by the car, I sat at a table under a shelter in a quiet area near the river and caught up more with my journal. Soon, an SUV parked nearby and out stepped a middle-aged Black gentleman wearing a dressy shirt and tie who approached me with a friendly greeting, then asked, "Are you familiar with the Lord's Prayer?" and I noticed him holding a copy of what looked like the Watchtower, which identified him as a Jehovah's Witness. I'd been approached by them before, and however much I don't buy into their beliefs, I like to be polite and responded, "Yes, I know the Lord's Prayer."

He then got into the meaning of "Thy Kingdom come, thy will be done..." and quoted from the Book of Daniel; then rambled on about how when the Kingdom of God finally arrives, everything will fall in order and humanity won't need its current governments.

I interjected: "You must be a Jehovah's Witness, and I've heard that they don't get involved in politics and are waiting for the coming of God's Kingdom to solve all the world's problems."

"Yes," he said, then offered me the Watchtower.

"No thanks," I replied. "I've seen it before, and I'm not interested."

Fortunately, he wasn't pushy and left cordially. Soon I thought I could have asked him if his denomination's belief about political activism meant that civil rights leaders like Martin Luther King should have done nothing and just waited for the Kingdom to come instead of fighting for equal rights and social justice for his people. But I also thought it better that I avoided such contentiousness because the man probably had a mindset that was very hard to change. I viewed meeting him as another example of the region's religiosity.

I resumed my writing for a while, then made and ate another sunflower seed butter sandwich with sliced banana at the table. While eating, I had somewhat of a "moment" as I was taken in by the simple beauty of the slow-flowing river and its verdant banks. The park was peaceful, and when I heard church bells and chimes in the distance, the feeling was enhanced.

I refilled a water bottle at a faucet, and nearby was a large public swimming pool that the flier I had said was new. Had it not been closed for the season, the temperature would have been warm enough for a swim. Before I left Ballinger, I wanted another look at its attractive downtown area.

I parked by the county courthouse, and on its spacious, green square was a monument to Charles H. Noyes—a twenty-one-year-old cowboy who was tragically killed by being thrown off his horse while working on his family's ranch in the area in 1917. In 1919, his parents erected this life-size bronze likeness of him standing next to his horse atop a large base of Texas granite. It's the work of the famous Italian sculptor Pompeo Coppini, which is "Dedicated to the Spirit of the Texas Cowboy."

From there I wandered down the main street called Hutchins Avenue and saw more red brick side streets, and the old downtown looked even more appealing in the bright daylight. I walked by some antique shops and an old movie house called the Texas Theater, which had reopened the previous year and looked very interesting, with its largely brick facade and disproportionately large sign displaying the name TEXAS vertically. Another noteworthy building was the restored Carnegie Library, which opened in 1911. It's one of the remaining four of the thirty-four libraries that Andrew Carnegie—the robber baron industrialist, but also philanthropist—funded in Texas.

During World War II, the second floor was converted to an entertainment club for Army Air Force cadets from the nearby Harman Training Center flight school.

Ballinger's rail origins go back to 1886 when the Gulf, Colorado, and Santa Fe Railway was extended westward. The original county seat was Runnels City, which wanted a proposed railroad terminal. But the town site that became Ballinger was selected because of its much better water supply from the Colorado River and Elm Creek for the old steam locomotives. The railroad company heavily advertised the sale of lots at the site, which sold quickly, and free property was even offered to those willing to move a home from Runnels City, and to any church that was built. Originally, the new town was called Gresham, then Hutchings. But it officially became Ballinger to honor William Pitt Ballinger, who was a railroad attorney besides a stockholder, judge, town site official, and distinguished veteran of the Mexican and Civil Wars.

Ballinger became a boomtown that attracted a lot of rough, transient characters during its own Wild West period. But it was soon tamed with more permanent settlers and was incorporated in 1892. By 1910, the town had three newspapers, and its population had grown to 3,536. It also had numerous businesses that included four cotton gins and a telephone company, but farming was the area's main economic activity. Later drought years that hurt agriculture led to a significant population loss in Ballinger by 1920. But it had a comeback when weather conditions improved, and there was steady growth that peaked when the town had 5,302 people in 1950. In the following decades, the numbers slowly decreased to 3,750 at the time of my visit.

What I saw, though, was an appealing community that had some vitality and apparent pride, which is the economic center of Runnels County besides the county seat. It also has two general hospitals and sixteen churches, according to a list I saw—giving it a completely lopsided church-bar ratio since there were no bars at the time. How different from Ballinger's wild early years when it was known for its saloons! On the last weekend of April, the town hosts the Texas State Festival of Ethnic Cultures and Arts and Crafts Show. And it used to have an annual rattlesnake roundup before it fortunately ended this ecological offense that removes and kills large numbers of a natural predator, which is still a tradition in some other Texas towns and other states with large rattlesnake populations. Hopefully, ecological wisdom will eventually prevail in these places. But many traditions die hard.

Heading south from "The Greatest Little Town in Texas," a very prominent cross appeared to the east of the road, and I stopped for a photo of this area landmark that's known to locals as "The Cross." The hundred-foot high, seventy-foot wide metallic icon of Christianity, which is illuminated at night, has been here since 1993 and was a gift to Ballinger from the Studer family—owners of a local fertilizer plant—who commissioned a local construction company for the project. The structure has an open-air pavilion by its base, along with a nearby chapel and grotto with a statue of Our Lady of Guadalupe—considered the patroness of the Americas by the faithful. I was satisfied to view The Cross from a distance, and it wasn't at all surprising to see a large monument to faith in a region where Christianity spread centuries ago and became as deeply rooted as the mesquite in its landscape.

The road surface ahead was still rumbly as I passed fields, trees, cotton crops, and flat-faced prickly pear cactus that often appeared along the roadside. Then, it was back to a mesquite forest with more strewn cactus before cruising through a more open stretch. I crossed several creeks with names like Fuzzy Creek and Brushy Creek, where a big truck got on my tail, and I pulled over to let it and another eighteen-wheeler pass my compact four-wheeler.

I stopped again to read a historical sign about John S. Chisum, who was a cattle baron in the area in the mid-1800s—not to be confused with Jesse Chisholm, who pioneered the Chisholm Trail. During the Civil War, John Chisum had a contract to provide beef to Confederate forces west of the Mississippi.

A water tower came into view that I thought must landmark the little town of Paint Rock, and I saw a sign for the Native pictographs that inspired the community's name, which cover about a half-mile wide area on a limestone bluff along the Concho River. These include over 1,500 colorful images of animals, human figures, and other forms that are actual paintings that used natural pigments sourced locally, unlike petroglyphs, which are engravings in rocks. It's believed this artwork may date back about a thousand years, and it continued for centuries. The site is completely on private land that's been owned by the same family since the 1870s, who give paid tours that require reservations. Despite their capitalizing on the attraction, I read that the landowners have been dedicated stewards of the site.

The Paint Rock "city" limit sign showed a populace of 273, and I crossed the Concho River on a rather long bridge that seemed to have more flow than the Colorado River, even though it's just a fifty-eight-mile tributary of the Colorado. Concho means "shell" in Spanish, and the name was prompted by an abundance of freshwater mussels in the river. There's a slogan: "You can't get lost in Paint Rock." But despite its diminutive size, it's the seat of Concho County, though one of the smallest county seats in Texas. I saw some brick buildings that included the old Wool Warehouse—a reminder of the area's sheep herding history—a homey-looking little restaurant that advertised breakfast burritos, and a small post office. An attractive stone courthouse with a reddish, Victorian-style roof stood out, though it was surely small by Texas courthouse standards.

Paint Rock was established in 1879, and a post office opened. Eventually, there were three churches, and the town became a shipping point for the pecan, sheep, and wool industries. Roads were built before rails arrived in 1910. By 1914, Paint Rock also had its own newspaper and water system. It survived serious fires in 1909 and 1922 and reached a population high of around 1,000 in 1931, which the Great Depression soon cut in half. Adding insult to injury, the railroad bridge over the Concho River washed out in 1936, but the town rebounded to about 800 residents in the early 1940s and remained quite stable through the 1950s. Another decline followed that led to a low of just 193 people in 1972. Since then, its numbers have crept up, but it still has less than the 323 that lived in the community in 1890. There was a lot more to this little town's story than what I saw there.

Concho County is in the large region of central Texas called the Edwards Plateau, which is considered the southern extent of the Great Plains. It's a geologically uplifted area composed largely of limestone, which formed from marine deposits about a hundred million years ago during the Cretaceous Period when the region was a sea bottom like so much of the Plains further north. Soils throughout most of the plateau aren't deep enough to be suitable for farming, which, along with a lot of rough terrain, makes grazing cattle, sheep, and goats a much bigger business overall. Even though a lot of the area appears natural, I learned that its original environment was greatly altered by settlers in the mid-1800s. Previously, the Edwards Plateau was largely grassland roamed by bison and pronghorn antelope, whose grazing habits, along with natural fires, maintained the grassland environment. But when the settlers introduced livestock that overgrazed, fenced pastures, and started controlling fires that had prevented the spread of trees and shrubs, the land transformed from grassland to brushland, with vegetation like mesquite taking over. Also, trees like cedars (actually Ashe junipers), which had ranged just along streams, rivers, and in canyons, have wildly proliferated into open areas and disturbed the once healthy diversity of flora. Fauna like bison and pronghorns diminished, and white tail deer that were rare when grassland dominated are now overpopulated, which hunters help control.

South of Paint Rock was more mesquite brushland with lots of cactus. An oil or gas operation appeared to the west of the road, with tanks and vertical structures that produced a noticeable odor. The chip-sealed road surface was rumblier and encouraged a lower speed. Soon I was surrounded by a sprawling mesquite forest in flat terrain that reminded me somewhat of the Pine Barrens in southern New Jersey. However different the vegetation, both must be among the worst places in the country to get lost in. With apologies to Texans, I have to say that I regard this "brushscape" of much of the interior of their state to be about the most scenically challenged landscape I saw along 83. For it lacks the liberating openness of the grassy plains, the bucolic charm of farmlands, or the visual appeal of the areas with elevations; and its shrubs and short trees lack the beauty of a real forest. I think aesthetics is another reason to better control the spread of mesquite besides its insatiable thirst for ground water.

A small water body was visible to the east and broke some of the monotony, and the road started to undulate a bit before knifing through some solid, tawny rock that was probably part of the region's primary limestone formation. The first windmill pumps I'd seen for miles stood out in the brush to the east. Then a spherical water tower came into view and two guyed radio masts—signs that I was nearing civilization again. The terrain became more open with lots of grass.

I approached the town of Eden, which I presumed was named after the biblical place where many still believe the first humans lived and got us all in big trouble. The name was displayed on the silver water tower, and a city limit sign stated a 2,766 population. I rolled by some nice ranch-style and older homes with well-maintained lawns, and some chain businesses like Sonic and Dairy Queen. Ahead was an intersection with U.S. 87—an original north-south federal highway that's a relative of 83 that runs almost border to border through five states—from Havre, Montana, to Port Lavaca, Texas, for 1,998 miles (3,215 km), making it longer than 83. However, much of 87 is co-signed with different interstates.

A sign for "Venison World"—a store advertising jerky and natural meats—caught my attention, and I stopped to check it out. Two nice ladies—young and middle-aged—let me sample some different types of jerky and said all the meat came from Texas and was processed down the road in Menard. All the dried meat samples were much more flavorful than the cheap, packaged stuff, and I decided to buy some strips of a spicy turkey jerky. The younger woman asked where I was headed, and I replied, "All the way to Brownsville and the Coast." As I left, the older one said, "Come back and see us,"—a genial variation of the "come back" often heard throughout the South.

Nearby was a small park with a gazebo and a sign with an image of Texas and EDEN in big letters along with "Experience the blessings." And in the D was an image of a bitten apple for a biblical association. I found out the town's name was derived from Frederick Ede—an early settler who moved to the area with his family about 1881. In 1882, he donated land for a townsite and town square, and the following year a post office opened with the modified name Eden to honor him. This was soon followed by a school, a Baptist church, and businesses and utilities that developed over the next two decades. When the town voted to incorporate in late 1910, its population was approaching 600. In 1912, a line of the Gulf, Colorado, and Santa Fe Railway reached Eden, so it was one of the highway towns without rail origins, though the later rails no doubt boosted its development. Sheep ranching, which had been introduced in the area in the 1870s, increased after 1925, and Eden became a trading center for wool and mohair. Cattle and goats were also raised by local ranchers, along with ponies for the polo market back East. Later in the twentieth century, Eden was considered the sheep capital of Texas, but as the demand for wool decreased due to more synthetic materials and Americans eating less lamb, the sheep industry declined.

A boost to Eden's economy came in 1985 with the opening of a detention center run by a private corporation that contracted with the Federal Bureau of Prisons to detain male undocumented immigrants convicted of felonies before they were deported. The center could house about 1,500 inmates, which was more than half the town's total population, and it became the city's biggest employer. This facility closed when the private company's contract ran out, but it reopened a couple of years later with contracts with two U.S. government agencies.

Eden is near the geographic center of Texas, though the town of Brady to the east is closer. So, I was now "Deep in the Heart of Texas," like the name of an old song. On the way out of town, I passed a golf course and a creek that didn't appear dry. The sun was low, and it was that time of glorious, golden light before it slowly faded to darkness. Soon I passed a ranch off the other lane, and cattle grazed to the west near my lane. There were groves of large dark trees I'd seen before, but no mesquite for now. The road became a four-lane expressway with a smooth surface, wide shoulders, and another grassy median, which led back into heavy mesquite. Soon it reverted to two lanes before I slowed down through a construction area.

Ahead, I stopped at a county marker about the Great Western Trail, which informed me that this historic cattle trail "lasted more years, carried more cattle, and was longer than any other cattle trail originating in Texas." It replaced the Chisholm Trail that had closed, and it operated from 1871 to 1890—moving about seven million head of longhorn cattle and horses through nine states and into Canada. Many cattle were sold and shipped east in railhead towns like Dodge City, Kansas, and Ogallala, Nebraska, and the rest were driven north to established ranches or Native reservations. It was the heyday of the legendary American cowboy, which led to romantic images and some misconceptions. The big cattle drive years were certainly a significant chapter in the history of the Lone Star State.

Next to the marker by a bunch of prickly pear cactus was a seven-foot-high cement post with "Great Western Trail" in vertical red letters. These posts have been set every six miles on the route of the trail by local Rotary clubs.

The sun was about to set when I reached Menard, with a population of 1,471, where 83 met U.S. 190 coming from the east. This east-west auxiliary route of U.S. 90 runs 875 miles (1,408 km) from the New Orleans area to near Bakersfield in West Texas. It's another 1926 road that originally had a short route in Louisiana that was greatly lengthened, and here it joined 83 for a very short distance before it would branch off west.

A friendly sign read: "Welcome to Menard—take a walk through time." I drove by some trailers and small homes, a large modern post office, some kind of power plant, and a gun shop called the Coyote Armory. Close to where 190 left 83, a sign for Motel 83 grabbed my attention by an old, apparently independent lodging. Attached to it was a country-type bar that enhanced its appeal to me. Though I'd splurged on a motel the night before, this first accommodation I'd seen named after the highway that looked like it might be economical and was right next to a bar was very enticing, and I decided to stop at the office.

Inside, I spoke to a sixtyish woman who looked very White and not Indian and spoke without a drawl. The single rate was a relatively low $45, and I decided to go for it after she showed me a room at my request. It was rather small, with a full-sized bed and a good-sized bathroom with just a shower. It also had a small refrigerator, a microwave, and an old TV without a flat screen. When I paid the woman, I got another old-fashioned key for Room 6, which I now expected in these indie motels. I found out the woman was a co-owner with her husband and asked, "How long have you been here?"

"Eight years," she replied.

"And where did you come from? If you don't mind my asking."

"From Las Vegas, which got just too crazy. I like the peace and quiet here."

"Well, I have my own Vegas connection since my sister lived and worked there for thirty years, and my parents spent their final years there. I flew there enough to visit the family."

"It's a better place to just visit now."

After getting settled in the room, I wrote for a while before walking over to the bar called Shifty's, where I found just the bartender and one customer seated at the bar—both older men wearing brimmed caps. Since I was wearing my own cap with the emblem of New Belgium Brewing in Fort Collins, I felt like I fit in. This sure wasn't a craft beer type of bar, though, and I bought a Coors Banquet.

The place had a big side area with a pool table that was dark and empty now, and overall, it looked like an old roadside bar that had probably been around and hadn't changed much since the 1950s. I started talking to the other customer, who had a heavy drawl and told me that he'd lived in Menard a while but was originally from another Texas town. He seemed hard of hearing, and I had to repeat myself a few times. Soon the man tending the bar, who'd been occupied with a laptop, joined the conversation, and I found out he was the office woman's husband and the co-owner of the motel and bar. He soon brought up a negative matter.

"The cops here are terrible. We have the Sheriff's department, though, and not local police. They're very tough on speeding—even one mile over the limit, especially for out of towners. Watch out for a speed trap by the bridge."

"Thanks for the warning," I said.

"The cops have given me a hard time with the business too, coming into the bar to check on probation people, which we have a lot of in this town. There's a lot of drug use, and 83 is used a lot for drug trafficking from Mexico. The cops are also very tough on DUI.

"Do you ever have any live music or other entertainment here?"

"Not really. It's hard to get enough of a crowd here for it. Plus, I'm sure the cops would be a pain about that too."

"Your wife told me you came from Las Vegas about eight years ago."

"Yeah, we got tired of it."

The conversation continued and somehow politics came up, and the owner had some very unflattering things to say about then President Obama and Senate leader Harry Reid. Wanting to avoid contentiousness, I managed to change the subject and talked about my trip. The owner knew how long 83 was and said the motel had been Motel 83 since the fifties. Since he'd talked about cops, I told him about my experience back in Hamlin. The other guy was a little slow to understand the kind of trip I was making, probably because of his hearing problem. Since the place was deader than I'd hoped for and I had enough conversation-wise, I decided to leave after one beer, though the hard of hearing guy encouraged me to have another that "would help me sleep better." But I told him I should still sleep fine, then said, "Have a good night" to both men as I got up to leave.

Near my room, I met another older guy who was staying at the motel, who had gray hair, a rather large belly, and another Texas drawl. After we greeted each other, he asked about the bar I just came from, and I told him it was almost empty and might be closing soon. I thought why not offer him a beer, and at first he hesitated, then accepted, and I pulled out two PBRs from my cooler. He told me he was heading home to Odessa, Texas, further west, from a church event near San Antonio.

"I'm involved with the Church of the Living God," he said, "and we just had our Feast of Tabernacles. We believe in a very strict, literal interpretation of the Old and New Testaments and merging them. Unlike most Christians, we don't celebrate Christmas and Easter because of their pagan influences."

"That sounds like the Jehovah's Witnesses from what I know about them." I thought he might start proselytizing, but he basically just mentioned some more of his group's beliefs, which I didn't challenge because he wasn't pushing his religion on me. I was also curious about his beliefs; however strange they might seem.

"I think I'll Google the name of your church," I said, which he encouraged, and he also gave me a website. He was a likable guy, and I also liked that he was having a beer with me and not being abstemious like many zealous Christians. We finally made introductions, and his name was Mike. He mentioned being sixty, and I admitted to having several years on him.

"We're both old now," he said somewhat kiddingly.

"Both Children of the Sixties, now in our sixties," I added.

The subject of my trip came up, and Mike was impressed by the distance I was traveling. The conversation ended on a good note, and he thanked me for the beer.

Then we wished each other safe trips before going back to our rooms. So, he was another religious person I met that day in this part of the Bible Belt, though one not trying to convert me. I had thoughts about the many different lenses that humans view the world through, and the Church of the Living God was the latest I encountered. My own views had evolved into accepting the mystery, more than seeking certainty.

I was hungry again after two beers but thought the local eateries had probably closed already in a town this size. So again, I resorted to my supply of sardines, and made another sandwich with a side of green beans, only this time rather awkwardly on a plate by the bathroom sink, since there was no table in the room.

After more journaling and watching the old TV till after midnight, I was tired enough to get into bed in a room of Motel 83 along U.S. 83 in Menard, Texas, and soon dozed off after hearing some sounds of traffic along the highway.

DAY 25

Menard and the Hill Country

Menard's history began in 1757 during the long Spanish Colonial period when a Spanish fort and mission were built several miles apart in the area. The fort became known as Presidio de San Sabá since it was located by the San Saba River and not far west of the present town. The mission—Santa Cruz de San Sabá—was destroyed by Comanches and other tribal raiders just a year after it was constructed, and the fort, or presidio, was abandoned in 1770 after repeated attacks by hostile Natives.

These conflicts discouraged settlers from coming to the area, and it wasn't until 1858, after Texas became a U.S. state, that a town site called Menardville was laid out after Menard County was established. The namesake of the new county and town was Michel Branamour Menard—a signer of the Texas Declaration of Independence from Mexico in early March 1836, who was also a member of the Texas Congress when Texas was an independent republic. In the beginning, three families lived in Menardville in log cabins protected by wooden palisades. The threat of Native attacks still deterred more settlement for some time, especially after Fort McKavett—now a state historical site twenty miles to the west—was closed in 1859, which had offered settlers protection. But the fort was reactivated after the Civil War, and there were spurts of growth that led to the small community becoming a trading post. In 1871, a county government was finally organized, with Menardville as the county seat, and the first court was conducted under a live oak tree before a two-story courthouse was built in 1872. In 1874, the town became an overnight stop on the Great Western Cattle Trail, and by the mid-1880s, it had a church, school, several businesses, and 150 inhabitants. Livestock, wool, and hide shipments were major goods in the small economy, and in the coming years four newspapers were published.

In 1899, the San Saba River, which flows right through the town, flooded and caused severe damage. But the residents rebuilt, and the town's growth continued. A boom came with the arrival of the Fort Worth and Rio Grande Railroad in 1911, and a few years later the town had about 1,000 people and became the county's shipping center. The name had been shortened to Menard at the request of the railroad company for the convenience of a shorter name on signs.

The population managed to grow a little during the depression years of the 1930s and reached a peak of 2,685 in 1950. After that was an overall decline that had decreased to 1,471 by 2010, but Menard still had more than half of the sparsely inhabited county's population. Improved roads had hurt the railroad's business, and in 1972 the Atchison, Topeka, and Santa Fe Railway discontinued service to Menard. The company donated their old depot to the county, and it became a historical museum in 1978. Today, the local economy is based on cattle, sheep, goats, grain, hay, and pecans, and eighty percent of Menard County is farm or ranch land.

Two annual events in Menard are linked with the legendary Jim Bowie—famous for having died at the Alamo in 1836 and for his Bowie knife—who came to the area with a party in the early 1830s in search of a storied silver mine. In commemoration, there are Jim Bowie Days in June, with a parade, rodeo, and other festivities, and a Jim Bowie Trail ride on horseback in late September.

After another great sleep and cereal breakfast in the room, I showered, then left the motel to explore Menard. On the way out, I talked briefly to a female housekeeper who I thought could tell me some more things about the town, but she cut the conversation short, probably because she was busy.

The day was heating up fast, and before I checked out the

downtown area, I drove west on U.S. 190 to see the remains of the Presidio de San Sabá, only about a mile away. I was following the Texas Forts Trail, and this historic fort—now owned and maintained by Menard County—was on the north side of the San Saba River, adjacent to the Menard Country Club. I parked in a lot near the walls of a wide stone fortification largely in ruins, though the center section had an arched entrance that looked intact. Beyond it was an open area that had been the interior of the fort, where I saw more stone wall ruins.

A sign informed me that an original wooden fort was rebuilt with stone. However, what's presently there contains few original materials. After the fort was abandoned, its condition deteriorated, and many of the stones were carried away and used by later settlers for various constructions, including the original courthouse in Menard. For the Texas Centennial in 1936, and more recently in 2011, the fort's walls were partially reconstructed with stones found around the location. The present structures did have an original look that included two round corner towers. And behind the arched entrance, a Spanish Colonial flag with the Cross of Burgundy—a serrated red X on a white background—flapped in the breeze.

The inside of the presidio once housed over 300 Spanish soldiers and civilians that included women and children. There were about fifty rooms and facilities, such as blacksmith shops, and outside the walls were corrals for horses and cattle. No one else was around when I roamed the ruins, except, perhaps, some ghosts from the eighteenth century.

In its brief period from 1757 to 1770, this presidio was the largest and most northern Spanish outpost in Texas. Its proximity to the mission run by Franciscan friars several miles away, which it was there to protect, is an example of the widespread pairing of faith and force in the vast territory claimed by Spain. The missions, of course, played a big role in attempts to convert Native people to Christianity and an agrarian way of life, which were often very unsuccessful.

When Spanish colonists first ventured north of the Rio Grande, they met strong resistance from tribes such as the Lipan Apache, who often raided and stole livestock. By the mid-1700s, they had more peaceful relations with that tribe, but the Comanches were an ascending power from the north and an enemy of the Apaches, who became a more serious threat to the Spaniards. So serious that in 1772, the Spanish authorities ordered a withdrawal from all the missions and forts in this part of Texas back to the earlier settlement in San Antonio. After the Comanches acquired horses through the Spanish from trades and raids, they developed an empire on the southern plains and were allied with some other tribes, besides having a trading relationship with the French to the north and east, who they obtained muskets from. These "Lords of the Plains," as they were fearsomely known, became some of the greatest horsemen in history, and were infamous for their belligerence and brutality.

On my way out of the presidio, I took a close look at the stone sides of the arched entrance, which are believed to be original. The right side had many carved letters and names of visitors through time. Some large letters spelled BOUIE, which is believed may have been marked by Jim Bowie, with an altered spelling, when he was known to be in the area searching for a silver mine. I was impelled to leave my own mark, and I used my Swiss Army knife to scrape my initials well above what could be the famous name.

Nearby was a large pavilion with tables, where I wrote in my journal while enjoying the peace of a place that had historically known violence. A young woman walking a dog came by, and my "Hi" didn't get much of a response. A colorful flower garden by the pavilion also got my attention, which had attracted numerous monarch butterflies and was a splendid sight. Like me, these beautiful flying insects—now tragically declining largely because of an herbicide used by humans—must also have been migrating south and resting here, since hundreds of thousands spend the winter far south of the border in mountain forests west of Mexico City. Soon I resumed my own movement.

Back on 83, I crossed the San Saba River and its verdant banks on a wide bridge into the old downtown of Menard. The San Saba is about a 140-mile-long east-flowing tributary of the Colorado River that's known for its clarity and not much development along its course. I parked in front of the old, limestone Luckenbach Building on the same block as the small city hall, then began a walk through a very quaint downtown.

There were lots of picturesque stone and brick buildings like in

Ballinger that I aimed my small Nikon at while wandering the streets. One was the light brown Menard County Courthouse. Near it was a small, weathered, wooden church and a blank sign out front, which looked like a real relic of the past. The well-preserved, former Bevans Hotel really got my attention—now a retirement and nursing home called the Menard Manor, where some residents in wheelchairs were sitting out in the Texas sun. I also encountered the vintage brick and stucco Mission Theater that looked like it might have had its last picture show back in the twentieth century. One of its sides had two murals, and the old theater was part of a row of buildings with some vacant storefronts. Business-wise, the town had certainly seen more prosperous days, though the decline didn't leave real eyesores.

On a nice, shady corner was the small and very visually appealing Sacred Heart Catholic Church—the oldest church in the San Angelo diocese, built in 1899 from limestone quarried about five miles east of town that was dug by hand and transported by horse and wagon. A plaque on the front of the church commemorated the Mission Santa Cruz de San Sabá that had been attacked and burned down by about 2,000 Comanches and their allies on March 16, 1758. Eight people, including two priests, were killed, but about twenty-seven others were able to escape from the mission under the cover of darkness when a Spanish force from the presidio arrived to rescue them. The actual mission site was about three miles east of Menard on an old farm to market road, which took years of archeological work to locate, where there's now a small monument. The church is right along what's called the Historic Ditch Walk, which follows a ten-mile-long irrigation canal that's provided hydration for the area's farms from the San Saba River since 1876.

Part of this old town's charm is its shade, with lots of tall pecan trees besides mesquite. The lofty pecan is the state tree of Texas, which ranges over a large portion of the state, especially in riparian areas. Menard is known for its "pecan houses" that sell the tree's tasty nuts.

Back at the car, I went into the Luckenbach Building for a look at the Burnham Brothers business, which *Road Trip USA* describes as "the oldest U.S. retailer of game calls," even though I've never had any real interest in hunting or regarded wildlife as "game." Inside, the place had a large assortment of animal calling devices, along with scents, decoys, and other hunting products, plus clothing, cassettes, and DVDs. There were also two taxidermized cougars, deer and elk heads, and separate antlers. A small sign by a counter stated: "There's no such thing as too much ammo." There I met a young guy about average height with short hair covered by a brimmed cap, who gave me a warm and friendly greeting. A conversation started easily, and I found out he was Steve Roberson, who was the son of the store's owner, Gary Roberson. In a strong Texas accent he told me his dad had bought the business in 1991 from the original Burnham brothers, who had started it in 1952.

"They were the originators of game calling devices that were improved by technology and made calling more popular," he said.

"I'm not a hunter," I admitted, "so all this is new to me," and he went on to inform me more.

"What started with Morton Burnham back in the 1920s, who used his hand to lip squeak to call predators, progressed to record players, four and eight-track tapes, cassettes, and now digital electronic callers like our Compucaller that has actual animal sounds recorded in the wild. We're the manufacturer of the products, and we've also produced videos and now have our own TV show called *Carnivore* that's the number one-rated predator hunting show. Our calls range from big predators to turkeys."

The conversation continued, and Steve had a very pleasant manner and said "Yes, sir" to some of my questions—a formality I was finding used by many Texans, regardless of their age. He was also very relaxed about some customers who came in and didn't seem to care that I didn't show interest in buying anything. He mentioned having gone to Texas A&M and that he'd worked in cinema photography. I told him about my journey down 83 and my intention to write a tome about it. He seemed impressed and interested and said that he knew someone who had also driven the whole highway.

"So has the local economy been declining?" I asked. "I saw quite a few vacant stores in town."

"They're trying to revive it more and having some success. An industrial plant that was closed for a while has reopened and is now making oil field drilling equipment and providing employment. Otherwise, there's no large businesses around here, and no local oil fields like in a lot of the state."

Before I left, Steve handed me a Burnham Brothers business card and a bottle and can holder—very appropriate for a beer drinker—with camouflage coloring and the name "carnivore." I was glad I checked out this rather unique store, where I met a very personable young fellow that I learned a few things about hunting from. Although I'd read that hunting has had a general decline in the U.S., it's apparently still a big part of the local culture in many rural areas, such as this part of Texas and many other places along U.S. 83. A flier I picked up referred to Menard as "Wild turkey capital of Texas" and said that over 400,000 acres were available to hunters in the area—also for quail, dove, and deer for those who regard these creatures as game.

It was almost mid-afternoon, and the temperature had risen to ninety-seven degrees like the early heat on the journey. I was hungry and thirsty and backtracked across the San Saba bridge to an appealing roadside restaurant called Mama Jo's, which touted "Home-cooking." The Texas heat urged me to crack an afternoon beer from my cooler that I drank in the car. Inside the restaurant, at this between lunch and dinner time, the only other customers were a heavy-set couple at another table with two young kids who were scurrying around. My server was a rather young and friendly woman with dark, Hispanic features, but no Spanish accent. I was hungry enough to consider ordering a chicken-fried steak—the popular comfort, if not health food—that's said to have originated in Texas and was influenced by the wiener schnitzel of German and Austrian settlers who arrived in the state in the 1800s. But when the lady confirmed that it was a cheaper cut of beef that was breaded, deep-fried, and greasy, I was afraid I wouldn't enjoy it enough to be worth the nutritional guilt I knew I'd have afterwards. So, I ordered a relatively healthy grilled chicken breast with mashed potatoes, a vegetable of the day, and a selection from a small salad bar.

The meal was very good and included a slice of thick, buttered Texas Toast I couldn't resist, and I finished with some fresh fruit from the salad bar. The whole meal cost just $10.50—an example of how you can eat well and cheaply on the American road if you stop at the right eateries. When I was done, the server asked me where I was from and traveling to.

"I'm from northern Colorado and driving down 83 to Brownsville and the Coast, and I started at the northern end of the highway on the Canadian border in North Dakota. Did you know that 83 runs border to border?"

"I knew it was long but didn't know it went that far. I used to live in Wisconsin, but moved here to be in a warmer place and close to my parents who are here. It only snows a little here occasionally, and never lasts long. Now I miss the snow and would prefer the winters in Wisconsin to the heat we have here."

When I left, she said, "Be careful," in a concerned way, and I wished her a snowier winter and less torrid next summer in Texas.

I made a last stop at a fairly large Lowe's Market—part of a grocery store chain I'd seen in some other Texas towns—then drove off toward the well-known Texas Hill Country.

U.S. 83 South climbed somewhat in an area without a lot of mesquite, where there were other hardwoods with dark green leaves, also junipers, and small grassy clearings. More mesquite reappeared, and a green ridge loomed in the distance that looked like the beginning of the Hill Country. Creeks continued to abound in this part of Texas.

The road got rumbly again and headed into a heavily wooded area with ups and downs, and sliced through some solid, light brown rock that must have been the regional limestone. I stopped for a closer look at a different type of hardwood tree with a short trunk, wide crown, and small oval-shaped leaves, which I realized was live oak—a species very associated with the South. The highway made more cuts through the limestone formations as the terrain transitioned to the Hill Country, where mesquite mixed with live oaks and junipers. To the southwest were low lying hills with heavy green cover. As I approached the town of Junction, the outside temperature read ninety-three degrees, even late in the day, and I could imagine what the summer heat must be like around here.

A sign indicated Junction's population was 2,574, and it was appropriately named for being where the North and South Llano Rivers converge to form the Llano River—another tributary of the Colorado River. The town is also a highway junction where 83 meets U.S. 377 and Interstate 10. The other federal highway is another north-south road that was commissioned in 1930 as a very short route connecting Fort Worth and Denton, Texas. Later it was extended to 478 miles

(769 km), from Stroud, Oklahoma, to Del Rio, Texas, on the Rio Grande border with Mexico. It joined 83 very briefly before continuing its southwestward course.

The community of Junction originated in 1876 after Kimble County was organized and was known as Junction City in its early years before its name was shortened in 1894. By 1927, the town had grown enough to be incorporated, and it became a commercial center besides the county seat. Its location on the Llano River and the edge of the Hill Country also led to attracting tourists and outdoor enthusiasts. The population increased rather steadily to a high of 2,654 in 1970 and has only declined slightly. Junction is also a ranching community and home to a branch of Texas Tech University. It's been given the appellation "Land of Living Waters" because of the steady flow of the Llano River and its tributaries. South of town is the South Llano River State Park, which is known to also attract wild turkeys that feast on pecans from the park's abundance of the state tree.

I came to a small commercial area with a Motel 6 by the intersection with I-10, where 83 enters the interstate on the north side of Junction. U.S. 377 left 83 and continued through the town, which I'd decided to bypass. I-10 is the first interstate that 83 joined since I-90 back in South Dakota, and it's the southernmost cross-country super-highway that spans 2,460 miles (3,959 km)—making it the fourth longest in the country after I-90, I-80, and I-40, which I'd all crossed. About a third of I-10's length is in Texas since it crosses the huge state's greatest width as 83 crosses its whole length. Here these two great roads run briefly together.

Junction has nice Hill Country surroundings, with prominent elevations covered by heavy greenery and lots of rocky outcrops. The expressway crossed the Llano ("plain" in Spanish) River over a long bridge, with a good stream of water flowing below. This spring-fed Texas river is known for its clarity and not drying up, which attracts fly fishermen. The road began a steep ascent and sheared through walls of light-colored limestone where there were more junipers and some mesquite along the road. Soon, 83 made its exit from I-10, and I was back on a rumbly, two-lane surface that also cut through some limestone. Something about these higher elevations also elevated my mood, and I was enthused about finally being in the Texas Hill

Country that I'd heard a lot about.

This region of south-central Texas is without distinct boundaries but is considered to include parts of twenty-five counties. It's the most rugged part of the Edwards Plateau that became elevated about fifteen million years ago from activity in the lengthy Balcones Fault Zone when the Texas Coastal Plain was also created. The present topography is called "karst"—a German word applied to landscape that was shaped by the dissolution of soluble rocks—like the limestone formed from marine deposits on the bottom of the inland sea that once divided North America during the Cretaceous Period. As a result, these hills have their share of caves, caverns, and aquifers—the major one being the huge Edwards Aquifer that supplies drinking water for two million people besides agriculture. The Hill Country is also a transitional area where West, Central, and South Texas converge. Most of its elevations range between 1,400 to 2,200 feet above sea level, with the highest over 2,400 feet.

The hills were once inhabited by the Lipan Apache, who were eventually driven out by their fierce Comanche enemies that also antagonized Spanish colonists. After the period of Mexican control from 1821 to 1836, Anglo settlers from hilly Southern states like Tennessee and Arkansas began arriving here. Many German immigrants also settled in certain areas, who were known to oppose the secession of Texas from the Union during the Civil War. The region also drew Polish, British, and Alsatian immigrants during the 1800s.

In recent years, the Hill Country has had about five million visitors annually, and it's also attracted large numbers of retirees who find it a bucolic refuge from the big and fast-growing cities in Texas. As a result of this influx, it's had a thriving economy that includes becoming the center of the Texas wine industry, and even the second-largest viticultural area in the U.S. Although the idea of Texas wines might seem strange to many, it shouldn't, considering the favorable, warm climate of much of the state, where raising grapes dates back to 1662, when Spanish Franciscan priests planted the first vineyard. Ranching and farming, which were major enterprises in the early settlement of the Hill Country, also continue to have roles in its current economy.

Further south of I-10, the hills had less rugged features and looked more rolling and very tree-covered. There were also some open grassy areas, and cactus, mesquite, and live oaks remained in the landscape. Heading up an incline, 83 made another deep cut through more limestone, and further ahead was a meadow with a group of grazing goats. I passed a ranch to the west, where a couple of windmill pumps appeared in the brush. The road undulated and led into a heavy juniper area with open meadows, and more live oaks were ahead. I thought of a special joy I heard about the Hill Country displaying in the spring, when it's a showplace of dazzling bluebonnets—the Texas state flower of the lupine family—which add spectacular color to many landscapes during that splendid season. The Texas bluebonnet—*Lupinus texensis*—is endemic to Texas, and it's on my bucket list to see its magnificent spring spectacle someday.

As I entered Real County, I was again lured by a sign at a place that sold "Fresh Jerky," and stopped at the Garven Store at the intersection of 83 and Texas 41—a small, vintage roadside establishment with a few gas pumps. Inside was an old-fashioned general store, and to add to what I had from the store in Eden, I bought some strips of beef and turkey jerky from a large variety that was prepared right on the premises, and from meat suppliers in Texas. One of the employees said the store had been there since 1932 and that the current family owners have had it since 1998. When I later searched where the name Garven came from, I was informed it was the surname of a young male Scotsman who came to America at the time of the Civil War and fought for the Confederacy and who eventually moved to this area. Before I left the store, I was encouraged to also try its much acclaimed barbeque, which I would have if I hadn't had a big late lunch in Menard. This was a mercantile full of local character with some real history, which innumerable travelers on 83 have no doubt stopped at over the decades.

Back in Wander, I ate a strip of the beef jerky and thought it may well be the "Best Dang Jerky in Texas," as claimed at the store's entrance. Though there was no name on my map at this crossroads spot, I found out it's part of a tiny, unincorporated community called Mountain Home, with a population of ninety-six, according to a rather old census figure. It's significant enough to have a post office, but it also has a black mark in its history because of hideous things that once happened at a local ranch, which became known as the Texas Slave Ranch.

Back in the late 1970s and early 1980s, the ranchers there were involved in a horrifying criminal scheme of luring vulnerable individuals like hitchhikers with offers of work, which turned into kidnapping for forced labor without pay under miserable conditions. The enslavement included making cedar key chains and cheap souvenirs that were sold locally, and the roughly seventy-five victims were often chained and sometimes even tortured with an electric cattle prod. When word got out about the atrocities from an escapee, lawmen raided the 3,500-acre ranch on April 6, 1984, and there were arrests and charges of aggravated kidnapping. The ringleaders' trial, a couple of years later, resulted in the conviction of father and son ranchers, but they received relatively light sentences—a mere probation for Walter Ellebracht Sr., and fifteen years in prison for Walter Jr., who remained free while the sentence was appealed. A ranch foreman was given fourteen years but served less than three. And although an Alabama man who was enslaved in 1984 died, and human bone fragments were found on the ranch, there were no murder convictions because the physical evidence was considered insufficient. Appropriate justice apparently wasn't given in this case in a state known for harsh justice.

It was now early evening of a perfectly clear day as I passed through a landscape heavily wooded with more live oaks and junipers, which transitioned to a much more open one with meadows, scattered trees, and prickly pear cactus. A sign indicated 83 was now part of the Texas Hill Country Trail, and there were continued changes between rolling, grassy, and open areas that looked Western—to hilly, woodsy ones that appeared more Eastern. Hills to the south and west, where the sun was descending, had heavy tree cover that gave them an Appalachian look from a distance.

The road climbed again and made several cuts through more limestone on a very scenic stretch through lush hills with rocky outcrops, where I stopped for a photo. Then the road descended, and for a while I drove straight toward the glaring, sinking sun until a ridge blocked the blinding light. Steep wooded ridges stretched on each side of the highway, and it almost looked like I was in a valley in Pennsylvania despite the very different vegetation.

A friendly sign ahead read, "Welcome to Leakey—Soaring for success"—with an image of an eagle. It was the first town on my map since Junction, and it's the seat of Real County with over 400 residents. Leakey is very tourist-oriented because of the nearby Frio River, which offers many recreational opportunities, and its proximity to Garner State Park. I passed the Real County Airport, crossed a bridge over the Frio River, and soon entered an appealing community in a scenic valley that was named after John H. Leakey—a pioneer from Tennessee.

With his wife and a few others, Leakey settled along the Frio River in 1856. But archaeological digs have revealed human habitation in the area going back thousands of years to Paleo Native peoples. During the settlement of the 1800s, a lumber industry developed due to the abundance of mountain cedar (actually Ashe juniper), and cypress trees. More settlers arrived after the Civil War, and by 1883 Leakey had a post office and the area's first school. In the early 1900s, ranching became a big part of the local economy, which included the raising of Angora goats. But the population fell to only about 120 in the mid-1920s, and it wasn't until 1951 that Leakey became incorporated. Since then, its numbers have experienced some fluctuations, with a modest increase since 2000. But it seems like one of those towns that will always have many more visitors than residents. One very established institution is the Alto-Frio Baptist Camp and Conference Center outside town that's drawn numerous people from the faith community since 1920.

The center of Leakey had a sidewalk canopy and some rustic Western storefronts. I also noticed a limestone building and an appealing Italian restaurant with a stone facade. There were some other eateries, art galleries, and antique shops that you'd expect to see in a tourist town, and a spirits and wine store showed it wasn't dry. I also passed an indie motel before I left the charming little community and headed for Garner State Park down the road, where I hoped to camp that night.

I crossed Flat Creek, and the roadway ran close to the Frio River toward the hills to the south. Frio means "cold" in Spanish, and this 200-mile-long river was aptly named for its spring-fed coolness. It has three main tributaries, and the East and West Frio branches merge near Leakey and flow southwest to meet the Nueces River. Before the state park was the tiny community of Rio Frio—the Spanish name for the river—that never had more than seventy-five inhabitants and is the location of the third largest live oak in Texas. Originally, it was known as The Ditch because of an irrigation channel constructed in 1868, until a post office was established in 1875 and it was given its current name. Earlier in 1871, the Lombardy Irrigation Company had opened a school here, and the first church was finally built in 1920.

The sun had set and left a gorgeous orange glow above the dark hills to the west. When I crossed Buffalo and Pecan Creek, I encountered a group of motorcyclists heading north. Ahead and off the east side of 83 was the entrance to Garner State Park. After turning in, I soon came to a visitor center and found a parking space in a very crowded lot, which wasn't surprising on a Friday evening and the start of a weekend.

Inside the center they were using a numbered system to handle all the visitors who wanted to camp, and I felt like I was at a busy motor vehicle agency. So, I took a number and sat in a waiting area. The park official organizing the crowd was an elderly man with a classic Texas accent and courtesy, who addressed me and other men as "Sir" repeatedly; and he wore a cowboy-style hat as part of his uniform. The wait seemed long, and a lot of the arriving people had reservations. I started talking to an older woman in the queue who told me this was the busiest state park in Texas, which was easy to believe. When I mentioned my trip, she said she'd always wanted to travel far up 83, but she didn't know it went as far as Canada until I informed her.

When my number came up, I paid a $22 fee that included $7 for the park entry, with the rest for a basic campsite with running water. I got written directions on a park map and drove off to find the site in the darkness that had fallen. It was a big park with lots of camping areas, and I was assigned to one called Persimmon Hill, which wasn't hard to find. I picked site 209, where there were no close neighbors. Several campfires glowed in the area with the pleasing smell of burning wood.

An awesome number of stars had come out in an extremely clear sky, which the nebulous Milky Way bisected in a vertical position like the last time I saw it. These hills were apparently far enough from San Antonio to the east to not be affected by its light pollution. The campsite had its own firepit, grill, table, and faucet, and a restroom was nearby. There was also a tall metal pole with a hook, which was a first for any place I'd ever camped, perhaps for hanging food for protection from scavenging bears or other animals. Instead of hassling with pitching my tent in the dark, I decided to just sleep in Wander again. The next thing I did was ignore a park prohibition of alcohol and pop a beer, which I imbibed discreetly in the driver's seat.

I ate some of the very tasty jerky I'd bought, then opened a can of spicy chili beans, dumped the contents into a bowl, and consumed it with some bread at the campsite table. The cold meal was quite satisfying on a warm evening.

I ambled around the area with my small flashlight and noticed that a lot of the other campers were families. Afterwards, I used my lamp on the table and wrote in my journal till around midnight. Then, gazing skyward, I saw the constellation Orion rising in the east, again reminding me of the approach of winter, despite my return to summer-like weather. I became even more awed by the Milky Way and countless stars, and saw multitudes more when I gazed through my binoculars.

The area was now completely quiet, and when I slipped into my sleeping bag, I felt safe and happy to be in the Texas Hill Country on such a beautiful night.

DAY 26

Garner State Park, palm trees and blackbirds

The morning sky had become overcast by the time I was up, but soon cleared and it was already seventy-one degrees. Daylight revealed a good view of some wooded hills to the west. After some breakfast at the campsite, I took advantage of a shower in the restroom facility.

Back at the site, a quite attractive, middle-aged brunette strolled by, and after greeting each other a conversation started. She mentioned being from Houston, and that her family had been in the oil business, not surprisingly.

"Is it usually this warm around here this time of year?" I asked.

"It's pretty normal. In Houston it really doesn't cool off until January."

"I'm not complaining. The older I get, the more I like warm weather."

"So, I noticed your Colorado license plate. I have relatives in Pagosa Springs."

"I've been in Colorado almost two years and came from New Jersey."

"Really?!" I lived in Wyckoff for a while."

"I know that's in Bergen County. I look forward to visiting Jersey again, but that's about it. I love living in Colorado."

"So where are you headed from here?"

"To Brownsville and the Coast. I'm traveling the whole length of U.S. 83 and started at the Canadian border in North Dakota."

347

"By yourself?"

"Yes."

"Wow. That sounds like quite an adventure. Is it something like *Blue Highways*? Do you know the book?"

"I sure do and read it years ago. A great travel story, and I plan on writing my own about this trip. There're some big differences between my journey and William Least Heat Moon's though. I'm now a retiree and a lot older than he was during his late 1970s adventure when he drove many back roads around the U.S. after a job loss and a marital separation. I'm single, and I wouldn't consider 83 a real back road or 'blue highway.' But I think it's a remarkable old U.S. Highway that should be better known, and I'm very focused on it."

"What's your name in case I hear of your book being published?" After telling her, she said: "So good luck with the rest of your trip and your story."

"Thanks."

As she walked away, it seemed like I could have easily had a longer conversation and made a good connection, but I noticed a ring on her left hand that indicated she was probably heading back to a husband. A familiar situation for single men.

As I sat at the campsite table with my journal, a flock of resplendent monarch butterflies passed through, presumably southbound on their own journey toward their winter refuge in Mexico. Monarchs are the only butterflies known to make a round-trip migration like so many birds do, since they can't survive the cold like other species. A squadron of turkey vultures also appeared, with some flying low, and one even landed on the table of a neighboring campsite that was unoccupied. But the vulture was soon airborne again, and I pondered the wonder of flight and how these common consumers of carrion are among the most graceful fliers and make it look so effortless.

The vegetation around my site varied and included mesquite and other short trees I couldn't identify, which gave it a light green, Southwestern look and not the look of autumn I was familiar with. I didn't leave the campground until near checkout time and drove off to see more of Garner State Park.

The history of the park goes back to 1934, when the land was acquired by the state to preserve a tract of the Hill Country for public use. The Civilian Conservation Corps, or CCC, made great contributions for posterity here too in the early development of the park, which opened in 1941 and was named after John Nance Garner—a local figure who was a two-term U.S. vice-president under Franklin D. Roosevelt. The park's size has increased through the years, and it draws about 400,000 visitors annually.

At a restroom stop in another part of the park, I chatted with a thirty-something guy who mentioned leading a cub scout hike early in the day. He lived in San Antonio and told me he came to Texas from Oregon to work in the oil fields and met and married a Texas girl that he had a family with.

"So do you like living in Texas?" I asked.

"I really don't like San Antonio, or Austin, or other cities. I'd really like to go back to Oregon and do logging, which I did there before, but the oil fields here pay more. Maybe I'll get back when I retire."

That still seemed far off at his age, and he came across as an Oregon country boy who also didn't say anything flattering about the Texas Hill Country—referring to the local elevations as just "bumps" compared to the mountains in his home state.

"I sure feel the same if these hills are compared to the Colorado Rockies near my home," I said, "but they must be special in Texas, and I appreciate their unique character."

Sometimes a short, casual conversation with a stranger can reveal something deeper about them—like this young man missing where he came from, who apparently felt pressured to live in Texas because of his responsibilities. I wished him well before I moved on with my relatively free lifestyle, which encounters like this help me appreciate more.

I found out about a dam area along the Frio River that flows through the park where swimming was popular; and with another Texas day heating up, I liked the idea of a cool dip. I drove some confusing park roads before finding the route to the dam on a scenic road that ran along the base of steep hills, with views of more distant ones. Then came a large touristy area with cabins before I got to my destination. When I arrived by the river, there was a huge weekend crowd with plenty of families and recreational facilities that included kayak and paddle boat rentals, which made this part of the park seem more like a people than Nature experience.

I managed to find a parking space near a large pavilion that's well-known for its long tradition of having nightly dances in the summer to the sounds of a Wurlitzer jukebox. It was constructed by the CCC from local limestone and is the only one the corps built in a state park where there's still dancing. The pavilion also has a very popular eatery called the Garner Grill, which dates to 1941 and has a slogan: "Where fat-free can take a hike."

I changed from shorts to swim trunks in the confines of the car, then grabbed my bath towel and walked toward the river swimming area in flip flops. For the first time on the journey, I saw some bald cypress trees all along the Frio River, which like live oaks are considered very Southern. This species is very associated with rivers and swamps inhabited by alligators and cottonmouths. But there were some swimmers and boaters above the dam where the river flowed slowly, and a lot more people were in the water below the low stone structure. Knowing that the American alligator's range extended well into Texas, I asked an older woman standing near the dam if she knew if there were any gators in this area.

"No," she reassured me, "but they're in rivers in Floresville to the east. My son hunts them there."

I took that as a sign that this might be a transitional area for wildlife, besides vegetation.

More tall bald cypress lined a narrow river stretch past the dam, enhancing the Deep South look of the whole scene. These stately trees can grow as high as 125 feet and live up to 600 years. Oddly, they're considered deciduous conifers because they shed needles that regrow in the spring, and the barren winter look is why they're called "bald." Some sizable sycamores also stood along the river, with their broad leaves turning yellow.

I joined a large group of bathers below the dam, where the water was above my waist. My first swim on the journey was comfortably cool and very refreshing—not "frio"—and I felt exhilarated to be somewhere warm enough to swim in mid-October.

Back near my parking space, I sat at a table and wrote more while admiring some beautiful reflections of trees in the river. Another group of monarchs flew in, and I wondered if these winged beauties might be traveling close to 83's route. High overhead, another group of turkey vultures soared, as if following the monarchs again. One also landed on a nearby table like back at the campsite and soon took off, giving me another close look at one of these usually high-flying scavengers.

The sun was getting low on another increasingly shorter day in autumn, and I felt it was time to head out of the very popular state park. I drove away on the same scenic road and stopped to savor and photograph a panorama of hills to the east in the glowing, late daylight, where I could also see the Frio River winding through the park. The road descended along a stretch of live oaks, and I saw the sun set over one of the ridges, casting glorious reflections on some overhead clouds. I found my way back to 83 on another confusing route, and stopped at a general store near the intersection where I bought some ice and bread.

A sign stated thirty-one miles to Uvalde—the next large town—and the highway climbed into a gap between two ridges. The clouds above the sunset dazzled me more with purple reflections that faded to dull blue, then dark gray. More of the Hill Country was ahead, including a long ridge with characteristic rocky outcrops.

I passed through the unincorporated community of Concan in Uvalde County, which had 225 residents in the last count. Like Leakey, it attracts many tourists because it's also on the Frio River and offers similar recreation. Birders are also drawn here in the spring, and hunters in the winter. The area has lodges, dude ranches, a lively bar and dance club, and an eighteen-hole golf course. Crowds are also drawn by the Rio Frio Fest in mid-March to be entertained by Texas musicians and enjoy Texas food. Concan was settled about 1840, and its name is thought to be derived from the Mexican card game "Conquian."

Several miles from 83 in this area is a cave, which at sunset in summer witnesses one of the largest flights of Mexican free-tailed bats in Texas—up to ten million of these airborne mammals. They prey on flying insects, and in turn are preyed on by raptors like peregrine falcons and merlins as they exit the cave. The bats are there from mid-March through September before they migrate south and return in the spring. So, they were probably gone before the time of my arrival. Texas has more bat species than any other state, and the Mexican free-tailed species became the official state flying mammal in 1995.

I crossed a bridge over the Dry Frio River, which seemed aptly named because of the riverbed's desiccation here. Some elevations looked lower and not as heavily wooded, and it appeared I was leaving the Hill Country. Soon the landscape was relatively flat, and there was a stretch with trees, shrubs, and grassy openings. Then came a cultivated area with huge dark fields and sprawling parked irrigators. Near Uvalde, 83 crossed the Leona River—an eighty-five-mile-long tributary of the Frio River—which, unlike the Frio, is said to no longer be clean enough for recreational uses.

It was dark when I entered the town and passed an industrial facility before a small commercial area where the Lone Star Saloon looked inviting. In *The Last American Highway—Texas*, Stew Magnuson describes it as one of the good-sized Texas roadhouses that the huge state is famous for and that have a long tradition. There was another sign for the Texas Hill Country Trail in this town that's considered the southern entry to the region. I crossed a somewhat arched bridge that went over some rails, and I could make out the figure of a water tower. Ahead was a nice residential area with different types of homes, and I saw a sign for the Garner Museum in the old home of two-term U.S. vice-president John Nance Garner. The namesake of the state park where I'd been was known as "Cactus Jack," and he spent his later years in Uvalde, where he died in 1967 at age ninety-eight—making him the longest-lived vice-president. An attractive downtown area was ahead, where I passed an old theater with vital signs. I also saw a Rexall Drug store that *Road Trip USA* said had an old-fashioned soda fountain, and the vintage Kincaid Hotel that looked very appealing to me.

U.S. 83 came to an intersection with U.S. 90—another of the 1926 originals that stretches 1,633 miles (2,628 km) between Jacksonville Beach, Florida and Van Horn, Texas, through five states. Although the 0 in a U.S. Highway number usually indicates an east-west, coast-to-coast route, U.S. 90 is one of the exceptions that was never that long. This is the "Highway 90" mentioned in the lyrics of the beautiful song "Gulf Coast Highway," written by Nanci Griffith, James Hooker, and Danny Flowers that was released in 1988. Different artists have covered this endearing song about this region of Texas.

The first palm trees on the journey appeared by the intersection of the two highways—a real sign of being in the subtropics and getting closer to the Coast. There were also cacophonous bird sounds from the trees, producing clicks, whistles, and rattles, which was unlike anything I'd heard before. I backtracked a little to the old hotel and parked to find out if it possibly rented rooms for the night. Near the entrance, I asked a young guy if he knew what the noisy birds were.

"They're some kind of blackbirds," he replied. "I've only been in town three weeks, but the birds have been around the whole time and are often noisy."

"Are you staying at the hotel?"

"Yes, and I'm renting weekly."

"Do you know if they rent rooms just for the night?"

"I'm not sure, but I can check on my phone since this entrance is locked now."

He called a number and found out they didn't rent nightly, but I thanked him for checking and asked where he came from.

"From Georgia," he said, "and I found a job here with a solar energy company."

"Great field to get into these days. So did you know about the company before?"

"No, I didn't."

"Well, good luck with your new career."

"Thanks." Then he set off on foot while I lingered to read a sign about the hotel's history.

I learned that this four-story, Art-Deco structure was built in 1927 and named to memorialize William Davis Kincaid—a prominent Uvalde citizen. It became a popular place for business meetings and social gatherings that also had many prominent guests, including former U.S. presidents Lyndon Johnson and Ronald Reagan.

I decided to rough it again and sleep in Wander, and I found a Walmart just a short distance east on U.S. 90 with plenty of parking spaces away from the store. I felt elated to be in a vagabond-friendly place in the balmy air of the subtropics, where it was eighty-three degrees after dark and there were palm trees around. I quaffed two beers in the car that went down smoothly, then walked over to a

Chinese eatery called Lin's Buffet, where for a modest price, I sampled a variety of tasty dishes and had a satisfying dinner that showed you could get good Chinese food in Uvalde, Texas.

When I finished it was near the restaurant's closing time, and I was the last customer. A group of employees were jabbering in what must have been Chinese near my table. At the checkout, I complimented the buffet to a young, Asian-looking hostess and asked if she had lived around here long.

"Only a month," she replied with a heavy accent.

"So do you like it here?"

"No," she replied without hesitation, "it's too hot here."

"Where did you live before?"

"I came from L.A."

"I know Southern California can be a hot place, but I guess not as much as here. I'm sure the winter here will be more comfortable."

"I hope so."

Apparently, she hadn't moved to South Texas for the weather.

While walking back to my car, a police car slowly rolled by with two officers and stopped just ahead of me. One of them stepped out, and I suddenly felt a surge of adrenaline, and my mind flashed back to the experience in Hamlin.

"Hi, Sir," this cop said cordially. "Where are you headed?"

"Just over to my car after leaving the Chinese restaurant."

"What are you driving?"

"A Toyota Corolla."

"Not a white Mustang then?"

"No."

"We got a complaint about one of those parked near the Walmart where it shouldn't be. So, you're OK."

He got back in the car, and they moved on, and I was relieved as suddenly as I'd been riled up. Close to the Walmart, I did see a white Mustang improperly parked by a cart collection area, and wondered if it might wind up getting towed. Before going back to my car, I took a short walk along U.S. 90 through more of the commercial area. Later, around midnight, I went into the Walmart restroom and did my end of day dental hygiene with a few others around and felt a little self-conscious again about doing it the vagabond way. But no one said anything.

Clouds had moved in, and I didn't see any stars above Uvalde that night. What a contrast to the dazzling stellar spectacle the night before at the campground in the Hill Country. So ended Day 26 as I progressed closer to the finale of 83 and the Coast.

DAY 27

Uvalde, meeting Popeye, some great brisket

By morning the sky had cleared, and I awoke and saw a radiant sunrise through the car window. After I was up, I went to a McDonald's inside the Walmart and had two of their small parfaits with yogurt, granola, and fruit for the first time.

I called my sister in Fort Collins, and an old New Jersey buddy who told me he'd been checking out my route on Google Earth. A rather large, dark bird, with a purple iridescence on its upper body and a long, rounded tail, was flitting around the parking lot, which I identified as a great-tailed grackle. My field guide showed this part of Texas was within the species year-round range and said these birds commonly congregate in towns. Now I realized that it was one of the noisy birds I'd heard but not seen the evening before, and I'd be seeing and hearing multitudes more in the miles ahead.

I drove back toward 83 and the center of town and stopped for a photo of a nicely landscaped stone monument with the inscription: "UVALDE, TEXAS—Tree City USA—Est. 1855." Originally the town was named Encina—meaning "oak" in Spanish—because of the presence of live oak trees, which was changed in 1856 after Uvalde County was organized and the town became the county seat. The new namesake was Juan de Ugalde—a governor and army general of the Spanish colonial period—and his last name was misspelled by Anglo settlers.

From a population under 800 in 1880, Uvalde has grown steadily to well over 15,000 current residents and is largely Hispanic. Though the town has a lot of railroad history, it's not of rail origin, and its first line—the Galveston, Harrisburg, and San Antonio Railway—didn't arrive until 1881. By then the town was well established, and residents successfully opposed the railroad going through the center of town like it did in other communities along its route. The old passenger depot was once about two miles from the city center, and in 1909 the two were connected by a streetcar service. Passenger trains ran until 1958, and huge freight trains now run an unobtrusive distance from Uvalde's attractive center.

The area has long had very productive farm and ranch lands, and Uvalde became a big shipping point for various fruit and vegetable crops, cattle, sheep, and goats. A lot of mild huajillo honey has also been produced locally, and Uvalde was even honored as the "Honey Capital of the World" during the 1905 World's Fair.

The town also produced some notable people besides the former U.S. vice-president, John Garner, such as 1970s Texas governor Dolph Briscoe; actor Matthew McConaughy; and actress-singer-songwriter Dale Evans—spouse of the famed Roy Rogers.

East of town is Garner Field—a municipal airport that was originally another of the U.S. Army Air Force training fields during World War II. It presently has a museum with vintage aircraft from the war. Regarding another type of aviation, Uvalde has a reputation for great soaring and was the location of the World Gliding Championships in 1991 and 2012.

I parked by the visually appealing old town square at the crossroads of 83 and 90, which was well-landscaped with green grass, shrubs, and tall shady trees. There was also a stone fountain that wasn't spouting. The square was faced by quaint brick buildings, with one being the Grand Opera House, which was built in 1891 and restored by the city in 1980. It's now on the National Register of Historic Places and has tours and many live performances.

I relaxed on a bench near the fountain, and just a few other people were around. The crossroads were busy and rather noisy, though. Soon I took a short walk down the street to the Rexall drug store to check out the old soda fountain my guidebook mentioned, but it was closed on weekends. A little further on was the old theater I'd noticed before, which I saw was now an art gallery and studio. Back at the square, I was ready to leave Uvalde, which seemed like a very nice and interesting town that was bigger and busier than the ones I'd been through recently.

Continuing south on 83, it was back into lots of mesquite and the very heavy brushland that Stew Magnuson's book refers to as "The Great Mesquite Forest of Texas." Like me, he considered such a mesquite-dominated landscape to be the least scenic along the highway. I wondered what it looked like originally before the activities of humans and their livestock might have spread the tenacious brush here.

The monotony of the scenery was briefly interrupted by the flyby of a scissor-tailed flycatcher—a songbird-sized bird with a remarkably long tail that I knew was common in the region. Ahead was a sign saying, "Picnic Area—Historical marker," and I stopped at a long pull-off by two small shelters and two signs from the Texas Historical Commission. One commemorated Camp Nueces, which was one of a chain of posts of the Confederacy's Frontier Regiment during the Civil War, established in 1862 to protect important traffic that crossed the Nueces River. That included cotton transported to Mexico and munitions and other vital supplies headed north for the Confederacy. The other sign was about the Bosque-Larios Expedition of 1675, which was an armed party that accompanied Spanish missionaries in an early attempt to Christianize indigenous inhabitants of Texas through peaceful methods. It apparently had some success when, on May 16, 1675, a High, or sung, Mass was celebrated by the Nueces River with over 1,100 Natives present. Fifty-five infants were baptized, and the crowd was proselytized. This was an event that led to establishing a system of missions in Texas, and I've wondered what methods were used in such conversion attempts when it involved abstract ideas and there were big language barriers. But I suppose there were good interpreters by this time.

I crossed a bridge over the Nueces River, and its large bed appeared arid. Its name means "nuts" in Spanish, which was given because of the abundance of pecan trees along its course. The headwaters lie in Real County in the Hill Country, and the Nueces meanders about 315 miles to Corpus Christi Bay in the Gulf of Mexico and is best known for having been the original southern border of Texas. But when the Republic of Texas became independent of Mexico in 1836, it claimed the further south and west Rio Grande as its border, and the controversy over the land in between continued when Texas was annexed as a state by the U.S. in 1845. U.S. president James K. Polk sent troops to the disputed area in 1846, which resulted in a skirmish with a Mexican force and some American casualties—triggering the very territory-driven American-Mexican War between April 1846 and February 1848. When it ended with a decisive victory for the U.S., Mexico was forced to accept the Rio Grande boundary and the loss of Texas, which it previously refused to do. And it's well-known that Mexico also ceded a mass of its northern territory, including California, to the U.S. because of its defeat. However, this giant territorial gain by the U.S. did involve a purchase price of $15,000,000, plus an assumption of over $3,000,000 of Mexican debt to the U.S. The huge land grab was very influenced by the belief in Manifest Destiny, which President Polk and much of the American public subscribed to at the time—the belief that the U.S. was truly destined, and even had a God-given right to expand to the Pacific Ocean. The Mexican War certainly accomplished much of that goal, despite strong moral objections from some of the American public and the tragic costs of war.

Agriculture reappeared close to the next town of La Pryor, with largely green and brown fields, long pivot irrigators, and storage bins. Mesquite was still around, but a lot had probably been cleared. La Pryor's water tower came into view, and I entered the town with a present population of over 1,600 that's at an intersection with U.S. 57. This federal highway, commissioned in 1970, is unusual for its short distance—a mere 98 miles (158 km) from the San Antonio area to the town of Eagle Pass on the Rio Grande border. Although it has a generally east-west direction, it's signed as a north-south highway because of its odd number. Originally, 57 was a state road that had its number changed for continuity with Mexican Federal Highway 57 across the border, which runs south all the way to Mexico City, and the number was retained when it became a U.S. Highway.

I passed the People's Cafe and a Family Dollar store and followed 83 near the center of the small town. La Pryor's origins go back to a large ranch owned by Colonel Isaac T. Pryor, who decided to sell small tracts of his holdings to farmers and started a development company.

In 1909, he negotiated with the Crystal City and Uvalde Railway to build a depot and cattle loading platform where a town was platted, and the land was aggressively advertised, which drew many prospective buyers from around the country. The promotion was enhanced by a very successful farm in the area that displayed the great variety of crops that could be cultivated locally, and many of the prospects were impressed and bought plots of land.

Soon the nascent town had a post office, hotel, school, and other establishments, and the farming became very productive—no doubt nurtured by the long growing season this far south. But the droughts of the 1930s had harmful effects, though that decade also saw the discovery of natural gas in the area. In 1969, there was a last big cattle shipment that ended major ranching in the area, and the railroad, which had played a vital role in local commerce and also brought many early settlers to La Pryor, has even been removed. The town's population had some fluctuations through the decades, and there were 1,643 people in the 2010 census.

The sun was descending, and the light became gilded as I drove through another forest of tall mesquite. Perhaps this arboreal pest, and not the pecan tree, should be the official tree of Texas because of its abundance. Some cultivated areas reappeared, and then the road rose over a crest through more mesquite brushland, with some grassy breaks strewn with cactus. The landscape undulated before I came to a sign with mileage—"Crystal City 7, Laredo 98"—then another: "Prison area—do not pick up hitchhikers." Soon I passed the Crystal City Detention Center, with towers, fences, and lots of wires, but later learned it had closed in 2012 after being run by a private company.

Just north of Crystal City, my Texas map showed 83 crossing the route of the historic El Camino Real de Los Tejas National Historic Trail, which was one of the Camino Reals or Royal Roads established during the Spanish colonial period that connected remote places in New Spain to the capital in Mexico City. This Texas route, which indigenous people had traversed for centuries for trade, was first utilized by the Spanish in the late 1600s and became extended all the way into western Louisiana. Despite its "royal" status, its condition was often primitive, and there was a regional network of Camino Reals with different names in Texas. The one I crossed was designated by the

National Park Service as a unit in the National Trails System in 2004.

The town of Crystal City came into view, with the local water tower touting its name. I started seeing palm trees again—some quite tall—that must have been planted. This seat of Zavala County calls itself the "Spinach Capital of the World" because of an abundance of the crop in the area, and this resulted in the city having a statue of Popeye—the classic cartoon character and world's most famous spinach lover. I found his representation under a large shelter with metal benches along the town's main street. The old "sailor man" whose character had entertained me in my childhood stood atop a high green pedestal rounded like a spinach can. His head with the familiar cap and massive chin was tilted up, while his left hand held his trademark pipe in his mouth. The front of the pedestal read: "Crystal City, Texas—the spinach capital of the world—founded 1907."

Popeye's source of strength became a major crop early in the town's history, and in 1936 a spinach festival started that has continued to the present in early November. Another Popeye statue was erected earlier than the one I saw, in 1937, in front of the city hall, with the approval of the character's creator, E.C. Segar. It's said that the Popeye character really had a big influence on increased spinach consumption and must have encouraged plenty of kids to eat something green—much, apparently, grown around Crystal City.

Near the shelter and statue were swarms of great-tailed grackles flying about and perching on power lines while making the same racket that sounded like a grackle convention. These birds and Popeye are my main memories of Crystal City.

Historically, Crystal City's origin is similar to La Pryor's. In this case, two developers—Carl F. Groos and E.J. Buckingham—bought a 10,000-acre ranch in 1905, platted a townsite, and sold most of the land in parcels for farms. It was along the same railway, and the new town was named Crystal City because of the clarity of the area's abundant groundwater from the expansive Carrizo-Wilcox Aquifer. It became incorporated in 1910 and was voted the seat of Zavala County in 1928.

The local agriculture did extremely well as part of the "Winter Garden of Texas," where, with irrigation, many vegetable crops can be grown in the subtropical climate during the winter months. Onions were the first crop grown before spinach, and Crystal City became a major shipping point for produce. In 1932, a vegetable cannery also opened. Huge growth in the agricultural industry attracted many Mexican and Mexican American migrant laborers, who made up most of Crystal City's population in the 1930s; and a big labor camp was constructed on the edge of town. But after the U.S. became involved in World War II in late 1941, this facility was converted into one of the now ill-regarded internment camps for groups thought to be a potential threat to national security. This camp had Japanese, German, and even some Italian nationals who were in the U.S. at the time and were arrested and detained. Texas had three such internment camps, and the one in Crystal City was the largest in the U.S. and the only one developed solely for families, which reached a peak of about 3,400 detainees in December 1944. When the camp closed officially in 1948, the city and school district took over the property.

The Postwar years brought an increase in Crystal City's population after the Del Monte Corporation opened a big canning plant just outside town, which became the area's largest single employer. The community reached its highest numbers in 1960 with 9,101 people, and there's been a slow decline since, with 7,138 in the last tally.

In the early 1960s, long-running tensions between the Mexican majority and the Anglo population came to a head when the civil rights movement gained momentum elsewhere in the country. Discrimination against Mexicans goes back to the days of the Texas Republic and worsened in later decades. Though not as well-known as the infamous Jim Crow laws that segregated and made second-class citizens of African Americans, there were very similar what's been called "Juan Crow" laws that Mexican Americans in Texas and other states where they were numerous were subjected to; and they were also victimized by mob violence and lynchings. Even after becoming a majority in Crystal City, those of Mexican ethnicity experienced segregation and lots of discrimination in the town for decades, when an Anglo elite controlled the local government and educational system. This entrenched political power was seriously challenged in 1963 when five Mexican American candidates known as "Los Cincos" ran for the city council and managed to win with a lot of energized grassroots support. This upset of an old status quo was a first for a Texas town and got plenty of publicity. But the Anglos regained control in the city in just a few years, only to be challenged again in 1969, when the local high school was the center of conflict because of discriminatory practices, exemplified by the way it selected cheerleaders and homecoming queens. It all led to a big student walkout that eventually won many concessions from the school board and resulted in a new balance of power in the school system and city government. A very dynamic young activist named José Angel Gutierrez was a key figure in both of these "Crystal City Revolts," and he became a co-founder of the La Raza Unida, or The United Race party that started in Crystal City in January 1970 to advance the interests of Mexican Americans, or Chicanos, better than they thought the Democratic Party could, which most of them had supported. The new party soon proliferated in Texas and other Southwestern states and had much influence. So, this relatively unknown town played a leading role in a big civil rights movement.

I drove past the eye-pleasing Spanish mission-style Sacred Heart Catholic church in town, and several downtown buildings had colorful mosaic murals with historic images.

The sun was setting through some overcast, and the next section of the highway had very smooth pavement that coursed through more brush country in the fading light. I crossed Turkey Creek—a tributary of the Nueces River—and, after entering Dimmit County, passed the very small community of Winter Haven just to the west on a farm road. Interestingly, it was established by settlers from Florida in 1911, who named it after a town in their home state that had an appropriate name for its subtropical climate. A post office opened here in 1927, and there were eight businesses in 1931, which declined to none by 1980. However, the number of residents rose from fifty in 1939 to 112 in the 1990 and 2000 counts.

Soon the lights of Carrizo Springs glittered ahead. The city limit sign posted a population of 5,602, and this town's name was also influenced by the area's pure artesian wells. "Carrizo" is a Spanish word for the tall cane grass that once grew here, which is a big invasive that's spread wildly and caused problems in a lot of the region. Some settlers from Atascosa County to the east got the town started in 1865, and in 1880 Dimmit County was organized, with Carrizo

Springs as the seat. By 1885 the community had well-constructed homes, a school, a courthouse, two churches, a newspaper, some businesses, and 900 inhabitants. Sheep and cattle ranching dominated the local economy in its early years, and then more agriculture developed that took advantage of the easily accessible wells for irrigation. In 1910, Carrizo Springs was incorporated, and the San Antonio, Uvalde, and Gulf Railroad arrived. By 1916, it had over 1,000 people and electricity. There was a steady rise in population in the following decades, which peaked at 7,553 in 1988 and has fluctuated since.

I came to an intersection with U.S. 277, which is the southern terminus of this auxiliary highway that 83 had first encountered much further north just before Anson. I pulled into a Stripes store lot to check out the possibility of spending the night there and parked in a back area with empty spaces. I got permission to stay there from a friendly young lady inside the store and asked her about ordering something from the Mexican menu this chain offers, but the food service had closed. However, she recommended a Mexican restaurant, or a place called the Red Dog Ice House that were both close by.

I took a walk and came to the Red Dog and was taken by its rustic appearance and the announcement of the words BEER and STEAKS. Lively sounds also carried outside. So, I went in and found a seat at the bar in a high energy atmosphere from a mainly young crowd that looked largely Hispanic. It was a good-sized place with a high ceiling that also had an outdoor eating area with a corral-type fence around it. I was served a beer by a thirty-something, dark-eyed woman with a Latina sensuality who called me "Hon," which was a boost for an older guy's ego. On the menu, a brisket sandwich caught my attention, with the description: "Brisket smoked over pecan wood for ten hours, sliced and topped with barbeque sauce..."—which sounded about as Texas as any food choice could be, knowing that brisket is a beef cut the state is famous for. It was another time to put any reservations and guilt about eating beef aside and indulge in this Texas specialty when I was there, and the price was very reasonable. When the sandwich arrived on thick Texas toast with a moderate portion of fries, I found the brisket extremely tender and delicious, and it's not an exaggeration to say it was one of the best sandwiches I ever had.

I bought another round of beer from the same female bartender, whose attractiveness was enhanced by a nice smile that she gave generously. But I was turned off by some of her tattoos—typical of her Branded Generation—because of my older sensibilities on this matter that doesn't find tattoos attractive on most of the female body.

I mentioned traveling 83 to the woman and asked, "Do you live in Carrizo Springs?"

"Yes, but I came from Crystal City."

"So is the warm weather now normal for this time of year?"

"Yes."

"Do you ever get snow here?"

"Not since 1989, and when it happens it's not much and is gone soon."

Then she smiled again and moved on to another customer. She had a slight Spanish accent that indicated what must have been her first language, and my bit of contact with this nice, sensual woman made my eating and drinking experience even more enjoyable. I also liked the energy of the younger crowd and got good vibes from the place, which made me glad they'd stopped serving food at the Stripes, or I might not have come here.

I walked further and discovered a smaller Walmart that closed at 10 p.m., which made me decide to stay at the Stripes, which was open all night with its facility. Back in Wander, I stayed up late catching up with my journal while some cars and trucks came and went around the backlot. When I was finally tired enough to call it another day, it was very early in a new one. I fell asleep easily, despite the lights in the lot. And some of my last thoughts while still conscious were about the irony of a Best Western lodging nearby, with its big beds and other comforts. But it was another time I was beating the pricey system.

DAY 28

Laredo, along the Border, a Motel 6

In the morning a border patrol vehicle was parked close to mine—a reminder of the proximity to Mexico. I went into the Stripes to check out what they served for breakfast and found out that this large convenience store chain, with many locations in Texas and neighboring states, had some good, economical food, and I ordered a breakfast taco. Before leaving the store, I saw two uniformed border patrol men from the parked vehicle. One looked Anglo and the other Hispanic.

I drove through another part of Carrizo Springs and saw yet another Stripes store, and a water tower with the town's name. There were more palm trees, mesquite, and numbered streets with some well-maintained older homes. A sign by a First Baptist church posted the question: "If you were on trial for being a Christian, would you be convicted?" I also passed the two-story, limestone Dimmit County Courthouse.

Back on 83 after a short stray from it, a sign said it was seventy-nine miles to the large city of Laredo. Ahead stood another water tower, a stretch of mesquite, and a sprawling green crop before I came to a somewhat industrial area with a big yard full of trucks. Soon I was back in more mesquite on both sides of the road and passed the appropriately named Mesquite Inn.

Down the road, I entered the city limits of Asherton and passed the Asherton Smokehouse, a Valero station with a Subway concession, another gas station with a small convenience store, but didn't see much else in the town, apparently because I didn't go into the main part of it.

In the 1950s, Asherton had over 2,400 people, and since then it's been another story of the slow decline of a Texas rural community, with the 2010 census figure down to 1,084. The town's name came from Asher Richardson—an ambitious local rancher who developed the town in the early 1900s after purchasing 48,000 acres in a state sale. Telephone service came in 1905, and a post office in 1909. The Asherton and Gulf Railway, which Richardson funded, began operating in 1910, and the new town became a shipping point for local farmers. By 1915, it had about 1,000 residents, four churches, and almost twenty businesses, and the area's irrigated farmland soon became one of the biggest producers of Bermuda onions in the U.S. The Great Depression of the 1930s took its toll on the town, which rebounded in the 1950s before a slide in numbers began. The community has a large Hispanic majority, like most in the region.

There's a view from 83 of the elegant Bel-Asher House that was built in 1910 with native sandstone, where Asher Richardson and his wife Belle lived; and it's remained in the family for generations. Ahead, 83 widened to undivided four lanes for a short stretch, with more sprawling mesquite to the west. A tank field appeared on the east side—another sign of the fossil fuel wealth of Texas, dominated in recent years by fracking. The state is still the biggest oil producer in the U.S., with about twenty-five percent of the nation's total production from old or legacy fields and new oil shale discoveries. A good share of this output is from the giant Eagle Ford Shale of South Texas that I was traveling through now, which wasn't discovered until 2008. Truck traffic had been very heavy since Carrizo Springs, probably because of the local industry.

I saw a sign for Catarina, with no population posted. On the west side of the highway, my attention was grabbed by two rectangular, red brick, two-story structures, with tall palms in between and shorter ones out front. HOTEL and RESTAURANT were painted on a side wall, and I parked across the road by a historical marker and walked over to the buildings, which had an attractive, vintage look but apparently weren't open. One section was undergoing some repairs or renovation, and a ladder and some window replacements were outside, but no one else was around. Some of the second-story windows had protruding air conditioning units. The tall palms were in a small courtyard, and a sign above a side door said, "Caterina Hotel-Cafe–family entrance–built 1926." I also saw "private property, no trespassing," which restrained my curiosity from leading me through one of the open doors. It was another old structure where I thought: "If those walls could only talk." The whole place was very photogenic, and I clicked a few pictures from across the road.

Later, a website revealed that this hotel is one of the few buildings left in Caterina, which was a thriving community in the 1920s. Like many old dwellings, this one has had stories of hauntings. The name Caterina was associated with the area as far back as the 1770s during the Spanish colonial period, when, according to legend, a Mexican woman with that name was killed in the vicinity by hostile Natives. But no town developed until Asher Richardson—the founder of Asherton—decided to fund a railroad link from Artesia Wells in the east to the new town he was developing. Richardson arranged to route it through the Taft-Caterina ranch along the way, and in return the ranch was able to build a depot with cattle shipping pens along the new line. After it began operating in 1910, the depot became the center of a small community when the ranch manager, Joseph F. Green, moved his headquarters there and started a small development that included a post office and schoolhouse. By 1915, there were also twenty-five residents. The area also had the Taft House—a mansion that was built by Charles Taft, who was the owner of the ranch and a half-brother of William Howard Taft—the U.S. president from 1909 to 1913. It's said that the mansion had larger bathtubs to accommodate the heavy president when he visited.

Caterina continued to develop, and electrical power and telephone service came. By 1929 it had about 2,000 people and a variety of businesses. But the Great Depression, combined with local artesian wells drying up, caused a serious downturn, and the population plunged to 592 in 1931, along with business closings. This was followed by decades of further decline, and by 1990 Caterina had been reduced to forty-five inhabitants. There was a spurt to 135 in 2000, but whatever the present numbers were had to be a small percentage of what was once here. And the same applies to the few buildings that remain.

However, it was encouraging to see the old hotel still intact and in some process of improvement.

A contemporary country music singer-songwriter named Max Stalling hailed from this area and wrote a long ballad called "Cowboy from Caterina" about a local cowhand who lived through most of the twentieth century, which remembers a character and way of life that was once here.

The historical marker near where I'd parked was a short block of granite marked by the Daughters of the American Revolution and the state of Texas in 1918, and it commemorates the Old San Antonio Trail that passed through here and was a Camino Real. However, a nearby information panel said that it wasn't a single trail because different routes were used, depending on conditions like weather and threats of Native attacks. The name San Antonio was used because trails converged there in its early settlement years. The trail history is long and complex, and some trails were originally used by tribal groups, as in many other places. Expeditions of Spanish colonists used this Camino Real to travel from Mexico to eastern Texas to establish and supply missions in the early 1690s. Eventually the routes were also used for commerce, cattle drives, and immigration, including the Anglo American settlers who started arriving in Texas around 1820. During the Civil War between 1861 and 1865, this "trail" became a supply line from Texas to the rest of the Confederacy, and to transport cotton to Mexico. When railroads later arrived and became dominant, the old paths of the San Antonio Trail were either abandoned or limited to local use.

U.S. 83 was at a crossroads here with a much more historic road, and I learned the stone marker was one of 123 that were placed along a route determined by a professional surveyor in 1915-1916, and that most markers have survived.

Past Caterina, 83 resumed a southerly direction and veered further from the Nueces River, headed for an eventual encounter with the Rio Grande. Ahead was a big oil extraction area with small tanks and other installations. The light gray road surface changed from smooth to rumbly, then back to smooth. What looked like a small oil refinery came into view to the west, and to the east was a vast terrain of solid mesquite. But despite all this heavy growth, gates for ranches appeared intermittently. So, there must have been enough grass amid the brush for livestock to graze on.

Before Laredo was a long, empty stretch where no towns were marked on my map. There was a break in the thick mesquite, where the landscape opened more and a low ridge appeared to the south. Bright yellow flowers lined the road, which headed toward the tree-clad ridge. Over the rise was a sea of brush that I was soon driving through, which had a lot of fossil fuel activity with familiar light brown, cylindrical storage tanks.

I stopped at the isolated Vaquero Pit Stop for fuel, where there was a store that served food and a 24/7 tire service, apparently for truckers. Since the gas prices were higher, no doubt due to the station's isolation, I didn't fill up the tank. There was some eyesore litter around, even close to a trash bin, which again motivated me to do a little volunteer clean-up. A few parked trucks were idling and fouling the air, and one had a huge round trailer like some others I'd seen in the area. When I saw its driver return, I walked over and asked what he was transporting, and he told me it was water from a Louisiana service company. I soon thought it was probably for the local fracking operations, which consume voluminous amounts of water. This pit stop also had showers, but I planned on getting a motel later.

I moved on through more brush country where mesquite continued to dominate, and there were some other shrubs that looked interesting. I found an FM radio station playing lively Tejano music—Tejano referring to Texans of Mexican descent. These sounds are part of that ethnic group's subculture that has influences from the accordion music of the German, Polish, and Czech immigrants in Texas. Later, Tejano music became more complex and was influenced by rock, blues, country, and other modern music.

I cruised under an overpass for Texas 255—a short, multi-lane toll road that connects with the Rio Grande border not far to the west. A small roadside tequila bar advertised having Karaoke, and further down the road I stopped at a sign about U.S. 83 in Texas also being the Texas Vietnam Veterans Memorial Highway—commemorating that tragic conflict like South Dakota also does. The sign had an image of Vietnam configured over the Lone Star flag of Texas, along with texts in English and Spanish:

"In gratitude to the thousands of men and women who served our country during the Vietnam War, the people of Texas dedicate this highway, which runs across our state from the southernmost tip to the northernmost point. It is our hope that all those who travel will pause to remember those who gave up their lives or their youth or their hopes in that long and bitter conflict. We vow not to forget those who did not return to us, and we pledge to remember the sacrifices of those who have come home."

As an old Child of the Sixties, who could have been sent to "Nam" myself if my circumstances had been different, these moving words had special meaning to me.

I came to a junction with I-35, which 83 joined and would run with to the far side of Laredo, and this was the southernmost section of this 1,569-mile (2,525 km) interstate that comes close to being another border-to-border highway. This stretch is also an unofficial part of the vast network of roads that make up the Pan-American Highway, which, in concept, connects Prudhoe Bay on the northern coast of Alaska with Ushuaia at the southern tip of Argentina. So, a small section of U.S. 83 is also part of that network. At first the expressway I entered had four lanes that coursed through more brushland, but there were signs of approaching civilization. Soon I was in the outskirts of Laredo and started seeing more businesses, including a big Trans America truck stop. The road widened to six lanes, and I passed an exit for the World Trade Bridge that crosses the Rio Grande into Mexico. The highway now ran closer to the river and border, which wasn't visible, however.

While cruising at a higher speed, an electronic warning sign inspired caution. "2,544 deaths this year on Texas roads." I later read online that the I-35 corridor across the state is one of the most dangerous stretches to drive in Texas. This is attributed to high congestion that's been affected by NAFTA, or the North American Free Trade Agreement, which brought a big increase in truck traffic between the U.S. and Mexico. I-35's dangers seemed to make it an exception to the notion that expressways are safer than largely two-lane roads like 83.

I entered the busyness of what's the largest city along 83, with a population of over 235,000. Laredo is also the tenth largest city in Texas and the seat of Webb County. Now the scenery was industrial and commercial, with billboards and familiar chain businesses, where lots of palm trees lined the expressway. Amid all the modernity was a sign for a historic district that *Road Trip USA* said had many vintage buildings around an old plaza that included a museum and cathedral—all at the site of the center of the original Spanish settlement started here in 1755, which came to be called Villa de San Agustin. Though I knew this now large city had a long and interesting history, it seemed too big and busy for me to want to get off the highway to explore any of it.

The name Laredo is familiar from some old movie and TV Westerns, and the city was named after a town on the northern coast of Spain. Almost twenty years after Mexico won its independence from Spain in 1821, the new country faced its own separatist challenge on January 17, 1840, when three Mexican states adjacent to Texas declared independence from Mexico and formed the Republic of the Rio Grande, with Laredo as the capital. The secession was prompted, as Texas had been four years earlier, by the harsh policies of Mexican president and general Antonio Lopez de Santa Anna—famous for leading the army that overwhelmed the defenders of the Alamo in San Antonio in 1836. Soon after Santa Anna was elected president in 1833, political turmoil led to his suspending the Mexican constitution of 1824 and making himself a virtual dictator. After some serious attempts to restore the constitution failed, the three northern states began the revolt, and for most of 1840, the Federalist forces of the breakaway republic clashed with the Centralist ones of the Mexican government, and the rebels lost. Their fighting forces included some Anglo Texans, and the brief-lived republic had a three-colored flag with three stars representing its states. So, while Texas, or parts of it, is known for having been under six different flags in its history—those of Spain, France, Mexico, the Texas Republic, the U.S., and the Confederacy—Laredo has seen seven, and is the only city in Texas with this distinction.

The Treaty of Guadalupe Hidalgo that ended the American-Mexican War in 1848 and finally settled the Rio Grande border dispute led to voluntary movement of many Laredo Mexicans across the river who still wanted to live in Mexico for cultural reasons. They established the city of Nuevo or "new" Laredo, which grew to the huge present population of over 373,000.

Laredo's rail history began in 1881, with the arrival of both the Texas-Mexican Railroad from Corpus Christi, and the international Great Northern from San Antonio. There was resulting economic growth, and by 1900 Laredo had a population of over 13,000. Oil and gas were discovered in the area in the early twentieth century, which led to more growth.

To promote American patriotism on the U.S. side of the Rio Grande, Laredo began what became its biggest festival and tradition on February 22, 1898 that remains strong—the celebration of George Washington's birthday, which turned into nearly month-long festivities. It's the largest celebration of Washington in the U.S. that includes parades, a carnival, an air show, fireworks, concerts, and even a jalapeno-eating contest. Laredo even has a Celebration Building that was designed to resemble Washington's Mount Vernon. While the town was founded during Washington's lifetime, he was certainly never anywhere near it, or even knew about the Spanish settlement. And it seems strange that a city with about a ninety-five percent Hispanic population would have such a relationship with totally Anglo George Washington. Perhaps it's mainly about celebrating, and the festivities attract about 400,000 visitors. Maybe I should join them one of these years, since my own birthday is the same as GW's on February 22, and I was middle-named George for that reason.

Laredo is one of the oldest crossing points along the U.S.-Mexico border and presently has four international road bridges. Consequently, it plays a vital role in trade between the two countries. The city's economy is based on this international trade, which was enhanced by the 1994 NAFTA Agreement. Laredo is also the largest inland port of entry in the U.S. Lots of illegal drug traffic also manages to enter the U.S. through Laredo, and Nuevo Laredo, which, though it has its charm, has been the scene of very violent clashes between rival drug traffickers in recent years like in many border towns. Nuevo Laredo also has its share of "maquiladoras" or assembly plants that are concentrated in these communities, which are run by multinational corporations to take advantage of cheap labor. Though often called sweatshops because of low pay and poor working conditions, I've read claims that many are really not so bad, and that the pay is significantly higher than minimum wage jobs in Mexico. A lot of these operations were in Mexico years before NAFTA, with its tariff-reducing benefits.

As a result of all the economic activity on both sides of the border, Laredo has been a very fast-growing city. And it's a young town that had a median age of twenty-seven in 2010. Inside the city limits is an international airport that had been another U.S. Army airfield during World War II that trained fighter pilots. Between 1952 and 1973, it was also a U.S. Air Force base.

After cruising through most of this sprawling city with low buildings, I reached the end of I-35 just before the Rio Grande and the Gateway International Bridge into Mexico, where I was careful to stay out of the lanes that would lead me out of the country. On the Mexican side is Federal Highway 85—a 753-mile (1,212 km) route to Mexico City that's a continuation of the Pan-American Highway that opened in 1936. The Rio Grande, like most rivers, has had floods in its history, and Laredo experienced very destructive ones in 1932 and 1954. I followed signs for 83 South, which continued as an undivided highway headed due east for a short stretch through an old residential section of the city, where some homes had Spanish tile roofs.

I stopped at a sizable H-E-B chain grocery store where the lot was very crowded. Inside were a lot of people with a Hispanic appearance that reflected Laredo's demographics. I bought three ruby red grapefruits that South Texas is famous for growing, and a few cans of King Oscar sardines spiced with jalapenos that I'd never seen before and must suit local Tejano tastes.

Moving on, this part of Laredo was still busy and commercial, and traffic moved sluggishly. Along the road were many Mexican restaurants. On the way out of the city, 83 was also the Zapata Highway, and I passed the South Campus of a modern-looking community college. It was good to be back in the breeze and brush, and the highway had four divided lanes for a while and still stayed close to the Rio Grande, which remained out of view. *Road Trip USA* says 83 follows a route here that was blazed by American general Zachary Taylor's army during the Mexican War.

The subtropical air was a balmy eighty-two degrees, and the humidity seemed quite high. Some light gray clouds started sprinkling on my windshield. A water tower to the west bore the name Rio Bravo, which was the next town with over 4,700 residents, making it the second largest in Webb County after giant Laredo. Its population is also overwhelmingly Hispanic, and Rio Bravo is the name given to the Rio Grande River in Mexico that's an abbreviation of the Rio Bravo del Norte, or "Furious River of the North."

The highway was back to a rumbly surface, and I saw a sign for the Texas Coastal Birding Trail in this region known for great bird migrations and numbers of avian species. The clouds stopped sprinkling, and I passed more cylindrical storage tanks for gas wells. The road narrowed back to two lanes and smooth asphalt.

Past the Zapata County line, I stopped by a stone monument for MISSION DOLORES A VISITA—Established in 1750 as part of Jose de Escandón's "project to settle the region and civilize and Christianize the Indians." Dolores was the name of a ranch near the historic mission in the area.

José de Escandón was the key figure in Spain's efforts to colonize the lower Rio Grande region in the mid-1700s, largely to discourage French and English encroachment there. He had spent his early years in the mother country and arrived in Mexico in 1715, which was part of vast New Spain. Escandón served in the Spanish military and worked his way up the ranks for his role in pacifying different Native tribes. By 1740, the viceroy of Mexico promoted him to colonel, and his leadership ability resulted in him being commissioned to establish the new colony, which he would name Nuevo Santander (New Santander) after his home region in northern Spain. After completing an expedition that explored lower Rio Grande territory and avoided violent clashes with the Natives—unlike the brutal Conquistadors of two centuries earlier—Escandón devised a colonial plan and was appointed governor-general of the new colony. He then enticed many settlers with descriptions of rich natural resources, monetary incentives, and promises of land grants; and between 1748 and 1755, he was involved in the founding of numerous missions and over twenty towns, including Laredo, which resulted in him becoming known as the "Father of the Rio Grande Valley."

A lot of road construction was ahead that looked like a section was being expanded to four lanes, with rows of bright orange barrels and road crews laboring. More monotonous brush bordered the long work zone. I passed a ranch with a Spanish name, and finally came to some cultivated land again where there were large sprouting fields bordered by more brush. A gullied land feature known as an arroyo was ahead, which was named on a sign. There was a sign for another arroyo, then denser mesquite before the landscape opened widely with a variety of smaller shrubs as I headed toward a dark cloud formation in the south.

The next community was San Ygnacio, with a populace under 700, which was named after the Spanish saint, Ignatius Loyola—the founder of the Jesuit order. It's the oldest town in Zapata County that goes back to 1830; and though small size-wise, it's very significant in history and architecture. A large part of it made the National Register of Historic Places as the San Ygnacio Historic District, which has thirty-six nineteenth-century sandstone structures that were built as a defense against Comanche attacks in the early years of the settlement. This is the last surviving group of such structures that were once numerous in South Texas. The oldest one here, known as the Trevino Uribe Rancho, was built in 1830, and a sundial was placed above its entrance in 1851. In 1998 it became a National Historic Landmark.

In 1839, leaders of the movement to establish the Republic of the Rio Grande met in San Ygnacio. During the American Civil War, Confederate troops saw action here, though not against Union forces, but those of the Mexican leader, Juan Cortina, who formed a large partisan-like force that fought against oppressive treatment of Mexicans in South Texas. Later, during what's known as the Garza War of 1891-1892, which was a failed uprising against the autocratic Mexican president, Porfirio Diaz, revolutionary forces struck Mexico from San Ygnacio. The town also saw conflict during the long and bloody Mexican Revolution and Civil War between 1910 and 1920, and some U.S. troops were involved when a Mexican force crossed the border and fought a U.S. Cavalry unit here.

Some scenes of the 1952 movie *Viva Zapata!* were filmed around San Ygnacio, which was about a heroic figure of the Mexican Revolution, Emiliano Zapata, who was played by Marlon Brando. Soon after this cinematic event, the town was about to face the same fate as some nearby communities that were being forced to evacuate because of the damming of the Rio Grande further south to create Falcon International

Reservoir. However, San Ygnacio residents petitioned to remain on their higher ground, which they believed would be safe from the flood waters, and they succeeded. However, a major flood in 1954 did cause some serious damage.

In 1982, the La Paz Museum, which is the official museum of Zapata County, was opened by a local elementary school. And in 1990, San Ygnacio's population reached a high of 895, but has decreased since. It's a community with a significance much greater than its numbers.

Ahead was Arroyo Grullo and, finally, the end of a lot of road construction, where 83 was four lanes with smooth new pavement and a wide, grassy median. For a while I was in another kind of brush country with smaller shrubs that resembled sagebrush and lots of cactuses. But the heavy mesquite soon returned.

I stopped along the east side of the road to read a sign about "Old Ramireno"—one of the several small communities that were evacuated before being drowned by Falcon Reservoir. I crossed the Arroyo Burro and a long bridge by the reservoir with no water beneath, though part of the large body of water became visible to the west, where it looked like a wide river. Soon a panorama of green brushland appeared, and I could see a good distance into Mexico.

Structures and operations of "Texas Energy" appeared in the vegetation ahead, and oil and gas production are a big part of Zapata County's present economy. Soon I arrived in the town of Zapata, where there was a hospitable greeting on a large stone wall with a cowboy figure—"Welcome to Zapata, home of Falcon Lake"—another name for the international reservoir. This is a relatively large town with over 5,000 inhabitants that grew from the relocation of the original Zapata on the north bank of the Rio Grande, which was evacuated because of the reservoir.

Both the town and county were named after Colonel Antonio Zapata—a cavalry commander of the revolutionary 1840 Republic of the Rio Grande—and not the later Emiliano Zapata who fought in the Mexican Revolution of the early twentieth century. Both were heroic figures who were killed. Emiliano was assassinated in 1919, and the earlier Antonio was executed while being held prisoner after his small force surrendered to an overwhelming one. It's said that the Mexican Centralist Army general, Mariano Arista, offered to pardon him if he swore allegiance to Mexico, but that Antonio Zapata refused; and on March 29, 1840, he was executed, then beheaded, with his head preserved in alcohol and transported to his home town of Guerrero, where it was impaled on a spike in the main plaza to terrify his family and residents there. Such a gruesome fate led to him being regarded as a martyr for his cause.

The modern Zapata is the Zapata County seat but isn't incorporated rather strangely. The origins of the old Zapata go back to 1767, and land grants from the Spanish government that resulted from José de Escandón's colonization campaign in the region. The new Zapata's population has been steadily increasing since 1960; and each year between November and April, its numbers are swelled by an invasion of snowbirds called Winter Texans, who migrate from the North with their RVs for the balmy temperatures and are no doubt attracted to sprawling Falcon Lake and its recreational opportunities. However, ninety-five percent of Zapata's permanent residents are Hispanic, not surprisingly.

Zapata has also been an attraction for serious hang-gliding enthusiasts in recent years because of excellent atmospheric conditions for the sport. An event called the World Record Encampment has been held at the Zapata County Airport since 2000, and more world records for hang gliding flights have been set there than from any other place in the world. One was a flight of 472 miles.

Driving through a commercial strip in Zapata with palm trees, I saw a drive-thru beer place that had a sign with the U.S. 83 white shield symbol. I stopped to snap a picture of it and of an eye-appealing Spanish-style church. Ahead were chains like Family Dollar, Pizza Hut, and McDonald's, and then another standout Texas county courthouse with a small dome. The 1901 courthouse in the old Zapata was submerged by the international reservoir.

I crossed a bridge over an inlet with a lot of marshy vegetation, and to the west was a wide expanse of water that the U.S-Mexico border runs through. Falcon reservoir is owned and managed by both countries through the International Boundary and Water Commission that was formed back in 1889, and it was developed to provide water, hydroelectric power, flood control, and recreation that's brought many visitors to the Zapata area. The name Falcon came from one of the small towns that was engulfed by the reservoir and relocated, which had been named after the wife of the town's founder—Maria Rita de la Garza Falcón.

Boating and fishing are popular on the reservoir, and Americans can cruise freely to the Mexican side if they don't land in Mexico or bring anything into the country. However, recent years had seen actual piracy on these waters, due to the infamous drug cartel, Los Zetas, which in May 2010 posed as Mexican Federal Police and made some armed robberies boarding boats. Two of the victims that month were a Colorado man and his wife who were jet skiing in Mexican waters and chased by boats with gunmen. The man was fatally shot, and the woman managed to escape and recount the terrible incident. It was thought that the couple may have unintentionally come close to drug trafficking that the reservoir has been used for.

Besides some old towns, a former section of 83 was also drowned by the rising waters in 1953 and re-routed. As with the huge dams much further north along the Missouri River, the project here was traumatic for the people whose lives were disrupted by the waters of progress and forced to move. Many of the homes had been in the same families for generations, and besides the emotional cost of being uprooted, the displaced people were offered poor compensation for all they had to give up, which led to protests in 1953.

Outside Zapata, 83 veered away from the reservoir and was back in brushland with undivided four lanes and a good surface. Overhead clouds sprinkled again, and the air had a refreshing smell. I passed a turnoff for the reservoir, and the road crossed a bridge over an arroyo named Tigre Grande (Large Tiger). El tigre is a Spanish name for the jaguar, which roamed this part of Texas historically, but has long been extirpated.

I came to Lopeño, with just 176 residents, which had about 500 in the early 1990s. It's another of the small towns that was relocated in the 1950s. The name is derived from an early settler and rancher with the surname Lopez; and like other towns in the area, its roots go back to settlers brought by José de Escandón in the 1700s with the promise of land grants. The residents of the original Lopeño and other local ranching and farming communities were largely descendants of the early Spanish colonists.

When I passed through the relocated Lopeño, I saw a sleepy little town with some modest homes and just a few businesses. But I'm sure the small population there could tell many stories about change.

The road crossed another inlet of the reservoir near the El Tigre Chiquito (The Little Tiger) arroyo. Some gas storage tanks appeared in the brush, and I passed another turnoff for "Falcon Lake," which wasn't visible as 83 coursed further from its shoreline. When I arrived in Falcon—one of the other relocated towns—I stopped at a roadside store with gas pumps for a break and went inside. A woman tending the store was speaking Spanish on a phone but greeted me with a smile. Just about everything in the store was in Spanish, including a TV station playing.

"Buenas tardes," I greeted the woman when she ended her conversation.

She answered something in Spanish I couldn't understand, and I responded, "Lo siento. No hablo mucho español" (I'm sorry. I don't speak much Spanish). "Habla usted inglés?" (Do you speak English?).

"No," was her short answer, and it looked like the three years of school Spanish I had many years ago wouldn't enable me to have much of a conversation. Mexico was across the river, but I'd run into a language barrier here. The woman seemed pleasant, though, and after a quick look around the store I left with an "Adios."

An abandoned Texaco station was up the road, and I passed through a residential area with some different styles of homes. It was a good thing I was driving slowly because I spotted a police car and what looked like a speed trap.

The history of Falcon is similar to Lopeño's, beginning with settlers enticed by land grants from the Spanish Crown in the 1700s. The town that developed was originally called Ramireño de Abajo after its founder, and the name Falcon, after the founder's wife, wasn't given until 1915, when a post office was established that needed a different name from the nearby one named Ramireño. The relocated Falcon that I saw had 191 inhabitants in the last count.

Down the road was a stone historical marker that commemorated "Mission Mier a Visita"—a local mission established in 1750 that was part of Escandón's colonization efforts. I came to a turnoff for the Falcon Dam and Falcon State Park at the southern end of the reservoir, but decided to pass it up. The state park just to the east of the dam is popular for varied recreation, and just below the park off a state road is Falcon Village—a miniature community with under fifty residents that's restricted to U.S. Government employees of the International Boundary and Water Commission and the Immigration and Naturalization Service. The dam to the west is jointly owned by the U.S. and Mexico, and it's a five-mile-long earth fill and concrete structure that stands 150 feet above the riverbed. A little over half of it is in Mexico, and there's a U.S. Port of Entry on the two-lane road that crosses it. The dam and the sixty-mile-long reservoir it created from the Rio Grande were dedicated ceremoniously on October 19, 1953, by U.S. President Dwight D. Eisenhower and Mexican President Adolfo Ruiz Cortines. Both countries have benefited from the hydroelectric power produced by the turbines and generators that each operate by the dam.

Just west of the dam on the Mexican side is Nueva Ciudad Guerrero, which was established on this higher ground when the old Guerrero was flooded by the reservoir. However, during serious droughts, the original's buildings, which weren't bulldozed like those of the submerged American towns, have had ghostly reappearances when reservoir levels have been low. Remarkably, some structures have remained intact after decades underwater, including a church and central plaza.

U.S. 83 South ran east of where the Rio Grande was released as a river again from the huge dam. I passed near the town of Salineño that's two miles west of the road and on the river near a historic crossing point used by indigenous people. The Spanish began ranching in this area in 1734, and ranch workers made up a good part of the town's Spanish-speaking population in the twentieth century, along with migrant laborers. Telephone service didn't arrive in the area until the 1960s, and Salineño's streets weren't paved until later. The town had 201 residents in 2010—a drop from 304 in 2000. But each winter thousands of birdwatchers arrive around here—many from great distances—to observe the abundance of species that concentrate in this part of what's called the Rio Grande Valley, although the region is too flat to be a true valley, and is actually more of a river delta. Brown jays, hook-billed kites, and Altamira orioles are but a few of the sought species.

About ten miles down the road, I saw a light-colored water tower for the next and much larger town of Roma, with a population well over 9,000. Next came a sign, "Welcome to Roma—National Historic Landmark," and I slowed down through a small commercial area with a Subway, Dairy Queen, and O'Maria's—a strangely Irish-themed eatery with a green roof in this very Hispanic area. The old part of town had a sign for the World Birding Center that my ornithological interest led me to follow. Along the way were some boarded up old buildings that at first reminded me of Paducah, but fortunately, this town didn't have such an amount of blight.

I parked close to the Roma Bluffs World Birding Center by an old plaza—one of nine such centers in this superb birding region where over 500 different species have been sighted. It displayed a "Welcome Birders" banner by the entrance, and there was an "Open" sign on the door, even though the place was closed. I walked back to the car and the plaza amid many brick and stone vintage buildings that were an interface with the past. Some scenes of *Viva Zapata!* were filmed in this plaza, as in San Ygnacio. While spooning out a sliced avocado from the shell in the car before I started a little exploration of the quaint surroundings, a police car appeared at the other end of the plaza near the old city hall. Still affected by the Hamlin incident, I thought, "Shit, is my Colorado plate going to attract this cop's attention and perhaps arouse suspicion?" The car did prowl around the plaza a couple times, but didn't stop to my relief.

I grabbed my camera and binoculars and stepped out for a close look at a sign with the heading, "National Historic Landmark District;" and I learned that since 1993, this core area of Roma has had this special status, which is the highest level of recognition for historic preservation in the U.S. Many of the old buildings are the work of a German-born architect, builder, and brickmaker named Heinrich Portscheller, who arrived in the area soon after the American Civil War and also designed and built distinctive buildings in some other local towns.

Roma has a lengthy history that goes back to Native Americans who used the nearby bluffs on the Rio Grande as a landmark for a shallow river crossing. In the mid-1760s, a Spanish rancher with the surname Saenz, who was part of Escandón's colonization of Nuevo Santander, founded a settlement at this location with some other ranchers that became known as Corrales de Saenz. Eventually, there were two neighboring settlements, and when the area officially became part of the U.S. after the Mexican War, the name Roma was used at the suggestion of the Roman Catholic Oblate order that established a mission at the location in the mid-1850s. Eventually, the town was incorporated as Roma-Los Saenz.

During the second half of the nineteenth century, Roma was a busy, westernmost port on the Rio Grande for steamships and flat boats that were able to navigate the river this far and carry cotton downstream. A railroad didn't arrive until 1925, and new roads were also constructed around the same time, which ended the town's isolation that resulted from the end of the river's shipping period. In 1927, a suspension bridge was built across the Rio Grande that connected Roma with what's now Ciudad Miguel Alemán on the Mexican side. This international bridge and port of entry operated until 1978, when a concrete bridge was built next to it. But the old bridge still stands and is one of the few remaining suspension bridges in Texas. Though it wasn't currently in use, there was an ongoing restoration effort and the possibility of reopening it to pedestrian traffic. Whatever the bridge's future, it became a National Historic Landmark of the U.S. and Mexico.

I started walking among the over thirty nineteenth-century buildings in the National Historic Landmark District and was captivated by the quaint atmosphere, though some structures were in serious disrepair, and most looked unoccupied. One was an old cantina with a favorite four-letter word—BEER—blurred on a weathered brick wall. A small group of men and women conversing in Spanish passed by the site, and I greeted them with an "Hola," which a few repeated.

Some of the buildings designed by Heinrich Portscheller had wrought iron balconies that were imported from New Orleans. One of his works is the colorful Pink House, which was once owned by a prominent resident who also sheltered refugees during the turbulent Mexican Revolution between 1910 and 1920. The old Roma movie theater with its light brown brick facade was closed and had a sign in Spanish. Resonant chimes sounded in the quiet atmosphere of the historic district, which emanated from the tower of Our Lady of Refuge church by the plaza. This church was constructed in 1853 by the French-born Oblate order priest Father Pierre Yves Keralum, who was also an architect, carpenter, and mason.

I wandered to the nearby river and the top of the sandstone bluffs where Roma is located by. Below was the closest view I had yet of the renowned Rio Grande, and this boundary between two nations was less than 200 feet wide here. I walked out on a ledge and got an even closer view of Mexico and could hear dogs barking and bells chiming in Ciudad Miguel Alemán—a city of about 20,000 in the Mexican state of Tamaulipas. There was a good view of the modern and old bridges to the south, and to the north was a bend in the river with heavy vegetation. The water had a greenish tint and a good flow.

I mused about the headwaters of this river so associated with Texas and Mexico, but which rises around 12,000 feet in the distant Rockies of south-central Colorado—beginning an over 1,800-mile course to the Gulf of Mexico. Thoughts about the river were distracted by a few rather high-pitched, repetitive bird calls, and I spotted a small bird perched on a nearby shrub with a sharp black and white contrast on its body, which my binoculars enabled me to identify as a black phoebe—a flycatcher species common in the Southwest. There was also a sign on the bluff about this being a site on the Great Texas Coastal Birding Trail.

Soon a whirlybird—or helicopter—made an appearance and flew low over the U.S. side of the river toward me, which I thought must be the U.S. Border Patrol, maybe even checking me out. I learned that the Rio Grande Valley has had far more apprehensions of illegal immigrants than any other region along the U.S.-Mexico border, and that this activity is particularly intense around Roma. So is drug smuggling from the cartel-infested Mexican state of Tamaulipas; and 2014 was also the year that many unaccompanied minors from Central America started arriving at the border. One of the Border Patrol's other vehicles are airboats that prowl the river, but migrants are known to hide in thick brush and carrizo cane and wait for the boats to pass before attempting to make the narrow crossing on inflatable rafts or Jon boats. Many were transported by smugglers who often abandoned them on the Mexican side. But if they make the crossing, they can hide or try to blend in Roma and find a connection to be off somewhere on U.S. 83. Others have turned themselves in to the Border

Patrol. It's all part of a sad and long chapter in the troubled history of the border region, which will seemingly continue until the conditions in the countries that migrants are so desperate to flee finally improve.

Back at Wander, a sprinkle that had started became rain, which I waited out in the car till it let up before driving off from the nineteenth-century charm of old Roma. *The Last American Highway—Texas* mentions accounts of ghost sightings in the town, which include a Burger King that's close to an old cemetery. I remain a skeptic about such paranormal claims, but it's no wonder that they originate in a place like this with many reminders of a colorful past. In contrast to the historic district, I passed a modern shopping center with some chain businesses and an indie motel called the Roma Inn.

Leaving town, 83 became a four lane, divided highway with a more eastward than southward direction as it followed the Rio Grande, and from here on, the towns would start coming in quick succession, with a big change in the character of the journey. One called Escobares ("brooms" in Spanish) was just ahead, with a recent population of 1,188. It wasn't incorporated until 2005, but it had more people before it was and has deep Spanish land grant roots. Presently, the poverty rate was extremely high, with big problems with unemployment and crime that efforts were being made to control. The community of Garceño was right next door with under 500 people, followed by diminutive Rosita, which originated with descendants of early colonists. I saw the first sign for the Texas Tropical Trail, which refers to what's actually a subtropical region at the bottom of Texas between the Rio Grande and the Gulf of Mexico—known for having flora and fauna not found elsewhere in the U.S.

Rio Grande City was a much larger community ahead, and a sign at the city limit showed 11,993 residents for this seat of Starr County. Another sign read: "Welcome to Rio Grande City, home of General Ricardo S. Sanchez"—a retired U.S. Army general who commanded troops in Iraq and was born in the city in 1953. The local water tower stood ahead and also a commercial area, followed by another quaint historic district with many brick buildings and another old movie theater. Heinrich Portscheller had designed buildings here also.

Like Roma, it's a very historic town, and its origins date back to a ranch established in 1762 by the Falcón family in Escandón's Spanish colony. But a town didn't develop until 1847 after an American military man named Henry Clay Davis, who was stationed locally during the Mexican War, married María Hilaria de la Garza Falcón—heiress to the land that became the townsite. Davis went on to develop a town that was named Rio Grande City after the river it was on, which soon grew into a port and hub of trade between Texas and Mexico, and with New Orleans. In 1848, the U.S. Army, under General Zachary Taylor, established what became Fort Ringgold next to the town, which was named in honor of an officer who was fatally wounded in the Battle of Palo Alto—the first major engagement of the Mexican War that occurred near Brownsville. The fort was at a strategic location for protecting the border's security, and it operated with some interruptions for close to a century, also contributing to the economy and stability of Rio Grande City. When Texas was part of the Confederacy, the city was occupied by a Union force in November 1863 after they captured Brownsville, but both were retaken by the Confederates in the spring of 1864.

After the Texas-Mexican Railroad further north connected Nuevo Laredo with Corpus Christi on the Gulf Coast in 1883, riverboat traffic on the lower Rio Grande sharply decreased. The short Rio Grande City Railway came to the city in 1925, and the oil and gas boom of the 1930s also expanded the city's economy. Its population has fluctuated but has been growing steadily since 1990. Currently, twenty-five percent of its residents are below the poverty level in a county that's one of the fastest growing but also poorest in the U.S.

Past the old downtown was a less charming commercial stretch and a turnoff for the site of Fort Ringgold and an international bridge to the Mexican town of Camargo. The standing buildings and property at the old fort site have been owned by the city school district since 1949, and in 1993 the site made the National Register of Historic Places.

U.S. 83 was back to two lanes for a short distance before it reverted to divided four lanes, and it would remain a multi-lane road for the remaining hundred miles to Brownsville, and soon run in tandem with an interstate.

Road Trip USA mentions the Rio Grande Valley's annual arrival of tens of thousands of Winter Texan snowbirds descending from the North to escape the harsh winters—like numerous avian species. Many of these seasonal migrants from the Midwest and other regions must travel down 83, and my guidebook said the area I was now in had an abundance of RV and mobile home parks, with some of the most economical rates in the country.

The day's light was fading over the brush and development I was passing through. A sign declared this stretch of 83 was also the Trooper Edwardo Chavez Memorial Highway, which honors a Texas Department of Public Safety officer who was killed in an accident while responding to a call in 2006. And closer to the Rio Grande was the Old Military Road, with dirt and paved sections through twenty-eight villages and towns. It dates to 1848, when it was the route between Fort Ringgold and Fort Brown in Brownsville.

I passed through tiny Garciasville, with just forty-six inhabitants, which has roots in the nineteenth century and was named after an early settler. Set south off the highway was La Grulla with 1,622 people—its name meaning "The Crane" in Spanish, which it was given because sandhill cranes were once common on the ponds north of town.

Sullivan City followed, where palm trees lined the road's median. The very un-Spanish name commemorates the owner of a huge local ranch. The city had a population of about 4,000 and got started in 1908 and was soon incorporated. One of its early residents was William Jennings Bryan—the three-time Democratic nominee for U.S. president and Secretary of State under President Woodrow Wilson, who is also known for his prosecuting role in the Scopes "Monkey Trial" of 1925. For decades, Sullivan City had a small population that didn't increase until the 1980s, presumably from more immigration from across the river. During that time a "colonia"—meaning colony or settlement in Spanish—named Rodriguez developed outside the city, which was one of these hundreds of unincorporated and unregulated communities of poor people near the long U.S.-Mexico border. The greatest numbers are in Texas, and most of the residents are Mexicans that include U.S. citizens and immigrants—legal and illegal. Developers were usually involved in starting these colonias outside municipal boundaries, often on former farmland where regulations and building codes were lacking, resulting in very substandard housing conditions frequently without basic utilities like running water and sewage systems, though these were often falsely promised. And the nearby towns have been reluctant to provide services without receiving revenue. The result has been a norm of squalid, Third World conditions in colonias, which must be one of the saddest examples of poverty in the Rio Grande Valley and in the nation that's considered to be the wealthiest in the world.

When darkness fell, a line of lights appeared to the south in Mexico. I passed a turnoff for the Los Ebanos Ferry that crosses the Rio Grande and is an official border crossing. It's the last hand-operated cable ferry on the river that can carry three cars and a handful of passengers, and it's been operating since 1950. But the location had been used for fording the river since 1740.

Right after entering the city limits of La Joya, an SUV traveling in the opposite direction cut in front of me way too close for comfort. I slammed the brakes and reacted with an expletive as well as a rush of adrenalin.

La Joya translates as "The Jewel," and the name was inspired by a small natural lake near the town that impressed early settlers by the way it shined in sunlight. It's said that many of La Joya's residents are descendants of colonists of Nuevo Santander. The original community was founded in the early 1800s and called Tabasco, which became thriving. But the Rio Grande flooded in 1908 and 1909, forcing residents to move north to higher ground. The new community that developed was incorporated in 1926 as La Joya. However, it stayed small with just a handful of businesses until the early 1970s, when the population began burgeoning. By the new millennium, it had over 3,000 residents, with over ninety-seven percent Hispanic. The high growth rate of towns in the Rio Grande Valley, due to immigration, is certainly a great contrast to the many declining Texas towns further north.

I rolled through Penitas ("small stones" in Spanish), which is a community of over 4,500 with storied origins about a small group of survivors from a Spanish expedition in 1520—well over two centuries before Jose Escandón—who were befriended by local Natives and decided to settle along the Rio Grande here. But the town didn't develop until the early 1900s and had very low numbers until after 1990. Two nearby colonias established in 1976 and 1986 had more people than the actual town.

After driving through a commercial area with a Walmart, I came to an exit for a Business 83 route that runs parallel to the main route till close to Brownsville, which happens to be the old route of U.S. 83. From here to Harlingen, about forty-seven miles to the east, the modern 83 is an expressway that was recently also designated as Interstate 2—part of a plan to expand the interstate system in South Texas. The old route was once called the "Longest Main St. in America" because of the string of towns it passes through. Although that seemed more interesting than an expressway, my intention was to stay on what's now U.S. 83 itself as much as possible for the continuity, and here it would also save me time and avoid stop and go in a busy area. The multi-laner I entered was built in the 1960s to accommodate lots of increased traffic that resulted from the area's growth.

U.S. 83-Interstate 2 expanded to an elevated six lanes, and it was now town after town with fewer distinctions, in a congested, highly developed area not unlike the huge northern New Jersey suburban area I grew up in. Palmview was the next community on my map, with over 5,000 people, which grew from only about 220 when it was incorporated in 1978. It was followed by much larger Mission—a city of about 80,000 that was founded in 1907 when two developers purchased 27,000 acres of land that included a ranch owned by the Oblate fathers, who had also established a mission in 1877 that the town was named for. Tracts were then sold, and a new town was incorporated by 1910, with farmers drawn by the irrigation potential of the Rio Grande. Citrus fruit was soon cultivated, and since 1921, Mission has been called the "Home of the Ruby Red Grapefruit." The city also hosts the annual Texas Citrus Fiesta in late January, which began in 1932 and includes a big parade through the city and the coronation of King Citrus and Queen Citrianna. Besides agriculture, oil discovery was a growth factor in Mission. One of the city's favorite sons is the late famous coach of the Dallas Cowboys, Tom Landry, who was born and raised in the city and was a star quarterback on its high school football team.

South of Mission along the Rio Grande is Bentsen Rio Grande Valley State Park—a 764-acre preserve of native subtropical forest and brush that's been spared the development that's overtaken its surroundings. Most of its acreage was donated to the state in 1944 by the parents of former U.S. Senator and 1988 Democratic vice-presidential candidate Lloyd Bentsen. The park is also the headquarters for the World Birding Center network, which, besides its own abundance of bird species, has attracted over 250 species of butterflies. That must be why the North American Butterfly Association located its National Butterfly Center adjacent to the park.

I cruised through more commercial sprawl and passed an amusement park on the north side, where a spinning Ferris wheel radiated colors in the darkness that had fallen. I saw a sign for the sizable city of McAllen and an international airport, then spotted a Motel 6 on the other side of the expressway that advertised one of this chain's relatively low rates. Now I knew where I wanted to spend the night and took the next exit and backtracked to the motel.

After a long day on the road, I was checked in by a nice middle-aged woman with Hispanic features, but no Spanish accent. I engaged her enough to find out that she moved here some years ago with her family from California.

"So do you like living near the bottom of Texas?" I inquired.

"No," she answered without hesitation, "mainly because of the summer heat, when it can be 110 degrees with 100 percent humidity"—which sounded similar to other complaints I heard about the region's heat.

"But I bet the winters are nice."

"Yes, but we do get some snow occasionally, and some sleet."

"That must disappoint the Winter Texans when it happens," I joked.

I told her I was traveling all the way down 83 and had left home almost a month ago. But she was another person along the highway who didn't know how long the road was and seemed surprised when I informed her. I was given a key card for room 102 instead of a real key like at the indie motels, and this was my first chain motel on the trip.

After my recent nights in Wander, I really appreciated even the basic, no-frills room that the Motel 6 chain is known for. This one had no carpet or wall decorations, no coffee machine, microwave, or refrigerator, and the TV was another old model without a flat screen. But there was a full-sized bed, a few other furnishings, and a decent-sized bathroom with a shower and tub; and I was soon in the shower to relieve my present grubbiness. Once again, soap and hot streaming water over my whole body left me with a rejuvenated, "born again" feeling. Then I relaxed in a wooden chair with a cushioned seat and imbibed two Miller High Lifes.

Later, I walked over to a big neighboring commercial area to find an open eatery and saw a Denny's restaurant, where I decided to get a take-out salad to combine with some sardines. I was waited on by a young Hispanic guy with a heavy accent.

I prepared the sardine salad on a small table in the room—another of the different ways to consume the small, strongly-flavored fish that I find very convenient for traveling. These were the ones with jalapenos that I'd bought at the H-E-B store back in Laredo, which gave the salad a spicy kick that I enjoyed with some bread.

After the meal, I turned on the TV and found a documentary about the ten worst hurricanes in history, which reminded me that I was now in a hurricane-prone region near the Coast during what was still the storm season. Then I switched to a program about a survival workshop in the Great Smoky Mountains before I got back to my journal. But well before I caught up, fatigue hit me and clouded my thinking. It was time for the comfort of a bed again at the end of what seemed like the longest day of the journey. I'd covered 262 miles through lots of places, and now Brownsville and the climax of 83 were only about sixty miles down the road.

DAY 29

Gunning for Brownsville, the finish line of 83

While having cereal in the room, I watched an Al Roker weather report on TV that mentioned a "nor'easter" about to hit the East Coast soon, and a tropical storm brewing near the Gulf that was supposed to move east and not affect where I was headed, fortunately. Check-out time wasn't until noon, and with the sound of rain outside, I was in no hurry to leave my comfort zone. So, I wrote more in my journal.

When I left, I asked another woman at the desk how the Motel 6 chain ownership worked, and she informed me that some of their locations were individually owned, like this one, and others company owned.

"I appreciate the low rate here," I told her.

"It used to be higher, but it was lowered to be more competitive. There's even another Motel 6 in the area."

Motel 6 is the original "budget" chain that at the time had over 1,000 locations in the U.S. and Canada, which got started in Santa Barbara, California in 1962 by two local building contractors set on providing more economical lodging. Back then, they charged a mere $6 for a stay, which inspired the company's name. A "no frills" approach was successful in the early years, and the business expanded outside California while other budget chains developed and became competitors. The ownership of Motel 6 changed hands several times during its history as the chain proliferated, with some policy changes that added more amenities. However, the company has basically remained committed to offering lower rates by making rooms more energy efficient and easier to clean to reduce maintenance and housekeeping costs. Many locations charge extra for Wi-Fi, and no breakfasts are served, though morning coffee is provided.

As much as I like what Motel 6 has been doing for decades to offer lower cost lodgings in a business geared toward providing frills and luxury, I wish their steps in the right direction went further so it would be easier to "sleep cheap" on the American road. I think what's really needed is a beyond-no-frills and more of a bare-bones alternative that would bring prices down closer to campgrounds. Often when traveling, all I've cared about was finding a clean bed and room that can even be small, and I wouldn't even mind sharing a bathroom and shower sometimes—especially if I'm going to just sleep in a place. And why can't more travelers carry their own towels, toiletries, drinking cups, etc., the way campers and RV people do? The frills and luxury approach certainly has its place. I just wish there were more alternatives for relative minimalists like myself. I'm glad that European-style hostels, where facilities are shared, have become more popular in the U.S., and I've stayed in some. But the lack of privacy isn't for everyone, though many enjoy the social experience, especially the opportunity to meet foreign travelers. It's not surprising that I didn't come across any hostels along 83, since they tend to be in touristy areas.

The rain had stopped but resumed right after I was back in the car and turned into another downpour that I didn't want to drive off in. While waiting it out, I took a close look at the cluster of communities on my paper map along the final leg of 83. This part of the Rio Grande Valley has become densely populated enough to be considered a metropolitan area.

I was in McAllen, which is the largest city in Hidalgo County, with a population of almost 130,000. It's situated near the Rio Grande, and across the river in Mexico is the much more populated city of Reynosa, with over 672,000 people. McAllen has a railroad origin going back to 1904, when an enterprising Scottish immigrant and ranch owner named John McAllen, along with his son James, donated land for an extension of the St. Louis, Brownsville, and Mexico Railway that reached their ranch that year. Both father and son were involved in a townsite company, and their surname was given to a new town along the railroad. However, the present city evolved from an early neighboring town that was called East McAllen, which grew more rapidly because of irrigation and farming and was renamed McAllen after the original one stopped developing. Its population increased to 6,000 by 1920, and over 9,000 by 1930 with the arrival of manufacturing and the oil industry. The construction of the McAllen-Hidalgo-Reynosa International Bridge in 1941 made the city a major port of entry and increased tourism.

The following decades saw continuing high rates of growth, and tourism from Mexico and the northern U.S. further increased. In 1973, the first inland Foreign Trade Zone in the U.S. was established on the border with Reynosa. Nevertheless, there were economic setbacks in the 1980s, including a freeze that damaged much of the local citrus crops. But the economy soon rebounded with the growing numbers of maquiladoras across the border and the 1994 North American Free Trade Agreement (NAFTA) that increased trade with Mexico.

McAllen has had a checkered past when it came to the treatment of its many residents of Mexican ethnicity, who were subjected to the segregation that occurred elsewhere in Texas through much of the twentieth century, which included schools and hospitals. The now disdained practice really took off in McAllen and the rest of the Rio Grande Valley in the early 1900s when the early Hispanic-dominated ranching economy was replaced by Anglo-dominated agriculture in the Rio Grande Valley after the arrival of the railroad, mechanized irrigation, and the purchase of old ranchlands by outside investors. In short time, the Tejanos were considered cheap labor and treated like second-class citizens by an Anglo minority in control. This led to social unrest and also some violence that resulted from the Plan de San Diego in 1915-1916—when a group of Mexican radicals came up with a manifesto that called for a race war and the repossession of most of the vast territory Mexico lost to the U.S. after the Mexican War. Fortunately, the violence stopped far short of a race war and its radical objectives, but there were raids and casualties.

McAllen has long been known as "The City of Palms" for the variety of these trees along its streets, though most of the palm species aren't native. The city has art and entertainment districts, the

International Museum of Art and Science, and a Heritage Center about local history in an old post office. It's also the location of the main campus of South Texas College and another of the region's World Birding Centers in a historic adobe home. And just to the south of the U.S. 83-Interstate 2 expressway is McAllen-Miller International Airport, which has non-stop flights to Mexico City and domestic destinations.

McAllen interestingly touts itself as the "Square-Dancing Capital of the World" because many of the thousands of Winter Texans who migrate to the warm "valley" during the cold months in the North are avid square dancers. Along with other local communities, McAllen offers an abundance of dance venues and opportunities, including in the RV and mobile home parks. Since 1987, the area has hosted the annual Texas Square Dance Jamboree in February, which draws tens of thousands of enthusiasts.

McAllen is also a big shopping destination from both sides of the border because of its many stores, and statistically, the city is one of the fastest-growing in the U.S. But despite outward signs of prosperity, over twenty-five percent of its population was said to be in the poverty bracket at the time, and a recent census had the McAllen metro area listed as the nation's poorest. This may have been affected by the large numbers of colonias in the area, with mainly poor agricultural workers. But for those who can afford a real home, the average cost in McAllen was the third lowest in the country in recent years. The overall cost of living was also significantly lower than the national average.

When the rain let up, I drove off from the motel on a frontage road that led to 83. While waiting at a light before getting on the expressway, a man with Hispanic features who had gotten soaked from the recent downpour crossed the road with a sign—"homeless and hungry," but didn't approach me. The light soon changed, and I drove off thinking he must have lots of unfortunate company in this troubled border region with its large share of impoverished people.

Traffic was heavy on the multi-laner, which soon backed up. Some rain resumed, and I found an FM station playing some upbeat Tejano music with accordion sounds. Rows of tall palms lined the highway, and ahead I could see flashing lights where there must have been an accident and the traffic was moving sluggishly. There was a sign for the Pharr International Bridge, and I gradually came to the accident scene, where a few emergency vehicles were still sitting in the left lane near some debris on the road. From there on it was a smooth cruise through the city of Pharr, which has over 70,000 residents and roots going back to a 1767 Spanish land grant. This city was established in 1910 and named after Henry N. Pharr—a Louisiana sugar cane grower who attempted a plantation in this locality that failed. But the new community developed successfully with the benefit of being situated along the St. Louis, Brownsville, and Mexico Railway that had arrived in the Rio Grande Valley.

I saw a sign for a hurricane evacuation route and could imagine the traffic gridlock if masses of people from this densely populated area hit the road at the same time. I rapidly passed through San Juan, with close to 34,000 people, which was also established in 1910. Its name originated from the prevalence of the male Spanish name "Juan" in the area prior to the community's founding, and it's included in the lengthy Roman Catholic name of one of the largest churches in South Texas in the town—The Basilica of the National Shrine of Our Lady of San Juan del Valle, which was built in 1908.

The town of Alamo was next—founded in 1909 and named after the renowned historic mission in San Antonio, where the legendary battle occurred. It had over 18,000 residents and is known for being a winter resort and having a retirement community in a region called the "Land of Two Summers."

The warm rain had let up again, and dark clouds moved to the south as 83 continued in an eastward direction—the direction now posted along the highway. There was a sign for the town of Donna, with land grant origins and a founding in 1904 along the new railroad. When a depot was built in 1907, the community was named Donna after Donna Hooks Fletcher—a divorcee who had run a cattle ranch and was later a postmaster. The town became a center for growing and shipping citrus and vegetable produce, which has continued. The present population is about 16,000, and the municipality has a motto: "The city with a Heart in the Heart of the Rio Grande Valley."

My appetite led me to exit the expressway, and I soon found a Stripes store that also sold Valero gas. I ordered a chicken fajita taco with beans in a soft tortilla that turned out to be another very good and economical Stripes meal. It got me thinking about how much I liked Mexican food and that it's no wonder the cuisine has become so popular throughout the U.S. But I remembered when it wasn't and was amused to think that I didn't even know what a taco was until I went to college in the West in the late 1960s. The employees in the store conversed in both Spanish and English, and I presumed a lot of the local population was bilingual.

Back on the six-lane highway through more commercial sprawl, I passed a sign for the Weslaco business district. This next town, with about 36,000 people, has a name that seems somewhat Spanish, but it's an acronym for the W.E. Stewart Land Company, which bought the real estate in 1917 where the town would develop. Unfortunately, the new town became a poster child for the segregation that the new Anglo minority instituted. In 1921, an ordinance designated the north side of the railroad tracks in town for Hispanic residences and businesses, and the south side for Anglos. Streets had Spanish and English names depending on which side they were on, and schools were also segregated and not officially integrated until 1961. Mexican women were even restricted to shopping on Saturdays in the Anglo section and had a curfew to be back in "Mexican Town." Despite such apartheid policies, Weslaco prospered in many ways and became a leader in agricultural businesses, and it had the first camp in Texas for housing migrant workers north of town. It also had other industries like sandbag production, which increased enough during World War II for Weslaco to call itself the "sandbagging capital of the world." Since the 1994 NAFTA agreement, a lot of the economy shifted from agriculture to international trade, retail businesses, and tourism. Weslaco also attracts lots of Winter Texans. Two significant residents of the town were Harlon Block—one of the U.S. Marines who famously raised the American flag over Iwo Jima in 1945 and was later killed in combat—and the late actor David Spielberg, who did films and TV but was no relation to famed director Steven Spielberg.

The commercial landscape along the busy expressway went on with more chain businesses that included some big box stores. A sign said, "Mercedes City Limit," and this town, known as "the Queen City of the Valley," or "La Runa del Valle," had a lower population of around 1,600. It was founded in the early 1900s by the American Land and Irrigation Company and was the first town to develop along the extending railroad, with previous names before it was called Mercedes—the origin of which is uncertain. The land company prohibited the sale of alcoholic beverages for fifteen years, but Mercedes still developed rapidly along with agriculture. Some manufacturing also became part of the town's economy and included boot-making. That must be why the town is known for its quirky public art of thirty handcrafted, five and a half feet tall cowboy boots scattered around town, which were individually painted with the logos of different colleges around the U.S. and Mexico. It's said that these oversized boots even attract some distant alumni from the represented schools who come to pose for photos with the symbols of their alma maters.

Between Weslaco and Mercedes, and close to the expressway, was something else quirky in present-day America—an open drive-in movie theater named the Wes Mer—an abbreviation of both towns. The *Last American Highway—Texas* has a long passage about this relic of Americana and a summary of drive-in history in the U.S., which mentions there having been approximately 4,000 drive-ins in the country in the 1950s, and that about 400, or ten percent, were in Texas. The Wes Mer is one of the sixteen that were still operating in the state, and it had closed in 1981 before being restored and reopened in 1994. Stew Magnuson says that this is one of the two remaining drive-ins along 83—the other being in Abilene, Texas—and that in their heyday, almost every town in the Rio Grande Valley had one. He also expressed his personal memories and love of drive-ins, and since I'm older than the other author, my own drive-in memories must go further back. They say, "everything comes back," and although this may be an exaggeration in the case of drive-ins, it's encouraging that some of these cultural landmarks have avoided extinction.

The next stretch was less commercial, with some fields, hay bales, and cattle. Then I rolled through La Feria (The Fair in Spanish) that's a community of about 7,300 that was established in 1909 through the efforts of a local developer, and the railroad arrived a couple of years later. La Feria's water tower stood prominently on the north side of the expressway and displayed the town's name.

Not far east of La Feria, nearby Business 83—"The Longest Main

St. in America"—ended and intersected with the U.S 83-Interstate-2 expressway in the city of Harlingen, which just ahead merged with multi-lane U.S. 77, where I-2 officially ended. From there, 83 and 77 would run together to the Rio Grande border and the terminus of both roads.

U.S. 77 is another of the 1926 originals that was co-signed with Interstate 69E in this area. The federal highway is a 1,305-mile (2,100 km) north-south route with its northern end in Sioux City, Iowa, and it courses through five states. It used to be longer, with sections in Minnesota and South Dakota that were decommissioned when Interstate 29 was completed.

At the busy intersection, I took an exit for a Texas Travel Information Center, which was a big modern facility with a wide tile roof and stucco exterior. Out front was a large group of diverse flags, and the inside offered an abundance of info about all parts of Texas. I helped myself to some maps and flyers and had a little conversation with an amiable young woman who worked there, who told me she was originally from the area. She was Anglo but lacked a Texas drawl.

"So how do you take to the summer heat here?" I asked.

"I don't. But the temperatures this time of year aren't that bad, and the winters are nice."

"I've heard about all the so-called Winter Texans that come down."

"There are a lot of them."

"I'm not one, though. But I've traveled all the way down 83. Did you know that it starts way up at the Canadian border in North Dakota?"

"I didn't know that. I knew it went north of Texas, but never really thought about just how far it goes. So, how much further are you going?"

"After I get to Brownsville and the end of 83, I plan on relaxing for a few days on South Padre Island before heading home to northern Colorado."

"That should be nice, and the island shouldn't be too crowded now. It's still early for most of the snowbirds to have arrived."

That sounded good, and I left feeling satisfied that I'd informed someone who worked in a travel information center off 83 about the length of the highway.

Harlingen is an interesting city that's the fourth largest in the Rio Grande Valley, with about 65,000 residents. It was oddly named after a city in the Netherlands by its founder and local developer, Lon C. Hill, in 1904. Hill's ambitions to introduce agriculture to the area with irrigation canals was very successful, and an agricultural town developed that was incorporated by 1910. An Army airfield outside town during World War II that was reactivated as an Air Force base in 1952 contributed to big increases in Harlingen's population, and the property eventually became the Valley International Airport. Harlingen's economy came to include manufacturing, service industries, and tourism, which led to more growth that was accompanied by many social organizations and cultural opportunities. In 1992, Harlingen even received an All-America City award—formerly called the Nobel Prize for Constructive Citizenship. The Winter Texans are big contributors to the local economy, and about seventy-three percent of Harlingen's permanent residents are Hispanic. In a region where immigration has long been a major issue, it's not surprising that Harlingen has one of the fifty-two U.S. Immigration Courts in the nation. Another World Birding Center is also located in the city's Hugh Ramsey Nature Park, and each November, Harlingen has been hosting the Rio Grande Valley Birding Festival for over twenty years.

After leaving the travel center, I got a little confused about how to get back on 83-77 in another congested area. Back on course, I cruised by car and motorcycle dealers and lofty signs trying to draw attention to businesses like Best Western, Valero, McDonald's, and IHOP. Tall palms also stood along the roadway.

The next town had a water tower near the road that announced, "San Benito—home of Freddie Fender," with an image of the Tejano Country and Rock musician, who was born in this town in 1937 and buried there in 2006. His original name was Baldemar Huerta, which he changed to Freddy Fender in 1958, thinking it would have more appeal to Anglo audiences. The name Fender was inspired by the guitar maker, and he liked Freddy for the alliteration. Fender was a singer-songwriter with a decades-long career as a solo and group artist, who covered a variety of musical genres and won three Grammy awards. He also had film and TV appearances. In 2007, a Freddy Fender Museum opened in San Benito in the same building as the San

Benito and Conjunto Music Museums—the latter referring to a musical genre related to Tejano music. Freddy's hometown is obviously very proud of him.

San Benito is the third largest city in Cameron County and developed on the site of a 1789 Spanish land grant. The railroad arrived in 1904, and the town became San Benito in 1907—though the namesake was not a saint, but a local rancher and one of the town's developers, whose name was Benjamin. Another name for the community is the "Resaca City," after the Resaca de los Fresno, which was a dry riverbed through town that became an irrigation canal from the Rio Grande and a water source for the community. Resaca is a Spanish name for former channels of the "Big River" in this part of the Valley. The first irrigation system was completed in 1906 and drew Anglo settlers as the brush environment developed into a big agricultural area where crops could be grown year-round, San Benito's growth has been basically steady like other towns in the Valley, with currently over 24,000 people that includes its share of Winter Texans and retirees. The permanent population is still predominantly Mexican in origin. Surprisingly, there's also a good-sized Japanese community outside the city limits along the Rio Grande, with roots going back to small numbers of immigrants who arrived in the Valley and some other parts of Texas in the early 1900s and engaged in farming.

The following community of Rancho Viejo has a very different character from others I'd passed through in the Valley, since it developed around a resort and country club that got started in 1968. The community's recent population was 2,437, with numbers increased seasonally by Winter Texans and Mexican nationals with summer homes at the resort. With a median age and income high for the state of Texas, this community is relatively affluent. It was given its Spanish name because two ranches that were established in the area in 1770 later became known as El Rancho Viejo—"The Old Ranch."

I was finally approaching my big destination of Brownsville at the end of U.S. 83, and the last town before it was Olmito (Spanish for "little elm"), which calls itself the "mesquite capital of the world." I did pass through a brushy landscape with lots of the now overly familiar vegetation that was very dense on the south side of the road, but I'd certainly seen more sprawling stretches of it in the miles behind me. Olmito had about a 1,200 population, and the town began with a post office in 1905. Then a depot on the St. Louis, Brownsville, and Mexico Railway was built in 1911. For years, it was a very small community with just a handful of businesses, and in the 1960s a colonia was established northwest of the town.

An interesting feature of Olmito is John Lennon Memorial Park, which honors the late, great musician and cultural icon, who was murdered in 1980. The park has an annual celebration around Lennon's birthday on October 9, with live music, a street dance, songwriting contests, cowboy poetry readings, and even a rodeo, which is quite a tribute to a very famous Anglo in this overwhelmingly Hispanic community. But Lennon was a great spokesperson for social harmony and "Give peace a chance."

This area, however, has sadly known violent conflict in its history. Just to the east of Olmito is Palo Alto Battlefield National Historical Park, where the first major clash of the American-Mexican War occurred on May 8, 1846—several days before the U.S. declared war on Mexico. The territorial dispute that preceded it resulted in troops of Mexican General Mariano Arista crossing the Rio Grande and besieging the American outpost of Fort Texas on May 3, 1846. U.S. General Zachary Taylor's army was then moved south to confront the Mexicans and managed to defeat a numerically superior force with a better-trained one and very superior artillery. Arista's force retreated south and was defeated and retreated again the following day in the Battle of Resaca de la Palma. I abhor war, but I'll admit to having some fascination with military history and would have liked to visit the Palo Alto battlefield if it were again not late in the day.

The six-lane 83-77 expressway had entered the Brownsville city limits, where there was still lots of mesquite and other vegetation along the road. Then the brush became sparse, and I saw a sign for "Brownsville Business District—next 8 exits," followed by commercial sprawl. Further on, another sign said, "Historic Brownsville—next 2 exits," which *Road Trip USA* commended for preserving its Spanish and Mexican architecture, which sounded interesting. But now, I was gunning for the finish line of 83.

Brownsville is another fast-growing city in the region with a current population over 175,000. It's been called the second most historic city in Texas after San Antonio and is also one of the southernmost municipalities on the mainland of the U.S., with just a small number in Florida further south. Although the city wasn't founded until 1848, the area had been explored by the Spanish in the 1600s, and settlement started in the latter part of the 1700s. In 1781, a Spanish land grant was given to José Salvador de la Garza that included the future site of Brownsville, where he established a ranch. By 1836—the year Texas declared independence from Mexico—a small settlement developed on the northern bank of the Rio Grande. When General Zachary Taylor's troops arrived on the scene in February 1846, before the Mexican War started, they constructed Fort Texas for a defensive position on the river. But after the Mexican attack on the fort that triggered the war, in which its commander, Major Jacob Brown, died from a mortal wound, the fort was renamed in his honor.

After the Mexican War ended in 1848 and finally settled the Rio Grande as the border between Texas and Mexico, an American entrepreneur named Charles Stillman bought local land and, with a partnership, formed the Brownsville Town Company that founded the town they named Brownsville after Major Brown. In 1849, the new town became the seat of newly formed Cameron County—the southernmost county in Texas—and it was incorporated in February 1853. The town then had about 3,500 people after surviving a serious cholera outbreak.

On July 13, 1859, an incident in Brownsville set off what became known as the Cortina Wars, when the wealthy Mexican rancher and military man, Juan Cortina, witnessed a city marshal physically abusing one of his former Mexican ranch employees after an arrest. Cortina wound up shooting and wounding the marshal and riding off with the man on horseback. On September 28, 1859, he returned with a force large enough to take control of Brownsville for two days, which released some Mexican prisoners thought to have been unfairly imprisoned, and they executed four Anglos who had killed Mexicans with impunity. However, the city and the rest of its inhabitants were unharmed, and a proclamation was made to pacify the population that called for the respectful treatment of Mexican residents. Nevertheless, there was a big backlash to Cortina's aggression and violence that escalated into conflicts in the next two years across a good stretch of the Rio Grande Valley, when Cortina's forces fought local militias, the Texas Rangers, the U.S. Army, and even the Confederate Army after the American Civil War began. Against such opposition, Cortina was not surprisingly defeated, but he lived until 1894 and was heavily involved in Mexico's military and politics.

During the Civil War, when Texas was part of the Confederacy, there was a Union naval blockade of Southern ports. Brownsville, being very close to the Gulf Coast, had a very strategic position because cotton was able to be shipped from the nearby Mexican port of Bagdad to Europe to maintain vital trade. To disrupt this trade, about 7,000 Union troops under General Nathanial P. Banks captured Port Isabel northeast of Brownsville in November of 1863, then marched toward Brownsville to attack Fort Brown. The outnumbered Confederates there abandoned and destroyed the fort. However, in July 1864, a Confederate force led by Colonel S. "Rip" Ford reoccupied the town and held it for the rest of the war. What historians regard to be the last battle of the Civil War occurred on May 12-13, 1865, east of Brownsville by the Rio Grande—over a month after the war officially ended with General Robert E. Lee's surrender in Virginia. Both sides had heard of the surrender, but glory-seeking Union commander Colonel Theodore H. Barrett was determined to drive the remaining Confederates out of Brownsville and ordered an attack, only to be humiliated when his numerically superior force was defeated by Rip Ford's Confederates. There was only one fatal casualty—Union Private John J. Williams—who's considered the last man killed in the Civil War, although it's been argued that the "Battle of Palmito Ranch" was a post-war action since the war had officially ended. A final truce was agreed on a few days after the battle, and Colonel Barrett had broken an earlier one with his attack. Post-war action or not, the Confederates had ironically won the last round in the terrible conflict they lost.

When the U.S. Army was back in control, Fort Brown was reconstructed and expanded. In 1872, a narrow-gauge railroad was built the short distance between Brownsville and Port Isabel. Brownsville developed and grew to a population of around 5,000 by 1885. However, a major rail connection to the north didn't come until 1904, when the St. Louis, Brownsville, and Mexico Railway arrived. This standard gauge railroad did much to shape the area's future by bringing in the many Northern farmers who developed the expansive, irrigated agriculture of the region, including the citrus fruit culture. In 1910, a bridge for both trains and autos was built between Brownsville and Matamoros across the Rio Grande.

The downside along with such progress was the worsening of relations between Anglos and Hispanics, influenced by the mainly White-Protestant newcomers, who were not inclined to assimilate with Mexicans as previous Anglos had, with resulting segregation. There was also a racially charged event known as the Brownsville Affair in August 1906 involving some African American troops stationed at Fort Brown, whose presence was resented by many of the city's White residents. The entire regiment of 167 men was dishonorably discharged by an order of none other than President Theodore Roosevelt for an alleged "conspiracy of silence" after some of the men were falsely implicated in the fatal shooting of a White bartender and wounding of a White police officer. However, many decades later, during the Nixon administration, a new investigation exonerated the troops and reversed the dishonorable discharges posthumously.

Brownsville's growth was very steady during the 20th Century, first spurred by the agriculture industry and a cheap land boom that increased the population to 22,000 in 1930. The Prohibition years also attracted many tourists who could consume alcohol legally across the border in Mexico. Infrastructure improvements like paved roads, a new international bridge, and an airport came in the 1920s, and later an Army airfield during World War II. Work also began on a seventeen-mile ship channel to enable deepwater vessels in the Gulf to dock near Brownsville, which was funded by the Public Works Administration of the New Deal years and local banks. The Port of Brownsville was officially opened in May 1936, five miles northeast of the city. During World War II, Fort Brown was a training base that brought many servicemen to the city, but the fort was deactivated in 1945 after a run of almost a century. In 1948, the city and Texas Southmost College acquired the property.

The Gulf Intracoastal Waterway was extended to Brownsville in 1949, and a big shrimping industry in the Gulf of Mexico developed during the Postwar years. In the Rio Grande Valley, citrus cultivation, vegetable farming, and cotton production increased, and for a while, the Port of Brownsville was even the leading cotton exporter in the world. The 1960s and 1970s saw the arrival of many new and diverse industries that provided lots of employment, and Brownsville grew rapidly for the rest of the century to about a 140,000 population by 2000. A lot of the growth came from Mexican immigration, but there was also an increased amount of Anglo retirees from the North, who were attracted to the subtropical climate and relatively low cost of living. The high growth continued into the new century, with the population pushing 180,000 at the time of my visit and remaining largely Hispanic. Anglos, however, still had a disproportionate share of the city's wealth, though the Hispanic middle class had grown, along with this huge ethnic group's role in local politics and civic affairs. Despite these gains and a thriving economy, about thirty-five percent of Brownsville's population was currently in the federal poverty level—again, probably because of the number of poor immigrants and the substandard colonias in the area.

In sharp contrast to this depressed side of Brownsville, there's been some very high-tech developments in the local economic mix, and 2014 was the year when tech entrepreneur-superstar Elon Musk planned the construction of his private space launch facility—SpaceX South Texas Launch Site—east of the city near Boca Chica State Park on the Coast—a very futuristic project close to a very historic city.

A highway sign showed the road's direction had changed from east to south again, and a billboard near an exit proclaimed: "Life is short, eternity isn't—signed GOD." I sure wouldn't doubt the first three words.

Soon the six lanes narrowed, and 83-77 crossed an intersection with multi-lane Texas Highway 4, then led toward one of the international bridges and the terminus of 83 just a short distance away. Along the way, I passed the campus of the University of Texas at Brownsville and Texas Southmost College—"U.S. southernmost campus"—at the site of historic Fort Brown. As I was about to accomplish driving from border to border, I mused more about the contrast between the placid plains where U.S. 83 began, and the bustling city where it ended.

The last section of the great old highway was divided by a concrete barrier, and I came to a bold sign: "Warning—illegal to carry firearms, ammunition, into Mexico, penalty prison." Ahead and just before the Veterans International Bridge into the big city of Matamoros, Mexico, was the Mexican Customs, and a U.S. Customs and Border Patrol station was off the other side of the road. With no intention to visit Mexico on this trip, which I'd done before, I turned off at my last opportunity to avoid the bridge and parked by the entrance of a truck lane, where I absolutely had to get a few photos of where 83 ended as I did at its other end at the Canadian border. I did it quickly and was able to turn around without having to deal with either of the Customs. I thought that such a significant road should have a sign or something to mark its finale more ceremoniously—something like: "Southern terminus of the 1,885 miles Border to Border Highway."

Backtracking north, I was greeted by a "Welcome to Texas" sign that reminded me I'd also driven from the very top of the Lone Star State to its extreme bottom, and this 906-mile distance of 83 is the longest of any U.S. highway in any state. I decided to park by a nearby Stripes store and walk back toward the border to get some more photos under a heavily overcast sky while there was still enough daylight. Heading there on foot, I felt more elated about reaching my big destination.

Palms along the road ranged in size from tall trees with wide crowns to short, stubby ones with shaggy bark. I snapped a few pictures of the last sign for 77-83, near where U.S.77 also terminated. Before the bridge, another sign declared: "End of state jurisdiction."

Rather suddenly, rain started descending from the dome of clouds, which quickly became heavy, and I was caught in the open without my raincoat or umbrella that I didn't have the foresight to carry. So, I started running toward the Stripes for a pretty good stretch. When I made it there, I'd been drenched by the warm, subtropical precipitation and hustled into the store instead of my car because I was about as soaked as I would have been from swimming across the Rio Grande. Feeling very self-conscious, I soon stepped outside and stood under a protective overhang while the rain continued to pour. When it finally let up, I scurried to my car and pulled out a small tarp from the trunk for my wet body to sit on in the driver's seat.

The heavy rain resumed, and I just sat it out in what now seemed like one of the low points of the journey, ironically right after an emotional high from my accomplishment. The idea of finding a comfortable, dry room for the night was extremely appealing, but I didn't want to drive in the downpour and continued to sit behind the wheel feeling depressed and inert as more driving rain pelted my small mobile shelter, accompanied by a few flashes of lightning and rolls of thunder.

When the rain let up again, it had gotten dark, and I awkwardly changed from my soaked shorts and tee-shirt into dry ones, after a towel wiping, in the confines of the car. Wearing something dry made me feel better if not comfortable, and I even started thinking about toughing it out in the cramper that night after spending the previous one in a motel. Staying at the Stripes was a possibility, but I really wanted to move on and went into the store to inquire about what else was around. A store associate told me there was a truck stop in the area and gave me some directions. After driving off, I had a problem finding it, though, and stopped at a Subway store for more directions.

The only person inside was a young male employee who looked Hispanic and informed me that there was also a Walmart nearby, which I preferred to a truck stop, and he even wrote down directions. After thanking him, he asked where I was from.

"Fort Collins, Colorado," I replied, "and I'm down here after driving all of U.S. 83 from the Canadian border."

"Wow! I used to live in Denver and moved there with my family. I liked a lot of things about Colorado, especially the mountains, and got used to the cold. But we moved back here."

"So how do you like being back?"

"I like it here too. But the summers are very hot"—more of the common complaint.

Then he asked how my trip was going, and I gave him a little summary of my exploits, mentioning sleeping in my motor vehicle more than motels. We could have easily chatted longer, but he cut it short to get back to his job. After leaving, I thought about how such simple contact with a friendly stranger can lift the mood of a solitary traveler, especially after the little ordeal I'd just been through.

The Walmart was a 24-hour store, and finding another vagabond-friendly place gave me a greater sense of relief from my recent emotional low. I was ready to celebrate completing 83, not with champagne, but with a bottle of Miller High Life, which has been long touted as "The Champagne of Beers" with its champagne-shaped bottle. As I imbibed one in Wander, I felt more relieved and satisfied with my accomplishment.

Quaffing another celebratory beer stimulated my appetite enough to not mind satisfying it at a McDonald's in the Walmart, where I ordered two of their tacos—my second Mexican meal of the day. Afterwards I sliced one of my ripe avocados in the car and spooned it out to complete my meal.

While I recorded more of the day's events, a security guy started making rounds in a small pickup truck around the lot, and even parked near my space in the outer area for a while. Some leftover anxiety about cops and their like made me feel uneasy and wonder if I was being watched. Like other Walmarts I'd stayed at, I saw no signs prohibiting overnight parking, but there were the usual ones saying, "security cameras in use," and in this case, there was an actual security person. He left me alone, though, and eventually drove off.

I caught up writing until after midnight when I was tired enough for the back seat. The rains had stopped completely, but no stars were out. My vehicle's gauge showed seventy-nine degrees even this late, which was very comfortable for sleeping in the car. I felt rather proud of myself for resisting the temptation of a motel after the miserable wet experience and again toughing it out and "beating the system." The next day, I still wanted to see the historic district of Brownsville and another attraction near the city before heading for South Padre Island on the nearby Coast for some relaxation and exploration before being homeward bound. Nevertheless, Day 29 had been a real climax.

DAY 30

The Brownsville Flood, a jungle, and the Coast

In the morning, it rained heavily again. I drove off from the Walmart after it let up and had to deal with what I'll always remember as The Brownsville Flood, which made Boca Chica Boulevard look like a tributary of the Rio Grande. I followed some other vehicles venturing on it and found out that Wander could be quite amphibious. Driving through the waters, however, resulted in a scraping noise from the front end that I soon found out was from a damaged inner fender piece that was rubbing the right front tire, and I wound up pulling the piece off.

After the unpleasant episode, I made my way to the drier and most historic part of Brownsville in the old downtown near the Gateway International Bridge—one of three such bridges that connect with the fast-growing Mexican city of Matamoros, which presently had about a half million people. I parked in a metered space on Elizabeth St. in the section where the old Spanish and Mexican architecture is especially well-preserved, and I started a leisurely walk with my camera. The many signs in and sounds of Spanish and all the Mexican faces made it seem like I was in Mexico—which it had been historically, of course—and the area bustled with pedestrians and traffic. I ambled by vintage buildings like the Old Capital Theater, which looked vacant, the Colonial Hotel, which was very viable, and an attractive, two-story, blue brick structure with a wrought-iron balcony known as "The Gem," built in 1848—the year Brownsville was established—

which was still in use. Some of the old downtown had a weathered look, but also a charm, and there weren't many vacant buildings.

Brownsville offers a lot to see and do, including the acclaimed Gladys Porter Zoo—one of the first zoos in the U.S. without barred cages. But I was anxious to get to South Padre Island, and the only other local attraction I'd decided to see was the Sabal Palm Grove Sanctuary southeast of the city. This sanctuary preserves the largest remaining grove of native sabal palms in the region and is an example of the original ecosystem of the Rio Grande delta. I headed out and stopped for some directions at an isolated Stripes store, which led me to a narrow road through very lush surroundings that culminated with an impressive, three-story Victorian structure with bright green lawns and palms around. This was the sanctuary's visitor center, and the elegant house built in 1892 had been the working headquarters of the Rabb Plantation owned by Frank Rabb—an agricultural innovator of his day. After his death in 1932, it went to his estate and second wife, and in 1971 the surrounding land was conveyed to the National Audubon Society, which was presently leasing it to the local Gorgas Science Foundation for public use. The sanctuary is near the southernmost point of Texas, and it's the most southern place in the state that's open to the public.

Inside the charming mansion, I met a fortyish Hispanic staff guy and paid a small admission fee. He mentioned some interesting birds and other things I could encounter on the trails in the sanctuary but also warned about mosquitos. After returning to the car for some repellent, I set out with my binoculars and field guide for an exploration along a wide, dirt path. A bilingual sign informed me that this area had been reforested with native plants in 1990, many years after the original palm forest had been cleared and the land was farmed for cotton and sorghum. There were trees draped with Spanish moss, and the tall, native sabal palms stood out in the jungle-like environment. The trail led to a still body of water that was part of a resaca that had once been a channel that connected to the nearby Rio Grande. Although the sanctuary is a birding hotspot, where I hoped to sight something exotic like a green jay or great kiskadee flycatcher that would have been life birds—or first time sightings—for me, the best I could do was see and hear a common belted kingfisher. Mosquitos were unfortunately common too. With the refuge about to close soon, I had to cut my exploration short.

Back at the visitor center, the staff guy said the birding can be slow some days, and he encouraged me to come back. He also informed me that the original ecosystem preserved here once extended about eighty miles north along the Rio Grande to where McAllen is—a huge contrast to the teeming human population there now. I mentioned my journey to him and that I was headed for South Padre Island next, and he said the birding was great there and that I should check out some trails behind the island's convention center. He also recommended an eatery called Dirty Al's—"They have good seafood and prices, and don't be turned off by the name."

After driving off, I passed through a big, open area by the Brownsville–South Padre Island International Airport, then hooked-up with Texas 48—the "South Padre Island Highway." The day was now very sunny with scattered clouds, and a delightful eighty-two degrees even while the sun was descending. The road ran near the Port of Brownsville to the south, which looked very industrial, and there appeared to be an old aircraft carrier in port. Four-lane Texas 48 ran parallel to the Brownsville Shipping Channel and soon led to the verdant coastal area with wetlands and a broad panorama to the south with trees on the horizon. I passed a body of water where I picked up the wonderful scent of salty air, accompanied by the sight of hovering seagulls. A mudflat followed, and to the north the expanse of Bahia Grande (Grand Bay) appeared. My excitement about reaching the coastal area heightened, and I crossed a bridge over a channel where there were fishermen. Memories of the New Jersey Shore were revived.

There were some sand dunes before Port Isabel, and I soon crossed a short bridge into the historic maritime town that lies just before the causeway to South Padre Island. The only lighthouse on the Texas coast that was presently open to the public stands there. Texas 48 terminated at the intersection with Texas 100, and I passed through the town's commercial center and noticed fishing shops and seafood restaurants.

I got on the Queen Isabella Causeway that crosses the lower end of the extensive bay called Laguna Madre between the mainland and long and slender Padre Island. To the north was a vast body of water, and the skyline of South Padre Island gleamed ahead, including a tall double tower structure. The first section of the 2.3-mile causeway—the second longest bridge in Texas—was arched, before descending to a level stretch. My old shore instincts were aroused even more as I crossed the bay that connected with the Gulf of Mexico, and it was exhilarating to be near the sea again.

A sign ahead proclaimed, "Entering Padre Island," which was near the lengthy barrier island's southern end. To the west was a great spectacle of the causeway and the almost setting sun above the bay I'd just crossed, which I stopped to gaze at and snap a few pictures before moving north on Padre Boulevard, keeping an eye out for motels. Turning east to drive closer to the Gulf side, views of the sea were obstructed by rows of high-rise hotels that looked too swanky for me. I drove back to Padre Boulevard and stopped at a liquor store and bought ice and a six-pack of Lone Star—"The National Beer of Texas" from Fort Worth. I asked a young Hispanic guy at the counter, who spoke with a slight accent, if he knew about any economical motels around, and he recommended one called The Flamingo and gave me directions. When I mentioned the recent flood in Brownsville, he said the island had no rain and that "The weather here can be very different from Brownsville."

On the way to finding the motel, I encountered a Motel 6 advertising a low weekday rate, which I didn't think any competitor could beat, and I immediately stopped and checked in with a nice young woman who also looked Hispanic. She also recommended a bar and eatery called Harpoon's that wasn't far and said: "If you go there, tell them Clara sent you."

After settling in room 711, the first thing I did was walk down a residential side street lined with palms to see the Gulf of Mexico while there was some lingering daylight. I entered a public beach access where I could feel sea breezes that were just wonderful, then saw breaking waves and stepped across a railed boardwalk over some small sand dunes. Suddenly I was overwhelmed by what now seemed like the real climax of my journey—finally making it to the sea after traveling through so much of the prairie sea and other spacious lands. Salt-scented breezes blew gently while light-colored puffy clouds hovered over a dark gray expanse of water speckled by the lights of boats. The sight and sound of the waves beckoned me to remove my shoes and walk barefoot across the smooth sand and into the warm surf, almost to my knees. For a while, I gazed at the white, breaking waves in the distance, reflecting on the size of the Gulf as I stood on an edge of the continent.

Back in the motel room, I uncapped a celebratory bottle of Lone Star, and this Texas beer had a light, refreshing taste suitable for the Texas heat, though not too much character. After a shower, I walked out to find Harpoon's but was enticed by the nearby Padre Rita Grill that advertised an enchilada special and live music. Inside was a lively, colorful atmosphere with a lot of Halloween decorations, and a female solo guitarist was playing. Most of the small crowd looked middle-aged and more Anglo than what I was getting used to seeing in the region. I ordered an enchilada that turned out to be pretty good and suited my spicy taste. A young server told me she'd just moved here from Tennessee because she thought even her Southern state got too cold. The young male bartender said he'd moved from Brownsville five years before and loved living right on the Coast.

After leaving, I still wanted to check out the other bar, and a little wandering led to Harpoon's Surf-Bar and Grill, which was a rather small place with a casual atmosphere. I sat at the bar close to two young women and a guy engaged in a conversation that indicated they were locals, and I bought a bottle of Rolling Rock from a tall, thirtyish bartender who had a very friendly manner. He said he was from "the North" and had also moved down here to escape the cold.

"So where in the North?" I inquired.

"Illinois."

"I'd call that the Midwest. But I guess from South Padre Island's perspective, at the bottom of the country, most of the rest of it is the North."

"I just don't like the cold weather," he said with conviction. "I even declined a wedding invitation back in Illinois because it was in the winter."

"So, I heard you get a lot of snowbirds from the North that are called Winter Texans."

"We sure do. A lot return each season, and I've gotten to know quite a few of them. They're mainly seniors and retirees, and the ones you don't know are terrible tippers. It's like if they don't know you, they won't tip you."

"I think most retirees are frugal, like myself, but there's certainly times when you shouldn't hold back and be that cheap."

"You're right about that."

"Are there many Winter Texans here yet?"

"Most start arriving in November, and there's a county park at the southern end of the island where a lot of them stay with RVs. Then we get a much younger crowd in the spring with lots of college 'breakers.' There's the usual bullshit with that age group, but they do bring lots of business, and some of them are even good tippers."

We made introductions, and his name was Jay. Then I ordered a salad from the menu, since I didn't have one with my dinner.

"The food is very good here," he reassured me. "*USA Today* was here recently and rated us in the top three for the region. The fish tacos are excellent and very popular."

"I'd love to try them, but I had an enchilada up the street a little while ago."

The salad that arrived included a generous amount of healthy roughage, along with some great-tasting cheese bread—all for just $3.00, to my amazement. While enjoying my second course, I told Jay that a woman named Clara at the Motel 6 recommended this place.

"I sure know Clara because she works here too. So, what are you doing on the island?"

"I'm here to relax and celebrate after driving all of U.S. 83 on the mainland—from the Canadian border in North Dakota to Brownsville. Soon, I'll be driving back to my home in northern Colorado."

"Wow! That's quite a journey."

"Are you familiar with U.S. 83?"

"Not much since I spend most of my time on the island."

An outgoing older woman who might have been the bar's owner or manager also joined some of the conversation, followed by a young guy who sat at the bar and was another local. The sociability made me feel very comfortable in this place, and I had a good little energy exchange with a few island residents. When I left, I told Jay I'd be back before I left the island for some fish tacos, and I made sure I left him a good tip. Back in the motel room, it was close to midnight, and I felt tired enough to get in my sizable bed soon. Before drifting into sleep, I had some pleasant thoughts about becoming somewhat of a Winter Texan myself some future winter on this alluring subtropical island.

DAYS 31-32

In the light and warmth of SPI, homeward bound

South Padre Island is actually not an island, but the name of the town at the southern end of 113-mile-long Padre Island—the longest barrier island not just along the Texas coast, but in the world, which extends up to the city of Corpus Christi. Seventy miles of this sprawling landform created by wave depositions and sea erosion was designated the Padre Island National Seashore in 1962, and only the southernmost five miles of the island were presently developed. It's the only subtropical island in Texas, and its namesake is Padre José Nicolás Ballí—a Catholic priest, rancher, and grantee of a Spanish land grant—who started the first non-Native settlement on the island in 1804. However, there wasn't much human habitation or development until after the first causeway was built in 1954, which was replaced by the present one twenty years later. So, the resort town of South Padre Island is relatively new.

It had a huge setback from devastating Hurricane Beulah in 1967, but the rebuilding led to greater development of the resort, and the town became incorporated in 1973 when it had a few hundred permanent residents. Presently, there are close to 3,000, and it attracts approximately five million visitors a year. The latitude is the same as Fort Lauderdale in Florida, and the resort offers plenty of activities and amenities, along with interesting annual events like the Kiteboarding Round-Up each May.

It was Thursday, October 23, and exactly a month since I'd left home, though it sure seemed longer, as is often the case when traveling with the stimulation of new places. I planned to stay at the motel another night and on the island until the weekend started. Day 31 began with doing some laundry at the motel while I did more journaling. Then I took a walk to explore the community a little more and bought a few postcards and tee-shirts for gifts at one of the touristy shops. Later I stopped at a grocery store and found out there was also a year-round farmer's market in town every Sunday.

Another sunny day with eighties temperatures encouraged me to take a relaxing swim in the motel's pool, and it seemed that life isn't always so tough. As the sun went down in the late afternoon, I walked in my swim trunks to the beach access where I was the evening before, named Bougainvillea after the very colorful ornamental flowers grown on the island, with the intention of also swimming in the Gulf. I left my footwear by some dunes, and with a towel tied around my waist, I started running barefoot along a white sand beach toward the south, which soon widened and was strewn with seaweed. I veered toward the shoreline, where my feet splashed in the surf, and reveled in the experience. My first run since I'd left home didn't feel like I'd lost any stamina.

While in motion, I watched gulls and terns flying above the blue waves, with some terns hovering and plunging headfirst below the surface in quest of a seafood meal. A flock of brown pelicans also made a pleasing appearance—circling and gliding gracefully before making their own dramatic dives for fish. And near the water's edge where I was running, small sandpipers that looked like sanderlings scurried around. This was just a small sample of the island's abundant avian life.

A long line of buildings, including high-rises, stretched near the beach behind low dunes coated with green growth. Soon, I started running back, and the golden light of my favorite time of day illuminated the seascape. Close to my starting point, I ran into the surf near where some other bodies were in the water and found its temperature comfortable and the bottom smooth and sandy. I ventured out up to my shoulders and rode a strong breaking wave back to the shoreline, which I repeated a few times and felt totally exhilarated, with thoughts of how much I loved the sea and how great it was to have reached the Coast on my journey.

I walked back to Harpoon's that evening, and Jay was there again and remembered my name. The older woman I'd also talked to asked what it was, which made me feel very welcome again. It didn't take long to start chatting with some other people at the bar too. One was a young guy from Maryland originally, who said he'd lived on the island "quite a while" and liked that there were no tacky amusements and commercialized boardwalks there like at so many East Coast seashore resorts, which certainly applied to much of the Jersey Shore. Another young guy asked what brought me here, and when I told him about recently driving U.S. 83 border to border, his response was: "That's the most interesting thing I've heard all day." He also didn't know how long the road was.

The fish tacos I ordered happened to be served by Clara from the motel, who recommended the place. She remembered me and said, "I'm glad you made it here."

"So am I. It seems like a very friendly place."

"It's like family here."

And that didn't seem too exaggerated.

The fish tacos were good-sized, with soft tortillas, sliced cabbage, parsley, and salsa, and the fish was mild-flavored and tasty. One little disappointment was that I found out from Jay that the fish, called Basa, was not from the Gulf but a type of farmed catfish from Asia. The bit of information didn't spoil my enjoyment of the meal, though.

A band was about ready to start playing in a nice back courtyard area with a fountain and tall palms, where there was a mainly young crowd, and I moved to a table there with another beer and listened to a set by a four-member band from Dallas. One of them expressed how glad they were to be out of the big city and on the island. Later I heard SPI had a notable music scene that also attracted good musicians from Houston, and that hotbed of talent—Austin. When I left, I went back to the bar to say good-bye to Jay in case I didn't come back before I left the island, and also caught Clara, who wished me a "safe trip."

I wandered a little further south along Padre Boulevard before heading back to the motel, then cut over to Gulf boulevard and found a beach on the Gulf side with some large dunes. There were strong sea breezes as I strolled out on the sand, and I quickly became entranced by the sight and sound of the surf in the dark, and a sky full of dazzling stars. Enhanced by a good little beer buzz, it was an ecstatic "moment" in a wonderful setting on what I was finding to be a wonderful island.

Back in my room, I stayed up a while writing. Besides this day marking a month on the road, it was the first and only day I didn't drive Wander at all. I suppose my Toyota deserved a rest, and I'd given my feet a good workout instead.

I checked out of the motel after deciding to spend a final night on the island in the car or maybe camp. It was another day of light and warmth, and I drove north on Padre Boulevard to explore what was in that direction. Past the South Padre Island Convention Center and Andy Bowie County Park, I entered an undeveloped area with large dunes heavily covered with grasses, shrubs, and some colorful flowers. The dunes obstructed views of the Gulf, but the bay was visible to the west. Ahead were pure white dunes right along the road on the Gulf side that were impressive, and grassy ones on the bay side. There was a feeling of wildness here, and it must have been what much of this part of the island looked like before all the development. Nevertheless, further on, a sign appeared, "Welcome to Island Adventure Park"—which was a family-owned, forty-acre recreational business between the Gulf and bay that offered horseback riding and ziplining among its activities.

Soon a sign posted in the pure white sand stated, "Road ends ahead," and I reached the end of the pavement. This point marked the end of civilization for a long stretch of the slender barrier island, though it's split over twenty miles to the north by the man-made Port Mansfield Channel, beyond which is the Padre Island National Seashore almost all the way to Corpus Christi. Some sun enthusiasts in folding chairs were out on the high grassy dunes.

After turning around, I pulled into a beach access area on the Gulf side where no one else was around. A sign warned, "Swim at own risk," and another announced: "Sea turtle nesting season—April–September—report turtles immediately." So, I'd arrived somewhat past the turtle season here. Beyond the breaking surf, some of the water had a turquoise tint reminiscent of my trips to the Florida Keys and the Caribbean, which was delightful to see here. Some great-tailed grackles that I'd seen in abundance in some South Texas towns had congregated on the beach but were much quieter here. Lots of seaweed and seashells lay scattered on the sands.

I had thoughts about the usual referrals in the U.S. to the East and West Coasts while overlooking that there's also a South Coast along the Gulf of Mexico. In fact, the 1,680-mile total distance in the five states along the Gulf is longer than the Pacific Coast, excluding Alaska, which is 1,293 miles; and the Atlantic Coast is 2,165 miles. So, I was now on the second longest coastline of the lower forty-eight states.

When I was back from the northern end of the island's main road, the temperature had reached ninety degrees, which felt even better to me. I parked in a vacant area of a lot by the modern-looking South Padre Island Convention Center and had two peanut butter and sliced banana sandwiches while sitting in my small folding chair. While eating, I watched an Osprey perched on a tall structure consume a fish it had caught for its own lunch. Afterwards, I walked over to the convention center and saw three walls with magnificent murals of colorful images of orcas and other marine animals, known as Whaling Wall #53. These were created as a tribute to whales and other sea creatures by the American artist Robert Wyland, who painted a hundred Whaling Walls around the world with life-size images, finishing in Beijing in 2008. Wyland's SPI creation was his fifty-third that was completed in 1994 and called "Orcas off the Gulf of Mexico." Orcas, or killer whales, are one of twenty-five species of whales and dolphins that live or migrate in the Gulf.

Just down the street, I stopped at Sea Turtle, Inc., which was founded in 1977 by a remarkable woman named Ila Loetscher, whose passion for protecting sea turtles led to her reputation as "The Turtle Lady" until her death in 2000 at the age of ninety-five. This hospital and rehab for injured turtles that have been found had many round and open water tanks where the genial reptiles—some very large—were submerged. I learned that about ninety percent of the turtles here are able to return to the wild, and all of the individuals were given names. The institution also had extensive educational programs, and a driving force behind these efforts is the serious decline of sea turtles in recent years—much, of course, due to human activities. The organization had turtle patrols that comb the beaches of SPI in ATVs in search of distressed animals, and there was even a Turtle Hotline phone number. So, humans have also been saviors of sea turtles on the island.

Right next door was the South Padre Island Birding and Nature Center—a large complex that's another of the nine World Birding Centers in South Texas—which had a five-story observation tower and a long boardwalk that extends into wetlands by the Laguna Madre. I went into the spacious building and checked out a white board with two long columns of recent bird sightings in the area, then asked a guy at the desk if there were any alligators in the nearby wetlands, since a tourist booklet mentioned a local one that had been named "Allowishes."

"There's a couple of resident gators here that weren't introduced," he said. "Gators are somewhat native to the island, but not in great numbers."

An inside exhibit was about to close, though the trails behind the building were still open with a fee. Then I remembered what the guy back at The Sabal Palm Grove Sanctuary said about the good birding behind the nearby convention center, and I decided to return there. So, with binoculars, camera, and field guide, I ventured out on a railed boardwalk called the Laguna Madre Trail, which led into a big wetlands area toward the bay. There I encountered a great egret preening itself, a majestic great blue heron, a pair of smaller Louisiana herons, and a hunched, black-crowned night heron. There was a wildness in the expansive salt and freshwater wetlands close to the bay, and I saw no other humans along the trail.

Reaching the bay, I spotted some fish jumping near the shore. The Laguna Madre is relatively shallow but rich in aquatic life, and waters around the whole island are home to approximately 600 fish species. The bay also has families of wild bottlenose dolphins that can be seen year-round and spend their entire lives in the local waters rich in their fish diet. I saw floating brown pelicans that have their own big appetite for seafood, and it didn't take long to see an airborne one dive into the bay and surface with a catch. Scanning the waters with my binoculars enabled me to see some even larger white pelicans, which, unlike the browns, are also an inland species, and they were floating and mingling with their close relatives. I also spotted a fisherman wading where the water was just up to his knees, which showed how shallow the bay was here. The boardwalk led to a shelter and blind, where I paused and became more absorbed by the surroundings, with balmy breezes and a low sun across the bay. A couple of diving ducks were also out toward the open water, where a pleasure boat made an appearance.

On my return, I read a sign about railroad vine, which seemed to be the widespread green vegetation I saw on many dunes on the Gulf side, which the rapidly growing, creeping vine was said to help stabilize. I next heard the rattling call of a belted kingfisher before the familiar bird that's another pescatarian species was in sight. At another shelter-blind, I finally encountered some other birders—a fiftyish couple who I first talked to about sightings. They mentioned being from Brownsville and were on the island for the weekend. I told them about being from Colorado and driving 83, and that this was my first visit to SPI.

"We love it here and come a lot," the woman said.

"I would too if I lived that close," I said, "and I hope to return someday."

Satisfied by my Nature experience here, I imagined how much more I could see if I spent a lot more time on the island, since its environs have impressively yielded over 300 bird species from being situated on a major migration route along the Gulf. But by now I felt the pull of home and thought I should begin the long return journey.

For dinner, I decided to find Dirty Al's that the guy at the sanctuary on the mainland had recommended, and I found it near the causeway. The sun was close to setting, and I parked on a side street close to the restaurant with a panoramic view of the bay and causeway and caught the glowing orange ball drop below the mainland, which was a great climax to the day and my visit to the island.

Right behind Dirty Al's was a campground with RV hookups, where some tents were also set up. But I had an urge to leave the island that evening to get a head start on my journey.

The smell of seafood cooking was enticing, and the restaurant had a stucco facade with a neon sign that said: "Sorry, we're open." I already liked the place for its sense of humor. Inside, I found a rather retro eatery that looked like a throwback to the fifties and sixties, with a cement floor, old-style cafeteria tables and barstools, and a great casual atmosphere. There was also a counter where fresh seafood was sold. I sat at one of the old tables, and my server was a forty-something Hispanic guy with a heavy accent. I bought a light beer and saw a lot of fried stuff on the menu that seemed in character for this type of place, but there were enough other choices. I decided on blackened shrimp tacos, and the server confirmed that the shrimp was from the Gulf and not somewhere in Asia, to my satisfaction. The meal arrived with fries, and the very flavorful shrimp was combined with lettuce, tomato, and onions in a soft tortilla.

"How long has this place been in business?" I asked the server.

"Fifty years, and it's been expanded. The family that owns it has other restaurants in the area too."

That was a continuity I liked hearing about.

I had some ambivalence about leaving SPI that evening; however, the pull of home was strong enough to win out. But back on the Queen Isabella Causeway, I was already looking forward to returning to this little seaside kingdom of escape—hopefully as a Winter Texan for at least part of a future winter. And my two days on the island had rejuvenated me from some road weariness, and I felt up to the many miles ahead.

A meditative mood must have distracted me from staying on Texas 100 in Port Isabel, which bypasses Brownsville and would have been the direct route to the lower section of 83 and 77 that I'd be traveling again. But by the time I realized it, I was on the way back to Brownsville on Texas 48 and decided not to backtrack. I thought I could find my way to the Walmart where I'd stayed and do it again.

The highway led right to Boca Chica Boulevard, where the store was, and the street had drained completely from the recent flood. I wound up parking in the same space next to a small divider in the Walmart lot, and after two nights in a Motel 6, I didn't mind sleeping in the car at all.

After more writing and using the Walmart restroom, I felt tired enough for the back seat sleeper again. The security vehicle that had made me a little nervous the first time I stayed here was now parked close to the store and well away from my space. One thing that did "bug" me though as I was trying to fall asleep was a buzzing mosquito that had entered the vehicle. But after opening a window wide, the tiny, bloodthirsty critter took the exit before it drew any of my blood. I was soon asleep on the first night of the return journey.

DAY 33

San Antonio, The Alamo, back in the Hill Country

It was a Saturday that was cloudless and continued summer-like, and I was back on U.S. 83-77 for the stretch up to Harlingen. Then I continued north on 77 (also I-69E), where 83 branched off, though this wouldn't be the last time I would see the great highway on my return. I was headed for San Antonio, where I'd connect with I-10, which I'd been on briefly in the Hill Country, for an express route home.

U.S. 77 North had four divided lanes, and once out of the congested lower Rio Grande Valley metro area, I passed through a long stretch that looked quite blank on my map that was flat and agricultural, where big roadside stands sold produce and numerous wind turbines towered over the landscape. I finally saw an armadillo—the odd-looking creature that's the official small mammal of Texas—only this one looked like roadkill. Approaching Kingsville, I was out of the agricultural area and had to go through a border patrol checkpoint, where a young officer just asked if I was a U.S. citizen and where I was headed. The landscape became brushy and grassy, and the highway led through a few very small towns. There were more roadside vendors, with some selling tropical freeze, brisket, and "fresh Gulf shrimp."

In Kingsville, a town with about 26,000 residents, I left U.S. 77 and headed west for a short stretch on two-lane Texas 141 through lots of mesquite. I soon reached the intersection with multi-lane U.S. 281 that would propel me north into San Antonio, which is the longest three-numbered, auxiliary U.S. highway in the nation that's 1,875 miles (3,018 km) in length—just ten miles shorter than U.S. 83. It's also a Canada to Mexico highway, commissioned in 1931, with a route that's east of 83 and also courses through six states.

I spotted another dead armadillo by the roadside and encountered a swarm of flying insects that looked like grasshoppers, with many crashing into and staining my windshield. There were also some oil operations before a junction with I-37, which 281 merged with and aimed toward San Antonio. I-37 is a mere 143-mile (230 km) long interstate, but from here on I would be cruising on interstates for the rest of the journey.

I took a break at a rest area and stepped out to stretch and relieve a somewhat sore butt. Litter was scattered around the site, despite the presence of trash cans, and I again wondered about the mentality that does such things while I cleaned up some of it. I also cleaned off a lot of the insect remains on Wander's windshield. The temperature had risen to the low nineties, and after driving away, I turned the AC on. There was more of a mesquite-dominated landscape, and a sign posted this as a hurricane evacuation route.

South of San Antonio, the concurrent highways split up, and I stayed on the interstate. Soon, the impressive skyline of the city appeared, which my map showed to be a sprawling metropolis. I-37 led to a connection with I-10 in the downtown area where the famous Alamo was, which I was set on visiting for the first time. I soon took an exit for the big historic attraction and saw names of familiar Alamo heroes on Bowie and East Crockett Streets, and the Crockett Hotel. I'd heard that contrary to impressions left from movies made about the legendary battle, the Alamo is now as surrounded by downtown San Antonio as it was by the Mexican Army in 1836. So, I wasn't too surprised by the urban environment. But when I drove by Alamo Plaza and finally saw the familiar figure of the historic Spanish mission building, it looked much smaller than I expected, as is often the impression, and seemed like a time capsule amid much modernity.

There was a huge weekend crowd, and I was lucky to find parking for a few hours nearby. The lines at the Alamo were long and sluggish at first, and a sign said there were about three million visitors a year—making it the most visited tourist site in Texas. The admission was free, which might add to the popularity, and the Alamo is appropriately owned and operated by the state of Texas,

The two-story mission building with a familiar hump on its top mid-section, which was added in the years after the battle, was constructed of local limestone and originally intended to be a church. Though it's often considered "the Alamo"—meaning "cottonwood" in Spanish—it's just part of what was originally a walled, four-acre mission compound that the 1836 battle occurred inside and outside of, and most of the other structures are long gone. The Spanish mission was developed near the San Antonio River in 1724, and later became a Spanish, then Mexican military post that was captured by insurgents of the Texas Revolution in December 1835. The siege and battle that followed and resulted in the massacre of approximately 200 Texan defenders by Mexican General and President Antonio López de Santa Anna's overwhelming force of over 3,000 troops occurred between February 23 and March 6, 1836. Besides Anglos, the defenders included some Tejanos, who opposed Santa Anna's dictatorial rule, and even a number of foreign-born volunteers. A small group of surviving defenders were executed by order of Santa Anna, and all the bodies were burned in a massive pyre. Although viewed as heroic martyrdom—especially by generations of Texans—for the cause of Texas independence from Mexico, it's rather well-known that the cause included the continuation of slavery in Texas, which the Mexican government had outlawed in 1829, and there were several African American slaves among a small group of Alamo survivors who were spared by Santa Anna. General Sam Houston's troops routed the general-president's army at the Battle of San Jacinto near present-day Houston on April 21, 1836, and Santa Anna was captured and pressured to accept Texas independence.

The long line finally moved into the iconic mission building, where the Alamo defenders made their final stand. No photos were allowed inside what has been designated "The Shrine of Texas Liberty," but I took enough outside and of other structures and the rest of the grounds. I also read information panels about the brutal battle that has evoked so much fascination, even internationally.

Back at Alamo Plaza, I gazed at the sixty-foot-high monolithic cenotaph—a marble memorial to the Alamo defenders that was dedicated on November 11, 1940. Above the base were sculptures representing the defenders that were created by Italian-born sculptor Pompeo Coppini. Below all the figures were long horizontal engravings of the names of many of those who sacrificed their lives for the Texas cause. When I thought about the fascination that draws hordes of visitors here, I supposed it had something to do with the Alamo symbolizing great heroism against overwhelming odds—a universal theme that many cultures must have their own stories of, which is exceptionally represented by the Alamo. I was glad that I finally made it to this revered site and learned more about one of the most dramatic events in the history of the state that I'd spent the most time in on my journey.

Despite the abundance of other attractions in San Antonio, I was anxious to leave the bustle of what was by far the biggest city on the whole route of my journey and continue homeward. But I had thoughts about returning someday and also visiting Austin to the northeast. I found my way back to I-10, then had to deal with a maze of expressways with lots of ramps, where I had to be very attentive to stay on course. San Antonio is a big crossroads of interstates and old U.S. and state highways, and I saw how sprawling this city has become. What began as a Spanish mission and colonial outpost in 1718 developed into what was presently the second largest city in Texas after Houston, with close to a million and a half people. It's also the oldest municipality in Texas and the most visited, which draws more than twenty million people a year to see a lot more than the Alamo. And it's long been a military town, with some bases and other facilities both inside and outside the city limits.

The traffic slowed while still in the urban congestion because of construction, But I was able to view a great sunset as I headed west on I-10. Further on in the remaining light, the Hill Country came into view, which the interstate approached. I was soon driving through these well-known elevations again, which became dark outlines as the light faded. The rises in the road occasionally cut through what must have been limestone formations like 83 did on my drive through the region over a week before, which I was glad to pass through again.

I cruised after nightfall, where the speed limit was eighty miles per hour. When I reached an exit for Segovia, I got off to check out a truck stop to spend the night, where there was also an open restaurant. I got another OK to park overnight and found a secluded spot where I drank a couple of Lone Stars—the start of Saturday night in Segovia.

In the restaurant, I ordered a chef salad with turkey, ham, and honey mustard dressing that was especially good. Like most truck stops, this place had showers, but I decided to wait till the morning. Outside, there was a chill in the air in contrast to the recent subtropical temperatures. I supposed it had something to do with the Hill Country's elevation besides being further north, and I didn't look forward to the colder temperatures ahead.

After more journaling in the car by lamp light, I walked around the lot where some eighteen-wheelers were idling. Then I was tired enough to sleep after driving 388 miles that day, which was a good start on the long return.

DAY 34

Into West Texas, Good Samaritans, an "old" twenty-five-year-old

Sunday morning had lots of blue sky, and it sure looked like I was back in the Hill Country, with white limestone outcrops and a tree-covered ridge in the surroundings. After a raisin bran with peanuts breakfast in the car, I walked to the showers that were surprisingly free, even for non-truckers. But an upstairs area was reserved for the modern-day teamsters, which had a lounge and laundry.

Segovia was essentially this truck stop, a motel next door, a few houses, and a population of less than twenty-five. It was named for a historic city in Spain and seemed just as remote from enormous San Antonio. Across from the truck stop was a state historical sign about an "Old Military Road" that once ran nearby between the U.S. Army headquarters in San Antonio and Fort Terrett further west, from 1852 to 1854, when there were numerous forts throughout Texas to protect settlers from widespread Comanche threats. After this fort closed in 1854, the former supply route was used by settlers as a road to San Antonio. The sign said some of the old road was still visible, but I didn't go looking for it.

Back on I-10 West, I soon arrived where it intersected and ran in tandem with good old U.S. 83 for a short distance near Junction. The road descended through the dramatic cuts in the limestone that I remembered well from ascending in the opposite direction, and there was a vista of some of the hills. After the long bridge over the strong-flowing Llano River, I saw the last U.S. 83 sign of the journey, where the highway left 1-10 and continued north. In what seemed like a ceremonious moment, I exclaimed, "Good-bye 83!" to the great old road that had been my inspiration for the journey.

Well west of Junction, a sign stated 432 miles to El Paso, and I was becoming more appreciative of Texas distances. The landscape gradually became less hilly, and what appeared to be junipers were mixed with mesquite and smaller brush. Some mesquite leaves were turning a seasonal yellow. I passed by the town of Sonora, with about 3,000 inhabitants, and ahead and south of the interstate were the Caverns of Sonora, which, though small, are said to be exceptionally beautiful with an abundance of calcite crystal formations.

The next town was Ozona, about the same size as the previous town, which on my map looked like the only town in Crockett County—named after Davey Crockett, the Alamo hero. Perhaps its isolation is why it calls itself the "Biggest Little Town in the World." It's also significant for being a national leader in the production of wool and mohair, according to Wikipedia. A little further west was a turnoff for the Fort Lancaster State Historic Site, which preserves the ruins of one of the mid-1800s Texas frontier forts. This one protected military supplies and immigrant traffic along the San Antonio-El Paso Road that developed after the Mexican War ended in 1848.

Soon the interstate crossed the Pecos River—a long tributary of the Rio Grande—and also entered sparsely populated Pecos County, where there was more rolling landscape, and junipers were scattered in a savanna-like environment that looked more arid and Southwestern. This impression grew stronger as I sped further west and saw more exposed rocks with different colorations, and some mesa-like landforms in a more varied and rugged terrain. After a warning sign for strong crosswinds, some gusts buffeted Wander while I was enjoying the scenery. By now, I was well west of the longitudinal hundredth meridian that so interestingly divides East and West in the landscape and climate, and the Texas heat was back in this more arid area.

After passing a congregation of wind turbines, I stopped at a rest area for a needed break and to check out a familiar noise from the front end of the car that had returned, which started right after I drove through the Brownsville Flood. A look under the vehicle showed that another part of the inner fender that had been damaged was loose and rubbing the right front tire. After spending some time on my hands and knees in the now ninety-five degrees heat, I was able to secure the piece away from the wheel with baling wire that I carried.

Just as I finished, a short and somewhat paunchy older guy came by and asked if I needed any help.

"Thanks," I replied, "but I'm done with a small repair."

Then we had a little conversation, and he told me he was moving to Los Angeles with his pickup truck after living in Houston for quite a few years. But he was originally from New York City, which was easy to tell from the accent he'd retained. I told him I was an old Jersey Boy now living in northern Colorado and headed home.

"This is my first really long road trip," he said, "and I wouldn't do it again."

"I've taken a lot of long trips and really enjoy being on the road. I guess you could say I'm used to it." When he was about to walk back to his loaded pickup, I said, "Have a safe trip, and I hope you start to enjoy it more."

"I don't know about enjoyment, but you have a safe trip too."

It was a cloudless day, and the intense heat led me to change into my swimming trunks at the rest area, which felt more comfortable. And after working under the car, I was thirsty for an early beer and quaffed a Lone Star discreetly in the car. Then I moved to a table under a small shelter and put together a sardine sandwich while harassed by some stiff winds. There were a good number of trash containers at the rest area, and just a little litter. So, it looked like the long-running, anti-litter "Don't Mess with Texas" campaign was working here.

Back on the interstate, a long line of wind turbines stretched along a broad mesa. Past this renewable energy operation came some fossil fuel activity, with bobbing pump jacks to the south. I was now in or near the Permian Basin, which is the top producing oil field in the U.S. Some rugged peaks appeared to the southwest, and there were more mesas. The scenery got very interesting and more Southwestern, including lots of short, dark green creosote shrubs in the open country that were very unlike mesquite.

I passed Fort Stockton—a real crossroads community with about

8,000 people that's the seat of Pecos County. As its name suggests, it was the site of another Texas frontier fort that originated in 1859 around a big source of spring water called Comanche Springs. It was occupied by the Confederates during the early years of the Civil War, and the U.S. Army was back in 1867. Some of the old fort is preserved, and there's a museum there.

Impressive mountains dramatically appeared due west, where my map showed a few small mountain ranges. Wander was soon shaken by more crosswinds.

Suddenly I saw a pickup truck stopped along the roadside in my direction, and a guy waving for help. I realized it was none other than the one I'd met back at the rest area who'd offered to help me. Of course, I had to stop, and I parked on the shoulder behind his vehicle. He was also surprised to see me again and thought I would have come by earlier. His Dodge pickup was crammed with whatever he was moving to Los Angeles and covered with a tied down tarp. He told me his truck had had two flat tires since I last saw him, and now he was stuck without a spare.

"I couldn't change my first flat because I didn't have a jack. But a police car came by soon, and the cop had one and changed the tire. Then I drove only about five miles and the spare went flat, even though it looked well inflated. I have to get the flats fixed, but don't want to have to pay for towing because I really can't afford it.

"So, you don't have any roadside assistance plan?"

"No. I need to call a service place, but my cell phone isn't working because it probably needs a charge. So do you have one I could borrow?"

"Yes, but it's a flip phone that won't give you tons of information but should have coverage in this area."

After lending him my phone, we introduced ourselves, and his name was Fred. Traveling with him was a small, white, floppy-eared dog that seemed calm about what was happening. While he called 911 to find out about getting service, I pulled out my triangle reflectors from the trunk and set them behind my vehicle for safety's sake. When I got back to Fred, he was finishing his conversation and had a dejected look on his face.

"A place just told me they can't come out because it's Sunday, and now I'm stuck. Man, I hate this trip! All the driving is bad enough, and now I can't even move!"

"Another highway patrol car is bound to come along, and maybe they can help some other way. Maybe you should call 911 again and try to get another service place."

"The cops will probably want the car towed, which I can't afford. I don't have a credit card, and not even a bank account now. Except for the money I'm traveling with, I'm pretty broke. I have a son in L.A. I'm planning to live with. and two other kids. One is a daughter in Houston that I lived with there. My only income now is Social Security, and I just turned sixty-three."

"You're almost as old as me since I'm sixty-four. So, what kind of work did you do before?"

"I've worn quite a few hats as far as employment."

But he didn't get more specific, and I didn't ask him to.

"I've had some health problems in recent years—a couple of heart attacks, and wound up getting stents."

He'd lit a cigarette, and I commented, "So you're still smoking?"

"I've cut down a lot. One every hour or two."

I gave Fred a little summary of my trip and told him I loved living in Colorado. He said he'd been there and also liked it a lot. Our conversation, which was a bit of a distraction from his problems, was interrupted by another pickup truck that stopped and parked in front of his and out stepped a middle-aged Hispanic woman who wore a Texas rest area service uniform. She spoke OK English and asked if she could help, and serendipitously she had a spare tire that looked the right size for Fred's truck, and also a large jack much better than what I had for my compact car. She was willing to lend her spare to enable the other truck to get to a repair shop and follow it, which was certainly very nice of her.

Before Fred and I got to work, I leaned the loaned spare against the back of his truck, not knowing that when I returned to my car for something, he moved his truck a little further from the traffic lane so the left rear tire flat could be changed more safely. When we were ready to use the jack, we realized the spare wasn't there, and Fred got very anxious and asked me what I did with it. I knew it must have rolled somewhere, and when I told my new friend, he ventured down an embankment and found the tire lying in the brush, to his great relief. The woman was amused, and I felt some embarrassment that was enhanced by Fred's joking accusation: "You did it! Never trust another old man!"

Then he asked if I didn't mind doing the jacking, but we disagreed on the best spot under the truck. He wanted me to put it under the fender where he said the cop had jacked it, which I thought was a weak spot that could dent the metal. But after his insistence, I started jacking there, which wasn't easy, though the rear end started lifting. However, before it was high enough, the jack collapsed and became pinned under the truck. I gave Fred a polite "I told you so," but he again mentioned the cop using a jack in the same spot. I still felt bad because the jack was really stuck and we needed another one to release it, but my car's jack was too small. I also felt bad for the woman who was being so kind and helpful, but she remained calm after what happened.

Fred went back to try to flag down a passing vehicle for another jack, and I called 911 for the police and wondered which kind of assistance would arrive first. There wasn't much traffic in this area with a lot of empty space on my map, and none of the vehicles that passed had another Good Samaritan. Nor did the highway patrol arrive soon. After a while, the woman decided to leave without her spare tire and jack—a truly Good Samaritan. She thanked me for my efforts, gave Fred a warm good-bye and best wishes, and he expressed a lot of gratitude to her. "God bless," were her parting words, and though I'm not religious, I was moved to say, "Vía con Dios" (Go with God) to this Hispanic woman, and she replied, "Amen."

It's too bad she didn't wait a little longer, when a highway patrol car finally arrived with a young Anglo officer who had a large jack. Since it looked like Fred was now in good hands and my parking on the shoulder was unnecessary, I thought it was time for me to move on. I handed Fred a card with my contacts and asked him to let me know that he made it safely to California, and I wished him a lot better luck for the rest of his trip. He thanked me a lot for my time and help and said he would get back to me. After removing my reflectors, I finally drove off.

Fred struck me as a rather hard luck guy who at least had some family support, though apparently no wife at the time. And he didn't seem that well prepared for a long road trip that he'd never done before. But now, at least, he would have a jack and another spare tire through the kindness of a stranger. I never did hear from him, and hopefully because he was just forgetful or neglectful after he made it to L.A. for the start of a new chapter in his life.

The episode set me back a couple of hours, and by now the sun had set behind the mountains to the west. The afterglow was mind-blowing and left a phenomenal blue cast on these elevations that was the most beautiful shade of color I'd ever seen on a mountain range. Meanwhile, the mountains to the south transformed to a gorgeous purple and magenta, with one peak having a painted appearance. The blue mountains turned a darker blue, and I was savoring every second of this ephemeral artwork of Nature. When the colors faded into dusk, the mountains became striking, dark silhouettes while a light orange glow still lingered from the sunset. The finishing touch to this magical transition was a dangling, thin crescent moon.

I passed a couple of exits for some very small towns and Balmorhea State Park, which boasts having the world's largest spring-fed swimming pool that was built by the amazing Civilian Conservation Corps between 1936 and 1941. Further ahead was an intersection with the western end of Interstate 20, which has an eastern end in Florence, South Carolina. To the north, in the darkness that descended, were the Apache Mountains, said to be a rugged range with remains of the largest fossil reef in the world that was formed in a sea that submerged this region during the Permian Period over 250 million years ago.

At the exit for Plateau, I got off the interstate to check out another truck stop to possibly spend this night at, since I didn't want to miss much of the dramatic West Texas scenery by driving further in the dark. I got their OK to park overnight, and once again found a space in a back area away from the behemoths. It had cooled to a very comfortable seventy-three degrees, and I relaxed while sipping another Lone Star and watching the lights of vehicles stream intermittently along I-10.

Next to a store at the truck stop was Lindsey's Cafe, advertising "Homemade Mexican Food," where I went in and sat at the counter and ordered a platter that included three chicken tacos with some rice and beans. My server was a cute twenty-something woman. At first, she wasn't too friendly, but after finishing a good, if not great meal, I was able to engage her in a conversation and found out she was a big pro football fan and that her name was Megan.

"Our family had been Cowboys fans like so many people around here. But we switched loyalty after my uncle died, who was a big Steelers fan."

"That sounds like honoring your uncle as much as the Steelers."

"I once saw the Steelers play the Cowboys in Dallas when I was a Steelers fan."

"So, did the Cowboys fans give you a hard time?"

"Actually, a few big Cowboys fans who came in here were more hostile when I was wearing a Steelers jersey, and actually wanted another server."

"I guess football is like war to some people, and I've heard Texas is a football crazy state."

"I like baseball too and have an eighteen-year-old cousin who's a very promising player who plays shortstop and also does some pitching. He has a choice of two colleges, and even the New York Yankees and Chicago Cubs have been interested in him."

Then she showed me a few pictures of her cousin on her phone.

"I went to one of his games not too long ago and cheered so loud for him that I lost some of my voice for a while."

"I hope that really helped him. It sounds like your voice has recovered."

"Pretty much."

Since business was slow, our conversation continued, and I mentioned my travels from Colorado while thinking that most of her customers must also be travelers in an isolated outpost like this, and that she's probably heard enough travelers' tales, especially from truckers. She said she lived fifteen miles away and had two young kids and a lot of bills that weren't easy paying. She wasn't wearing a wedding ring and didn't mention a husband. So, I thought she may have been a single mom.

"I'd like to travel more myself," she said.

"Well, you're young, and should have plenty of time to do more of that eventually."

"But I'm not young. I'm twenty-five and feel old"—which jolted me to hear.

"But that is young! And you'll sure think it is when you get older." I wondered what she'd think of my pushing sixty-five, which I didn't dare mention, and I was glad she didn't ask my age. After a little more conversation, I concluded with: "It was really nice meeting you, Megan, and please don't think you're old at twenty-five when you should have most of your life ahead of you."

"Thanks for the encouragement. And have a safe trip."

I left her a very good tip to help a little with her bills, and she was very grateful.

The night was extremely clear, with an immense amount of stars illuminating the West Texas sky. After ambling around the truck stop, I did more journaling in the car. When I was ready to slip into my sleeping bag, I realized this could be my next to last night on the road, and I soon fell into slumber despite the sounds of some running trucks.

DAY 35

El Paso and "The Land of Enchantment"

The little outpost of civilization called Plateau is also located on a subdivision of the Union Pacific Railroad, which had previously been the Missouri Pacific. From a population high of about fifty in the early 1940s, it decreased to merely five in the last count, and I didn't see much around besides the truck stop. After another cereal breakfast in the car, I took an $8 shower there, thinking it would probably be my last one on the road.

Back on I-10, the surroundings were very mountainous, and all the elevations looked arid and Southwestern. The flat brushlands were dominated by green creosote shrubs. Another cruise control stretch brought me to Van Horn—the seat of Culberson County and a community with about 2,000 residents, where I-10 intersects with the western end of lengthy U.S. 90, which I'd crossed paths with back in Uvalde, and also Texas 54 that continues north toward the Guadalupe Mountains and Carlsbad Caverns National Parks, making Van Horn a town many tourists pass through. There was some Western Theater Civil War action near here in 1861 when a Confederate force captured a Union post that was south of where the town is now. The Union garrison's commander was Lt. James Judson Van Horn, who was taken prisoner and later became the namesake of the town that developed here, which was spurred by the arrival of the Texas and Pacific Railroad. Culberson County, in contrast, was named after a Confederate.

Just west of Van Horn, I left the Central Time Zone I'd been in for weeks and was back on Mountain Time, gaining an hour. This stretch of I-10 ran parallel to a frontage road and single railroad track on the north side. A sign showed the distance to El Paso had decreased to ninety-seven miles. The mountains ahead were very impressive, and to the north stood a peak called Sierra Blanca, or "white mountain" in Spanish, which had a very light appearance. It looms over a town with the same name and about 550 inhabitants. Oddly, half of this town stays on Central Time, and it also has the only adobe courthouse in Texas.

I-10 veered in a northwestward direction and coursed very close to the Rio Grande and the Mexican border, passing a string of small towns with mainly Spanish names. To the west was spacious rangeland and a long chain of barren mountains that must have been in Mexico. On the east side was more shrubby, open land with stubby yucca. The interstate entered El Paso County and approached the large city, cutting through some formidable reddish rock formations.

I stopped at a rest area and had some lunch at a table under a shelter, which didn't protect it from some West Texas winds. I talked to a trucker and asked why so many in his occupation let their parked vehicles idle so long, and he confirmed that it was mainly to charge accessories like heaters and AC. "But some states like California don't allow it," he added.

The sparsely inhabited spaces gave way to a commercial landscape along I-10 in the outskirts of El Paso. Then the spread out city came into view, and the expressway widened to four lanes in my direction. Soon, I passed an oil refinery within the city. Rugged, arid mountains speckled with shrubs dominated the surroundings, and the city stretched toward the mountains in each direction. The interstate ran near El Paso International Airport and Fort Bliss to the North—a U.S. Army post that's one of the largest military installations in the nation and dates to 1849. To the south was the downtown area with some rather tall buildings, and residential areas reached into the hills.

El Paso's population was now over 650,000, making it the sixth largest city in Texas, with a good share of cultural and other attractions that include 242 municipal parks. Franklin Mountain State Park, within the city limits, is the largest urban park in the nation. It has an aerial tramway where passengers can ascend to the summit of Range Peak on the only commercial tramway in Texas. Like a lot of West Texas, El Paso lies in the Chihuahuan Desert—the largest desert in North America that also extends into six Mexican states.

The city has a long history, and evidence of human habitation in this region reaches back 10,000 to 12,000 years to a Paleo Native culture. When three different Spanish expeditions arrived in the late 1500s, several Native tribes lived in the area. Juan de Oñate's expedition of 1598 named a passage of the Rio Grande between two local mountain ranges El Paso del Norte (The Pass of the North), which became shortened to El Paso. Spanish missions and settlements came in the 1600s, and by the mid-1700s, the area had the largest population on New Spain's northern frontier. Agriculture was established with irrigation from the river, and vineyards. In 1789, a presidio, or fort, was built to defend the settlements from Apache attacks. After the end of the Mexican War in 1848, El Paso developed on the American side of the Rio Grande across from El Paso del Norte in Mexico, which was renamed Juarez in 1888. Fort Bliss was occupied by the Confederates in 1861 and re-taken by a Union Force from California the following year. El Paso grew after the war, especially with the arrival of three railroads, and the town had a rowdy Wild West period when it was known as Six-Shooter Capital and Sin City, in contrast to the Sun City of modern times. From the early 1900s, El Paso evolved into a respectable industrial, agricultural, commercial, and transportation nexus with a rapidly growing population.

At a bridge by the Mexican border in the city is the southern end of U.S. 85, which joins I-10 and is the close relative of U.S. 83 that's also a border-to-border highway that I'd traveled a lot of early in the journey en route to 83. U.S. 85 is 1,479 miles (2,380 km) in length, through six states, like 83, with its northern end at the Canadian border in Fortuna, North Dakota. Much of its route is concurrent with I-10 and I-25, however.

El Paso is situated in the westernmost corner of Texas, and in his *Travels with Charley,* John Steinbeck had this to say about the giant state: "Once you are in Texas, it seems to take forever to get out, and some people never make it." But I finally was, after spending fifteen days there out of the thirty-six of my journey, and I certainly had a new appreciation of its size. I also experienced the "many kinds of country, contour, climate, and conformation..." in the Lone Star State that Steinbeck also referred to in his famous story.

I-10 crossed the state line where I was greeted by, "Welcome to NEW MEXICO—The Land of Enchantment," with images of two colorful chili peppers, which are significant in the state's agriculture and cuisine. Mesquite was still part of the landscape, mixed with the dark green creosote. I also rolled by some green, cultivated land as the road continued near the Rio Grande and a cluster of small towns.

Not far ahead was the city of Las Cruces and the strikingly jagged Organ Mountains to the east. It was time to depart from I-10, which turned west, and continue north on I-25 all the way to an exit for my home in northern Colorado. Once on I-25, I suddenly felt closer to home on this familiar interstate, even if it was still hundreds of miles away. This was also the southern terminus of the 1,062 mile (1,709 km)-long interstate that runs as far north as Buffalo, Wyoming. Las Cruces is the second largest city in New Mexico, with a population of about 100,000, and it's the big business center of the southern part of the state. It was founded in 1849 when the U.S. Army was there to protect settlers after the Mexican War.

I'd passed through this area exactly thirty-eight years before, in October 1976, on my motorcycle odyssey around the U.S. during the Bicentennial year, while headed east toward my then home in New Jersey. Some memories of the scenic surroundings were revived by this second passage from another direction.

Cruising north on I-25 near the Rio Grande and the route of the historic Camino Real de Tierra Adentro, I didn't think the "Land of Enchantment" moniker for New Mexico was hype at all. There were more jagged, arid mountains to the east, other elevations in the west, great shrubby plains, and other eye-appealing landforms. In this region, the Rio Grande's course is accompanied by heavy vegetation known as "bosque"—from the Spanish word for "woodlands"—which are found along many rivers and streams in the Southwest. Here was a very long bosque that extends all the way to Santa Fe in the north.

I stopped at a rest area near the Fort Selden State Monument that commemorates an 1865 U.S. Army fort to take some photos of the impressive San Andres mountains to the east, which had a gorgeous, reflective glow from the descending sun in the west. A state historical sign there read:

JORNADA DEL MUERTO—on the Camino Real

This stretch of the Camino Real leaves the Rio Grande and cuts across 90 miles of desert with little water or shelter. Despite its difficulty, the dreaded 'Journey of the Deadman' was heavily used by Spanish, Mexican, and Anglo travelers between El Paso and the northern New Mexico settlements.

Another sign mentioned that trail parties would fill up with water from the Rio Grande before the desert trek. The Jornada Del Muerto appeared on my map to the north, east of I-25.

In the parking lot I met a motorcyclist—an older guy wearing blue jeans and a black leather jacket, who was riding a K model BMW with good-sized saddlebags, a large rear trunk, and a Michigan license plate. I asked where he was headed.

"I'm on my way home to Michigan now. I was in San Diego for a U.S. Navy commemoration for my uncle and his crew who were killed in the Battle of Leyte Gulf in the Philippines during World War II, exactly seventy years ago in October 1944."

"Wow, that's interesting. Wasn't that one of the biggest naval battles in history?"

"Yes. It was the biggest in World War II, and some historians regard it as also the biggest in history in some respects. There were about 200,000 naval combatants on both sides. It was a very decisive victory for the Americans and Australian allies that crippled the Japanese Navy. But my uncle and more than half of his crew were among the casualties on the destroyer USS Johnston. The ship was shelled and sank by a powerful group of Jap warships after putting up a heroic fight that damaged the enemy. My uncle was my mother's brother, and I was born three years after he died."

"So, you never knew your uncle, but sure honored him by attending the commemoration."

"That's why I went, and it was a great experience. I didn't even know that much about my uncle's war experiences until recently."

"My dad was a World War II vet who fought in Europe with the U.S. First Army, and I've often thought how I wouldn't be here if he'd been killed. Of course, today most of the Greatest Generation is gone, and it's sad."

I next told him I was the original owner of a vintage 1976 R75 BMW motorcycle.

"Really! My first Beemer was a '76 R75 that I had for two years. This K bike is an '04. I've done a lot of long trips and even ride in cold weather, and I got my 300,000 Mile Award from BMW."

"That's impressive, and it leaves me well behind with about 153,000 miles on my bike's odometer. I got my 100,000 Mile Award back in 1993."

He'd also been to a good number of BMW rallies around the country like I had through the years, which prompted me to say, "Maybe we've crossed paths before." When I mentioned my U.S. 83 journey, he asked why I wasn't on my bike, and I told him one reason was the advantage of being able to sleep in my car, which I'd gotten used to in recent years. Then we introduced ourselves; his name was Bob, and he was sixty-seven and retired from a company that manufactured auto parts. He said he'd been married twice but had no kids. He was an interesting and articulate guy who was quite a talker. When the conversation finally concluded, we left the rest area at the same time after mutual wishes for a "safe trip." I didn't envy him for heading so far north at this time of year on a motorcycle. But he was a high mileage rider who said he also rode when it was cold, and it was great to see him still making trips like this at his age.

Further on, I became even more enchanted by the Land of Enchantment, as the changing light of late day had its magical effect on the rugged landscape. After the sun sank behind the mountains to the west, it created as awesome a spectacle as in West Texas the previous evening—with a deep blue in the afterglow that transitioned to purple before the mountains became silhouettes under a remaining orange glow. And the eastern elevations had an earthy, brownish coloration. Some daylight lingered for quite a while, and the transformation also had spectacular effects on the open brush country. I again reflected on how beauty makes me happy, and how it had been a companion on much of the journey.

Darkness descended, and the interstate ran near a series of very small towns on a state road along the Rio Grande, then by two state parks by the southern end of long and narrow Caballo Reservoir—created from a dam on the river. From here on, the river would be on the east side of I-25 for a long stretch. Not far ahead was another reservoir and state park named Elephant Butte, and a town of about 6,000 people with the quirky name of Truth or Consequences, which was originally called Hot Springs because of the numerous, local, mineralized thermal springs that led to the development of spas there. But in 1950, the town took up a whimsical offer from Ralph Edwards—the host of the old radio quiz show *Truth or Consequences*—to be the first town to rename itself after the show for the reward of his appearing and broadcasting the show from the renamed town on the show's tenth anniversary, which Edwards did in the renamed Hot Springs; and he even continued to visit Truth or Consequences, New Mexico for the next fifty years.

Further ahead in the darkness, I passed the Fort Craig National Historic Site, where another U.S. Army fort once stood that was built in 1854 and was the largest fort in the Southwest that quartered over 2,000 soldiers. Ahead, the interstate passed through the western side of the Bosque del Apache National Wildlife Refuge on the Rio Grande floodplain—known to have one of the best-preserved sections of the river's bosque that attracts a great diversity of bird species, including sandhill cranes in the fall and winter.

I passed a very small town with the name San Antonio, with less than 200 residents, which is significant for having been a meeting place for scientists who conducted the first atomic bomb test twenty-eight miles to the southeast at Trinity site in the Jornada del Muerto desert on July 16, 1945. The community experienced earthquake tremors from the blast and some radioactive fallout. This tiny San Antonio is also the hometown of Conrad Hilton, who founded the huge hotel chain bearing his name.

I spotted a Walmart from the interstate and got off at the next exit for the good-sized town of Socorro. I was ready to call it a day, and this store turned out to be a 24-hour one that was better than another noisy truck stop for what I expected to be my last night on the road and car camping. I parked in the big lot near a few RVs, then popped a beer and just relaxed in the driver's seat. My supper that evening was canned chili beans that I didn't mind eating cold again, along with some bread and leftover jerky that I ate in the car.

Afterwards I walked some streets of Socorro and felt a definite climate change this further north and at an elevation over 4,500 feet. I'd changed from shorts to jeans earlier, and now needed my hooded sweatshirt again over a long-sleeved shirt for what felt like a return to autumn. The town's mountainous surroundings weren't very visible in the dark, and my map showed a well over 10,000-foot peak not far to the west. What I did see at first was a commercial area near the Walmart with other chains like Denny's, McDonald's, and a Phillip's 66 station. The proliferation of such businesses does make parts of so many American towns look similar, especially at night, and I didn't walk far enough to see Socorro's historic district and plaza. I picked up quite a bit of litter on my walk—another thing in common with many other towns—and I contemplated all the wandering I'd done on foot in so many communities around the country in my decades of travel; and this was my first presence in Socorro.

Back at the Walmart, I was in my sleeping bag by 11:30 p.m., with pleasant thoughts about being in a comfortable bed again the following night—only this time at home. As much as I now looked forward to it, I also felt a little melancholy about my odyssey approaching its end.

DAY 36

The Big Push, "There's no place like home."

I woke up early enough to see a red-orange glow in the east before a brilliant sun rose over a low ridge in the distance. With daylight, I could much better appreciate Socorro's rugged, mountainous surroundings, and it looked like another bright day for the desert region that began with a cool fifty-one degrees. After having a breakfast sandwich in another Subway store in the Walmart, and an orange, I was ready to begin the big push to make it home that day, which I estimated to be close to 600 miles.

Socorro is a very interesting and historic community with about 9,000 people that I would have explored more if I didn't feel a haste to make it home by the end of the day. The local history goes back to the 1598 expedition of Juan de Oñate, which arrived near here after crossing the hazardous Jornada del Muerto; and the party met a hospitable group of Natives of the Pueblo culture known as Piros, who helped sustain them. A local Spanish mission named San Miguel was soon founded, but the town of Socorro didn't start developing until about 1815. A boom came after the arrival of the railroad in the 1880s. Today, the community is known to be artsy and outdoorsy, among other things.

Back on my way north, I-25 was co-signed with U.S. 60 for a stretch—a road I'd previously connected with in Canadian, Texas, in the Panhandle. The expressway ran by more very small towns with Spanish names along the Rio Grande to the east, and many autumn-colored hardwoods were visible in the bosque along the river. Trees and shrubs to the west were also changing color, and in the open spaces, pale blue sagebrush was replacing the dark green creosote. Verdant cultivated lands near the river continued for miles, along with the mountainous terrain. By now it seemed I was out of the Chihuahuan Desert region I'd entered in West Texas, which also covers a good portion of southern New Mexico. I-25 crossed the Rio Puerco close to where this river flows into the Rio Grande, and U.S. 60 left the interstate and shot east.

I breezed by Belén—an old town with over 7,000 residents that was founded by Spanish colonists in 1740 and given a name meaning Bethlehem in Spanish. In February 1862, the Civil War came here when a Confederate force that had captured Fort Bliss in El Paso marched up the Rio Grande Valley and briefly occupied Belén while advancing north in what's known as The New Mexico Campaign. In later years, Belén became an important rail hub, and the railroad is still very active there.

Albuquerque was ahead—by far the most populous city in New Mexico. Just south of the city, I-25 cut through the Isleta Indian Reservation, also called Pueblo of Isleta (isleta meaning "little island" in Spanish). This reservation has one of the largest surviving pueblos, or adobe dwellings, in New Mexico, which has existed here since the fourteenth century. The interstate crossed the Rio Grande, which had a strong flow and coursed back on the west side of the road. I drove through a heavy bosque area with lots of cottonwoods, and the sprawl of Albuquerque lay ahead, with a mountainous backdrop toward the east and some high-rise buildings standing out to the west. I passed the city's international airport and adjacent Kirtland Air Force Base, then the University of New Mexico stadium and campus. A sign appeared for Historic Route 66—formerly part of famous U.S. 66 that runs through the city.

I crossed transcontinental I-40 at a complex interchange known as the "Big I," and I-25 has been named the Pan American Freeway in Albuquerque since it's a segment of the approximately 30,000-mile (48,280 km) road network that connects Alaska with Argentina.

This very fast-growing city with over half a million people—about a third of New Mexico's population—is a very energetic and ethnically diverse place that was founded in 1706 by a Spanish provincial governor and named in honor of the Spanish Viceroy of Mexico. Albuquerque was also briefly occupied by the Confederates during their northward advance in early 1862, and again a month later during their retreat when they also had a local engagement with a Union force.

North of the city limits, I-25 crossed the small Sandia Indian Reservation—the home of another Pueblo group—and ran near 10,678-foot Sandia Crest—the highest elevation in the Sandia Mountains to the east. To the west of the road was the old Spanish and Native community of Bernalillo, and north of it were six adjacent reservations of Pueblo peoples. The interstate veered to the northeast, away from the Rio Grande, and I stopped for gas at the San Felipe Travel Center, where there was a large casino. I also added another layer of clothing at the stop since it felt chillier as I progressed north. It remained a very bright day, though, in this sunny climate.

Nearing famed Santa Fe, there was a vista of the big mountainous area north of the city, which is generally considered the southern extent of the Rocky Mountains, though other mountain ranges continue far to the south, as I'd seen. I passed the exit for the Santa Fe Regional Airport, and soon cruised by the very historic small city that I'd visited a few times. From the interstate, I saw many adobe-style homes and buildings very characteristic of Santa Fe, and there was another sign for Historic Route 66.

This capital city of New Mexico with over 70,000 residents—renowned for its Southwestern architecture, art, music, cuisine, and overall culture—was founded in 1607 on the Santa Fe River after the conquistador, Don Juan de Oñate, established Nuevo (New) México as a province of New Spain in 1598. In 1610, it became the provincial capital and has had a remarkable continuity as a seat of government. It's not surprising that it's the oldest state capital in the U.S., and also the highest at 7,199 feet. For centuries before Spanish colonization, Pueblo people had occupied the area, including where the city developed. In its long history, the city has been under the flags of Spain, Mexico, the U.S., and the Confederacy during the New Mexico Campaign in 1862. Beginning in 1821, it became the end of the line for the close to 900-mile long commercial, and later immigrant, Santa Fe Trail from starting points in Missouri, which was replaced by the railroad bearing its name in 1880.

I-25—concurrent with U.S. 285 and U.S. 84—made a bend toward the south and wound through a mountain forest of pines and junipers at the southern end of the Sangre de Cristo range that terminates the Rockies. The highway ran close to the route of the Santa Fe Trail and the BNSF Railway—formerly the Atchison, Topeka, and Santa Fe Railroad—and through 7,500-foot Glorieta Pass. This is where the Confederate army's northward advance toward other regions of the West was thwarted on March 28, 1862, by a force of Union volunteers from the New Mexico and Colorado territories. The Confederates were able to force a Union retreat, but their supply train was found and destroyed by a Union unit, which forced their own retreat southward toward Texas.

The road headed east for a stretch before turning northward, and the next large town it passed was Las Vegas, with over 13,000 people, which is older than the famous tourist mecca in Nevada with the same Spanish name meaning "the meadows" or "plains." It's a very interesting and historic town that dates to an 1835 Mexican government land grant to a group of settlers, and the community that developed was influenced by being along the Santa Fe Trail and later the railroad.

Ahead were sprawling, tawny grasslands, and the bright afternoon sun gave the Sangre de Cristo range to the west a cast of blue, unlike the reddish coloration of late day that may have inspired these mountains' Spanish name—"Blood of Christ." I loved this landscape's colors and all the grassy openness, where some cattle grazed peacefully.

I passed an exit for Fort Union National Monument—the site of a U.S. Army fort that the Confederates had intended to capture before their retreat at Glorieta Pass. Ahead was a butte visible from the road named Wagon Mound, which was a landmark for the wagon trains that rolled along the Cimarron Cutoff of the Santa Fe Trail and is now a National Historic Landmark. The plains ahead had yellowish, short grasses that were about the lightest colored grass I'd ever seen. In the west, the Rockies stretched northward and soon appeared more rugged with some snow-capped peaks. I-25 intersected with the western end of U.S. 56 and crossed the Cimarron River in the small town of Springer. Soon the Canadian River, which 83 had crossed in the

Texas Panhandle, meandered close to the interstate for a while, which passed by the Maxwell National Wildlife Refuge that's a haven for migratory birds. Ahead, I interrupted my momentum toward home with a lunch break at a rest area.

Just a short stretch of New Mexico was left before I was back in Colorado, and I'd already seen distance signs for Pueblo and Denver. I-25 ran concurrently with U.S. 64 to where the latter exited eastward in the small city of Ratón, and U.S. 87 joined the interstate and is co-signed with it all the way to northern Wyoming. Ratón is just south of namesake Ratón Pass, and it developed from what had been a stop on the Mountain Route of the Santa Fe Trail after the AT&SF Railroad arrived in 1880.

I-25 began climbing toward the 7,834-foot pass, which cuts through a row of mesas of volcanic origin along the state line. Soon I saw a wooden sign with the words WELCOME TO COLORFUL COLORADO by a turnoff, where I pulled off for a photo. Being back in my now home state stirred a very homey feeling, even almost 300 miles from my own home.

To the west was a panorama where the double Spanish Peaks stood prominently and speckled with snow, which were a leading landmark on the Santa Fe Trail visible from great distances. Signs referring to the historic trail were along the roadway, and some others warned about elk and even bear crossings. The route here was part of the Santa Fe Trail National Scenic Byway, and Ratón Pass has National Historic Landmark status. I stopped at another scenic turnout with a great view of rocky, 9,626-foot Fisher's Peak to the east—the highest point of Raton Mesa. A sign said the early Hispanics in the area originally named the peak Ratón (meaning "mouse"), possibly because of an abundance of small rodents on the mesa's slopes. The sign also informed me about a temporary rail line that operated over the pass in 1878-1879 that used the world's largest locomotive at the time, and a tunnel that was constructed at 7,588 feet, which was the highest point on the AT&SF Railroad. The route is presently used by Amtrak and limited freight service of the BNSF Railway.

I-25 continued along what had been the Mountain Route of the Santa Fe Trail, passing the tiny community of Starkville that was once a company-owned coal-mining town where a terrible explosion in a local mine killed fifty-nine miners in 1910. Close by was the attractive and scenic town of Trinidad ("trinity" in Spanish) on the Purgatoire River in this area originally explored by Spanish and Mexican traders. Trinidad was a big coal town for decades after being founded in 1862, and the area was the location of what was called the Colorado Coalfield War of 1913-1914 between striking workers and anti-union forces, which resulted in much violence and around 200 deaths.

U.S. 160 also joined the interstate from the east, where the Santa Fe Trail route split off northeastward toward the Arkansas River. The next sizable town was Walsenburg on the north side of the Cucharas River, and U.S. 160 left I-25 and headed west into the mountains. This community of about 3,000 started as a settlement in 1859, and there was coal mining near the town for over a century, resulting in some casualties during the coalfield conflict.

About eight miles north, I stopped by Huerfano Butte, which rises 200 feet above the plains near the Huerfano River. Early Spanish explorers named the butte, which means "orphan," apparently because of the butte's solitary appearance. It has a volcanic origin, like much of this region's geology, and resembles a pyramid. Historically, it's been another natural landmark for travelers.

There were hardly any towns along a good stretch of I-25 before the old industrial city of Pueblo on the Arkansas River. The mountains to the city's west are the southern extent of the Front Range of the Rockies that rises along the western edge of the High Plains. This city with a population over 100,000 had a humble beginning as an adobe trading post established by a group of fur trappers on the Arkansas River in 1842. One of them was James Beckwourth—an amazing half-Black man and freed slave who played diverse roles for decades in the Old West. By the early 1900s, Pueblo was the only steel-producing town west of the Mississippi, as well as Colorado's main industrial center that attracted many immigrants and led to much ethnic and cultural diversity. Today it has a branch campus of Colorado State University. I-25 crossed the Arkansas River in the city where it also intersected with cross-country U.S. 50, which 83 had crossed in Garden City, Kansas along with the same river.

Another landscape turned golden late in the day, and the high peaks to the west became beautiful silhouettes from the setting sun.

To the east, the BNSF Railway now ran close to the interstate. I passed sprawling Fort Carson on the west side—a U.S. Army installation established in January 1942, soon after the U.S. entered World War II. Ahead were the city limits of huge, rapidly-growing Colorado Springs—Colorado's second most populated city with well over 400,000 people—where heavy traffic moved sluggishly because of an accident that left just one lane open for a while. But there was enough daylight left to enjoy the sight of 14,110-foot Pikes Peak—the great natural landmark named after Zebulon Pike, whose expedition route I'd also encountered in Kansas. A crescent moon hung in the direction of the majestic peak, enhancing the beauty of the spectacle.

"The Springs," as the city is often called, was once part of the stomping grounds of the indigenous Ute, Arapaho, and Cheyenne tribal groups. The year 1859 brought the Pikes Peak Gold Rush, and a mining settlement named Colorado City was established at the future site of the city. When a railroad arrived in 1871, a different community planned for the wealthy sprung up just a few miles away, which was named Colorado Springs after the nearby mineral springs. Eventually the two communities merged under the latter name, and the population has grown steadily ever since. The modern city is known for being a big military town, a sports town that's the headquarters of many sports organizations, and a center for many religious organizations that have especially drawn big numbers of Evangelical Christians. It's also a college town with a branch campus of the University of Colorado, and tourism is a leading industry because of the splendid mountain scenery.

I was relieved to be out of the large city as I breezed by the U.S. Air Force Academy to the west of the road, and I was soon back in open spaces. When I reached the town of Castle Rock it was completely dark, and I made a final gas stop at a Conoco station. The air at this town's 6,224-foot elevation was a chilly forty-five degrees, and I added another sweater. Had I been through Castle Rock in daylight, I would have been able to view the butte near town that's been thought to resemble a castle. I'd heard it's a very nice town, with lots of open space and parks, and a population well over 50,000 that's been growing rapidly like so many communities along the Front Range. Its origins go back to 1874 and a development spurred by the discovery of rhyolite—a volcanic, igneous rock that has industrial uses and was quarried locally.

Ahead was the sprawl of the Denver Metro Area, where the Mile High City is just one of multiple contiguous municipalities. A broad plain of lights glittered in the distance, including the skyline of downtown Denver. I was looking at the center of the Front Range Urban Corridor, where most of its population and business is concentrated, and the whole corridor is home to about eighty-five percent of Colorado's population. The Denver Metro Area has about three million inhabitants, with Denver itself—the state's capital and most populous city—approaching 700,000 and counting.

The Mile High City got started as a mining camp in November 1858 during the Pike's Peak Gold Rush and was connected with the ambitions of two land speculators from the Kansas Territory that the region was part of at the time. A townsite was first named Denver City after the then governor of the territory, James W. Denver, and it was the speculators' intention to develop a large community. What was later called just Denver must have greatly exceeded their expectations in the long run—especially with the modern city being such a hub of manufacturing, distribution, transportation, energy development, and education, which is racially and ethnically diverse, and rich in cultural and recreational opportunities.

I cruised easily on I-25 through the center of the city, passing the gold-leaf domed state capitol building to the east. The interstate crossed the South Platte River, which I'd connected with in North Platte, Nebraska, then ran by Mile-High Stadium and Coors Field before it intersected with I-70, where U.S. 85 finally made an exit after its long concurrent run with I-25. Out of the city limits, there were intersections with I-76 and U.S. 36, and I saw a mileage sign for Fort Collins—now under seventy miles—and also picked up a favorite FM station from the city that was playing some good music.

I drove on through the lights of the suburbs north of Denver when the snowy peaks of the Front Range to the west were concealed in darkness. Eventually, I was out of the congestion of the Metro area. Reaching Loveland—another fast-growing community south of Fort Collins on the Big Thompson River—the interstate intersected with U.S. 34 that 83 also had in McCook, Nebraska. The Fort Collins exits weren't far ahead, and I took the one for Mulberry St. and headed west, where it was about five miles across town to my home. I felt a little incredulous that I was so close and back in such familiar surroundings.

There's so much I could say about the town that became my new home a couple of years earlier, but I'll just summarize. First, Fort Collins is an amazing place that's had its own long journey from its beginning in 1864 as a U.S. Army outpost on the Cache La Poudre River—a tributary of the South Platte—which was established to protect the Overland Trail during the Indian Wars and was named after Colonel William O. Collins, who authorized its location. The fort was short-lived, but a settlement soon developed that grew into the present vibrant city with about 160,000 people that's been growing at a fast rate, to the delight of some, and dismay of others, which became the fourth most populated city in Colorado, besides the long-standing seat of Larimer County. Its residents come from far and wide, with many drawn by the main campus of Colorado State University, which was originally an agricultural college founded in 1879. What was considered a very conservative community for much of the twentieth century, which had an alcohol prohibition until 1969, has evolved into a cosmopolitan and cultured city, brimming with events, activities, festivities, and epicurean delights—including abundant eateries and breweries. It's the kind of place I was happy to return to, and the city was celebrating its Sesquicentennial, or 150th anniversary, during the year of my journey.

I pulled into the driveway of my small house on the edge of Fort Collins' Old Town just before 9 p.m.—having accomplished my big push of 572 miles from Socorro, New Mexico—the most mileage of any day of the journey. I had a great sense of completion, accomplishment, and relief from a safe return. It was Tuesday, October 28, and the evening temperature was thirty-nine degrees, with some later frost likely. I felt grateful to Wander for running so reliably, and the Corolla had just a bit of damage from the Brownsville Flood. My next drive would be to a car wash to cleanse the grime and stains from hundreds of highway miles, and it was definitely time for an oil change.

Entering my home, I was ready to imbibe some celebratory beer waiting in the refrigerator before I started unpacking or did anything else. And I looked wonderfully forward to a long soak in my bathtub before returning to the comfort of my own bed, which would be more appreciated than ever after more backseat sleeping than I'd ever done in my travels.

It's great to wander and have the freedom to do so, but feels just as great to return. And my mind lapsed back to the Land of Oz creation in Liberal, Kansas and the famous, time-honored words: "There's no place like home."

Epilogue

In thirty-six days, I'd traveled 4,749 miles (7,643 km) through nine states, with six along the route of U.S. 83. Though it was nowhere near the longest of my journeys in distance or time, I regard it as one of three what I consider epic journeys that I've made in my lifetime. The first was my four-month, over 15,000 miles (24,140 km) motorcycle odyssey through thirty-six states in 1976 to celebrate the nation's Bicentennial; and the second was my six-week over 10,000 miles (16,093 km) adventure on the same motorcycle in 1992 to celebrate the Fiftieth Anniversary of the Alaska-Canada Highway. These journeys were made in different stages of my life: the first at age twenty-six while still in my youth; the second at forty-two in middle-age; and the third at sixty-four in what I consider young old age.

In the recent one, I'd learned a lot about U.S. 83—"The Road to Nowhere"—and now know that the open, uncrowded lands of the Plains states are really a fascinating "somewhere"—full of beauty, history, and many things of interest. If I ever drive all of 83 again, I'm sure it would be a similar, yet very different experience due to the contingencies of travel, of course. I really hope that the highway remains less altered than most other old U.S. highways, so it continues to be a great route down the Spine of America. But just what travels on it and some of its environment is destined to change. The near future will probably and hopefully see a great popularity of electric vehicles, with charging stations replacing gas stations. And perhaps self-driving vehicles aren't that far-fetched.

I've mused about making a future journey on 83 later in my "golden years" to see what's changed and what hasn't, and also about roaming more old U.S. highways and other interesting alternatives to the haste and relative dullness of the interstates and other expressways. I believe I'll continue to hear the call of the open road, and hope to make some future epic journeys. So many roads, so little time.

Acknowledgments

Writing a book is known to be usually a very solitary experience. But now I know first-hand that publishing one always involves a lot of teamwork. I have a heap of gratitude for the great team at Atmosphere Press, who brought my dream of publication to realization. I'd first like to thank my developmental editor, Nathaniel (Nate) Lee Hansen, PhD, who I worked with closely, for his expert advice on improving the manuscript and help with some technological matters that were new to me. A special thanks to Managing Editor, Alex Kale, for all her assistance; to Chris Beale for his astute proofreading; also to Art Director, Ronaldo Alves, and his department for some great graphics. And a big thanks to everyone else on the team who were players in the publishing process. This, of course, includes Nick Courtright, PhD—the founder and CEO of Atmosphere Press—whose "author-friendly" policy was well lived up to.

I also owe a lot of gratitude to David Duhr, a co-founder of Write By Night—a great writers' services organization I fortunately found out about—who arranged a special connection for me with Atmosphere Press.

Some friends and family members who showed interest in my book and read portions of it and offered feedback also deserve my gratitude. I'd specifically like to thank my friend, Dan Meyer—a children's story author—for his ongoing interest and encouragement; my lifetime buddy, Joe Hall, for reading different chapters and giving honest and helpful feedback; my friend Reg Sprik—a recently published memoir author—for his reading, interest and advice; my cousin, Christine Dymkowski—a retired professor with an English literature background—for her valuable input on some sample chapters; and last, but not least, my sister, Donna Brown, and her husband, Jud Brown, for their helpful readings and encouragement.

I also feel grateful to many of the people I met on my 83 Odyssey—especially the now late Herbert Wilson, MD—who added much to my story.

A Note on Sources

I used a lot of online, non-primary sources for the many historical, geographical and other facts presented as part of the narrative. Much came from Wikipedia, which I understand has improved considerably, and the seemingly omniscient Google. I referred to many websites, including those of different historical organizations like "The Handbook of Texas"—the digital encyclopedia of the Texas State Historical Association or TSHA.

Certain print sources were also useful and also non-primary. Most significant were *Road Trip USA* by Jamie Jensen, Avalon Travel Publishing (2002 third edition); the three volume *The Last American Highway* series by Stew Magnuson, Court Bridge Publishing (2014-17); *Slow Road to Brownsville* by David Reynolds, Greystone Books (2014); and *Great Plains* by Ian Frazier, Picador (1989). I also used information from various pamphlets, booklets, and other literature I picked up along my route.

About Atmosphere Press

Founded in 2015, Atmosphere Press was built on the principles of Honesty, Transparency, Professionalism, Kindness, and Making Your Book Awesome. As an ethical and author-friendly hybrid press, we stay true to that founding mission today.

If you're a reader, enter our giveaway for a free book here:

SCAN TO ENTER
BOOK GIVEAWAY

If you're a writer, submit your manuscript for consideration here:

SCAN TO SUBMIT
MANUSCRIPT

And always feel free to visit Atmosphere Press and our authors online at atmospherepress.com. See you there soon!

About the Author

CHARLES ROAMER is an old Jersey Boy who found a great new home in Fort Collins, Colorado, which has also been a great base for his roaming. This is his first book publication. He can be contacted at cgroamer83@gmail.com or through atmospherepress.com.

Milton Keynes UK
Ingram Content Group UK Ltd.
UKHW012329290524
443431UK00004B/178